World of Faith and Freedom

World of Faith and Freedom

*Why International Religious Liberty Is
Vital to American National Security*

THOMAS F. FARR

OXFORD
UNIVERSITY PRESS
2008

3/9/09
Lon
$29.95

OXFORD

UNIVERSITY PRESS

Oxford University Press, Inc., publishes works that further
Oxford University's objective of excellence
in research, scholarship, and education.

Oxford New York
Auckland Cape Town Dar es Salaam Hong Kong Karachi
Kuala Lumpur Madrid Melbourne Mexico City Nairobi
New Delhi Shanghai Taipei Toronto

With offices in
Argentina Austria Brazil Chile Czech Republic France Greece
Guatemala Hungary Italy Japan Poland Portugal Singapore
South Korea Switzerland Thailand Turkey Ukraine Vietnam

Copyright © 2008 by Oxford University Press, Inc.

Published by Oxford University Press, Inc.
198 Madison Avenue, New York, New York 10016

www.oup.com

Oxford is a registered trademark of Oxford University Press

Library of Congress Cataloging-in-Publication Data
Farr, Thomas F. (Thomas Franklin), [date]
World of faith and freedom : why international religious
liberty is vital to American national security / by Thomas F. Farr.
p. cm.
Includes bibliographical references and index.
ISBN 978-0-19-517995-8
1. United States—Foreign relations.   2. United States—Foreign relations—Islamic countries.
3. Islamic countries—Foreign relations—United States.   4. National security—United States.
5. Freedom of religion.   6. Globalization—Religious aspects.   7. Terrorism—Prevention.
I. Title.
JZ1480.A5F37 2008
323.44'2—dc22   2008026671

1 3 5 7 9 8 6 4 2
Printed in the United States of America
on acid-free paper

For Cara and Wilson
Requiescat in pace

For Betsy
For Hilary, Natalie and Cara

For all who suffer persecution because they seek God.
Sing praise to the Lord, you his faithful ones,
and give thanks to his holy name…
At nightfall, weeping enters in,
but with the dawn, rejoicing.

Acknowledgments and a Disclaimer

This book has been several years in the making. I owe a debt of gratitude to many people who have either read parts of the manuscript at some stage or who have discussed with me the arguments presented herein. I am particularly indebted to those who have disagreed with me or pressed me to be clearer. Lucidity, it seems to me, is the preeminent writer's virtue. Whether I have achieved it only the reader can judge. Any errors, obscurities, miscues or misjudgments in this book are, of course, mine alone.

I'd like to thank those who have read and commented on elements of the manuscript or versions of it: Khaled Abou El Fadl, David Abramson, Steve Artner, Peter Berger, Judd Birdsall, Delane Clark, Cara Cook, David Cook, John F. Cullinan, William Craig Davidson, Bradley T. Deatherage, Robert Destro, Cole Durham, Margaret Farr, Natalie Farr, John Farr (RIP), Hillel Fradkin, Mary Ann Glendon, Brian Grim, Philip Hamburger, Carol Hamrin, Laura Bryant Hanford, James Hitchcock, Dennis Hoover, William Inboden, Patrick Kelly, Julia Kirby, Alex Kronemer, Fr. Lawrence Kutz, Phil Lawler, Steven McFarland, Paul Marshall, Ken Masugi, Steve Naplan, Fr. Richard John Neuhaus, Marcia Pally, Keith Pavlischek, Daniel Philpott, Aaron Pina, Tina Ramirez, Robert Royal, Rabbi David Saperstein, M. Allen Saunders, William L. Saunders, Jr., Chris Seiple, Robert A. Seiple, Timothy Samuel Shah, Russell Shaw, John Shattuck, Kamal Sidhu, Tad Stahnke, Knox Thames, Hilary Towers, Jon Towers, Lawrence Uzell, George Weigel, Kenneth Whitehead, Eric Wind, Joseph Wood.

I'd also like to thank others who have assisted me in developing my arguments through direct discussions or email exchanges: Elliot Abrams, Akbar Ahmed, Alexandra Arriaga, Sandra Bunn-Livingstone, Thomas Banchoff, Kit Bigelow, Scott Carpenter, Archbishop Charles Chaput, Richard Cizik, Ted

Constantine, Joseph Crapa (RIP), Michael Cromartie, Patrick Fagan, Carol Finerty, Felice Gaer, Robert George, Reuel Marc Gerecht, Walt Grazer, Joseph Griebosky, Jeremy Gunn, John Hanford, Charles Harper, Kevin Seamus Hasson, Allen Hertzke, Nancy Hewett, John Hittinger, Victor Huser, Philip Jenkins, Douglas Johnston, Joe Loconte, John Kamm, Firuz Kazemzadeh, David Killion, Harold Koh, Daniel Kurtz-Phelan, David Little, Karen Lord (RIP), Theodore Cardinal McCarrick, Faith McDonald, Laila al Mariyati, Jennifer Marshall, Paul Martin, Janet Mayland, Coleman Mehta, Rebecca Yael Miller, Mark Milosh, Philip Mirrer-Singer, Steve Moffit, Daniel Moloney, Seyyid Hossein Nasr, Senator Don Nickles, Michael Novak, Jerry Powers, Elizabeth Prodromou, Ben Rogers, Austin Ruse, Nina Shea, Congressman Chris Smith, Abdulkarim Soroush, Alfred Stepan, Julie Sulc, Dorothy Taft, Dennis Teti, Mervyn Thomas, Kristina Wahl, Joshua White, Congressman Frank Wolf, Christopher Wolfe, Angela Wu, Michael Young.

Additional thanks go to my students at Georgetown University whose vigorous classroom discussions have sharpened my argument; to Kyle Layman, my Georgetown graduate student assistant; to Thomas Banchoff, Director of the Berkley Center for Religion, Peace and World Affairs, who has generously provided a stage for my teaching and writing; to Dean Robert Gallucci and the Edmund A. Walsh School of Foreign Service; and to the Henry Luce Foundation, for providing funds that have supported my work through the Luce/School of Foreign Service Program on Religion and International Affairs.

My deep gratitude goes to my editor at Oxford University Press, the veteran Cynthia Read, and to her assistant Meechal Hoffman, for their persistence and cheerfulness in dealing with the manifold dilemmas presented by a first-time author.

Finally, my sincere thanks go to Mark Ramee, a foreign service colleague at the Department of State who shepherded the manuscript through its review by that sometimes thorny institution with nary a scratch.

In that regard, I have been asked by the Department of State to issue the following disclaimer, a request with which I gladly comply, noting only that it is hardly necessary, a fact that the reader will discover soon enough: "The opinions and characterizations in this book are those of the author, and do not necessarily represent official positions of the United States Government."

Preface

My interest in the issue of religion as an object of U.S. foreign policy began late in my career—in 1999, to be precise, after sixteen satisfying years in the American Foreign Service. Until then my work had involved the typical pursuits associated with diplomacy. I had issued and denied visas to people seeking entry into the United States. My family and I had been quickly evacuated from a foreign country after a terrorist threat (alas, not all that unusual for diplomats these days). During the Cold War I helped develop U.S. nuclear arms control policy, parried with Soviets over President Reagan's "Star Wars" initiative, and negotiated agreements with the Greek and German governments. In the 1990s I taught foreign policy at the U.S. Air Force Academy and served in the State Department's intelligence bureau. It was there I first read—in highly classified reports—about the activities of a man named Osama Bin Laden.

As the millennium closed, the rhythms and norms of diplomatic life began to shift dramatically for me. Nearing the end of my assignment in the intelligence bureau, I was scanning the list of available positions when my eyes ran across a word rarely seen in State Department personnel documents: "religion." A new office had been created by the 1998 International Religious Freedom (IRF) Act, and it was seeking a deputy for Robert Seiple, the man who would become the first IRF Ambassador at Large. I became Seiple's deputy and the first director of the State Department's office of international religious freedom. Thus began a new chapter in my career: crafting and implementing a policy concerning religion in one of America's most avowedly secular institutions.

During the next four years (1999–2003) I worked with Seiple, his successor, Ambassador John Hanford, and many others to plant a solid religious freedom policy in the infelicitous soil at Foggy Bottom. We and our staffs traveled to dens of persecution, places like Riyadh, Tashkent, and Beijing. For about 20 months spanning the Clinton and Bush administrations the ambassador's position was left unfilled, and I had the distinction of being the State Department's senior religious freedom official. Looking back over that period I sometimes see myself as the admiral of a leaky skiff with a tiny crew of happy but hardy souls, all of us rowing fiercely to avoid sinking beneath the waves. The reader will in due course learn the basis for that memory, including its revealing, and occasionally humorous, milieu.

In our travels abroad my colleagues and I met with, and sometimes wept with, victims of religious persecution from all over the world. We learned that their travails, and their destinies, are affected by what the United States says, what it does, and what it does not do. We negotiated with officials autocratic, theocratic, and democratic. They had little in common except their general dislike for what we had to say. Religion, let alone religious persecution, is not an easy subject to discuss over tea and cake.

But our problem was not (or not simply) that our message offended. Sometimes our problem was that we—representatives of the most powerful country in the world—were not taken seriously when we talked about religion. Some ministries of foreign affairs thought they could assuage our demands by sitting with us for hours discussing their countries and their systems, which they never failed to defend. These staid diplomatic dances, run by specialists in America management, were too often accepted at the State Department as "movement" or "raising the issue." Sometimes our interlocutors, having consulted their betters, would bend to a prisoner release, or even several, so that we had "deliverables" to take back to the small band of people in Washington who did human rights for a living.

None of these things, mind you, are bad in themselves—certainly not the removal of someone from harm's way, no matter how infrequently it occurs. I will later recount one of my most gratifying experiences as an American official, the case of an extended family of Iranians who fled their country because they had left Islam for another religion. As apostates, they faced death in the nation of their birth. After enduring hostile refugee camps and the fear of being returned to Iran, they encountered the bewildering, and sometimes maddening, procedures of the United Nations High Commissioner for Refugees, and, later, of what used to be called the U.S. Immigration and Naturalization Service. Bad policies have many step-fathers. Among them is bureaucratic inertia.

But in its policy of promoting international religious freedom, the world's most powerful nation can do better. It can achieve more than endless discussions of persecution with foreign ministries and the rescue of a few souls in the bargain. It can attack the very structures of persecution by promoting religious liberty as it was understood by America's own founding generation. To those men and women religion was not a private matter but a natural, powerful human pursuit with inevitable public consequences. It could destroy or it could create. Properly nourished and channeled, the religious enterprise in their view could benefit not only the individual but also the common good. Religion could sanction ideas of ordered liberty, justice, and equality and, in short, become the very engine of a liberal political order.

Some will object that these ideas and institutions are uniquely Christian or Jewish or Western, and cannot be grown in Cairo or Beijing. They will cite America's failure to export stable democracy, manifest in the bloody sectarian killing fields of Baghdad. Others will angrily insist that Baghdad merely demonstrates how *all* religion is toxic to the liberal project, something we should have learned from the events of September 11, 2001. They will insist that Enlightenment rationalism, not religion, made liberal democracy possible precisely by banishing religion from the pubic square.

This book presents the case that such arguments, which occur in many guises and across the ideological spectrum of American life, are both ahistorical and tendentious. More to the point, they are endangering the national security of the American people by underwriting a diplomacy of unreality. Our foreign policy in general, and our approach to religion and human freedom in particular, exhibit a dangerous disarray and confusion. We must do better. Our security and well-being depend upon it.

It is my sincere hope that the arguments set forth in this book will appeal to those with whom I served for over two decades, the men and women of the American Foreign Service, some of whose particular judgments I may call into question, but never their love of country. U.S. foreign policy is made by the president and the president's appointees, and aided or obstructed (as the case may be) by Congress, think tanks, and interest groups. But, as we shall see, American policies are framed, fed, and implemented by American diplomats. It is they who must be persuaded, their culture that must be changed, and their approach to American foreign policy that must adopt a new realism about the religious practices of other men and women around the world.

Contents

World of Faith and Freedom

Introduction

Why Religious Freedom?

The Duty which we owe our Creator, and the manner of our discharging it, can be governed only by Reason and Conviction, not by Compulsion or Violence; and therefore all men are equally entitled to the full and free exercise of it according to the dictates of conscience, unpunished and unrestrained by the Magistrate....
    —James Madison

Despotism may govern without faith, but liberty cannot.
    —Alexis DeToqueville

The problem came briefly but sharply into focus during the spring of 2006. The news had been dominated for months by the terrible sectarian violence in Iraq and the fragility of that country's struggling democracy. But this particular week's spotlight shifted to a courtroom in democratic Afghanistan where a man named Abdul Rahman was in grave danger of being found guilty of the crime of changing his religion. If convicted, Mr. Rahman would be beheaded.

It had been over four years since U.S.-led forces had invaded Afghanistan and ousted the cruel, theocratic Taliban government, one which had not only harbored Osama Bin Laden and Al Qaeda, but had also sanctioned the stoning of women and the brutal execution of men for the slightest deviation from its version of Islamic purity. After the overthrow of the Taliban, Afghans had elected a parliament and a president and had drafted and ratified a democratic constitution. The 2006 U.S. National Security Strategy proudly observed that the constitution guaranteed for Afghans "rights and freedoms unprecedented in their history."[1] The implications for America's national security were clear:

3

"Through the freedom agenda, we...have promoted the best long term answer to Al Qaeda's agenda: the freedom and dignity that comes when human liberty is protected by effective democratic institutions."[2] The wretched rule of the Taliban, and with it Islamist extremism, seemed to have been banished like the memory of a nightmare.

But now, in democratic Afghanistan, Abdul Rahman was being tried for apostasy—converting from Islam to Christianity—a crime meriting death under the prosecution's interpretation of the constitution. What happened in the days surrounding his trial revealed a great deal about Afghanistan and about the foreign policy of the United States. It suggested something troubling about the way both governments viewed the issue of religion, including its proper role in a democracy, the true meaning of religious freedom, and the relevance of those issues to Islamist extremism and the stability of democracy.

For one thing, the trial afforded a glimpse into the debate among Muslims over what their religion requires of them and of a democratic government, a debate sometimes referred to as the "war of ideas" within Islam. For another, it demonstrated the confusion that often reigns in U.S. policy precincts when it comes to the subject of religion. For most U.S. officials the Rahman trial was a high-profile humanitarian case.[3] But it was in reality much more than that. The trial pointed to a flaw in Afghan democracy that directly affected the national security of the American people.

When the apostasy charge became public, the U.S. State Department's initial response was to insist on a fair and "transparent" trial.[4] Calls from outraged Christian and human rights groups soon flooded the White House and the Congress. A congressional hearing was held. One influential evangelical Christian, Charles Colson, asserted that the trial called into question "the whole credibility of our foreign policy."[5] Soon the president said publicly that he was deeply troubled by the Rahman affair and the State Department swung into action. After pressure from the United States and other countries Mr. Rahman was released. He immediately fled Afghanistan in fear of his life.

In one sense the freeing of Abdul Rahman was a success for the U.S. policy mandated by the 1998 International Religious Freedom (IRF) Act. In the years since the passage of that law, a new religious freedom office at the State Department had managed cases of religious persecution, incidents which prior to the law had not always been pursued with alacrity. Now, in the wake of Mr. Rahman's escape, the head of that office told a congressional hearing that he had "never been more proud of our government's work than I was with regard to this case." Both the president and the secretary of state, he said, had made it clear to the world how important this issue was to the United States.[6]

But what *was* the issue? Saving Mr. Rahman was certainly a humanitarian act worthy of our nation. But there was a far more serious problem. The United States had, in two successive National Security Strategies, declared its intent to implant democracy in Afghanistan and Iraq as a means of fighting Islamist extremism by "draining the swamps" of the pathologies that fed radicalism. The Afghan constitution was heralded as a major step in that direction, and it was indeed a very progressive document. It created a presidential system, a parliament elected by universal adult suffrage, and an independent judiciary. It guaranteed free expression and equality under the law. In its own words, the constitution sought to create "a civil society free of oppression, atrocity, discrimination, and violence and based on the rule of law, social justice, protection of human rights, and dignity, and ensuring the fundamental rights and freedoms of the people."[7]

These were noble goals. But they did not affect the Afghan court's understanding of Mr. Rahman's crime. Nor did U.S. officials pay much attention to the bizarre inconsistency—Afghan democracy had officially declared that there was no contradiction between protecting human rights and the judicially required execution of a man for his peaceful religious practices. The justice system had endorsed the use of violence by the democratic state to coerce the religious conscience. Afghanistan was not a Saudi theocracy, where public beheadings for religious crimes were not unusual. It was a democracy, brokered by the United States and celebrated for its nascent liberality precisely because it would provide an antidote to extremism—the kind of extremism that had produced the Taliban and provided a safe haven for Bin Laden and Al Qaeda.

The Americans had worked hard to make the drafting of the constitution a success. They had pulled together an impressive international effort almost immediately after the events of September 11, 2001. In October the Taliban had been overthrown, and by early December, U.S., UN, and other officials had helped broker the Bonn Agreement which provided the legal framework for a transitional government and mandated a commission to draft a new constitution. By January 2004 it was ratified and became law.

That month the U.S. ambassador to Afghanistan, in an op-ed in the *Washington Post*, hailed the new constitution as a milestone on the path to democracy and stability. It set forth, he wrote, "parallel commitments to Islam and to human rights. While embracing Islam as the state religion, the document provides broad religious freedom—allowing adherents of other faiths to practice their religions and observe religious rites."[8]

Clearly something was missing here, a disconnect or a misunderstanding. How could an American official so confidently declare religious freedom secure in a document that others read to permit the execution of a man for his peaceful religious beliefs? It wasn't a slip of the pen. The same assertion—"the constitution provides for religious freedom"—was made almost two years later in the Department of State's *Annual Report on International Religious Freedom*.[9]

Nor was Mr. Rahman's case an anomaly. In 2002, just after the formation of the transitional government, Afghanistan's Chief Justice Fazul Hadi Shinwari had publicly denounced the new women's affairs minister, Sima

Samar, for telling a magazine that she did not believe in *shari'a*. She was formally charged with the crime of blasphemy, and ultimately resigned for fear of her life. Under U.S. pressure the charges against Samar were dropped but the problem did not go away. Muslim journalists were tried and convicted for blasphemy, for the crime of offending Islam.[10]

After the constitution was ratified, the supreme court created within its administrative structure a "Fatwa Council," composed of Islamic clerics who reviewed questions of Islamic law. The council soon began, on its own initiative, to issue rulings in matters not brought to the supreme court.[11] In a 2003 meeting with the U.S. Commission on International Religious Freedom—a watchdog agency created by the IRF Act—the chief justice explained that he rejected religious freedom, freedom of expression, and equality of the sexes.[12]

In the State Department, officials knew that such incidents were not good for Afghanistan's image, or theirs. The IRF Commission held public conferences and publicly implored the president to require the State Department to pay more attention to the issue of religious freedom.[13] But within Foggy Bottom all these problems were viewed as unfortunate humanitarian discrepancies that the Afghans were going to have to work out. The American embassy complained privately to the new government about Shinwari and the continuing blasphemy charges. But it had sprung both Rahman and Samar, had it not? It had the larger problem of pulling the country together after decades of oppression.

It did not occur to most American officials that these were not mere incidents, nor the actions of a single rogue jurist, but indicators of a much larger problem. In fact, the constitution had not guaranteed religious freedom. For non-Muslims it protected the right "to perform their religious rites within the limits of the provisions of the law. In Afghanistan," the constitution noted pointedly, "no law can be contrary to the sacred religion of Islam...."[14] This was a pinched version of religious freedom indeed, a "right to rites," as one observer wryly noted.[15] It wasn't much better than what non-Muslims were permitted to do in Saudi Arabia, which was to worship in private.

For some U.S. officials, this "right to rites" constituted the sole content of religious freedom. If people could pray and worship together, what more did they need? Besides, there was only a handful of non-Muslims in Afghanistan. The "other religious groups," as the State Department put it, consisted of "Sikhs, Hindus, and one Jew." As for Christians, there was "a small, hidden Christian community;...estimates ranged from 500 to 8 thousand." Together the non-Muslims comprised less than one percent of the population.[16] When the IRF office and the IRF Commission complained about the lack of religious freedom, some officials wondered whether they weren't really trying to pave the way for missionaries. That would hardly be helpful to the new government.

The central problem for American national security, however, was not missionaries (although, as we shall see, missionaries raise the problem of proselytizing, which must be resolved if democracy is to endure). The fates of Mr. Rahman, Ms. Samar, and the others were indicators that Afghanistan was not moving toward the kind of democracy that would contain Islamist radicalism and remain stable. The constitution had created a window through which extremism could lawfully enter, contend with the reformers and the moderates, and stand an excellent chance of defeating them. In fact, no one had true religious freedom in Afghanistan, including the Sunni and Shiite Muslims that constituted 99 percent of the population. Like the others, they were generally free to perform rites—to worship and attend to the private imperatives of Islam. They could attend mosques and follow the pillars of their religion.

But religious freedom means more than private activity. Among other things, it means the right to speak and write publicly about religion. It apparently did not occur to U.S. policy makers that "draining the swamps" of extremism would require establishing a public space in Afghanistan for facilitating such a discourse and ensuring that the constitution protected it. As it stood, there were compelling reasons for Muslims (let alone non-Muslims) not to express themselves publicly on Islam, its proper relationship with the state, and its value to democratic stability. The courts had virtually unchecked power to decide what the undefined values of Islam were, and to apply them in the Afghan public square. Afghanistan's president and its legislators had their own platform, but the court's undefined power was far greater. It would take courage for a Muslim to suggest publicly, as some had done, that Islam did not require the execution of apostates, or that *shari'a* itself permitted broad religious freedom, including freedom of expression and women's rights. Most Muslims would not take the risk.

In short, the U.S.-brokered Afghan political order was blocking precisely what it was intended to energize—democracy as a sustained agent of moderation. In Washington, however, policy makers simply didn't see it that way. In deciding what was important to make democracy endure and drain the swamps of extremism, they paid little attention to the religion-state issue. In endless discussions of the "war of ideas" raging within Islam, they saw the issue of religious freedom in Afghanistan as largely irrelevant.

Culture Matters

In the wake of the American experience in Iraq, it seems clear that some cultural groundwork must be laid before a nation can achieve the kind of durable self-government sought by the Bush administration as an antidote to Islamist extremism. History provides ample evidence that lasting democracies do not emerge from elections and constitutions alone, and they are rarely imposed from without. The United States has long accepted a version of this "culture first" argument. In the early 1980s the Reagan administration and Congress established the National Endowment for Democracy (NED) to implant the institutions of liberal civil society around the world. The goal, in other words, was to seed democratic cultures. But the programs funded by the NED were by and large secularist. They tended to avoid faith communities, as if religion had nothing to do with culture, or had to be separated from society in order to grow democratic institutions.

Until 9/11 most of those dollars were spent outside the Middle East, in large part because Arab and Persian versions of Islam were considered antithetical to democracy, and because the United States equated "political Islam" with Islamist extremism. With the adoption of President Bush's "foreign strategy of freedom" in Iraq, Afghanistan, and elsewhere, however, U.S. democracy funding began to pour into the broader Middle East. Programs such as the State Department's Middle East Partnership Initiative focused on women's movements and other important aspects of civil society. But until quite late in the Bush presidency, it remained largely taboo to engage directly the subject of religion.

The influence of religion on culture and politics, of course, is not limited to Muslim nations. The consolidation of stable self-government in virtually every society will depend in some measure on the role played by religious communities and religiously informed norms and actions, as well as whether a state can successfully construct a regime of religious freedom.[17] This is true of non-Muslim nations as diverse as Russia, China, and India. Indeed, it is true of virtually every nation on earth.

A handful of officials at the State Department, in the White House, and in Congress worried about this habit of not thinking systematically about religion—the tendency not to take it seriously unless it was pointing a gun at you or driving aircraft into your buildings. These officials understood that culture drives politics, and that in a growing number of societies, religion drives culture. They believed that the political reform pushed by American foreign policy could influence but was unlikely to transform the cultures of the greater Middle East, at least not in the course of a few years. They supported the president's freedom agenda, including its premise that democratic procedures and economic growth could help destroy the tyrannies that wracked that region and fed Islamist extremism. But they also feared that political and economic liberties alone were insufficient to alter attitudes shaped by the extremists and their ideas.

Largely because of their concerns over this issue, these officials had helped to generate more than one "engaging Islam" initiative among U.S. foreign policy agencies.[18] But in the end they had not succeeded in focusing the policy process on the religious aspects of culture. Internally they asked but failed to elicit answers to an increasingly critical policy question: how can the United States succeed in promoting stable self-government in Muslim nations unless it can influence the religious climate of opinion? There were useful American experiments to engage religious ideas in a few countries, such as Indonesia and Nigeria. But these were exceptions that proved the rule. In the end, there was no official answer to the question. It was just too hard.[19]

In a 2006 book former Secretary of State Madeleine Albright noted that diplomats and policy makers in the 1990s ignored the role of religion in shaping the world. To them, she wrote, the subject of religion "was above and beyond reason; it evoked the deepest passions; and historically, it was the cause of much bloodshed. Diplomats in my era were taught not to invite trouble, and no subject seemed more inherently treacherous than religion."[20] By 2006 Albright was long gone from Foggy Bottom, but the diplomatic mindset she described was well rooted and still dominant.

The tendency to see charges of apostasy and blasphemy as little more than isolated humanitarian problems unconnected to the stability of democracy stems from a culture as embedded in the State Department as Islam is in Afghanistan. Most American diplomats and foreign policy makers do not think of public human affairs and political structures in religious categories. This does not mean that they are irreligious. To the contrary, some are deeply religious men and women. But for many in the field of foreign affairs, religion is understood as properly a private matter, largely unconnected to the processes of reasoning, and therefore unsusceptible to rational analysis. They tend to understand politics and culture in modern "realist" terms, that is, that people and nations are "rational actors," which means less that they apply reason in any classical sense than that they are mainly motivated by power and economic interest.

Developments in the broader Middle East ought to have provided evidence that a hands-off view of religion is a highly unrealistic basis for U.S. attempts to encourage stable democracy. It not only reinforces the tendency to treat an apostasy trial as a humanitarian issue rather than an indicator of deep cultural and political problems. It also reflects an incomplete understanding of how to root liberal norms and institutions in highly religious societies. Afghanistan is a multiethnic and tribal nation that presents many challenges to an aspiring midwife of democracy. Foremost among them is the fact that some version of Islam has a deep and abiding influence on many of the Afghan people, whether or not the Taliban is in charge. Indeed, an Afghan Islamism willing to employ the democratic state to coerce religious consciences suggested a continuing affinity with Taliban-like belief and practice that should not have been ignored.

Amid all the strategies adopted by the United States to undermine Islamist terrorism and to encourage stable liberal governments in the Muslim world, we have thus far failed to credit a critical objective: the religious rationale for violence must be turned on its head. Mainstream Muslims who reject violence and coercion not in spite of Islam, but because of it, must move to the fore. Until that happens, U.S. policy in Afghanistan and Iraq, and its counter terrorism efforts around the world, are unlikely to succeed.

To put the issue in this way raises some sympathy for the religion-avoidance syndrome common among American foreign policy officials. The obstacles involved in thinking about how to influence the religious aspects of culture are daunting in the theological realm, let alone the policy world. For any policy maker to consider the direct engagement of Islamic and other religious communities—for example, how to facilitate the processes of internal reform—would require serious thought about the role of religion in human affairs. It would also require fresh thinking about a concept that Americans of all political persuasions talk about with great conviction: religious freedom.

Part of the problem is that both religion and religious liberty are often understood as nonpublic phenomena. This orientation is reflected in the frequent use of phrases such as "freedom of worship" and "religious tolerance" as in the 2002 U.S. National Security Strategy.[21] But these formulations for the most part leave unaddressed the issue of *public* manifestations of religion in a democracy. Moreover, American foreign policy officials routinely use terms such as "religious liberty," "freedom of conscience," and "freedom of belief" as though everyone agreed on what they meant. But they do not agree.

Those who have had responsibility for U.S. foreign affairs since the end of the Cold War have not attempted to reach a consensus on the meaning of religious freedom any more than they have agreed that they must pay serious attention to the religious beliefs and practices in other societies. They have not internalized the reality—of which the Rahman trial was merely one bit of evidence—that the world in which America is engaged is increasingly affected by public manifestations of religious conviction.

The attitudes that have handicapped American foreign policy in Afghanistan have echoes in the War on Terror. During the 2006 and 2008 elections Democrats and Republicans disputed the question of whether the U.S. invasion of Iraq had exacerbated Islamist terror, and whether the resources used in Iraq would have been better employed finding Bin Laden and fighting Al Qaeda and its offshoots elsewhere (including in Afghanistan). Reasonable people might disagree over the answer, but it is the wrong question. At the very least, it is not the only question. What we should be asking ourselves is how to influence the religious war currently taking place *within* Islam over its meaning and its future. And we should be asking similar questions about the religious aspects of other national security issues, such as those presented by China, India, Russia, and even Europe.

Desecularizing Diplomacy

This book presents three distinct but overlapping arguments. First, for the foreseeable future religion will have a significant and increasing impact on public matters in virtually every region of the world.[22] The vast majority of the world's population will not only be committed to a particular religious tradition but also their beliefs will influence social norms and political behaviors, government policies, regional trends, and transnational movements. A world of public faith will continue to have serious implications for the interests of the United States abroad and the security and prosperity of the American people at home.

For those reasons, the religious teachings and actions of other peoples and other nations should be integrated into the official American understanding of the world and our strategy for engaging it. This does not mean that diplomats must be theologians, any more than they must be lawyers or economists. It means that they must rediscover the first principle of true realism, which is to understand things as they are and to call them by their right names. They must attain the capacity to know and to address human behavior in all its forms, including beliefs and practices formed by religion.

Second, the American foreign policy establishment is at present ill-prepared, both philosophically and bureaucratically, to address a world of public faith. A whole variety of principles and habits from across the ideological spectrum of American society feeds a secularist diplomatic culture. The distinction between secular and secularist is important. The United States is a secular society in that it seeks to maintain a proper differentiation between the overlapping spheres of government and religion. Vigorous debates continue about whether the balance has tipped too far in one direction or another in domestic politics and in the influencing of American foreign policy.[23]

But among many of the professionals and scholars in the American foreign policy community itself, there has long been a *secularist* approach to religion—an official, if sometimes implicit, reticence about addressing the religious factors in other cultures and indeed in seeing culture as an expression of religion at all. The explanations are varied and cut across the red-blue, political-cultural divide in America. Our diplomatic tendencies in such matters clearly flow in some respects from what is commonly referred to as modern liberal secularism, that is, the suspicion of religion in any public manifestation. But diplomacy's religion deficit is also nourished by habits of mind, including theological habits of mind, present in the American right. More importantly, as we shall see, the various schools of thought in the U.S. foreign affairs establishment struggle mightily either to avoid the subject of religion or to assume it away, albeit for very different reasons. The fact is that no matter which political party has been in charge, and which version of foreign affairs in the ascendant, American diplomacy has been largely passive and ineffective in its engagement with an international order influenced by faith.

A 2007 study by the Center for Strategic and International Studies examined this problem. After surveying the treatment of religion across the spectrum of American foreign policy agencies, it found that

> U.S. government officials are often reluctant to address the issue of religion, whether in response to a secular U.S. legal and political tradition, in the context of America's Judeo-Christian image overseas, or

simply because religion is perceived as too complicated or sensitive. Current U.S. government frameworks...are narrow, often approaching religions as problematic or monolithic forces, overemphasizing a terrorism-focused analysis of Islam and sometimes marginalizing religion as a peripheral humanitarian or cultural issue. Institutional capacity to understand and approach religion is limited due to...lack of religious expertise or training, minimal influence for religion-related initiatives, and a government primarily structured to engage with other official state actors.[24]

Ironically, this policy deficiency persists amid a significant increase in the numbers of scholarly books and articles concerning religion and foreign policy. One of the unanticipated results of 9/11 was an added momentum to something already under way in some academic disciplines—the abandonment of the so-called secularization theory, according to which religion was inevitably withering with the advance of modernity. A few scholars have questioned the theory for years but its assertions were for the most part too comforting to be challenged by mere facts. The attacks of September 11 proved to be, at least for some, the fact that would not be ignored.

Since 2001 we have seen a proliferation of publications and programs dealing with religion and international affairs, especially among policy-oriented think tanks, such as the Pew Forum on Religion and Public Life, the Rand Corporation, and the Center for Strategic and International Studies (all of which existed prior to 9/11, but whose interest in religion and foreign policy has increased). And yet, as late as four years after the terrorist attacks on the American homeland, the Henry Luce Foundation found it necessary to *entice* selected U.S. academic institutions specializing in international affairs to apply for grants on religion and foreign policy. Its purpose was to get them to pay attention to an issue that they had largely ignored.[25] Although the relationship between religion and foreign policy is getting greater emphasis among some policy institutions, it is still struggling for attention among academic institutions who seek to educate and train our future diplomats—those who will carry out America's engagement with the world. Among the goals of this book, one is to assist in that worthy enterprise.

Third, although correcting these deficiencies will not be easy, a potentially effective and even potent vehicle is at hand. America's existing statutory policy of promoting international religious freedom should be recalibrated, detoxified (at least in the minds of its objects, who view it as U.S. imperialism), broadened, and integrated throughout our foreign policy apparatus to help the United States meet the challenges presented by a world of faith. Such a change will require fresh thinking about religion, about freedom, and about the relationship between the two. It will require new policy mandates from a president, the urging of Congress, a determined secretary of state, strongly supportive political appointees at Foggy Bottom, and new training, incentives and career opportunities for America's diplomats.

To some extent, however, this project will constitute a work of recovery. U.S. policy makers and diplomats will need to recall the success that their own country has had in balancing the competing authorities of religion and state. On June 1, 1660, magistrates from the Massachusetts Bay Colony hanged Mary Dyer on Boston Common for her persistence in believing and proselytizing the Quaker faith.[26] In 1791, the first sixteen words of the Bill of Rights guaranteed the free exercise of religion at the national level. What had happened in the intervening 131 years was not the secularization of American society or politics, or the triumph of Enlightenment rationalism, but the mutual development of religious doctrine and political culture. Rediscovering this experience will be important for American diplomacy, not in order to impose the First Amendment on others, but to overcome the crippling assumption that religion and freedom, or faith and reason, are irreconcilable. U.S. diplomats cannot sell snake oil, not only because consumers won't buy, but also because the salesmen won't believe in the product.

As noted, a major obstacle to this project will be the premises and habits of thought present in U.S. diplomacy's various schools, such as realism, liberal internationalism, and neoconservatism. These schools are repositories of what ought to be our best thinking on how America should engage the world, but until very recently they have had little to say about religion as a policy issue. In the past decade their reluctance has been challenged by the 1998 International Religious Freedom (IRF) Act, the emergence of Islamist terrorism and rising concerns on the American left about the influence of the Christian right on foreign policy.

Those factors have in some ways actually increased resistance among foreign affairs thinkers and the general public to considering religion as a policy matter. As we shall see, the IRF Act has focused the State Department on the humanitarian objectives of denouncing persecution and saving victims, not promoting freedom in any long-term political sense. As such, IRF policy has neither had a significant impact on worldwide religious persecution nor overcome the perception that it is designed to make the world safe for American missionaries. Islamist terrorism has elicited a wide spectrum of responses, from a denial that religion has anything to do with the terrorists' actions to the arguments that Islam is too evil or too violent to engage. Fears on the left about the resurgence of religion in America have deepened suspicions about any official policy, including foreign policy, that treats religious beliefs as a public matter.

The moral and legal framework for official America's hands-off approach to religion in foreign policy is provided by the concept of a "wall of separation" between religion and public life. Many Americans, religious and not, liberal and conservative, have come to understand religious liberty as embodied in that phrase. The wall, thought to be established in the constitution, was puta- tively built to protect us from the divisiveness and (a more recent fear) the moral judgmentalism of religious groups in America. So understood, "reli- gious freedom" requires that religion-based belief and practice be protected but privatized. Because religion and religiously informed moral judgments are based on absolute truth claims, and such claims and judgments endanger the compromises necessary for democracy, faith-based "absolutism" must be cor- doned outside the public square in order to protect the democratic system.

This idea of religious liberty is both ahistorical and tendentious, but it is highly influential in the foreign affairs establishment. Not long ago I queried a lawyer in a foreign policy agency about why U.S.-funded democracy programs in the Middle East avoided direct engagement with religious communities. By way of explanation he cited parts of the Supreme Court's "Lemon test." We must determine, he wrote, "whether there has been a violation of the consti- tutionally required separation of church and state, [... i.e.,] whether the funded activity has a secular purpose and, even if it does, whether the funded activity has a primary effect of advancing or inhibiting religion."[27] In other words, a court test for determining cases inside the United States is cited as a reason for restraining America's engagement of religion abroad.[28]

That view of religious freedom is, of course, controversial as a domestic matter, and has in some ways been abandoned by the Supreme Court itself. Moreover, it is slowly being challenged in foreign affairs by intermittent U.S. programs that do engage religious belief and practice. But in the 21st century a policy of ad hockery concerning religion is destined to fail. Unfortunately, the wall of separation understanding of religious liberty (also known as "strict separationism") and its parallel insistence on the privatization of faith tend to be accepted by most members of the permanent bureaucracy in Washington, D.C., by the professoriate, the media, and Hollywood. In American universities it has become so encrusted in academic orthodoxy that a Harvard curriculum committee implicitly made the extraordinary admission in 2006 that Harvard graduates were not being educated to know "the role of religion in contempo- rary, historical or future events."[29] More to the point, it is the view assumed by most senior members of the U.S. Foreign Service, many of whom were educated in elite institutions like Harvard, charged with "promoting religious freedom" as part of American foreign policy.

But skepticism about official U.S. involvement with foreign religious com- munities is not the exclusive preserve of strict separationists. Some who reject the "wall of separation" at home believe that our government, especially the State Department, is simply incompetent to address the issue abroad. This view was embraced by some who led the campaign for a new international reli- gious freedom policy and still has its adherents. Responding to my advocacy for more U.S. engagement with Muslim jurists, a veteran conservative religious freedom activist told me he had "no faith in the U.S. government's ability to do this sort of thing intelligently: Washington will end up subsidizing the Islamic counterparts of Hans Kung [a Roman Catholic dissident]."

The upshot of all these views is that, while most of the world is steeped in religious thought and action, the agencies charged with understanding the world and furthering American interests in it are not yet up to the task. And, for the most part, there is little public pressure for them to change. There are, of course, exceptions—foreign affairs thinkers, policy officials, or active diplomats who for whatever reason happen to have an interest in the subject.[30] Indeed, there are signs that their numbers are growing, especially in the wake of the debate over radical Islam, and we will meet a few of them in the story to come. But although religion as a topic of discussion in foreign policy has certainly increased, the increased volume has not overcome diplomacy's religion deficit.

In the 21st century, this simply will not do. Creedal commitments have too much impact on the public behavior that affects American security for our diplomats to avert their eyes, treating religion as a private matter or addressing it only if they happen to have a personal interest. Our diplomacy should treat faith much as it does politics or economics—as factors that drive the world of men, women, and nations in important ways. Diplomats must begin to engage the various aspects of religion systematically, not as it suits, or doesn't suit, the fancy of whoever happens to be on the spot. The quality and effectiveness of America's engagement with a world of public faith should not depend on whether a Baptist, a Rawlsian secularist, or a lapsed Catholic is in charge.

That said, this is not a book about the religious right or the religious left or any other direction of religious persuasion. Much has been written about the impact on American national security policy from lobbying by Christians of one sort or another, or Jews of one sort or another, or, increasingly, Muslims of one sort or another. This is not that kind of book. Although the influence of religious interest groups will play a part in the following chapters, my purpose is not to lionize or demonize one or another. In the course of telling the story, I will have a few nice and a few critical things to say about many of them. But that is not the point I am trying to make.

The starting point from which American foreign policy should encounter the world of religion is not the dogma of any particular religious tradition or any particular secularist philosophy. The starting point should be that of American national interests, of religious realism, and of religious freedom properly understood. The United States should address the public effects of religion, both positive and negative, by promoting religious freedom in the fullest sense of that term, including the advancement of solutions to one of the foremost national security issues of our day—achieving a stable and liberal balance between the overlapping authorities of religion and state. The failure to achieve such a balance has in many states fed religious persecution, led to social and political instability, and encouraged the religion-based terrorism of groups like Al Qaeda and Hezbollah.

Religion has also had an important but little noticed influence on the nation many experts believe is the most consequential for American interests—China. There the Communist government fears religion so vehemently that it admits capitalists into the Communist party but not religious believers. Chinese attempts to control religious practice have led to grave persecution and injustice and have triggered a significant humanitarian reaction within religious and human rights circles in the United States. Those policies, as we shall see, have also reinforced the American diplomatic habit of addressing cases and seeking prisoner releases.

But U.S. policy has virtually ignored a more strategic problem: an economically and militarily powerful, regionally ambitious, and nuclear-armed China also has an exploding population of religious adherents. The communities they represent, especially evangelical forms of Protestant Christianity, but also Catholicism, Islam, and Buddhism, present a growing dilemma for Chinese authorities. China's surge of religion cannot successfully be repressed or controlled short of another brutal and destructive Cultural Revolution. The trajectory suggests that either the Chinese will find a way to accommodate religion or turn it into the very thing they (and we) most fear: deep social and political instability. The United States must begin to address this problem.

There are, of course, limits to what U.S. foreign policy can and should do with respect to the religious convictions active in other societies. American officials cannot fruitfully engage directly in the theological and religious debates taking place within various areas of the Muslim world—or for that matter within other influential religious communities, such as Russian Orthodoxy or Indian Hinduism. To do so would invite scorn and suspicion and would undermine the mutual respect that must undergird a successful U.S. policy. Muslims must decide on the authoritative interpretations of the Koran and the hadith, Christians the Bible and its teachings.

But America is not served by ignorance, indifference, or confusion about the impact of religion on the moral and political norms necessary to protect the nation's security in the 21st century. American diplomacy must not only understand the religious traditions of the world and their adherents, but must have a clear policy with which to engage and influence them, and the governments under which they live, in ways that further American interests. We must find ways to demonstrate that public religion and liberal governance are not only compatible but can be mutually supportive. We must learn how to engage in respectful discourse with religious actors and their political theologies. We must be able to make the case that societies willing to construct democracies based on religious freedom are more likely to last, their citizens to flourish, and their religious communities to have a legitimate influence on democratic policy.

Eliminating Persecution with Ordered Liberty

Promoting religious freedom properly understood must be a central element of a refurbished American engagement with a world of faith. Since the passage of the 1998 International Religious Freedom Act the United States has nominally been committed to advancing religious freedom around the world.[31] In fact, with few exceptions, our government has not pursued such a policy. The State Department has instead focused on countering religious persecution and freeing religious prisoners. Even so, a decade after the passage of the IRF Act, worldwide religious persecution has not substantially abated, and in those few areas where it has abated, U.S. IRF policy has usually not played a role.[32]

Part of the reason for the relative ineffectiveness of U.S. IRF policy is that even the focus on religious persecution has been isolated from larger national security strategies. IRF actions have too often consisted of fruitless rhetorical denunciations of persecuting governments. It is true—and important—that religious prisoners have been freed by State Department efforts. Each removal of a human being from harm's way is a noble achievement worthy of our nation and the American diplomats who have helped to bring it about. But in the world of persecution prisoners are, alas, fungible assets; victims liberated after U.S. pressure are easily replaced by others.

More to the point, opposing persecution and freeing prisoners, however successfully, is not the same as advancing religious freedom. Clearly religious freedom and religious persecution are incompatible, and it is entirely appropriate and commensurate with American values for U.S. human rights policy to condemn this degrading abuse of human dignity, just as it does others (such as torture of people because of their ethnicity or gender). Further, it makes sense to develop policies that can have a chance of altering or ending persecutory behavior, whether it is by governments or private actors sanctioned or ignored by governments.

But to repeat, a decade of U.S. IRF policy has for the most part not succeeded in altering, much less ending, persecutory behaviors by governments or private actors. Nor does IRF policy as currently configured seem likely to produce such an outcome. Since the passage of the IRF Act, it is arguable that U.S. intervention has significantly reduced levels of religious persecution in four countries—Vietnam, Serbia-Kosovo, Afghanistan, and Iraq. U.S. IRF policy has clearly had a positive impact in Vietnam (see chapter 7). But in the other three cases the effects were due to military action, not IRF policy. In each, human rights abuses on the basis of religion fell dramatically after the respective despotic regimes were overthrown, but in the ensuing years levels of persecution have crept back up. And in none of these cases has the United States sought in any comprehensive way to "promote religious freedom." Its IRF policy has only been involved in any of these countries in an ad hoc and inconsistent way.

Religious persecution is generally associated with egregious abuse of persons—e.g., torture, rape, unjust imprisonment—on the basis of religion. A political order centered on religious liberty is free of such abuses, to be sure, but it also protects the rights of individuals and groups to *act* publicly in ways consistent with belief. This positive understanding of religious freedom implicates justice for individuals and communities, *and* the long-term stability of the democratic state. It includes, most importantly, the right to influence public policy within limits roughly similar to those that apply to other individuals and associations in civil society. Helping religious communities see those limits as part of a democratic bargain they otherwise desire—and as compatible with, if not mandated by, their teachings—is a critical step in creating stable self-government, and in countering religious extremism, especially in societies with powerful religious groups. It is a step that current U.S. policy ignores.

Where religious liberty truly exists, citizens are certainly free from torture and abuse, but something far more transformative and durable has occurred in the political order. A useful way to think about this issue is provided by political scientist Daniel Philpott in his notion of "consensual differentiation," that is, a harmonious, overlapping autonomy between religion and state that works to the advantage of both.[33] In such a polity the natural tensions between the claims of religion and the claims of the state are continually reconciled and rebalanced by setting reasonable limits on both. These limits free both minority and majority religious communities not only to practice their religious rites but also to contend peacefully within the public square on the basis of their claims to religious and moral truth. Religious freedom grounded in consensual differentiation is not the same thing as "strict separation" or French *laicite*, both of which seek to banish religion from the public square. Rather, it is a mutual accommodation of religion and government which serves the common good.

As we shall see, consensual differentiation and religious freedom have been major components of democratic development among nations formed historically by Protestantism. Moreover, since the 1970s the movement of most Catholic nations toward democracy has been driven by a doctrinal embrace of religious freedom and consensual differentiation, that is, the abandonment of any claim on the state's coercive powers. In recent years a handful of Muslim nations—most notably Indonesia and Turkey—have moved toward greater differentiation, and, more haltingly, toward religious freedom. These politico-religious developments have both humanitarian and strategic significance for the United States. They do herald a decrease in persecution, but they also mean an increase in the prospects for the kind of stable, ordered liberty that can further American interests and reduce threats to American security.

Among successful, mature democracies levels of differentiation between religion and state will vary, but a few generalizations about benefits and boundaries are warranted. If powerful religious communities in the Middle East, for example, are to accept consensual differentiation and, ultimately, full religious freedom, they must perceive advantages for their adherents and their teachings. Some of the benefits are demonstrated by history and social science. A growing body of scholarly work is adducing evidence that religious freedom is the key element in a set of "bundled freedoms"—political liberties such as free speech and assembly without which democracies cannot mature and survive, let alone flourish. In nations with powerful or significant religious communities (that is, most nations on earth), religious freedom seems to be the lynchpin. Without it, the other freedoms cannot do their work. When religious liberty is absent, the result is religious violence and conflict. When it is present, the result is more social capital and economic development, more critical social progress such as increased female literacy, and—perhaps most important—the consolidation, maturation and longevity of democracy itself.[34]

In political terms, consensual differentiation and religious freedom can convey benefits on religious communities that seek to influence political authority and legal systems. A democracy based on consensual differentiation does not require the banishment of religion from the moral judgments that inform public policy and shape the laws and norms designed to promote the common good. In fact religious liberty renders democracy more stable by encouraging religious individuals and communities to contend within the political order on the basis of the rationality and persuasiveness of their views, rather than through coercion or violence. In other words, Afghan Muslims, Afghan democracy, and the various forms of Afghan Islam will benefit from differentiation and religious freedom, including from a public debate over blasphemy and apostasy laws. This argument will be resisted by Islamist extremists, which is precisely why it must be made by Muslims themselves, encouraged by the United States.

In some cases the very experience of democratic governing will provide its own incentives for differentiation and religious liberty. Iraqi Shiites, for example, have exercised majoritarian power over minority Sunnis and non-Muslim Iraqis, but the difficulties of governing may eventually lead Shiite leaders to accept greater differentiation and some degree of religious freedom as means to stabilize Iraqi democracy. Over the long term, however, it will be critical for religious and political actors in the Middle East and elsewhere to understand the empirical benefits of differentiation and religious freedom—social, economic, political and religious. American IRF policy should put itself in a position to help them reach this kind of understanding, a point to which we return in chapter 9.

The flip side of differentiation is the limits on the power of religious communities within civil society, limits critical to democratic stability and longevity. Those boundaries will vary from country to country, but some are foundational. Religious actors and groups must agree to forswear coercion or violence. They must reject any claim on civil authority to privilege membership in their organizations, prevent exit from (or entry into) their and other religious communities, advance their forms of worship, or coerce acceptance of revealed truth claims not subject to rational public discourse and assent. Christians in a liberal democracy, for example, may not use the laws to require baptism or belief in the Trinity. Governments in democratic Muslim nations may not mandate legal penalties for apostasy or blasphemy, nor condition citizenship on being a Muslim. Nor may they employ religious norms to disadvantage women, non-Muslims, or disfavored Muslims in civil society by denying them the vote or equality under the laws. As difficult as the acceptance of these ideas may be, history (especially that of the Roman Catholic Church) is replete with evidence that privileged access to legal and civil power by religious communities works to their disadvantage over time. The union of political and religious authority corrupts both (a lesson that many citizens of Iran may have begun to discern).[35]

In sum, the United States can attack the very structures of persecution by advancing ideas and institutions of religious freedom that support the same goals as liberal governance—the flourishing of citizens in a well-ordered civil society. In order to accomplish this, however, America's international religious freedom policy must recognize the particular role that religion often plays in public lives, and the role that it can play in the public life of a liberal democracy, always taking into account variations in culture, ethnicity, nationality, politics, and economic development.

How Can We Talk to the Neighbors about Their Religion?

A fruitful way for American diplomacy to discuss religious freedom in a democratic political context is to focus on who we are rather than who God is.[36] First, two caveats. This approach need not require anyone to deny their own theological principles, least of all diplomats acting on behalf of the United States. Indeed, the American democratic system is steeped in a powerful theistic truth claim—that, in the words of Supreme Court Justice William Douglas, American democracy "presupposes a Supreme Being."[37] Moreover, even though Islam is less doctrinal than Christianity, it is difficult to speak to Muslims about politics without taking into account their understanding of God and what God requires of them.[38] In my travels to the Middle East, I employed to good effect my understanding of the theistic underpinnings of American democracy in discussions about the relationship between religion and democracy. In such situations it is neither necessary nor desirable to banish God from the conversation. Among those who do believe in God or gods, a reasoned discussion of divine nature can help, witness the Christian-Muslim dialogue that has developed out of Pope Benedict XVI's 2006 remarks concerning the nature of God in Islamic theology during a speech in Regensburg, Germany.[39]

Second, the focus on the person and his or her nature, rather than on theology itself, should not cause us to overlook what Harvard scholar Michael Sandel has usefully labeled the "encumbered self." Sandel has criticized both modern American jurisprudence and liberal political thought for defining religious freedom as merely another measure of human autonomy. Religious beliefs are in the modern liberal understanding merely one category of choices in the supermarket of possible choices. Sandel points out that the American founders did not see religion as a choice, but a duty, and defined religious liberty as the right to fulfill the duty. He also notes that many Americans still see religion not as a choice but a response to something beyond themselves, something that beckons with a force that binds the conscience.[40]

In Sandel's words, the modern liberal understanding of religion as mere choice "fails to capture those loyalties and responsibilities whose moral force consists partly in the fact that living by them is inseparable from understanding ourselves as the particular persons we are...."[41] The modern liberal understanding of religious freedom has handicapped America's international religious freedom policy, in particular in those parts of the world where religious individuals see themselves as responding to something metaphysical rather than choosing among lifestyles. This is a particularly important caveat in our approach to religious freedom in Muslim-majority nations.

But there are also distinct advantages to focusing on the nature of human beings rather than the nature of God. It admits into the conversation those whose religious beliefs are not monotheistic, such as Hindus, or not theistic at all (some versions of Buddhism and Taoism). Within the United States, this approach also accommodates those who deny that theistic principles underpin American democracy, or those who argue that such principles once existed but are no longer relevant under conditions of contemporary religious and moral pluralism. It includes those who, like former Secretary of State Madeleine Albright, may accept the role of God in the American story and are calling for more attention to religion in American foreign policy but still fear that public religion in America has resulted in our leaders confusing their own will with God's.[42] Our anthropological approach relieves us of the necessity of agreeing on the precise content of God's will while focusing us on the human quest to understand it.

To assert a right of religious freedom in this fashion is to affirm a truth claim about human nature and on behalf of human beings. This claim, of course, may be challenged by secularists or others, but many will acknowledge its rationality and potential for American foreign policy. The claim is that people naturally seek to know ultimate, transcendent truths. Following James Madison and most of the American founders it assumes a duty and therefore a "natural" right to seek those truths. Unlike civil rights (such as the right to vote), natural rights are not created by governments. Madison believed those rights came from God. But he would also agree that they are rooted in justice and intrinsic to the well-being of every person because of human nature, because each of us is "hard wired," as it were, to seek ultimate truth. Natural rights must therefore be recognized and protected by any government constituted to serve the interests of its citizens.

The reality is that virtually all human beings share a thirst for transcendence. Wherever we live, however we are situated socially or economically, most of us are naturally impelled to ask the questions that lie at the heart of personhood: What are the origin, meaning, and destiny of my life? Is there something or someone beyond my personal existence, a transcendent reality that accounts for my being, or influences me and the world in which I live, or determines my fate in an afterlife? If so, what is its nature and what does it require of me?

The desire to answer such questions is for the most part so natural and so powerful in human nature that addressing them in some fashion is utterly necessary to our private and public well-being (another way of expressing Madison's notion of "duty"). If I conclude that such a transcendent being exists, it is quite natural—indeed, quite reasonable—that I should want to know and communicate with that being. This is the religious quest, and it has been pursued by human beings from ancient Greece and Persia to modern China and contemporary France.[43] The questions may be asked in different ways and the answers quite obviously vary widely. A few skeptics, mostly secularists living or educated in the West, despair of discovering answers at all or simply conclude that any certainty about them is impossible. A smaller minority, also mostly in the West, quite remarkably manage to achieve certainty that there is no God or that there are no answers.[44]

An under secretary of state once told me that his most powerful existential questions had to do with his tennis swing, not the existence of God. This was a cordial but pointed jest, designed to refute my argument that the search for transcendence is universal. It reflected a point of view that should not be trivialized, much less ignored. Such attitudes, unusual outside the West today, are perhaps disproportionately represented in the U.S. State Department. Whether or not that is true, it is beyond dispute that the world which the State Department must engage on behalf of the American people is religious. The vast majority of the world's people appears to believe they have discovered or are in the process of discovering answers to the religious questions.

Properly understood, then, freedom of religion is the right to pursue the religious quest, to embrace or reject the interior and public obligations that ensue, and to enter or exit religious communities that reflect, or do not reflect, one's understanding of religious truth. If people are not free in all these senses, they cannot be said to be living a fully human life. To restrict this right unduly, or to persecute someone for exercising it peacefully, is to mount an assault on human dignity. In political terms religious freedom is the right of every person to an immunity from coercion by civil or other human authority in pursuing, or not pursuing, the truths of religion.

So defined, the right is grounded initially in an interior and personal dimension, namely the right of conscience (to believe or not) which cannot be touched by any government or other human agency. The right of conscience, however, also has a natural public dimension. Moral obligations flow from a conscience that is bound by its apprehension of religious truths, whether derived by faith, reason, or both. Those obligations often require a religious believer to take or refrain from taking certain actions. Accordingly, freedom of conscience implies a right to live publicly in accord with the truths one has discovered during the religious enterprise and to enter the public square with those truths, bounded by the kinds of limits discussed earlier in this chapter.

The enterprise of holding and manifesting religious truth claims can induce charity and winsome persuasiveness, compassion and respect, fidelity and sacrifice—characteristics and virtues that can underwrite positive social, economic, and political forces, liberal institutions, and stability. As noted, social science data demonstrate that societies embracing religious freedom induce high levels of social capital from religious individuals and communities, that is, the attitudes and actions that both benefit societies and help consolidate democracies. But human commitment to religious truth claims can also yield self-righteousness, hatred and intolerance, instability, persecution, and, when combined with modern technologies and weapons, transnational terrorism. It is all the more important, therefore, that any liberal polity address this bivalent potential of religion successfully. Any U.S. strategy designed to advance democracy must also advance religious freedom, including the limits which harness it to the common good.

For American diplomacy there are at least two difficult but critical implications of religion's potential for good and ill and the public dimension of religious freedom. The first is that religious liberty implies a right peacefully to persuade others that one's beliefs are true and that they should be embraced. Often labeled "proselytism," this is one of the most controversial aspects of religious freedom but one that goes to the core of its meaning. The right to convince others of the truthfulness of one's religious beliefs is in one sense a subset of freedom of expression, but it is far more than that. Religious people usually hold their beliefs not simply as "opinion" but as objective truth. The very nature of apprehending religious truth often includes the utter necessity, the duty, of sharing it with others.

Religious truth claims, in other words, are not generally understood as personal possessions, generated by human agents for themselves. Especially in Christianity and some interpretations of Islam those claims are seen as universal, belonging to and applying ipso facto to everyone. This is why they are so powerful and so volatile. Proselytism can be mercenary and can exploit ignorance, poverty, and emotional loneliness. It can interrupt or damage existing family and social relationships and disrupt communities of faith. In states with historically dominant religious traditions, the arrival of foreign missionaries can trigger severe reactions within those traditions, sometimes with the support of the state. This has occurred, for example, in Russia where the Russian Orthodox Church has allied with Russian civil authorities in resisting missionaries. The net result has been increased barriers to differentiation and a decrease in religious freedom. No American religious freedom policy can succeed if it is, or is perceived to be, designed to undermine traditional cultures or to privilege American missionaries.

But if proselytism is understood as peaceful persuasion, necessarily respectful of human dignity, culture, and tradition as intrinsic to the activity, it can contribute to stable, liberal, and just governance, especially in highly religious societies. The evidence suggests both that government restrictions on proselytization and conversions lead to religious violence, and that permitting such activities within reasonable limits can yield social, political, economic, and—perhaps most important—religious advantages.[45] The question for political and religious leaders in any country, and for American foreign policy, is how proselytism as an aspect of religious freedom can be encouraged so that its benefits might be realized while at the same time limited to avoid its costs. Such limits can be imposed by the state through laws of general applicability against violence and coercion, and restrictions on conversions of minors without the consent of their parents. Even more important is the exercise of restraint on the part of proselytizers who understand and respect the societies and individuals that they are engaging. Teasing out these tensions is a task for America's international religious freedom policy—a subject to which we shall return.

The second public aspect of religious freedom is of equal and perhaps even greater consequence for the long-term social and political harmony of a nation, and for American diplomacy. Most people do not live their religious lives in isolation. They worship, teach, raise their children, seek and celebrate religious truths, and attempt to influence laws and norms, in community with others of like mind. That is to say, most religious people are members of confessional communities that tend to increase the validity and the power of the truths that bind them in conscience. Accordingly, the right of religious freedom must extend to religious groups just as it does to individuals.[46] Both individuals and religious communities must have access to the interior and exterior rights of religion, including the right to influence the political arrangements under which they live in an attempt to make them consistent with belief. In short, religious communities must have the same rights of autonomy and political engagement as other elements of civil society, albeit bounded by rules that take into account the unique value and power of religion in the lives of human beings. So defined, religious freedom for groups is both a matter of justice and of democratic political stability.

It is also true that the significance of religion in the modern world goes beyond its status as a set of beliefs. Religion sometimes constitutes a source of social identity into which people are born and remain for reasons that cut across the search for transcendence—reasons such as family ties, ethnicity, nationality, language, or status. Within religious groupings that themselves are defined by belief, there are inevitably differences over theology and politics. Moreover, the most apparent differences between religious communities are often over power, and not simply views of God and salvation. Although

American foreign policy has not dealt effectively with religious communities on any level, the "rational actor" model of human behavior (as we shall see) encourages diplomats to address religion as little more than a quest for power and wealth. It is far more difficult, and far more important, to understand and engage the religious ideas within which those quests operate and which lend them meaning and potency.

Politics is the way we order our lives together. Liberal democracy is premised on the equal right of all individuals and groups within civil society, both religious and secular, to influence the constitutions, laws, norms, and regulations that order individual liberty to the common good. If the United States is to continue the quest to undermine religious extremism through the institutions of self-government, it must address this issue forthrightly. The history of religion and democracy, not least in the United States, suggests that the two can flourish together and strengthen each other, provided they arrive at a covenant that regulates their respective, overlapping authorities. A democratic government constituted by citizens with strong religious beliefs cannot bypass this step if their society is to be truly liberal, stable, and free.

This is how American foreign policy should understand the twin goals of advancing religious freedom and, at the same time, engaging a world of public religion by enticing religious communities to the advantages of liberal governance. There are, of course, different ways to achieve these goals. In some cases, it will be necessary or prudent to pursue modest, interim objectives, for example in theocratic societies such as Saudi Arabia. In other cases it will continue to make sense to convince a dictator such as Uzbekistan's Islam Karimov that continuing his persecutions will cost more than they are worth. But such punitive approaches should over time occupy a smaller and smaller place in our religious freedom policy. Not only have they proven ineffective in reducing persecution over the long run, but they obscure and threaten America's need to adopt a new realism in a world of faith.

Making religious freedom properly understood the centerpiece of U.S. policy does not mean abandoning the humanitarian goal of reducing persecution and the suffering of victims. Quite the opposite is true. Success in a broadened policy would reduce religious persecution, as well as other human rights abuses. Nor would a broadened policy mean placing its entire burden on one office headed by one ambassador—the State Department's office of international religious freedom and the ambassador at large established as its head by the 1998 International Religious Freedom (IRF) Act.

In order to succeed, America's policy of advancing regimes of religious freedom must be mainstreamed within U.S. diplomacy and embraced as a policy that serves the national interest broadly understood, rather than as it is widely seen now—a humanitarian effort that is acceptable, even nice to have, so long as it is absorbed into other human rights efforts and will cede the way when other more strategic interests are involved. That is what has happened to U.S. policy in Afghanistan and much of the Middle East.

For this reason and others, as we shall see, it will be important to elevate the role and authority of the State Department's office of international religious freedom, even as a broadened IRF policy is integrated into U.S. national security strategy and mainstreamed within American diplomacy. Currently, that office is the only institution within the foreign policy establishment of the United States whose job it is to engage religious communities and to think about religion systematically. It holds this mandate by law, a considerable advantage in a culture resistant to thinking about religion at all.

Moreover, the fervent (if fragmented) religious rights movement that produced the IRF Act has for the most part moved on to other foreign policy issues, such as trafficking in persons and the horrific problem of Sudan, but these groups could quickly be reinvigorated to support the office and its work. They remain a potentially powerful base for support among the American public for a broader religious freedom policy, one that benefits their co-religionists abroad more effectively than at present. And then there are those religious groups who resisted the policy, in particular Muslim Americans, as aimed against their coreligionists overseas. This resistance remains to this day and has increased with the abandonment of the dialogue begun with Muslims under the first IRF ambassador at large. Winning American Muslim support for U.S. policy would be a major step forward and could have some benefit for U.S. efforts in the greater Middle East.

In sum, a policy of actually advancing political regimes of religious freedom as a centerpiece of U.S. foreign policy could have a broad spectrum of benefits. It could strengthen American national security by undermining Islamist transnational terrorism and regional or national extremism. It could help stabilize struggling democracies throughout the Muslim world and beyond in nations such as Russia and India. In China, it could help encourage a transition to political reform without domestic upheaval. It could reduce the perception abroad that America is imperialist, hedonistic, and peddling a value-free form of democracy that is intrinsically anti-Islam. It could encourage a broadening of U.S. interest group advocacy and encourage cooperation among U.S. religious groups, such as Catholics and Muslims or Muslims and Jews.

The following chapters are arranged into three sections. Part I examines the various dimensions of what has long been thought to be a fundamental contradiction: the simultaneous spread of democracy and of religion. Chapter 1 explores the dimensions of religion's "return from exile," as one group of international affairs scholars puts it, and what this means for American national security. It maps out a key element of the secularization theory that has disproportionately influenced policy makers—the conviction that religion is inherently irrational. Chapter 2 explores the sources of the "religion deficit" among the major schools of American foreign policy. Here we engage the question: Why do they (and the U.S. foreign affairs establishment writ large) tend to set religion aside as a category of discourse and analysis? Chapter 3 examines how a more realistic and historical understanding of religion and democracy can increase the effectiveness of U.S. foreign policy in influencing the natural desire of peoples around the world for freedom and for religious autonomy.

Part II explores an unprecedented political phenomenon—the passage and implementation of a law that *requires* the executive branch, and in particular the Department of State, to advance religious freedom as a core element of U.S. foreign policy. Chapter 4 describes the genesis and adoption of the 1998 IRF Act, a process that previewed some of the fault lines that would later emerge—including the shortsightedness of both the American left and right. Chapters 5 through 7 examine the accreted habits and bureaucratic instincts that effectively enabled Foggy Bottom (a moniker for the State Department) to do very little about advancing religious freedom in any real sense but that also laid the groundwork for future progress.

Although the liberal internationalists in the Democratic Party were highly suspicious of the law and its supporters, the Clinton administration was in some ways more supportive of the new policy than the Bush administration that followed. Surprisingly, George W. Bush's undoubted devotion to the issue of religious freedom had few policy tentacles. U.S. international religious freedom policy was not integrated into the administration's freedom agenda, with consequences that appear in retrospect to have been significant. Nor did the president's team see any reason to elevate the policy within the State Department, where it had been effectively quarantined.

And yet significant tracks were laid for a more comprehensive strategy of actually advancing religious freedom in ways that would promote America's interests in places such as Saudi Arabia and China. Part II is partly autobiographical in that it draws upon my adventures serving with two brave souls— the first and second ambassadors for International Religious Freedom in the U.S. Department of State.

Having set the stage with manifold problems and possible solutions, the book descends to the particular in Part III. It begins with an exploration of what is perhaps the most imminent challenge to American well-being: the multilayered and bewildering phenomenon of Islamist extremism. Chapter 8 is built around my pre-9/11 trip into Saudi Arabia, and examines Islam from within the region of its birth. Chapter 9 attempts to demonstrate what might be accomplished in the lands of Islam by religious realism and the advancement of religious freedom properly understood. Chapter 10 turns to perhaps the most important non-Muslim country affecting American national interests—China. It argues that the control and suppression of religion in China is more than a humanitarian, rights-based issue. It also implicates the well-being and security of the American people.

Along the way I pay due regard to the significant obstacles to a more realistic U.S. policy on religion, including the "poison hand" problem—the perception that other nations are going to resist what the United States offers simply because it is the United States that is doing the offering. Some of this problem is endemic. It goes with the territory of being the most powerful country in the world. But some of the problem is self-inflicted. It derives from a perception, however inaccurate, that America is dismissive of the cultures of others and intends to remake the world in its image.

One of this book's themes is that promoting true religious freedom can help counter that perception. There are several reasons that this is so, but the primary one is straightforward: if the United States stops peddling strict separation and privatization of religion and begins to address the way religions can flourish within liberal states, it will be perceived as grounding its policy in respect rather than in hostility or in arrogance.

PART I

Intimations

1

⸺∞⸺

Confounded by Faith

The consistent need to find explanations other than religious ones for the [9/11] attacks says, in fact, more about the West than it does about the jihadis. Western scholars have generally failed to take religion seriously. Secularists, whether liberals or socialists, grant true explanatory power to political, social, or economic factors but discount the plain sense of religious statements made by the jihadis themselves.
—Mary Habeck, *Knowing the Enemy*[1]

I want my lawyer, tailor, valets, even my wife, to believe in God. I think that if they do I shall be robbed less and cheated less.
—Voltaire[2]

"Sociology."

With that damning label the CIA had dismissed the only intelligence analysis of Iran during the 1970s that discerned a religious basis for the opposition brewing against the American-backed Shah. The word was, according to one scholar of international affairs, "used in intelligence circles to mean the time-wasting study of factors deemed politically irrelevant." By contrast, most credible attempts to explain Iranian social and political ferment were securely grounded in a secularist world view: the unrest was caused by political opposition to tyranny, the economic dislocation of the newly urbanized, the social resentment of the traditional merchant class, or some combination of such factors. Religion, if it had a role at all, was seen to be marginal or reactionary. Reports indicated a distinction between "pious" and "modern" Iranians, the former inevitably in decline, the latter moving with the tide of history toward triumph.[3]

From the vantage point of the early 21st century, as Iran's clerical autocracy resists internal democratic reform, pursues nuclear weapons, and supports Islamist terrorism, it is clear that the premises driving America's official understanding of events in Iran were severely deficient. Although the CIA and State Department had experts on the shah and the Iranian political elite, they had virtually no contacts with religious leaders and little understanding of the influence of Ayatollah Ruhollah Khomeini. As one observer put it, our foreign service officers lacked "mosque time."[4] American diplomacy simply did not believe that mastering a culture meant mastering "cult" or religion.

These assumptions also meant that American policy makers gave little consideration to the range of possible relationships between religion and state in this overwhelmingly Shiite nation. There was no policy to understand the variants of Iranian Shiism or encourage thinking about Shiite democracy among the theologians in places like Qom. That city was then a major center of Iranian religious thought; today it is home to some 300 seminaries and 50,000 seminarians, including men and women.[5] But there was ample reason for at least considering such a policy. Iran's 1906 constitution had been a remarkably liberal document, one which had vested more political sovereignty in the people than in God. Popular sovereignty had been supported by most of the Iranian *ulema* (religious scholars), led by Ayatollah Muhammad Husayn Na'ini, as compatible with Shiism. A century later, Grand Ayatollah Ali al-Sistani, an Iranian who became the most influential cleric in Iraq after the American invasion, took essentially the same position during the 2005 debates over an Iraqi constitution.[6]

One reason the United States did not seek to engage religious communities in Iran was that it tended to associate those communities with terrorism. When Shiite radicals held U.S. diplomats captive in Tehran for over a year, the connection between political Islam and extremism was rooted in the American diplomatic psyche. The spread of Islamist extremism during the next three decades did nothing to ease those concerns. Beginning with the assassination of Egyptian President Anwar Sadat in 1981, followed by suicide attacks on U.S. diplomats and marines in Lebanon two years later, American diplomacy witnessed, and fell victim to, a growing tide of religion-based terrorism.

Other failures of analysis and policy were fed by a similar tendency to discount the role of religion. In Lebanon, the U.S. for years insisted on ignoring the confessional basis for political affiliations, and tended to explain Lebanese divisions in classic "right-left" political terms. Today an extremist Shiite group, Hezbollah (the "party of God"), is emerging as the dominant political force in Lebanon. In Vietnam during the 1950s and 1960s, religious differences were generally ignored by U.S. policy makers in analyses of Vietnamese political behavior.[7] Today the Vietnamese government periodically commits or ignores abuses against religious communities of all stripes, from indigenous Hua Hao and Buddhists to more recent arrivals like evangelical Protestants in the central highlands.[8]

In Sudan a twenty-year civil war was often seen as the result of ethnic or racial differences, when in fact an Islamist government had widely broadcast its intent to impose its version of Islam on Christian and animist minorities, as well as Muslims that failed to measure up.[9] By the 1990s the Islamist Sudanese government was harboring Osama Bin Laden while he planned Al Qaeda attacks on American interests. Today Khartoum continues its campaign for Islamicization.

Nor was official America's religious myopia confined to areas where Christianity was a minority religion. In Cold War Poland, the U.S. embassy's understanding of the Catholic Church was so thin that embassy officials were caught off guard by its contribution to the events that were to alter Polish history and trigger similar changes in Europe and the Soviet Union. Typically, American diplomats did have connections with the Polish labor movement but were insufficiently familiar with its grounding in Catholic theology and social teaching.[10] In his history of Solidarity's nonviolent revolution against the Polish communist regime, Timothy Garton Ash observes that the workers' movement kept its sights on "the higher plane of human rights and political participation."[11] Neither the revolution nor its animating vision of human rights would have occurred, writes George Weigel, "without the steady catechesis of human rights preached by the Church since the 1960s."[12]

U.S. democracy promotion programs begun in the 1980s generally ignored the powerful connections between religion and democracy. The hesitation to engage directly with religious communities was in part the result of a secularist diplomatic culture, but it was also buttressed by a vague sense that such activities were unconstitutional. In retrospect it seems reasonable to ask whether this linkage might have played a more productive role in U.S. thinking about how to encourage and influence democratic institutions. The "third wave" of democratic development during the 1970s and 1980s was heavily influenced by Catholic doctrine.[13] Political reformers from Spain and Portugal to Chile and the Philippines were influenced by the Second Vatican Council's embrace of religious freedom in the civil order and, by implication at least, democracy itself.[14] There was also considerable evidence that Protestantism had long been associated with democratic development.[15]

Despite these trends, U.S. democracy programs have until recently avoided the subject of religion in their objectives and implementation. With some exceptions, nongovernmental organizations funded by the United States have tended to emphasize democratic procedures such as holding elections, developing political parties, and drafting statutes.[16] They have also focused on seeding civil society institutions, such as a free press, professional associations, women's movements, and trade unions, which limit the power of government and encourage the habits of trust and cooperation that are vital to a free citizenry. Our experiences in Iran, Lebanon, Sudan, and elsewhere should have taught us that religious teachings and institutions are often a very important part of political culture and, prospectively at least, of civil society.

This tendency of American diplomacy to avert its official eyes from issues of faith is not new. "Since the founding of the republic," writes Douglas Johnston, a preeminent scholar of religion and American foreign policy, "diplomacy has essentially placed religion beyond the bounds of critical analysis." As policy failures of the late 20th century tended to confirm, religion had become a "missing dimension" of U.S. international statecraft, and handicapped the nation's ability to understand and address the religious sources of human behavior abroad, both individual and collective.[17]

The Resurgence of Religion

If American diplomacy is to succeed in its mission of engaging the world in pursuit of U.S. interests, it must recognize that the world is, as sociologist Peter Berger put it in 1999, "as furiously religious as it ever was, and in some places more so than ever." The phenomenon to be explained, he noted dryly at the time, "is not Iranian mullahs, but American university professors" who persist in ignoring the evidence.[18] He might have added diplomats, who are often on the same wavelength as professors.

Berger was one of the first Western scholars to challenge the secularization theory, of which he himself had been a leading proponent, that religion would wither as modernity advanced. During the 1970s and 1980s he and a handful of other scholars began to pay attention to the evidence reflected in the third wave of democratization, the Shiite revolution in Iran, and elsewhere around the world. That evidence strongly suggested that religion, far from diminishing, was playing a growing role in human affairs, even as modernization proceeded apace.

Tellingly, however, the work of Berger, David Martin, Jose Casanova, and other sociologists of religion was not replicated in the scholarly world of international relations (IR) until quite recently.[19] The thought of IR scholars and their counterparts in the foreign policy establishment has long been framed by the international system of nation states created by the Peace of Westphalia in 17th-century Europe, in which religion was subordinated to the ruler and the state. By and large, religion ceased to be a bone of contention in international relations during the next three and a half centuries. As a result, political scientist Daniel Philpott has observed, most in the field simply "assumed the absence of religion among the factors that influence states."[20]

With the attacks of September 11, however, it has proven extremely difficult for any objective scholar to argue that secularization is a global phenomenon. Several IR scholars have begun a post-9/11 call for reexamining the question of religion in international relations—a "return from exile" as one book put it in 2003.[21] It has been a long exile indeed. Today IR experts are belatedly but rapidly discovering that modernity has not only failed to consign religion to the sidelines of human affairs but that modernity has in some ways actually underwritten the importance of faith to human flourishing. Indeed, one might say that the process of desecularization has confounded the very notion of modernity. "There is a global resurgence of religion taking place throughout out the world," notes Scott M. Thomas, "that is challenging our interpretation of the modern world."[22] "Ironically," agree Jonathan Fox and Shmuel Sandler, "rather than cause religion's demise, modernity has caused a resurgence of religion."[23]

The reasons for integrating religion into our foreign policy are overwhelming. Philip Jenkins, a leading authority on religion's international growth, predicts that the 21st century is likely to "be regarded by future historians as a century in which religion replaced ideology as the prime animating and motivating force in human affairs, guiding attitudes to political liberty and obligation, concepts of nationhood, and, of course, conflicts and wars."[24]

Of greatest moment to U.S. national security is the deadly peril of transnational Islamist terrorism. That threat is abetted by nation-based extremist interpretations of Islam such as Saudi Wahhabism (which we explore in chapter 8). Wahhabism has been widely exported from Saudi Arabia to Muslim communities in the Middle East, Europe, Asia, Africa, and the Americas, including the United States. Wahhabism, which provided much of the theological oxygen for Al Qaeda, is by no means the only variant of extremist Islam. But it has facilitated a steady stream of fanatics willing to kill as a means of satisfying what they believe to be a religious obligation.

Religion is combining with other forces to drive the fate of America's investments of blood and treasure in Iraq and Afghanistan. In Iraq the teachings and practices of Shiism, accepted by a majority of the population, remain a major factor in the country's fate. Shiism will help determine whether a fragile Iraqi democracy succumbs to an internal religious war, adopts the theocratic structures of neighboring Iran, or embraces the norms of liberal governance that can heal its divisions and create a model of Muslim democracy. In one sense, the issue is whether Shiite Iraq will follow the pro-democratic teachings of Grand Ayatollah Ali al-Sistani, which have since 2003 been in competition with the radicalism of Moqtada al-Sadr, or the dictatorship of the theologians that has emerged from the life and work of Iran's Grand Ayatollah Ruhollah Khomeini.

The beliefs of minority Iraqi Sunnis will also heavily influence the outcome, especially the continued influence of Islamist extremism, most notably (but not exclusively) that of Al Qaeda. Ancient Christian Iraqi communities, including the Chaldeans and Syriacs, have much at stake, and much to offer an Iraqi political order should they find reason not to separate themselves into enclaves or to flee the country for good. Not least would be their contribution in Iraq to what has emerged as one of the cornerstones of religious freedom around the world—genuine religious pluralism.

In Iran, clerical despots following the Khomeini line have for almost three decades moved that nation in a radical direction by supporting terrorism and, more recently, seeking the capability to build and deliver nuclear weapons. Iranian interpretations of Islam range from the potentially catastrophic (President Mahmoud Ahmadinejad's suggestions that nuclear weapons are associated with the imminent return of the Hidden Imam) to the creatively democratic (the belief of some conservative Iranian clerics and lay leaders, following the Iranian born Sistani, that theocratic structures are incompatible with Islam).[25] Religion dominates powerful political forces—for better or for worse—in other Muslim majority countries vital to American interests, such as Egypt, Saudi Arabia, Lebanon, Pakistan, and Indonesia.

Underlying all the political and religious developments in the greater Middle East is the renaissance of Shiite Islam triggered by the U.S.-led attacks on Afghanistan and Iraq. The overthrow of the Taliban and of Saddam Hussein freed Shiite Iran from the restraints imposed by two bordering regimes, and has enabled the Khomeinist government to contend for hegemony in the Middle East. Sunni Arab governments, in particular Saudi Arabia, Jordan, and Egypt, fear the Shiite resurgence and are positioning themselves to counter it. Meanwhile, the departure of Saddam's Baathist regime has also empowered the Iraqi Shiite population, with consequences that are not yet clear. It is safe to say, however, that Iraq will never again be ruled by the Sunni minority that was dominant under the Ottomans, the British, and the Baathists. Whatever happens in Iraq, it is clear that the crisis in the greater Middle East will be increasingly defined by the Sunni-Shiite competition for the soul of Islam.[26] Within Shiite precincts, there is likely to be a competition between the teachings of Sistani and Khomeini on the question of the role of religion in the political order.

The importance of religion in the international order is not confined, however, to Muslim majority countries or Islamist movements. China's fate is of critical significance to the world economy, the stability of East Asia, and the security and prosperity of the United States. China has the world's second largest population, one of its fastest growing economies and markets, a huge standing army, a growing navy, and a bevy of operational intercontinental nuclear weapons, all being precariously managed by a Communist government trying to ride the dragon of economic development while stifling political reform. One of that government's greatest fears is popular movements that it does not understand and cannot control. Few internal developments are a source of greater concern among Chinese officials than the explosion of religious devotion among Chinese Protestants and Catholics, and the tenacity of religious belief among the Buddhists of Tibet and the Uighur Muslims of Xingjiang Province on the country's northwest borders.

In India, Hinduism helps account for both the strength and fragility of democratic institutions in the world's largest democracy, one with a huge

Muslim minority population. The continued habituation of that minority to liberal political institutions, including its participation in the enormous economic
growth India is experiencing, will play an important role in the future development of Islam, both in the subcontinent and worldwide. Moreover, confessional differences drive the volatile, decades-long rivalry over Kashmir between
a nuclear-armed India and its nuclear-armed Muslim neighbor, Pakistan. No
resolution of that rivalry will be possible without substantial support from religious authorities on both sides.

Religion will continue to influence democracy's fate in Russia, where
Russian Orthodoxy has emerged from its 20th-century travail under siege
from new spiritual competitors as diverse as Muslims, Roman Catholics,
and Jehovah's Witnesses. Orthodoxy's temptation has been to ally with anti-
democratic forces to regain its privileged position in Russian society. Other
nations of the former Soviet Union face similar challenges.

Religious beliefs help shape and may help solve the Israeli-Palestinian
crisis, so critical to American interests, which involves Jews, Muslims—
including the extremist Hamas party—and the ancient Christian Palestinian
community.[27] The latter is slowly dwindling from emigration, its population
increasingly under pressure both from Palestinian extremists and Israeli security measures. Nearby, tensions between American allies Greece and Turkey,
long fed by interreligious hatreds, have interestingly seen some respite under
Turkey's Islamist-led government, although this rapprochement remains quite
fragile. The perennial problem of Cyprus, in which Turkish and Greek Cypriots
are geographically but not ethnically divided, has always had an underlying, if
muted, Muslim-Christian component. Religion could play a positive role in the
continued healing of that troubled and volatile island.

In the other Asian countries of the Communist world—Vietnam, Laos,
North Korea—religion is viewed as a dangerous threat by ruling elites. In sub-
Saharan Africa, a conflict looms between Islam and Christianity. In Sri Lanka,
the political landscape includes a group most Westerners have never heard
of or thought possible: Buddhist extremists. In Latin America powerful and
energetic Pentacostal Christian movements are challenging the centuries old
monopoly of the Roman Catholic Church.

Even in Western Europe an official aversion to religion has yielded a
bizarre historical amnesia about the Christian sources of European culture,
and—partly as a result—placed religious liberty at risk. Western Europe has
seen itself as a laboratory for the secularization theory, but religion, in the form
of Islam and pockets of Christian revival, simply will not go away. Outside
Europe, some authoritarian governments—Uzbekistan and Turkmenistan,
to name two—have employed the French model of managing and restraining
religion as a pretext for abuse and persecution.

From a global perspective three transnational religious movements are
having a dramatic impact on societies and politics. They are Islam, evangelical

Protestantism, and Roman Catholicism.[28] In some cases, such as sub-Saharan Africa and South America, two of the three seem bound to clash. In others, such as the Vatican-Islam dialogue, there is at least the hope for peaceful disagreement, although these waters were roiled by remarks on Islam from Pope Benedict XVI in late 2006. As noted, both Catholics and Protestants have been associated with the spread of democracy, and the Catholic Church has been credited with initiating a human rights revolution in the late 20th century.[29]

Viewed as a whole, the international order of the 21st century is literally overflowing with religious ideas, movements, and communities, many with enormous implications for fundamental American interests abroad and the security of the American homeland. And there is little reason to believe that this state of affairs will change any time soon. One powerful datum from social science should help drive that point home. Two leading demographers of religion recently surveyed evidence from a variety of sources on the incidence of religious commitment around the world and the prospects for its growth. Their conclusion is striking and—one would think—difficult to ignore: "demographic trends coupled with conservative estimates of conversions and defections envision over 80 percent of the world's population will continue to be affiliated to religions 200 years into the future."[30]

The implications for America of the reappearance of religion on the world stage are varied. Religion has both bolstered and undermined stable self-government. It has fed political reform and support for human rights, as well as irrationalism, persecution, extremism, and terrorism. But the response of American diplomacy to the religious scaffolding so apparent in international relations has been at best inconsistent, and often incoherent. Only in two cases—religious persecution and transnational Islamist terrorism—has it been compelled to address the issue of religion in any direct sense. In both cases the response exposed the difficulties posed to American foreign policy by the religious avoidance syndrome that at times seems endemic to the foreign affairs establishment.

The Ineffective Humanitarian Response to Religious Persecution

"As a child," she told the American lawmakers, "my only ambition was to become a nun." Tsultrim Dolma had taken her vows at the age of 17 and left home to enter a convent in Lhasa, the capital and spiritual center of Tibet. The trouble began when she joined demonstrations protesting the arrests of other Buddhist nuns and monks. Taken into custody by Chinese military officials, she was subjected to four months of brutal interrogation and torture. After her release, she was raped by Chinese soldiers.

Concluding that she had lost her purity and could no longer live with the other nuns, she decided to flee to northern India. "I thought if only I could reach him, if only I could once see his face, he would provide me with a solution." When she finally met the Dalai Lama, she told her audience, "He patted my face gently. I could not say anything. I could only cry.... In Tibet, so many long to see him."[31]

It was the fall of 1997. Washington's hardwood trees were on the verge of turning to gold and red, and members of the 105th Congress had just returned from the summer recess. As Tsultrim Dolma and other victims of religious persecution told their stories of horror to the House Committee on International Relations, some hoped that a major correction in American policy toward persecution was beginning to take shape.

During the Cold War the U.S. State Department had yielded to congressional pressure for more attention to human rights, including the problem of religious persecution, and had to some extent integrated both issues into the nation's policy of containing Soviet Communism.[32] With the end of the Cold War, however, abuses of religious minorities seemed to increase, in part because the lifting of Soviet oppression tended to loose long-standing ethno-religious rivalries (as in the Balkans and Central Asia) and in part because religion itself was spreading and having a greater impact on societies and governments.[33] Oddly, however, American diplomacy had during the 1990s almost reflexively subordinated its efforts on behalf of religious victims. Abuses against people of faith had become, in the words of one informed observer, "the neglected stepchild of the human rights movement."[34] The result was a campaign led by conservative Christians and Jews to solve the problem of diplomatic reticence through legislation.

The House Committee gathered on two days that September to hear testimony on a proposed "Freedom from Religious Persecution Act" sponsored by two Republicans, Frank Wolf (R, Virginia) in the House and Arlen Specter (R, Pennsylvania) in the Senate. Wolf-Specter, as it came to be called, was pushed by a coalition of groups that were highly suspicious of the Department of State. The centerpiece of their bill was a new office in the White House with a new function: to ensure that the foreign policy of the United States paid more attention to the plight of the millions around the world suffering because of their religious faith, especially (but not exclusively) members of the religious group they argued was the most persecuted—Christians. Under the coalition's proposed legislation the head of the White House office would have unprecedented authority to punish persecuting governments with near automatic economic sanctions.

But Wolf-Specter was strongly resisted by the Clinton administration. On the day before Ms. Dolma's appearance, Assistant Secretary of State for Democracy, Human Rights and Labor John Shattuck told the House Committee that the proposed law would do more harm than good. For one thing, Shattuck asserted, the administration was already increasing its efforts against governments that mistreated people of faith. The State Department was requiring more reporting on the issue from American embassies and consulates abroad. An advisory committee on religious persecution would soon make recommendations to the Secretary of State.

A separate law, the assistant secretary argued, would reduce the department's flexibility, damage U.S. relations with key allies, and risk hurting those whom it was designed to help. Then, reaching deep into the foundations of Foggy Bottom's worldview, Shattuck warned against creating what he called "a hierarchy of human rights" in which religious rights were given preference over others. The department was, he said, "particularly concerned" about this problem.[35]

Congress was not persuaded. The following year it unanimously passed the International Religious Freedom (IRF) Act, which appeared to be an even more comprehensive approach to persecution than Wolf-Specter's. The IRF Act sought to incorporate rather than bypass the State Department by placing the new office at Foggy Bottom. It provided the department a long menu of measures to address religious persecution.[36] It even established a watchdog agency—the U.S. Commission on International Religious Freedom—to ensure the department did its job. President Clinton, whose negotiators had won several concessions in the final bill, decided to sign it into law.

Within the State Department's building at C Street in Washington, however, skepticism about the impact of the law remained strong. There was a generalized fear that it would needlessly complicate U.S. foreign policy and reduce the secretary of state's flexibility. Since the end of the Cold War, official American advocacy on behalf of victims of religious persecution had been conducted either in multilateral institutions, such as the United Nations, or in private, ad hoc bilateral discussions. These talks usually occurred in the larger context of U.S. human rights diplomacy and at a time and venue of the department's own choosing. The State Department's annual Human Rights Reports covered religious persecution, but the issue was always situated among the other human rights.[37] Now, however, the United States would be required to aim a spotlight—focused, public, and unilateral—on a single, controversial human rights issue. As one prominent liberal internationalist scholar had put it during the IRF debate, "to press this right is to alter the human rights equation."[38]

Other concerns became clearer as the law began to be implemented. One was the department's continuing resistance to establishing the "hierarchy of human rights" mentioned by Shattuck. Secretary of State Madeline Albright herself had addressed this issue in a Washington, D.C., speech attacking the proposed legislation.[39] Internally, some voiced the worry that a policy of actually "promoting religious freedom" might clash with other rights, such as those of children or women, being pursued by the Clinton administration through the United Nations and other international forums. There was a fear that traditional religious communities, in pressing their religiously informed moral claims about how human beings should live, presented obstacles to what the Clinton foreign policy team had labeled the new "nontraditional" human rights.

Skepticism also flowed from the "realist" understanding of America's interests abroad that remained influential at C Street. Was the department now to increase pressure for religious changes in countries whose cooperation was vital to U.S. national security? Was it, for example, to subordinate the need for Egyptian or Saudi support in the Middle East peace process in order to highlight religious persecution in those two countries? To engage in harsh and public criticism of their human rights records might embolden Islamist radicals in the region and endanger U.S. interests.

Still others thought the new law placed at risk important commercial relationships and the prosperity of American businesses. China, for example, was already a huge importer of American products, and a major U.S. debate was under way over whether it should be granted permanent status as a "most favored nation" for purposes of trade concessions. Some argued that admitting China to the world of international economic norms, such as granting it membership in the World Trade Organization, would do more for human rights over the long run than the kind of pressure represented in the IRF Act.[40]

In short, there were a variety of conflicting views on the goals, strengths and weaknesses of America's new "international religious freedom" policy. But it was now law and would have to be implemented in some fashion. It soon became clear that there was one approach on which most could agree. Realists, liberal internationalists, and conservatives of all stripes, inside and outside the State Department, could sympathize with the plight of Tsultrim Dolma and the other victims of persecution around the world. As a result, their contending views about the issue of religion in U.S. foreign policy tended to converge on a lowest common denominator, ad hoc, humanitarian approach that all could accept, even if they occasionally criticized its failures: denounce the persecutors and threaten them with punitive actions; take no serious action that would jeopardize other vital U.S. interests; rescue the victims of persecution whenever possible. Many disagreed with parts of this strategy but no one opposed it as a whole.

In fact, the implementation of the International Religious Freedom Act did not involve any serious attempt to "advance religious freedom" as the law nominally mandated. Not only did all sides agree on what was essentially a humanitarian policy, rather than a policy of promoting religious freedom, but the statute itself stressed mechanisms that consisted largely of denunciations and threats of punitive action. Such vehicles were simply not designed to promote regimes of religious liberty in which the respective authorities and roles of religion and state were accommodated and balanced.

But as IRFA neared the end of its first decade in operation, it was becoming increasingly clear that U.S. IRF policy was not succeeding even in its narrower goal of reducing international religious persecution. Hundreds of human beings around the world, perhaps more, had been rescued as a result of the new policy, but millions remained under persecuting regimes. It was simply too easy for governments such as China or Uzbekistan to release religious prisoners in response to U.S. pressure without changing the systems that would unjustly incarcerate, and abuse in even worse fashion, many more.

In the sense that it called upon the American government to "stand with the persecuted" around the world, the IRF Act certainly reflected the deepest values of the nation's creed. For those suffering for their faith who knew of the American policy, it was doubtless a source of hope. But the law proved ineffective in achieving its humanitarian objectives on any large scale.

Transnational Islamist Terrorism

Eight months before the passage of the IRF Act, a London newspaper published a statement by Muslim leaders little known outside American intelligence circles. The statement was drafted in Arabic so powerful that one eminent scholar of Islam has called it "a magnificent piece of eloquent, at times poetic Arabic prose."[41] The document was entitled a "Declaration of the World Islamic Front for Jihad against the Jews and the Crusaders," and its primary authors were Osama Bin Laden and Ayman Al Zawahiri.

Some of the declaration's eloquence derived from its liberal use of quotations from the Koran and from the sayings of the Prophet Mohammed. But its analysis was entirely contemporary and aimed squarely at the United States, which it said was engaged in a crusade against Islam. "For more than seven years," it declared, "the United States [has been] occupying the lands of Islam in the holiest of its territories, Arabia,...humiliating its people, threatening its neighbors, and using its bases in the peninsula as a spearhead to fight against the neighboring Islamic peoples." This was a reference to the U.S. invasion of Iraq from the territory of Saudi Arabia during the Gulf War.

After condemning the economic sanctions that followed the war and the presence of U.S. troops in Saudi Arabia, Bin Laden gave an assessment of America's objectives. "While the purposes of the Americans in these wars are religious and economic, they also serve the petty state of the Jews, to divert attention from their occupation of Jerusalem and their killing of Muslims in it." The United States sought "to dismember all the states of the region..., whose division and weakness would ensure the survival of Israel and the continuation of the calamitous Crusader occupation of the lands of Arabia."

Then came a judgment of U.S. actions. According to Bin Laden, those actions constituted a "clear declaration of war by the Americans against God, His Prophet, and the Muslims." The remedy provided by Islam was unambiguous: a defensive jihad. "In such a situation, it is the unanimous opinion of the *ulema* throughout the centuries that when enemies attack the Muslim lands, Jihad becomes a personal duty of every Muslim."

What followed was a "fatwa"—an Arabic word then only vaguely familiar to many Americans, but one that would soon enter the common vocabulary as an authoritative Islamic edict.[42] The declaration asserted that "to kill Americans and their allies, both civil and military, is an individual duty of every Muslim who is able, in any country where this is possible, until the Aqsa mosque [Jerusalem] and the Haram mosque [Mecca] are freed from their grip, and until their armies, shattered and broken-winged, depart from all the lands of Islam, incapable of threatening any Muslims."

Following additional Koranic citations, the fatwa now reached its climax. "By God's leave, we call on every Muslim who believes in God and hopes for reward to obey God's command to kill the Americans and plunder their possessions wherever he finds them and whenever he can. Likewise we call on the Muslim *ulema* and leaders and youth and soldiers to launch attacks against the armies of the American devils and against those who are allied with them from among the helpers of Satan." The declaration and the fatwa then concluded with more quotations from the Koran.[43]

When Adolf Hitler wrote *Mein Kampf* during the 1920s, a book which laid out his program for the future, he was generally ridiculed or ignored in the West.[44] Osama Bin Laden, while relatively unknown beyond government circles, was not ignored. Indeed, by the late 1990s there was much discussion within the U.S. government about him, his goals, and his fatwa.[45] But on this side of the divide known to history as 9/11, it is clear that the influence of Bin Ladenism was tragically underestimated. Before the end of the century, Al Qaeda would carry out deadly assaults on two American embassies in Africa and on the U.S.S. *Cole,* a naval vessel anchored in the gulf of Yemen. On September 11, 2001, Al Qaeda terrorists successfully attacked sites in Manhattan and Washington, D.C. Other attacks planned for that day were diverted by intelligence and good fortune—and by the heroic actions of a handful of Americans on a commercial airliner above the fields of Pennsylvania.

During the eight months between the publishing of the Bin Laden fatwa and the passage of the International Religious Freedom Act, there were several congressional hearings on the subject of religious freedom and U.S. foreign policy. Most of them focused on religious persecution of the kind represented by the Buddhist nun or by a Sudanese Christian who had escaped slavery. Few, if any, in Congress, the White House, or the State Department discerned or articulated a connection between the international religious freedom policy they were devising for the nation and the problem presented by Islamist terrorism. Nor, despite America's own history, did policy makers perceive a nexus between religious freedom and the kind of democracy some would come to identify as the best long-term antidote to terror.

In the years that followed, and especially after September 11, 2001, the issue of religious motivations for human behavior came forcefully into America's collective consciousness. The events of that terrible day threatened to force a debate over U.S. policy with respect to Islam, religion, democracy, and the promotion of religious freedom abroad. But the debate was never quite joined. It seemed to lurk just below the surface of national policy discourse, and the issue of religion remained uneasily in the background.

On 9/11 there had been no senior Muslim officials in American embassies overseas or in the Department of State. The department's Arabic specialists, many extraordinarily accomplished and experienced, tended to focus on the nonreligious aspects of Middle Eastern political culture. To its credit, the department knew there was a problem, so the secretary of state's office of policy planning spearheaded in 2003 an interagency examination of how best to "engage Islam" in the Middle East and elsewhere.

Meetings were held at the State Department and at the headquarters of the National Security Council. Memoranda were written to senior officials. A major conference of Muslim leaders was conducted in the Middle East. Recommendations for policy changes were vetted that might improve America's understanding of the role of Islam in international affairs. But the initiative came to naught and in due course was abandoned. Resurrected in 2004, under the title of Muslim World Outreach, the outcome was similar.[46] All in all, the countervailing cultural tendencies at the State Department—the extreme reluctance to get too deeply into a religion's guts—overcame even the imperatives loosed by 9/11.

The office of the ambassador at large for international religious freedom played virtually no part in these projects. Despite its significant connections in the Muslim community—the result of an ongoing Islamic Roundtable begun by the first ambassador in 1999—the office's mission was not perceived within the U.S. government as having any substantial connection to the task of engaging Islam.

Other events revealed the same problem. In 2003 a much-awaited report on how to counter Islamist extremism by means of the department's "public diplomacy" programs, submitted by the Advisory Commission on Public Diplomacy, paid virtually no attention to religion and made no mention of U.S. international religious freedom policy.[47] In a 2004 congressional hearing on State Department strategy in dealing with the phenomenon of Islamist terrorism, eight senior department officials testified. These eight men and women represented the diplomatic expertise deemed relevant to the question at hand. The ambassador at large for international religious freedom was not one of them. As the eight testified over the course of several hours, none addressed the issue of religion in any substantive way, notwithstanding the nation's six-year-old, legally mandated policy of promoting international religious freedom.[48]

Although many foreign affairs officials viewed the promotion of liberal democracy as a viable strategy, and even as an antidote to terrorism, few perceived an organic relationship between religious freedom and democracy. The department's primary program for developing democracy in the Middle East was the Middle East Partnership Initiative (MEPI), a well-funded clearing house for ideas (some quite good) to encourage democratic institutions. But in the years after 9/11 MEPI programs evinced no systematic interest in religion or religious freedom. As late as 2006, no programs involving religious groups or religious freedom had been funded under MEPI.[49]

Reactions to the 9/11 terrorist attacks themselves also revealed official America's profound confusion and disarray as it tried to articulate the causes of the attacks, Islam's role in terrorism, and the role of U.S. diplomacy in responding to the problem. One reaction was to blame strong religious beliefs for the terror unleashed by Al Qaeda. To many, as one observer put it, "the events of that day seemed to confirm their contention that religion is incorrigibly toxic, and that it breeds irrationality, demonization of others, irreconcilable division, and implacable conflict."[50] Two months after 9/11 former President Clinton suggested in a speech analyzing the problem that religious people with absolute truth claims posed a danger to freedom.[51]

Confusion and Culture Wars

This theme would become more prominent as the "red-blue" cultural divide seemed to widen with the 2004 reelection of George W. Bush. Many on the left began to see 9/11 as merely the Muslim variant of a worldwide phenomenon reflected in Bush's reelection—the growth of religious fundamentalism. On the day after the election, the *New York Times* ran three op-eds that articulated this fear. Maureen Dowd wrote that the president "ran a jihad in America so he can fight one in Iraq." Garry Wills asserted that Bush's America was, like Al Qaeda, captive to "fundamentalist zeal, a rage at secularity, religious intolerance, fear of and hatred for modernity." Even the venerable Tom Friedman wrote that "Mr. Bush's base is pushing so hard to...extend the boundaries of religion that it felt as if we were rewriting the constitution, not electing a President."[52]

Some on the left were more open to dealing with Islam as an influence in Muslim democracies than they were evangelical Christianity as part of American democracy. This was doubtless a product of the liberal emphasis on the value of multiculturalism, at least when applied outside the United States. It also reflected a tendency present at Foggy Bottom. In a 2000 study of U.S. policy toward Islamism, Robert Satloff noted that despite being "profoundly reluctant to view...the organic connection between religion and state that exists in many other societies...U.S. officials tend to evince an exaggerated deference to religious sensibilities when they are claimed by others."[53]

There was also a conservative version of the "blame religion for 9/11" line of thinking. Many on the right believed that Christianity had been demonized by American secularists and unjustly banished from the public square by Supreme Court decisions in the latter half of the 20th century. Some of these conservatives were powerful advocates for religion-based norms in the American public square, but they believed Islam was simply incapable of contributing to democracy in the Middle East. Evangelists such as Pat Robertson and Franklin Graham were quick to condemn Islam as an evil theological system, a virtual launching pad for terrorism. An influential Catholic intellectual, Father Richard John Neuhaus, used his editorials in the journal *First Things* to express hope that Islam could develop toward liberal norms, but also extreme skepticism that it was capable of doing so.[54] Neuhaus's argument was in part an extension of Samuel Huntington's assertion in the mid-1990s that the problem was not Islamist extremism, but Islam itself.[55]

Perhaps the most typical official reaction to 9/11 was to acknowledge in some fashion the religious roots of Islamist terrorism but to avoid addressing them as a policy matter or to incorporate religion into policy solutions. Some standard of analysis, it seemed, required euphemism and indirection when it came to religion. The 9/11 Commission, appointed by President Bush and Congress to analyze the attacks and to recommend policy changes, submitted a comprehensive report in 2004. In a chapter entitled "The Foundations of the New Terrorism," it candidly discussed the Islamic context of Bin Laden's actions. In its recommendations, however, the report in effect declared the subject of religion out of bounds: "Lives guided by religious faith, including literal beliefs in holy scriptures, are common to every religion and represent no threat to us."[56]

On more than one occasion in the early years after 9/11 the president asserted that "Islam is a religion of peace."[57] These kinds of statements were understandably designed to counter the charge that American military actions in Afghanistan and Iraq were anti-Islam, but they also served to discourage any official discussion of the religious roots of what the United States was encountering in the Muslim world.

As the second Bush administration neared its end, this official reticence seemed to be shifting, at least rhetorically. As sectarian conflict in Iraq worsened and the threat of transnational Islamist terrorism continued, President Bush began to speak publicly of "Islamic fascism." He openly asserted that the enemy was a distorted offshoot of Islam, thereby implying that the United States needed a better understanding of its nature in order to defeat it.[58] But the president's rhetoric did not seem to augur substantially new thinking about religion in foreign affairs. For one thing, it was roundly criticized by Muslims as defamatory, and by his political opponents as well. By 2008 any terminology connecting terrorism to Islam was officially being discouraged by the U.S. Department of Homeland Security.[59]

Even some conservatives insisted on continuing to avert their eyes from the religious component of terrorism. The lead story in a 2006 issue of the *National Interest* argued that extremist "jihadists" were not motivated by religion at all. According to this article, not only had Osama Bin Laden made "a geopolitical, rather than a religious, call to arms," but the jihadists themselves were essentially nihilists with a hormonal imbalance (a reference to the sexual gratification they believed awaited them in the next life), rather than people seeking to achieve religious goals.[60]

Thus did the American culture wars conspire with long-standing diplomatic habits of thought to keep religion off the policy table. It was, of course, not a planned conspiracy. It was an inadvertent concord of avoidance that cannot even be called a disagreement. "Disagreement is a rare achievement," observed the American Jesuit John Courtney Murray. "Much of what we call disagreement is simply confusion."[61]

Understanding the U.S. Religion Avoidance Syndrome

What accounts for the secularist tendencies in American foreign policy? Why have American diplomats so routinely assumed that religious belief and practice is properly a private or personal matter with no legitimate, systematic place in policy thinking? Why have those whose job it is to engage the world in the pursuit of American interests not been more alert to the resurgence of religion as a major force driving the behavior of men, women, governments, and transnational movements?

We have already encountered some of the reasons, including the reflexive association of political Islam with extremism after the Iranian revolution of the late 1970s, the belief that engaging religious communities in our foreign policy is somehow unconstitutional, and the failure to abandon in toto the secularization theory as a policy assumption. We return to some of these themes in due course. In the next chapter we will examine the climates of opinion underlying the dominant U.S. foreign policy schools of thought, all of which tend to reinforce the religion avoidance syndrome.

Underlying all those views, however, is a central aspect of the secularization theory that has proven particularly resilient among foreign policy practitioners, namely the idea that religion is inherently irrational and emotive. The core premise of the secularization theory was, and remains, that religious belief constitutes little more than a grasping for meaning that cannot survive the maturing of human knowledge. A milder contemporary version of this view in the West, held by some who identify themselves as religious, is that religion is essentially a psychological process, an internal, therapeutic search for meaning and self-esteem that has little if anything to do with the intellect, no metaphysical referents, and few if any public policy implications. In both cases the implication is that religious beliefs should be tolerated, even protected, in a democratic system. But because they are irrational, or intensely personal and individuated, they should be permitted no more influence on public policy than alchemy or psychoanalysis.

Modern American versions of such sentiments abound—from the *Washington Post*'s infamous caricature of evangelical Christians as "largely poor, uneducated, and easy to command," to *New York Times* columnist Nicholas Kristof's alarm at a poll showing that 91 percent of American Christians actually believe in the virgin birth of Jesus, up 5 percent from the previous year! This, Kristof wrote, was a sure sign of the "withering" of the intellectual traditions of Christianity, akin to the crisis in the Muslim world that, he implies, led to 9/11.[62] In making such an argument, Kristof was revealing an astonishing ignorance of Christian history and theology, but he was also reflecting the modern certainty that faith and reason are irreconcilable.

A more sophisticated example of this phenomenon can be found in the highly influential work of Harvard political philosopher John Rawls.[63] We look again at Rawls' views in chapter 3's exploration of religion and democracy, but for present purposes it is important to note how his writings have reinforced the assumption that religion is inherently irrational and thus divisive. Rawls argued that religion was the preeminent example of what he called "comprehensive doctrines" that cannot not be reconciled in conditions of modern pluralism. Accordingly, such doctrines must be left out of public debates over issues essential to democracy, such as what the constitution means. In short, according to Rawls democracy cannot flourish unless citizens agree to abandon, for purposes of public discourse, premises or arguments drawn from religion. They must instead give "public reasons" for their positions, based on "political values that others as free and equal also might reasonably be expected reasonably to endorse."[64]

Rawls' theory, which has had an enormous impact on modern American understandings of political liberalism, treats as self-evident the view that religious beliefs are inherently incompatible with "public reason."[65] It has reinforced the tendency in American foreign policy circles to exclude religion from U.S. strategy, especially democracy-promotion strategy. His theory fails to credit not only the emphasis on reason present in both Catholic and Protestant traditions, but also the religious foundations of democratic principles and institutions in both Europe and the United States.

Democratic theorist Alfred Stepan has pointed out that "the Rawlsian normative map" to liberal democracy ignores the actual contributions to liberal democracy made by Christianity precisely because of the development and application of religious "comprehensive doctrines."[66] In other words it was often because of religion's public reasons, not in spite of them, that European democracy developed. Political philosopher Robert George argues that Rawlsian secularism is especially vexed by Roman Catholicism because Catholics understand liberal democracy as the best political system for promoting the dignity of the individual and the protection of the common good, and they make reason-based, religiously informed public arguments accordingly.[67]

Rawlsian assumptions about the inherently anti-liberal and anti-rational characteristics of religion are widely shared among intellectuals in the West and in the United States, including both secularists and many Protestants and Catholics. They have encouraged a highly selective and often simplistic reading of European political and intellectual history that has been influential in senior State Department circles. Without question that history provides evidence that religion can be divisive, irrational, and the enemy of human freedom. But as the work of scholars such as Stepan, George, Timothy Samuel Shaw, and Daniel Philpott demonstrates, history reveals ample evidence of vital contributions by religion to the development of liberal democracy.[68] At the very least, the story is far more complex than secularists would admit.

The stage was set for the idea that irrational religion was a danger to modernization and modernity by the 16th- and 17th-century wars of religion in Europe that followed upon the Protestant Reformation. At the end of those wars (which were fought for many reasons, religion preeminent among them), the 1648 Peace of Westphalia inaugurated the international system of sovereign states and subordinated religion to the rule of princes and kings. The religio-political ideal of "Christendom," long in decay, was now supplanted by a state system in which religious communities largely understood themselves as subordinate to political communities.

Modern Western scholars often cite 1648 as the point at which a political notion of "religious freedom" entered history. What they mean by this, however, is the subordination of religion to the state, not the liberty to practice religion as constitutive of human dignity or an accommodation between religion and state that fosters religious freedom.[69] This new system of national sovereignty did help end the wars of religion but it also facilitated the replacement of religion by the state as the primary arbiter of the public good.[70]

What truly transformed Europe's understanding of the relationship between faith and reason, however, was the combined effect of the Scientific Revolution and the French Enlightenment. Growing confidence in the empirical methods of science fed a conviction among elites that the claims of religion were not only unprovable but entirely subjective. This was a fundamental break with the classical understanding of faith and reason as expressed in the classical tradition, perhaps best captured by St. Augustine in the 4th century: "No one believes anything unless one first thought it believable.... Everything that is believed is believed after being preceded by thought."[71]

The French Enlightenment firmly rejected this long-established marriage of faith and reason. It enthroned human rationality as the sole arbiter of truth and relegated faith to the realm of superstition—and private superstition at that. The core meaning of the Enlightenment, as expressed by one of its most authoritative historians, was "the rise of modern paganism." According to Peter Gay, French Enlightenment philosophers believed that Christianity's "central myth was incredible, its dogma a conflation of rustic superstitions, its sacred book an incoherent collection of primitive tales, its church a cohort of servile fanatics as long as they were out of power and of despotic fanatics once they had gained control."[72]

By the 20th century, the separation of religion and rationality, and the privatization of religion, were considered complete by many in the Western intellectual community. In a series of lectures at Yale University in 1931, the eminent American historian Carl Becker told his audience that "It is true we may still believe in Zeus [the biblical God]; many people do. Even scientists, historians, philosophers still accord him the customary worship. But this is no more than a personal privilege, to be exercised in private…."[73] Thus was the divorce of *fides et ratio*, and the relegation of *fides* to the private realm, trumpeted as the liberation of mankind.

But the classical tradition of faith and reason working in tandem was closer to human experience. Most human beings do accept as a matter of faith some revealed truth claims that cannot be conclusively demonstrated by reason, such as the virgin birth of Jesus or the Shiite belief in the return of the Mahdi. These and other propositions about revealed truths, for example, that the Koran is divinely and eternally created, or that God is three persons, cannot be *proven* by reason but can nonetheless be examined and tested by reason. Thomas Aquinas, the great medieval theologian and philosopher, reasoned carefully in the *Summa Theologica* that Mary "conceived as a virgin, gave birth as a virgin, and remained a virgin after the birth."[74]

Typically, such claims of faith can be buttressed by reasoning, but they also rely on trust, which is itself subject to rational scrutiny. People tend to accept propositions that cannot be proven because they trust the messenger or prophet who proposes them, as well as those who are the direct companions or witnesses of the prophet. It is in this additional sense that revelations not directly accessible to human reason can be tested by reasoning: How do particular revealed truths accord with human experience? Are the actions of the prophet and the witnesses reasonable and moral? What does the history of lived religion demonstrate about the community of adherents?[75]

Within the Christian tradition, the marriage of faith and reason depended on a belief that God is a rational being who reveals himself more fully as human history progresses. Sociologist Rodney Stark notes the logic and its implications for modernity: "because God is a rational being and the universe is his personal creation, it necessarily has a rational, lawful, stable structure, awaiting increased human comprehension."[76] The very intelligibility of God in his creation led to a Christian belief in progress and to the rise of modern science.

Pope Benedict XVI, in a 2006 lecture in Regensburg, Germany, enraged many Muslims by quoting a Medieval Christian emperor who asserted that the Islamic concept of God was an irrational, capricious deity. The pope's speech engendered a firm denial on this point from an international set of Islamic religious leaders and initiated what one can hope will be an ongoing Christian-Muslim dialogue. The incident revealed, however, that the issue of rationality in God, man, and religion is not an obscure theological matter. It goes to the very heart of the role of religion in modern liberal democracy and the potential contributions of theistic religious communities to stable self-government.

But the secularization theory did not rest exclusively on the marginalization of faith as irrational belief. The combined effects of the Scientific Revolution and the Enlightenment also radically transformed the very meaning of reason and rationality itself.[77] Heavily influenced by the work of Immanuel Kant, modern reason became identified with mathematics and the scientific method, according to which the only truths knowable by human beings are the empirically demonstrable truths of science. By the 19th century, writes historian Owen Chadwick, "[t]he conflict was hypostasized, Science and Religion were blown up into balloon duelists, Science containing all knowledge, Religion containing no knowledge, and the two set side by side, with know-nothing using saber from keeping know-all from his place."[78]

This, too, constituted a radical break with the past. Beginning with the ancient Greeks, philosophy had applied reason in the search for truths not scientifically verifiable but nonetheless knowable—truths about human nature, ethics, beauty, the existence of God, and the role of reason itself. After Kant, philosophers began to accept that whatever was not scientifically verifiable lay outside the realm of reason.

Those in the foreign affairs establishment who continue to accept, even inadvertently, the secularization premise that religion is by its nature irredeemably irrational, and that the processes of reasoning about the world cannot legitimately encompass the religious traditions of others, are closing their thought prematurely to the possibilities present in a world of public faith. At the very least, they are declining to grapple with the most dynamic aspect of the 21st century—public manifestations of religious belief—and its potential for good or evil, for peace or war, for stability or chaos. If American foreign policy is to contribute to the growth of stable self-government and to the war on terror, it must begin to think systematically about the role of religion in human affairs and the relationships between religion and state in places such as Egypt and China.

Before investigating that potential, it is worthwhile to look at some of these crippling secularist premises in action, as it were, in the thought of some of the nation's premier schools of foreign policy. It is to those schools that we now turn.

2

—⚬⚬⚬—

The Intellectual Sources of
Diplomacy's Religion Deficit

Iraq has relegitimized realism, which is a good thing. But without an idealistic component to our foreign policy, there would be nothing to distinguish us from our competitors.
      —Robert D. Kaplan[1]

The Bush Doctrine has reminded the country and the world that there are options beyond an idealism untethered by reality or a crackpot realism susceptible of premature closure in its thinking about what is possible.
      —George Weigel[2]

Intellectual history has its limits. In 1983 President Reagan's Middle Eastern envoy, Donald Rumsfeld, cut a classic realist deal with Saddam Hussein: if Iraq would continue to counter the growing menace of radical Islamist Iran, the United States would not complain about the chemical weapons it knew Saddam possessed. Iraq continued its war with Iran for five more years, ultimately employing its chemical weapons against both Iran and its own Kurdish citizens. In 2003 the same Donald Rumsfeld, now secretary of defense under President George W. Bush, sent U.S. forces to depose Saddam and plant democracy in Iraq, an effort widely labeled as a repudiation of classical realism and an embrace of neoconservative ideas. In late 2006, after Democrats had regained control of both Houses of Congress, Rumsfeld was fired. His former boss, James Baker, who had been Ronald Reagan's chief of staff, headed a task force on Iraq that argued for a return to realist goals in the Middle East.[3]

It is often misleading to understand the actions of any one person, whether a president or a diplomat, in terms of the intellectual climate that is thought to be dominant in a given period. To put it differently, labels rarely capture the range of motives and purposes of political thinkers or practitioners. Although he may have presided over a neoconservative strategy for the Middle East, Donald Rumsfeld was no neoconservative. Nor is support for the spread of democracy merely a neoconservative, or even Reaganite, idea. It can be said to have originated in Wilsonian idealism, and its descendants reside as much in the Democratic Party and in liberal internationalism as they do among Republicans. If neocons can be considered Wilsonians with guns, liberal internationalists are Wilsonians with treaties.

Acknowledging the limitations of labels, it will nevertheless be useful to examine how all three of the foreign policy schools of thought operative since the end of the Cold War—realism (under George H. W. Bush and the pre-9/11 George W. Bush administration), liberal internationalism (under the two Clinton administrations), and neoconservatism (under the post-9/11 Bush administration)—approach the subject of religion in the international order. Notwithstanding their very different views of the world and how America should engage it, it is striking that they all arrive at a similar conclusion about the religious beliefs and practices of others: except in extremis, those beliefs and practices should not affect in any substantive way how the United States conducts its foreign policy. Religion may help with enemy identification, but even then it should if possible be kept off the policy table.

Understanding why this premise has dominated our foreign policy thinking can help us evaluate the weaknesses of American diplomacy and suggest remedies for its more effective operation in a world of public faith.

Realism, Power, and Passion

Realists are most clearly defined by the view that the international order is a Hobbesian system of competition among nations for power. It is, in effect, a system of anarchy, defined as such by the absence of any common external power.[4] An effective foreign policy maneuvers within this anarchic power structure to maintain balance and stability. In general a realist will sanction military force only when vital national interests are threatened. Many have isolationist predilections that lead them to worry about overreaching, and are skeptical about excessive involvement in the internal affairs of others. Typically, realists do not view the domestic circumstances of other states and the internal policies of their governments as a major factor in U.S. foreign policy decisions. They tended to view the Cold War more as a great-power struggle between the United States and the Soviet Union than as an ideological struggle between communism and freedom. Internal developments, realists have traditionally argued, are poor guides to the external behavior of governments, which must occupy our attentions.[5]

The beliefs and actions of religious individuals and communities are therefore not terribly relevant to the realist's understanding of international affairs unless they drive the policy decisions of governments or help us understand the levers of power. This caveat should in theory permit realists to credit some role for religious actors, if not their ideas. Moreover, many of the realists of the post–World War Two period were not so much moral skeptics as they were pragmatists who were skeptical of pursuing idealist goals. Reinhold Niebuhr and George Kennan, for example, accepted the existence of objective moral truths but did not believe it feasible to spread democracy or human rights.

And yet, as we have seen, realist categories did not prove useful in understanding the rise of Khomenist Shiite theocracy in Iran. Realists have often misunderstood or overlooked in the early stages other contemporary manifestations of religion, including the Taliban in Afghanistan, the role of Confucianism in East Asia, Hinduism in India, the growth of religious communities in China, the Wahhabi faction in Saudi Arabia, or the emergence of transnational Islamist terrorism.

The world order assumed by realists has also contributed to their subordination of religious ideas and action. That order was created by the 17th-century Peace of Westphalia, which ended the European wars of religion. As noted in the last chapter, the Westphalian system institutionalized the relationships between sovereign nation-states, and the destructive power of religion was brought to heel by the power of governments. Henceforward governments had no warrant to interfere in the internal affairs of other sovereign states, especially on behalf of or against a particular religious community.[6]

Realism proved reasonably effective as the intellectual substructure of U.S. containment policy during the Cold War, but there were also weaknesses. Most realists failed to predict or even conceive of the collapse of communism and the Soviet empire. Realists tended to assume the permanency of both, as well as the bipolar world of U.S.-Soviet ascendancy within which their theory operated so comfortably. But the internal dynamics of the Soviet Union, and in particular the appeal of political freedom and human rights both in Russia and its satellites, proved unexpectedly powerful in the collapse of the empire that took place between 1989 and 1991.

In the early 21st century some realists have attempted to recalibrate their worldview to account for the threat of Islamist terrorism and the popularity of democracy.[7] The spread of democratic movements has in particular generated a greater, if still limited, realist focus on developments within societies, including the impact of confessional communities. But religion's place in the realist analysis is usually as a gauge of power-seeking behavior. Almost nowhere do realists credit the religious impulses of men and women as anything more than a manifestation of political appetite.

The quintessential realist of the Cold War, former Secretary of State and National Security Adviser Henry Kissinger, kept up a remarkable level of commentary in the post-9/11 world. In a 2005 essay he warned the Bush administration against applying Western political models, created over centuries among what he called "homogeneous" Western societies, "to ethnically diverse and religiously divided societies in the Middle East, Asia and Africa." In multiethnic societies, he noted, majorities will naturally subjugate minorities unless the political system prevents it through divided powers and checks and balances. Achieving such systems through negotiations between hostile ethnic groups is "an extraordinarily elusive undertaking."

An example of the problem, wrote Kissinger, is Lebanon, where past foreign interventions by the United States, Syria, and Israel have prevented the nation's collapse into sectarian violence between Christians, Sunnis, Shiites, and Druze. What is required today, he argued, is an agreed political framework among these parties brokered by and overseen by the international community "to guarantee that the conflicting passions do not once again erupt into violence...."[8]

This is classical realist analysis applied to contemporary problems. It applies the balance of power model to internal communities, as well as external state policies. It is open to the role of the international community, albeit in a restrained way. It acknowledges the importance of democratic political institutions and the difficulty of sustaining them. But it also reflects realism's secularist principles by failing to envision, or even imagine, any role for the doctrines of domestic religious communities in bringing about the political framework that can resolve Lebanon's problems. It thus has nothing to say about how American diplomacy might influence those communities. They are, in Kissinger's analysis, little more than repositories of "passions," which necessarily will come into conflict unless managed by outside forces.[9]

Kissinger is surely correct that a long-term political solution to conflict in any multiethnic and multireligious society must involve some system of federalism, separation of powers, and carefully constructed checks and balances. But where religious communities are powerful political players, as they are in every country of the Middle East and much of Asia, it will be important for them to sanction the political framework as consistent with their religious teachings, or at least acquiesce in political institutions as compatible with their beliefs. These teachings and beliefs are not, of course, the only factor in the decisions of political or religious leaders, but recent history should have taught us not to ignore them or assume them away.

Kissinger's secularist assumptions are also revealed in his comment on the "homogeneity" of Western societies. Here he simply assumes that American religious communities—products, after all, of the Westphalian system of sovereign states in which religious strife had been defeated—were passively compliant because colonial Americans were ethnically and religiously homogeneous. Although it is true that Anglo-Saxon ethnicity dominated the colonies prior to the 19th century, the conflation of religion and ethnicity is a mistake typical of foreign policy elites and is misleading (as it is in Lebanon, where confessional groups are not divided along ethnic lines). It underestimates the fierce doctrinal contentions that beset 17th-century Anglo-Saxon Protestant America, and which had to be addressed within and among the various religious groupings in order to create the 18th-century United States' regime of religious freedom.

We will return to the American regime, but it is important to understand why realists continue to avoid the issue of religion in the international system, even after 9/11, except as a lever of power. In part the answer is that they are trapped in the intellectual construct they have adopted and in the assumption that religion is inherently irrational. Religion is ordinarily productive of "passion" and little else. As such, religiously motivated behavior is a unit of analysis only in understanding the drive to power. Kissinger's own perspective on this point was highlighted in a review of U.S.-India policy, in which he praised Indian Hinduism for its passivity (the opposite of passion). Both Indian democracy and the long-term stability of Indian culture were in some sense attributable to "the impermeable Hindu culture." "The Hindu religion," he asserted, "is the only major faith that does not accept converts."[10]

By contrast, Kissinger noted, Americans have traditionally seen democratic institutions as "both unique and relevant to the rest of the world as guarantees of universal peace." This led to "crusades on behalf of democracy" from Woodrow Wilson to George W. Bush. Hinduism has never conceived of democracy as part of itself but as "a practical adaptation, the most effective means to reconcile the polyglot components of the state emerging from the colonial past." In other words, Hinduism is virtually alone among world religions in not producing the passions that feed the quest for power.

There is clearly some truth to this interpretation. Hinduism has made a major contribution to the successful balance of religious communities in India, including minority Muslims, Sikhs, and Christians. In order to appreciate the achievements of Indian democracy, one need only recall the horrific interconfessional massacres that attended the coming of India's independence in 1948. Doubtless much of this achievement has to do with Hinduism's practical, ecumenical strain and its traditional rejection of the missionary impulse.

But Kissinger's analysis overlooks other critical factors in India, most notably the accommodation to democracy of the huge Muslim minority, and the tiny but influential Christian community, which has had an important role in retaining aspects of British liberalism. Moreover, although it is true that Hindu teaching does not typically seek converts from other religions, that teaching has not always induced passivity. Some Indian provinces have instituted harsh anti-conversion laws to prevent Hindu apostasy, and puritanical Hindu nationalists have been responsible for terrible violence against Muslims and Christians. The continued social power of the Hindu caste system still consigns millions of Indian citizens to the status of "untouchables."

It is difficult to avoid the conclusion that Mr. Kissinger simply wanted to fit Hindu religion into his worldview by crediting what he saw as an atypical aspect of religion—spiritual passivity—for the stability of Indian society. Here religion without passion becomes a positive force, a counterweight to the push for power. But this represents a flawed understanding both of religion and the achievement of Indian Hinduism. At its best, as represented in the life and work of Mohandas K. Gandhi, Hinduism has reflected an understanding of human nature and swaraj (self-rule) that supports the regime of religious freedom holding Indian society together. Gandhi's hope for India was grounded in his religion-based (and highly reasoned) conviction that a common human spirit could animate the political actions and institutions of men.[11]

A second example of the religion deficit in post-9/11 realist thinking is an important 2005 article by two influential realist thinkers. In "Realism's Shining Morality," Robert F. Ellsworth and Dimitri K. Simes provided their prescriptions for foreign policy under the second George W. Bush administration. As the title suggests, their treatment was designed in part to overcome a standard charge against realism, that it "offers no vision beyond power. It is all means and no ends."[12]

Ellsworth and Simes argue for a "high-minded realism" that avoids the neoconservative tendency undermining the Bush administration's foreign policy, namely the temptation "to play fast and loose with the facts in order to create the appearance of acting morally." The article does not refer to the growth of religion's influence around the world, but it does suggest that religion is one cause of the Bush administration's tendency toward moralism. Neoconservative influence on President Bush, the authors imply, has led him to overemphasize his own religious faith and that of the American founders. The result has been an illegitimate intrusion of religion into foreign policy.

But history shows, they argue, that the "genius of the American experiment was based on the fact that great ideals [represented in faith traditions] were combined with an equally great pragmatism and that strong belief in one's cause was also measured by a decent respect for the passions of others." Religious belief, in other words, yields "great ideals" and "passion" but must be counterbalanced by pragmatism and respect for other passions [i.e., religious beliefs].[13]

Once again the analysis rests on the assumption that the American experiment in democracy was achieved in spite of, or in compensation for, the teachings of its various religious communities, whose deepest beliefs and emotional commitments had to be overcome by the political system. In this sense we have returned to the classic realist worldview: religious belief and religious communities cannot be integrated into the system in any authentic way (unless they lack the missionary impulse) but must be managed and controlled if the system is to work.

A third example of realist thinking drives this point home more explicitly. Rachel Bronson, a senior fellow at the Council on Foreign Relations, wrote in

2005 an essay from within a realist perspective entitled, "Rethinking Religion: The Legacy of the U.S.-Saudi Relationship."[14] In it, she argues in distinctly unrealist fashion that "the role of religion in the U.S.-Saudi relationship has to date garnered far too little attention." Importantly, she is not referring to American religious influences but those operating in Saudi Arabia. But neither her analysis nor her policy prescriptions stray from the classical realist view of religious communities as a purely negative factor feeding power politics.

Bronson focuses on the rise of Saudi Wahhabism during the last two decades of the 20th century. This brand of Sunni Islam, named for the puritanical and violent 18th-century theologian Muhammed ibn al Wahhab, has exported its extremist interpretations of the Koran and hadith for years, with devastating results for the Muslim and non-Muslim world. The House of Saud had retained power throughout the 20th century in part by manipulating and controlling its indigenous Wahhabis.

After the 1979 Shiite revolution in neighboring Iran, Bronson writes, Wahhabism was viewed within the kingdom as a barrier to the potential destabilization of Saudi Arabia's Shiite minority. The Saudi government thereafter permitted "the unconstrained radicalization of Saudi Arabia's elaborate [Wahhabi] religious machinery." The United States aided this development indirectly by supporting Wahhabis during the Cold War because they were anti-Communist. U.S. aid was extended to the Wahhabi-inspired Arab mujahadeen opposition to the Soviet invasion of Afghanistan, which had tragically facilitated the rise of Osama Bin Laden and Al Qaeda.

Within Saudi Arabia, Bronson notes, the growth of Wahhabism led to anti-U.S. and anti-Israel fanaticism and harsh laws against women. Ultimately, it fed religious forces within the kingdom that turned against the Saudi royal house itself. Bronson quotes a Saudi national's assessment of the problem: after 1979, Saudi "society was given an overdose of religion."

The implicit bargain between the Saudi government and Wahhabism began to change in the early 21st century, she notes, beginning with the Al Qaeda attacks of September 11, 2001. The attacks were carried out by 19 men, 15 of whom were Saudi nationals, most of them with some connection to the Wahhabi understanding of Islam. But the real turning point came with the May 2003 bombings by Al Qaeda within Saudi Arabia itself. This led to a deepening sense of crisis and a conscious decision by the Saudi government to crack down on the radical religious establishment, an attempt to disband Al Qaeda, the toning down of mosque sermons, and new financial and banking policies to interrupt the flow of Saudi funds to radicals inside and outside the kingdom.

What, then, is Bronson's prescription for U.S. foreign policy given this altered landscape in Saudi Arabia? She understands its implications for U.S. interests, and goes beyond the classical realist focus on access to oil and Saudi support for U.S. policies. She subscribes to the view that Saudi Arabia will play a major role in either blocking or continuing to facilitate the spread of Islamist terror. Whether the Saudi government will take action "to diffuse the spiritual context that nurtures radical and violent groups" is difficult to assess, she writes, but it must be done. Key issues include "how the House of Saud resists and co-opts its religious opposition," whether the government can avoid the "politicization of religion," and whether it can "help encourage opportunities [for Saudi citizens] outside or alongside religious pursuits."

Bronson is clearly right about the importance of new opportunities, especially secular education for men and women. She recommends, for example, more U.S.-Saudi educational cooperation and student exchanges. She writes persuasively that "broadening human capital will help wean some away from radical religious pursuits...." But like other realists and neo-realists, she apparently gives no thought to a deeper proposition. There is little suggestion in her writing that religion—especially religion in the birthplace of Islam—is something more than an impulse to be controlled by government action, or educated away by modern science and social science. The thing to be avoided at all costs is the "politicization of religion." Nowhere is any consideration given to the central theme that characterizes American history: properly mixed and differentiated in a political framework, religion and liberal government can support one another.

Bronson, like other realists, believes that the only feasible solution to the Wahhabis is their control by the Saudi monarchy, as if the former were nothing but a particularly troublesome interest group gone awry. But Wahhabism did not simply emerge after 1979. Its influence on Saudi Islam runs deep and it is unlikely to be extirpated by the actions of a monarchy whose legitimacy is itself subject to challenge within the kingdom. If Wahhabism is to be contained as a destructive force in Saudi Arabia and the world, Muslims must reject its theological premises. American policy must begin to acknowledge this reality in its dealings with the Saudis, a subject to which we will return in chapters 8 and 9.

A final example of realist single-mindedness in excluding the possibility of religious reform in engaging the problems of the Middle East can be seen again in an op-ed by Henry Kissinger in early 2007. The elder statesman had reportedly by then become an unofficial advisor to the Bush White House in its attempts to recover momentum in Iraq. Under urging from Kissinger and James Baker (coauthor with Lee Hamilton of the report of the Iraq Study group),[15] the administration had persuaded the Iraqi government to agree to two international conferences. These, it was hoped, would form the basis for cooperation by Iraq's neighbors, especially Iran and Syria, in playing a more productive, or at least less destructive, role in the deepening Iraq crisis.

At the end of his op-ed this storied student of Metternich and the Congress of Vienna referred to another seminal international conference—the one that assembled in northern Europe between 1644 and 1648 to produce the Peace of Westphalia and ended the religious wars that had devastated much of continental Europe. Should America fail to galvanize the international community, including Iraq's neighbors, in a Westphalia-like diplomatic effort, Kissinger wrote, the result might well be a religious war of comparable impact, leaving the international community to face a situation of "exhaustion and despair" in the Middle East. Such a development would lead to "a period of extreme turbulence, verging on chaos" that would threaten global oil supplies and could result in "jihadist fanaticism...driving the world toward an ever widening conflict."

Kissinger's call for an international and regional concord of powers to forestall chaos in the Middle East echoes realist recommendations by the Iraq Study Group and others.[16] It is perhaps an initiative worth trying, although it raises questions about why regional powers such as Iran, or world powers such as China and Russia, will cooperate in strengthening America's hand in Iraq and elsewhere. Perhaps they can be persuaded to act by the argument that Islamist terrorism affects their interests just as it does America's. But a central problem remains, one that other powers may be as reluctant to acknowledge as we seem to be. Islamist extremism cannot be defeated merely by military means, or by pressures from external powers alone. The sources of Islamist extremism lie in the cultures that produce the ideas of Wahhabism, Khomeinism, and other aspects of radical Islamism. America, and any partners it can muster, must find ways to encourage the cultural changes necessary to contain or extirpate extremism. That can only be accomplished by Muslims themselves, through political and religious reform.

At the end of the day, even post-9/11 neorealists find it difficult to see religion as anything other than a negative, irrational force. They've got the story half right. But in ignoring the possibility of a positive, rational role for religion in liberal governance, and in simply refusing to address the natural desire of men and women to live in accord with the religious truths they believe they have discovered, "realism" remains an utterly unrealistic basis on which to ground American foreign policy in a world of faith.

Liberal Internationalism

Although realism has traditionally exerted great influence at Foggy Bottom, the tenured chairs among the senior permanent cadre at the Department of State are today often occupied by liberal internationalists, or those who see wisdom in both schools. A descendant of Wilsonian idealism, liberal internationalism has been influential at the State Department in part because it places heavy emphasis on the tools that diplomats are trained to use, such as negotiating and persuading, crafting agreements and treaties, and working within multilateral organizations to induce cooperation from other states.

Liberal internationalists, like most diplomats, have a natural interest in the domestic policies of states (something that realists typically lack) and believe that U.S. policy should attempt to influence those policies through the medium of international organizations and norms. They also tend to be more interested than realists in public diplomacy, which liberals believe should emphasize international norms as a means of convincing foreign societies of the wisdom of the U.S. position.

Liberals generally believe that the United States should rarely if ever employ military power unilaterally, but should seek and gain the imprimatur of international organizations such as the United Nations in order to achieve the kind of legitimacy they believe flows from the international community and international law. As the U.S.-led NATO intervention in Kosovo demonstrated, liberal internationalists are capable of acting without the agreement of the United Nations, especially when urged by U.S. neoconservatives (many of whom supported the Kosovo war) and when acting within the context of another multilateral organization (in this case, NATO). Realists do not reject multilateral organizations but are more likely to see them as means to achieve American national interests than as institutions that lend legitimacy to U.S. actions.

But the popularity of liberal internationalism at Foggy Bottom derives from more than its emphasis on diplomatic methods and its Wilsonian quest for international legitimacy. Senior American diplomats have often been educated in elite academic institutions and, partly as a result, tend to have a modern liberal worldview. The policies they seek to encourage in other countries often reflect this orientation. Although most foreign service officers pride themselves on carrying out the instructions of any administration, it was my experience that the policies of the Clinton State Department were more often welcomed than those of the more conservative Reagan or Bush administrations.[17] The embrace of Clinton's liberal internationalism also extended to some degree to the military interventions in Bosnia and Serbia. Although neither was welcomed unconditionally at Foggy Bottom, those military actions were deemed acceptable because they were seen as humanitarian in nature. They were not conceived or defended by the administration as examples of American exceptionalism.

When it came to human rights, Clintonian foreign policy tended to emphasize modern liberal concerns such as population control as a means of addressing the social and political problems of nations and mitigating damage to the world's environment. The population problem was viewed under the two Clinton secretaries of state (Warren Christopher and Madeleine Albright) as a major human rights issue. At two international conferences focusing on women's rights, international family planning was eagerly supported by the State Department bureaucracy, both as a means of furthering women's rights and as a prudent approach to the problem of population growth.

When it comes to religion, liberal internationalists share with realists—albeit for very different reasons—a reluctance to incorporate the spiritual dimensions of other societies in their analyses and policies. Whereas realists see religion as relevant only to understanding the drive to power, liberals understandably tend to see traditional religious communities as obstacles to the adoption of liberal policies. Examples of liberal skepticism about the political role of religion abound; they increased exponentially as a result of the rise of Islamist terrorism and the 2004 reelection of George W. Bush. Some critics of the Bush administration (both liberal and conservative) have seen Islamist extremism and red-state evangelicalism as two aspects of the same worldwide trend toward fundamentalism, and consequently as a threat to Western values.[18]

An example of the intellectual basis for these concerns appeared in a 2003 article in one of the venerable American foreign affairs journals, *Foreign Policy*. Two liberal scholars, Ronald Inglehart and Pippa Norris, argued that Samuel Huntington had in his "clash of civilizations" argument fundamentally misunderstood the nature of the conflict between Islam and the West. Huntington had argued that Islam was deficient in its capacity for political democracy, but the World Values Survey (which Inglehart directed) indicated overwhelming support for democracy in the Muslim world.[19]

What truly separates Islam and the West, according to these scholars, is the West's commitment to "gender equality and sexual liberation," two factors that prove "time and time again to be the most reliable indicators of how strongly [a] society supports principles of tolerance and egalitarianism."[20] Neither is present, they point out, in countries where Islam exercises a strong influence on society and politics.

To demonstrate their argument, Inglehart and Pippa cite the answers given in Muslim nations to questions on the World Value Survey's "Gender Equality Scale." Some of the questions clearly have probative value in determining whether a society sees women as inherently inferior to men and therefore whether such attitudes form obstacles to liberal governance. For example, most Muslim populations in the survey believed education more important for boys than girls, that men should have a greater right to work than women in a situation of high unemployment, and that men make better political leaders than women. Although there may be economic factors that mitigate the gender biases revealed in the answers, there can be little doubt that the equality of women is a major stumbling block to political, social, and economic development in many Muslim nations, and that Islamic teachings have considerable influence over Muslim views on that issue. For example, the Culture Matters Research Project at the Fletcher School of Tuft's University has found a correlation between low levels of female literacy and low levels of development in nations formed by Islam.[21]

But one of the World Value Survey questions—the first in a sequence of five—highlighted the tension between modern liberalism and all traditional religions. "If a woman wants to have a child as a single parent but she doesn't want to have a stable relationship with a man, do you approve or disapprove?"[22] Disapproval was seen as a deficiency in progress toward tolerance and egalitarianism. But the question stipulates as normative the modern liberal understanding of human autonomy, namely that all persons are "unbound by moral ties antecedent to choice."[23] Protecting women's rights, in this view, requires the elevation of human will—in this case what a woman wants—such that other moral obligations involving the family and the child are subordinate. Most religious traditions, however, and not just Islam, embrace a notion of prior human obligation, and the value of the traditional family, that represents a serious threat to the modern liberal project reflected in the World Values Survey.[24]

It is not difficult to see that diplomats and policy makers who share these assumptions about human freedom and human rights may have difficulty engaging, let alone influencing, mainstream worldviews in most Islamic societies. Such modern liberal views are unlikely to appeal to the Muslim women they presume to represent. The negative reception that the modern liberal project is likely to receive can be seen in the principles being espoused by Islamic feminists. Muslim feminism is a religiously and geographically diverse movement, united by a belief in the inherent dignity of all women. While universally condemning the anti-woman practices often associated with Islam, such as inequality under the law, force marriages, and genital cutting, many Muslim feminists believe Islam rightly understood provides no warrant for the subordination of women. These women seek to establish Islam rightly understood through exegesis of the Koran and hadith, in other words from the heart of Islam.[25]

But Islamic feminists do not seek the liberation of Muslim women by embracing the values represented as progressive and democratic in the World Values Survey. In writing her book *In Search of Islamic Feminism*, Elizabeth Warnock Fernea encountered throughout the greater Middle East what she labeled "family feminism." Muslim feminists, she discovered, see the family, and the relationships between men and women within the family, as the centerpiece of feminism, not its solvent.[26]

A striking example of the conflict between traditional religion and the modern liberal project appears in an extraordinary essay published in 2005 by Human Rights Watch (HRW), one of the world's oldest human rights institutions and widely respected in the liberal internationalist community. HRW has long been associated with the secularist left, but unlike other human rights organizations has also actively advocated for religious individuals and groups suffering persecution, even when those groups may be hostile to the HRW view of freedom.[27]

The essay in question examines whether there is a "schism between the human rights movement and religious communities." It engages in an unusually candid analysis of religion's negative and positive impact on human rights advocacy, and admits that "the secular human rights movement sometimes sees conservative religious movements as an artifact of history and itself as contemporary, ahead on the 'infinite road of human progress and modernity.'" Some human rights activists are "tempted to dismiss such [traditional] faiths and cultures as obstacles to economic or human rights modernity."[28]

The authors call for more openness to religion and more cooperation between human rights and religious activists. But they also conclude that there is a deep divide between human rights properly understood and religiously informed moral judgments, a divide that must not be breached. Although human rights activists should stand for the rights of believers to be free of persecution, activists must also "directly oppose pressures from religious groups that seek to dilute or eliminate rights protections.... Human rights groups should oppose efforts in the name of religion to impose a moral view on others when there is no harm to third parties and the only 'offense' is in the mind of the person who feels that the other is acting immorally." A footnote emphasizes that the principles of "no harm to third parties" and the subjectivity of moral judgments are "essential to safeguarding the dignity and humanity of lesbian, gay, bisexual and transgender people." Genuine human rights advocacy requires "a distinction between private religious morality and religiously motivated public policy that infringes rights."[29]

A failure to maintain that distinction, the essay argues, has not only led to human rights abuses by governments and groups influenced by religious judgmentalism, but also to a disordered emphasis on religious freedom. In the 1998 International Religious Freedom Act, the U.S. Congress had capitulated to Christian and other religious groups in making religious freedom "a unique yardstick of foreign relations." This law, the essay argued, was analogous to King Louis XIV's 1649 declaration of French protection for Lebanon's Maronites, or "19th century European powers' 'humanitarian interventions' against the Ottoman Empire to 'protect persecuted Christians.'"[30]

As we shall see, there is a grain of truth in this criticism. To some extent the 1998 religious freedom law was seen by many of its leading supporters as a means of protecting their co-religionists abroad—mainly Christians—from persecution, and this factor evinced skepticism and hostility from some at the State Department. But the deeper liberal objection was not to saving Christians or those of other faiths from torture or abuse. Indeed, as already noted, that approach was quickly adopted at Foggy Bottom as the best way to manage an unwanted, congressionally imposed mandate.

The real problem among liberals at the department was the fear evoked in the Human Rights Watch essay, namely, that public manifestations of religious freedom could frustrate the aims of the liberal internationalist project, including its social objectives of sexual liberation and the determinative value of human autonomy. For that reason, among others, liberal internationalists, like their counterparts in the human rights community, are content to view the "promotion of religious freedom" as the protection of religious people from violence and persecution. They are hesitant to promote it as a right to adduce religiously informed moral arguments as one means of shaping public democratic institutions, or of persuading others to adopt a religiously informed understanding of individual flourishing and the common good.

As John Rawls, Ronald Dworkin, and other liberal political theorists have put it, the individual right is prior to the common good. Accordingly, "government should be neutral on the question of the good life or of what gives value to life," and should seek to maximize the autonomy of the individual.[31] This view was reflected in a volume of essays, which included several liberal internationalists, on the subject of democracy and human rights. The volume was edited by Harold Hongju Koh, the State Department's assistant secretary of state for democracy, human rights, and labor (DRL), when the nation's new international religious freedom law began to be implemented in earnest.[32] One essayist was his predecessor in DRL, John Shattuck, who was the Clinton administration's primary spokesman against religious freedom legislation.[33] Liberal political theorists included Thomas Nagel, Ronald Dworkin, and Jeremy Waldron.[34]

The essays address the questions of how to ground human rights and what makes them universal, how constitutions can preserve human rights in a way compatible with democracy and stability, and the relationships between human rights and democracy, voting, and deliberation. The volume is rich with discussion of human autonomy, including sexual expression as a fundamental right[35] and the grounding of individual rights in Kantian philosophy.[36] Other than a discussion of the role of the Catholic Church in Argentina, however, it nowhere grapples with the religious sources of human rights or the potential contributions of religious communities to democracy. Following Rawls, the essays assume that religious doctrine is incompatible with constitutional arguing in the public square.[37] These views do not necessarily reflect hostility to religion, although in some cases they may. More generally, they manifest the liberal internationalist assumption that religion is irrelevant to politics—unless it mistakenly insists on its own involvement, drawing from its own truth claims, in the public square.

Neoconservatism and the Bush Administration

Of all the approaches to American foreign policy, neoconservatism might well be considered the one most open to the question of addressing religion, particularly its role in the neoconservative's core theme—the supreme value of democracy at home and abroad.[38] Its roots can be traced to the 1930s, when a group of leftist intellectuals abandoned Soviet communism as a failed experiment and a grave threat to American democracy. The latter came to be invested by neoconservative thinkers with a sacred character, its exceptionalism being attributed to the wisdom of its political institutions and its protection of religious minorities through the separation of church and state.

By the 1960s and 1970s the movement, while remaining staunchly anticommunist, had also begun to focus on the shortcomings of the Great Society and government-induced social engineering. Neocons such as Irving Kristol, Daniel Bell, James Q. Wilson, and Daniel Patrick Moynihan were taking positions at American academic institutions, and their views were being articulated in the pages of neoconservative journals such as *Commentary* and the *Public Interest*. After the Vietnam war many liberals concluded that U.S. involvement resulted from what President Jimmy Carter later called an "inordinate fear of communism," but neocons argued that communism was both a moral evil and a mortal threat.[39] The ranks of the movement were religiously diverse, but the intellectual interests of members were largely secular in orientation. Many neocons, while more open to the role of religion in public policy than liberals, were nevertheless skeptical about the aggressive entry of evangelicals into American politics.

The neocon ambivalence over the role of religion in American society was to be challenged in later years when leftist Christian intellectuals such as Michael Novak and Richard John Neuhaus became disenchanted with modern liberalism and their ideas became influential in neoconservative circles. Dubbed "theocons" by detractors, these thinkers argued for the value of religiously informed moral judgments as key to the success of democratic institutions. They, too, were skeptical of the Christian right but saw the greater threat to American democracy from liberal secularism.

Many were Catholics, such as Novak, George Weigel, and Robert George (Neuhaus, a Lutheran, later converted to Catholicism), but their appeal to the importance of religion in democracy was nonsectarian. They tended to write from within the Catholic natural law tradition, which asserted that certain truths about human nature and objective morality were intelligible to all people of good will, of whatever religious conviction, or none.[40] With the notable exception of Weigel, however, most of these Christian thinkers did not write in any systematic way about U.S. foreign policy.[41]

During the 1980s, other neoconservatives were applying their ideas about democracy and American exceptionalism to foreign affairs, ideas that influenced the development of President Reagan's international democracy programs. For example, the National Endowment for Democracy was designed to channel funding into nongovernmental efforts to seed democratic development overseas. Prominent neoconservatives such as Elliot Abrams helped mold that policy. Abrams served as assistant secretary of state in three positions during the 1980s: inter-American affairs, human rights and humanitarian affairs, and international organizations.

But much of the movement's influence was in the area of defense policy. Some of the younger neocons had positions of importance in the Reagan administration, such as Richard Perle and Douglas Feith in the Office of the Secretary of Defense. Paul Wolfowitz was under secretary for political affairs at the State Department. All were strongly supportive of Reagan's military buildup as well as his strong moral condemnations of the evils of communism and the Soviet empire.

For their part, classical realists tended to support President Reagan's military buildup as necessary to counter balance Soviet power. Many liberal internationalists, however, did not. Many condemned, for example, Reagan's decision to develop a new generation of mobile intercontinental ballistic missiles. Most liberals (and many realists) were supremely skeptical of Reagan's Strategic Defense Initiative (SDI), which rejected in principle the doctrine of "mutual assured destruction" long supported by the foreign policy establishment. In U.S.–Soviet Defense and Space Talks in Geneva, the U.S. negotiating team was divided by mutually contradictory goals. The State Department's representatives wanted to compromise with the Soviets on SDI, whereas Defense Department officials sought to protect it.[42] Furthermore, both realists and liberals scorned what they viewed as moralism on the part of President Reagan, who referred to the Soviet Union as "an evil empire" and the United States as "a city on a hill." Many rejected as simplistic his premise that neither communism nor the Soviet empire was permanent.

Most realists and liberals were, to put it mildly, caught off guard with the sudden collapse of the Soviet Union, its proxies in eastern Europe, and their abandonment of communist ideology. Few if any foreign policy observers had understood the intrinsic weaknesses of Soviet communism, the potential effects of Reagan's military buildup and his persistent moral pressure, or the possibility that a man like Mikhail Gorbachev, in seeking to reform and preserve the communist system, could unwittingly trigger its collapse. And virtually no one in the West predicted that a religious doctrine of human freedom, articulated by a charismatic Polish pope, could assist in the process.[43]

Although neoconservatives were part of the policy that contributed to the end of the Cold War, it is safe to say that most of them were gratified but surprised by the speed and completeness with which it ended. In fact, some may have taken the wrong lesson from the events of those remarkable years. Francis Fukuyama, a neoconservative who later abandoned the movement, has emphasized this point as a likely explanation for what he believes to have been critical neoconservative mistakes in Iraq. Having observed the rapid movement toward democracy among many nations of the former Soviet empire, Fukuyama argues, neocons erroneously concluded that the removal of Saddam Hussein in Iraq would lead to a similar result. The fatal flaw was the assumption "that democracy was a default condition to which societies would revert once liberated from dictators."[44]

Fukuyama's larger point is a reasonable one. The desire for freedom, dignity, and prosperity may well be a "default condition" for human beings, but achieving the stable political arrangements that order and protect those aspirations, such as liberal democracy, cannot be seen as automatic, as the long travail of Western history surely demonstrates. But if Fukuyama is correct about the shortsightedness of the neocon vision in Iraq, it is in another sense quite surprising. Neoconservatives were thought to have developed a deeper appreciation for the role of culture and social institutions in political development than their counterparts in the schools of American foreign policy. Neocons were said to differ from realists in rejecting the latter's "amoral" approach to human behavior and in having a greater appreciation of the varieties of human and political experience. According to foreign affairs scholar Andrew Bacevich, writing in the late 1990s, neocons tended to view "the human person as something more than the sum of his or her appetites," and were interested in the connections between democracy and character.[45]

At this writing, the American experiment in seeding stable self-government in Iraq remains in peril. After their impressive adoption of democratic procedures during 2005 and 2006, including the elections of transitional and permanent governments and the ratification of a permanent constitution, the Iraqis were plunged into a series of crises, including a religion-based civil war. Pundits rushed into print with post mortems, many of them centered on U.S. military mismanagement, especially the failure to secure the country in the first weeks after the invasion. Others argued on various grounds that the reasons for war were fatally flawed: for example, because of inaccurate assumptions about weapons of mass destruction or the belief that Iraq had a role in Islamist terrorism or the idea that democracy could be implanted by force.[46]

It is both premature and beyond the scope of this book to predict the fate of Iraqi democracy. But it is worth exploring in a preliminary sense whether the American diplomatic habit of downplaying religion, reinforced by neoconservative goals, may have contributed to the problems encountered by the United States in Iraq. It seems highly likely that the religion-based hatred loosed in that country can only be curbed by fierce and efficient political oppression, such as Saddam provided, or by a politico-religious agreement among the Iraqis to stop it. American involvement has provided an opportunity for the latter, but its diplomatic influence over the outcome has been weak. Could it have been otherwise?

It is now obvious that those neocons who helped define American strategy in Iraq relied too much on military power (however ineffectively applied after the initial invasion) and gave too little thought to what would be necessary to develop a democratic political culture after the overthrow of Saddam, including the influence of Islamic teachings on key players and groups. If Fukuyama is correct, it appears they did not make the proper distinctions between what had happened in Eastern Europe and what could be expected in the Middle East. After all, Samuel Huntington's thesis, influential among neoconservatives at the time, was that, in substantial part because of religion, democracy would emerge more easily in the countries of Latin Christianity than it would in the Islamic nations of the Middle East. Did the neocons not accept that a political key to implanting democracy in Iraq was the role of religious individuals and communities, especially the Shiite community and its spiritual leader, Grand Ayatollah Ali al-Sistani?

In retrospect it is reasonably clear that the neocons did not view Iraqi civil and political society as fundamentally religious in nature. Heavily influenced by secular Iraqi émigrés such as Ahmed Chalabi, Paul Wolfowitz and other policy makers appear to have concluded that a secular Iraqi middle class would provide the manpower for a secular democracy.[47] The neocons saw Kemalist Turkey as the religio-political model for their thinking. In Turkey religion was by law and decades of practice in effect cordoned outside the world of politics. The rise to power of the Turkish Justice and Development party—an Islamic democratic political party—does not appear to have influenced the administration's thinking about Iraq.[48]

Policy makers were utterly convinced that the only secure protections for liberty in Iraq, and for larger American interests, would be a secular state and a secular constitution. The possibility that Iraqis would, with virtual unanimity, reject this idea apparently did not carry much weight in U.S. planning for the debates over drafting of the initial constitution, the Transitional Administrative Law (TAL). One participant in that process has written that "neoconservatives (in Washington and Iraq) began to argue to the Iraqis involved in the constitutional process that state secularism was desirable." In the end, this did not happen. Both the TAL and the permanent constitution that succeeded it established Islam as the state religion of Iraq.[49]

The constitution contains other guarantees, including religious freedom, which are quite liberal. Neither that constitutional provision nor any other, however, has prevented Iraq from disintegrating into religious factions; Sunnis and Shiites fight each other, opposing Shiite militias vie for superiority, and Christian and other religious minorities are severely threatened. The deeper question is why the neocons did not foresee the need to work with Islamic and other religious communities and parties within the country until so late in the game.

One way to get at this issue is to ask why the ideas of Christian intellectuals (the so-called theocons) apparently had little influence on the neoconservatives in the Bush administration who were responsible for post-war planning in Iraq. On the one hand, it seems clear that some conservative religious leaders, including many evangelicals, had a definitive fear of Islam in power. Many pressed the president and the State Department to ensure that strong guarantees of religious freedom were accompanied by the political marginalization of Islam.[50] On the other hand, scholars such as Novak, Weigel, and Neuhaus had written at length of the moral underpinnings of stable democracy and the importance of the religious element of human nature.[51] Although none were scholars of Islam, their ideas might have signaled the dangers of a secularist view of Iraq—that is, the view that liberal democracy could be implanted there or anywhere else without due regard to the political theologies of dominant religious communities.

It is important to recall that most senior members of the Bush adminis-tration were not neoconservatives at all but realists and pragmatists of vary-ing sorts whose views had been altered by 9/11. They included Vice President Richard Cheney, Secretary of Defense Donald Rumsfeld, National Security Advisor (and later Secretary of State) Condoleeza Rice, and Secretary of State Colin Powell. President Bush himself was not a neoconservative (at least not initially), as his early foreign policy pronouncements made clear.[52] It is pos-sible that for these senior policy makers, the realist tendency to focus on power overcame the need to understand internal forces and led to an underestimation of postinvasion difficulties, including the role of religion. But even this argu-ment fails to explain why neither these senior leaders nor the neoconserva-tives in other influential positions were influenced by the ideas of the Christian thinkers.

One explanation may be that the Christian intellectuals had their greatest impact on administration policy in areas that did not directly affect postwar planning. These thinkers were often consulted for their views on domestic U.S. religion-state issues, such as judicial nominees, and on the Catholic vote. When it came to the war, Novak and Weigel in particular became engaged in defending the American invasion on classical Catholic just-war grounds.[53] But their views about religion and state were, it appears, not sought during the planning for what should happen on the ground after the invasion took place and the task of building a state began.

The ideas of at least one of these thinkers could have provided, at least in principle, a different path to American post-invasion policy. In the early 1990s George Weigel had pondered in remarkably prescient fashion the role of revivalist Islam. He had concluded that "[t]he heart of the issue of Islam and democracy, indeed of Islam and the West, is not the development of new political traditions, but the possible evolution of a new (or reformed) Islamic theological tradition."[54] Weigel's 1994 book *Idealism without Illusions* exhorted a return to nonutopian moral reasoning in foreign policy, reasoning that would serve America's national security by, inter alia, accepting without illusions the possibilities of human progress.

In that book Weigel articulated his views on the barriers to Islamic reform, and therefore to Islamic democracy, including the Muslim conviction that Islam had entirely superseded Christian and Jewish revelation and the absence of Koranic warrants for religion-state differentiation or religious pluralism.[55] Later, in 2007, Weigel's moral reasoning about the justness of the Iraq war, and about mistakes made *post bellum*, were widely circulated among Bush policy makers.[56] Some of those views doubtless met with approval. But his cautions about American "tone deafness" on the subject of religion had been ignored too long to make much difference by that late in the administration.

In a 2008 book intended as a call to action for the next presidency, Weigel provided a pointed critique of Bush administration planners and the American foreign policy establishment. He noted that policy makers had been "tone deaf for too long to the religious dimensions" of the intra-Arab Sunni-Shiite divide in Iraq.[57] More broadly, he decried the blinding secularity of the foreign policy establishment that derived from, among other things, the belief that modern concepts of freedom began with the Enlightenment. This belief, he wrote, "is mistaken as a matter of the history of ideas." Western history, including modern democracy, "was formed from the fruitful interaction of... biblical religion, philosophical rationality and law."[58]

Worse, he argued, ignorance of the religious dimension in modern notions of freedom played into the hands of Islamist extremists "who are all too eager to claim that democracy, civil society, and the rule of law... are the by-products of decadent, godless cultures." Recovering the "religious roots" of civility and persuasion, Weigel admonished, can help the United States engage Muslims "who want for themselves political communities that respect the dignity of the human person [and] in which government is both responsible and responsive."[59] American diplomacy must abandon the conceit that such government "will only follow some form of secularization."[60]

Had those views been incorporated into U.S. policy, American diplomats might have carried to Iraq in 2003 a comprehensive, multifaceted strategy on religion and democracy. Such a strategy could have included the premise that long-term democratic stability would depend on a gradual movement toward differentiation between religion and state, religious pluralism and religious freedom. The United States would have made efforts, before the invasion and after, to discern which Iraqi religious and political actors might be open to that premise. It would have made systematic efforts to convince those actors of the advantages of a differentiated democracy leading to religious tolerance and ultimately to religious freedom. It is impossible to know, of course, whether such a policy would have made a difference. Conceivably it could have weakened the early appeal of the Sunni insurgency and Al Qaeda, encouraged further development of Sistani's democratic political theology, and increased the political influence of the Grand Ayatollah himself. At a minimum, this kind of engagement would have elicited less scorn and suspicion than early U.S. attempts to implant a secularist democracy widely perceived as a godless western Trojan horse.

As it happened, however, such ideas, if they were ever considered, were not part of U.S. policy. One well-connected Catholic activist with ties to the religious intellectuals and the neocons, Nina Shea of Freedom House in Washington, D.C., consistently urged the administration to ensure that the Iraqi constitution protected religious freedom. Although her work (along with that of others, including the State Department's office of international religious freedom and the U.S. IRF Commission, on which she served) clearly had a positive effect on the constitution, it did not alter the administration's resistance to a longer-term strategy of engaging religious groups in Iraq.

In the end, there was simply too much resistance among neoconservatives to thinking in policy terms about religion and state. This reluctance is reflected in the thought of Francis Fukuyama himself. Fukuyama was not in the George W. Bush administration, and he opposed the Iraq war. But he had provided some of the intellectual scaffolding for neoconservative thinking about democracy, its intrinsic superiority, and the value to the United States of its proliferation around the world.

During the late 1980s Fukuyama had served in the George H. W. Bush State Department. He had been a member of Foggy Bottom's "think tank"—the office of strategic policy planning for the Secretary of State (James Baker). While there Fukuyama wrote an article in the *National Interest,* later turned into a well-received book, that posited the "end of history" in the sense that "there are no serious ideological competitors left to liberal democracy."[61] With this work Fukuyama laid a theoretical base for the supreme neocon confidence in democracy.

But as *The End of History and the Last Man* (1992) and later writings make clear, Fukyama's understanding of liberal democracy and its constituent elements tended to relegate public religion to the status of an "obstacle" rather than an integrated part. Although he acknowledges religious communities as elements of civil society, and although a key weakness of liberal democracy in his writings is radical individualism and the loss of a sense of the common good, Fukuyama does not see the public dimensions of religious freedom—the involvement of religious groups and their claims—as a means of rebalancing the ledger. In his work religious communities and their truth claims appear as interlopers in the modern democratic project. Notwithstanding his concerns over a loss of moral certainty and the dangers of moral relativism, Fukuyama makes no connection between those problems and the possibility that religious claims, contending with others in the democratic order, might contribute to a solution.[62]

This dismissal of the religious possibility is perhaps clearest in the work that formally declares his independence from the neoconservative movement. In *America at the Crossroads* (2005) Fukuyama takes to task his former ideological brethren for their utopian assumptions about the ease with which democracy would be embraced in Iraq and elsewhere in the Muslim world. In one revealing section of the book, Fukuyama discusses the work of Leo Strauss, an American philosopher of the mid-20th century often seen as the intellectual godfather of neoconservatism.[63]

Fukuyama's logic in this section seems to demand some treatment of religion as normative in democracy. He notes that neocons correctly took from Strauss the idea that "certain political problems can be solved only through regime change."[64] But they had failed to understand Strauss' deeper argument, namely that "regimes...are not just formal institutions and power structures; they shape and are shaped by the societies underlying them. The unwritten rules by which people operate, based on religion, kinship, and shared historical experience, are also part of the regime.... Founding a new political order is, therefore, a difficult business, and doubly so for those who are not immersed in the habits, mores and traditions of the people...."[65]

In a long and detailed chapter of prescriptions for a new American foreign policy, Fukuyama delves deeply into the kinds of economic development and international cooperation he believes necessary for the emergence of democracy—a goal he has certainly not abandoned as an element of American foreign policy. But nowhere in his discussion does he entertain the possibility that Islamic communities can, indeed must, embrace as consistent with Islam the democratic institutions and habits that he continues to see as their salvation. Despite his acknowledgment of the centrality of religion in the life of any society, Fukuyama apparently sees no policy connection between Islam's religious teachings and the consolidation of Muslim democracies.[66]

The theme that religion and democracy are in the end irreconcilable can also be seen in the recent work of a neoconservative "elder statesman"—James Q. Wilson. Wilson has spent much of his illustrious career working on the theory and practice of public policy. In two articles after 9/11 he turned to Islam and what is necessary for the development of liberal societies and democratic institutions in the Muslim world.

Drawing from Western history Wilson argues that liberalism results from freedom of conscience, defined as the capacity for "doubt and self criticism" which are "the source of human progress." As a source of moral and metaphysical certainty religion constituted the major obstacle to human progress, an obstacle that was removed in the West not by "theoretical argument but political necessity." In American history political necessity was epitomized by the constitutional ban on establishment of religion. The "wall between church and state" created by the ban, though controversial, brought about a "profound change in the relationship between governance and spirituality," which was necessary for the establishment of freedom of conscience in America.[67]

Applying this model of liberalism and religion to Islam, Wilson concludes that the most liberal Muslim regimes (Turkey, Indonesia, and Morocco) have succeeded by banishing religion from the public square through strong leaders, an army committed to secularism, and the absence of ethnic conflict. Wilson skeptically cites the goals of exiled Tunisian Muslim leader and reformer Rachid Ghannouchi, who "says he hopes somehow to preserve the Muslim faith while allowing personal freedom." Ghannouchi decries the West's concept of absolute individual freedom, which is grounded in no "absolute value that transcends the will of man." This understanding of freedom, according to Ghannouchi, has yielded "greed, deception, and brutality."

Wilson notes that religious Westerners might agree with this "in some metaphorical sense," but argues that "the historical lesson of the liberal West is that freedom trumps absolute values. This creates a problem that Ghannouchi [and other Islamic reformers] cannot solve." Western history suggests it will take time, but in the end "the proponents of 'Islamic democracy'...[must] abandon their efforts and realize that no nation can be governed effectively simply on the basis of Islamic law."

Wilson's argument is certainly correct at a general level: Islamic law cannot be the basis for effective, let alone liberal, governance. But he is saying much more. He is arguing that liberal democracy means that human freedom and absolute truth claims are irreconcilable, that "freedom trumps absolute values." Although he acknowledges the high cost of this excessive individualism in the West, he sees it as the price of religious tolerance.[68] It appears that, in Wilson's worldview, the meaning of the American founding has little to do with liberty ordered to the truths articulated in the Declaration or those natural duties and rights derived from God to which James Madison and the other founders appealed.[69] Democracy and human rights are achieved by political processes that move religion off the stage of politics altogether.

In this sense, then, Wilson joins Fukuyama and other neoconservative thinkers not only in accepting a highly secularist view of American history, but also in applying it to the imperatives of American foreign policy in attempting to foster stable, liberal societies in the Muslim world. Such an achievement is possible, both seem to agree, only if Islam is marginalized in the democratic political culture. Joshua Muravchik made this even planer in a defense of the neoconservative democracy agenda written in late 2006. The root cause of terrorism in the Middle East, he wrote, was its political culture. But, he noted pointedly, "[p]olitical culture did not mean Islam. Rather, it meant a habit of conducting politics by means of violence." In other words, Islam had nothing to do with the problem of violence. By implication, at least, it had little to do with the solution. "The neocon solution," he observed, "involved overhauling the way the region thinks about politics, so that terrorism would no longer seem reasonable."[70] It seems reasonable to ask whether that worthy goal can be accomplished without the religious sanction of Islamic leaders in those countries where terrorism has flourished.

Finally, neoconservative assumptions about religion, and in particular about Islam, are reflected in the strategic documents that define the Bush administration's goals for U.S. national security. The 2002 version of that plan is where, critics have noted, President Bush's faith in democracy and freedom was laid out in language that appealed to evangelicals. What was not laid out, however, was the relevance of religion to any of the threats or tasks identified in the document. Indeed, almost nowhere does the National Security Strategy mention religion. "Global terrorism" was identified as a major strategic threat to the security and well-being of the United States, but there was no discussion of the relationship between Islam and Al Qaeda (the word "Islam" does not appear in the document). As we have seen, the 9/11 Commission's report at least pursued that link but denied that religious beliefs had any implications for U.S. action. The 2002 National Security Strategy, by its failure to discuss that link, came in effect to the same conclusion.

Nor does the document even hint at any relationship between religion and democracy, even though the promotion of democracy was the major initiative coming out of the 9/11 attacks. There was absolutely no suggestion that the two had a relationship that needed exploring or that U.S. policy should address it. The only references to religion were pro forma tips of the hat to the need for "freedom of worship" and "religious and ethnic tolerance" and "freedom of religion and conscience"—phrases which if nothing else had become part of the American human rights catechism since the passage of the 1998 IRF Act.[71] If critics are correct in identifying a "marriage" of Bush's evangelical theology with neoconservative secular evangelism about democracy, it certainly did not produce a policy of engaging Islam as part of U.S. strategy.[72]

Why this avoidance of religion on the part of a president widely charged with precisely the opposite impulse? It may well be that to an evangelical president and to the various people advising him, including secular neoconservatives, the direct engagement of religion as a factor in national security was simply too thorny or too personal. If the president's evangelical grounding had any impact on his view of strategy, it may have been his instinct that religious belief is a matter of private conscience. As for the U.S. policy of promoting religious freedom, its goal was primarily humanitarian rather than political. To protect freedom of religion meant opposing the persecution of individuals and minorities. It did not automatically require U.S. policy to address the relationship between Islam and democracy, or delve into the political implications of Iraqi Shiism, in order to determine how to proceed in the aftermath of Saddam.

If this analysis is accurate, one might reasonably expect that the experience of confessional strife and of the important political role played by religious leaders and Islamic political parties in Iraq might have had an impact on presidential thinking and the views of his advisors. Looked at through the window of U.S. national security strategy (NSS), there are indications that experience did begin to have an impact in the last years of the administration. With the publication of a new NSS in March 2006, the resistance to considering the broader role of religion in political development seemed to show signs of receding. One veteran foreign policy observer noted the shift, and wrote that the reticence about religion in 2002 had come from the president himself.[73]

The changes occur in the second goal of the 2006 document: "champion aspirations for human dignity." Under the heading "Promoting Effective Democracies," which in the 2002 NSS made no mention of Islam or of religion (other than the aforementioned pro forma references), there were two new phrases that perhaps foreshadowed a change in U.S. thinking about religion. The first is the assertion that effective democracies protect "the institutions of civil society, including the family, *religious communities,* voluntary associations, private property, independent business and a market economy (emphasis added)." The second is the following statement: "In effective democracies, freedom is indivisible. Political, religious and economic liberty advance together and reinforce each other."[74]

In some ways, these statements seemed little more than rhetorical shifts. For one thing, the document's later discussion of "building the infrastructure of democracy" did not return to the contributions that might be made by religious communities in civil society, or to the notion that religious liberty can have an impact on the advancement of political liberty. For another, the Bush administration did not allocate funds for religious freedom programs, either before or after its final NSS. And yet, as we shall see, there were in 2006 and 2007 indications that some American embassies and U.S.-funded programs were beginning to challenge the religious avoidance syndrome that has prevented engagement with religious groups on the basis of their beliefs. The ambassador at large for international religious freedom had in those years begun to use the IRF Act in a creative fashion, suggesting the possibilities inherent in the law.

But it remained unclear whether such changes augured any systematic change in policy. As the Bush administration neared its end, serious questions loomed about the direction the nation would take in its approach to Islam, religion in general, or the issue of the relationship between religion and democracy. The war in Iraq, which threatened to become a religious war between Sunnis and Shiites, seemed to have dealt a setback to the belief that America could succeed in encouraging the growth of stable self-government in the greater Middle East. But the critical role of democracy in human flourishing and world peace was widely accepted in the United States. The question loomed: what could American diplomacy do that it was not doing to facilitate stable democratic development in a world of public faith? To that question we now turn.

3

---☙☙☙---

Religion and Stable
Self-Government

Alongside every religion lies some political opinion which is linked to it by affinity.
    —Alexis de Tocqueville, *Democracy in America*

We're going to show a vision to the world of...what democracy and freedom is all about. It works. The other systems do not work. We're not going to shove it down your throat. We're going to give you the power of our example.
    —Secretary of State Colin Powell, Inaugural Remarks,
    Department of State, January 2001

It's my job to teach these natives the meaning of democracy, and they're going to learn democracy if I have to shoot every one of them.
    —Colonel Wainwright Purdy, U.S. Army, *Teahouse of the August Moon*

The United States has actively supported the growth of democracy around the world for over 25 years. It has an obvious interest in continuing to do so, especially in the greater Middle East, provided democracy leads to prosperity and peace rather than instability and conflict. The American experiences in Iraq and Afghanistan suggest that U.S. military force can overturn a despotic regime and that U.S. diplomats can help broker a democratic constitution and democratic elections. It also suggests that the durability of democracy depends on factors essentially beyond the control of U.S. military force and U.S. diplomacy, including history, geography, and culture.

But acknowledging our incapacity to control or manipulate the larger forces that determine democracy's fate can be liberating. It can relieve us of the burden of arrogance and help us perform the hard analytical task of understanding

79

what works. If we have learned anything in Iraq it should have been that religion drives culture, for good or ill, that we did not fully comprehend that reality, and that we still have not absorbed its implications for the democracy project.

American diplomacy must learn to think more systematically and creatively about the relationships between religion and culture, and religion and state.[1] This will be important for U.S. policies in all regions but especially in the greater Middle East. Allowing for economic, political, and cultural variations in each country, we must understand better than we have the factors that increase the likelihood of a healthy, mutually beneficial balance between religion and state. And we must decide what role American diplomacy can productively play in affecting the outcome.

Majority rule is the heart of democracy. A successful democracy necessarily reflects the values of the majority.[2] The recent history of Iraq suggests, however, that unless the majority accepts limits on its capacity to enforce its will, democracy will remain unstable or collapse into tyranny. In either case, the forces of extremism will profit. A compact between religion and state that works to the benefit of both, and to the benefit of all citizens, including religious minorities, will be critical for the transition of mere democratic procedure into stable self-government.

In part III we turn to the matter of how U.S. diplomacy might influence Muslims as they decide such questions for themselves. For present purposes, it will be useful to do some stage setting on the subject of democracy and religion. The two have been growing in tandem for decades. American foreign policy has given a great deal of thought to freedom and democracy but has barely noticed that one of freedom's constant companions has been religion. We have thought very little about the relationships between ordered liberty and faith and how they affect our security. Such issues are no longer academic questions to be fought over by theologians and legal scholars. They are directly related to the security of the American people.

The reality is that despotism in the greater Middle East has nourished, not repressed, Islamist extremism. Whatever tactics the United States adopts in the short term to address problems in Iraq and Iran, it cannot afford to continue underwriting the system of failed authoritarian states in that region. It must become more adept at identifying, influencing, and supporting the forces that can move the region toward stable self-government. Only durable democracy can increase human flourishing and economic development, create peaceful stability within nations and regions, and undermine the pathologies that yield extremism and terrorism.

Democracy and Its Discontents

Like public religion, democratic forms of government spread rapidly during much of the late 20th century, no doubt reflecting the natural desire of peoples to influence their own destinies. In retrospect, two forces once thought antagonistic—public manifestations of religious belief and democratic reform—appear to have been moving in tandem. In some cases, religion emerged as the handmaiden of freedom. In others, it emerged despite authoritarian attempts to subdue it. In the lands of Arab and Persian Islam, authoritarian regimes prevented the development of anything like a democratic political Islam. What did develop was Islamist extremism of a fearfully rich variety.

Across the world democracy's growth, while dramatic, was less resolute than religion's. By the end of the 20th century the rate of increase in the number of democracies was slowing and perhaps stalling. Dictatorships and authoritarian regimes, it seemed, had learned how to counter their democratic adversaries. Worldwide, the numbers of both electoral and liberal democracies remained essentially unchanged between 1998 and 2006.[3] Electoral democracies are characterized by free and fair elections, but lack protections for civil liberties and human rights. Liberal democracies have both democratic procedures and protections for liberties.

Until the late 20th century the trend toward democracy had been unmistakable. Even liberal democracy had been spreading with vigor. As late as 1975 only 40 countries around the world, about 25 percent of the total, could be characterized as liberal democracies. Most of them were in Western Europe and former British colonies, including the United States. The Soviet empire was responsible for much of the lag outside the West, but even so a mere quarter of the world's nations having achieved liberal democracy that late in modern history seems in retrospect a modest number. After all, the world had for over two centuries witnessed a profusion of democratic theories, democratic reform movements, and democratic revolutions. Two 20th-century world wars had defeated anti-democratic forces, and after each war a new group of democracies had struggled to emerge.[4]

In the 1970s, however, the doors opened and liberal forms of self-governance seemed to be racing from the stalls. The Soviet imperium notwithstanding, a "third wave" of democratization appeared during the late 1970s and 1980s. Then in the early 1990s the Soviet Union dissolved and communism began its retreat. By the end of the 1990s, the numbers of liberal democracies had stabilized at around 88 countries, more than double the number in 1975 and 46 percent of the total number of countries. If electoral democracies were included, the number stabilized at around 117, or two-thirds of all nations.[5]

Democracy's popularity is not difficult to understand. As the 20th century entered its final years an age of totalitarianism seemed to be coming to an end. There was a growing public awareness that alternatives to tyranny existed, and that representative government was not only the best of the political options on offer but that it was achievable. The democratic alternative was now on constant display worldwide via radio, satellite television and the internet, and through increased international travel. It seemed clear that, in the words of democratic theorist Robert A. Dahl, nondemocratic forms of government had "fatally declined in legitimacy and ideological strength."[6]

Today it is almost undisputed that liberal democracy creates the possibility for human flourishing more than any other political system. The fortunate people who live in such nations not only have free and fair elections in which political parties and elected officials vie for their support, but also their societies possess the attributes that make democracies stable and lasting: the rule of law applied equally to all, an independent judiciary, a climate of respect for civil liberties and human rights, a civil society of voluntary associations, and a free press. Most have free market economic systems and an entrepreneurial middle class. It is these kinds of nations that are responsible for what is called the "democratic peace"—the reality that liberal democracies do not as a rule wage war with each other, and that they are also likely to generate economic prosperity for themselves and their commercial partners.[7]

It doesn't take a foreign affairs expert to see why the continued spread of this kind of democratic society would benefit the security and well-being of the American people. If U.S. foreign policy could successfully encourage the growth of such polities, especially in those areas of the world where tyranny and repression still breed discontent, instability, and aggression, the results would be good for the citizens living under them, good for world peace, and good for America. The chances of military conflict within and between nations would decrease. The governments of Iran, North Korea, and China, for example, would see their roles in the world quite differently were they subject to popular sovereignty and constitutionally ordered liberties rather than the ideologies and whims of their authoritarian political masters. Protections for human rights and incentives for economic development would increase. And very likely the spawning, growth, and success of Islamist extremism and transnational terrorism, grave threats to U.S. interests, would be significantly reduced.

As we have seen, such reasoning has not led most American realists to endorse programs of democracy promotion. It is not that they oppose democracy but that they are skeptical of America's capacity to manage democracy's emergence or its development. However, democracy programs were generally supported by conservatives and neoconservatives under the Reagan administration, who saw the programs as a means of countering communism. After the Cold War, liberal internationalists of the Clinton administration supported the expansion of democracy as a moral and humanitarian imperative and worked to create an international community of democracies.

The Al Qaeda attacks of September 11, 2001, elevated democracy promotion to a national security imperative. The Bush administration concluded that past American support for anti-democratic regimes in the greater Middle East (a region that includes Afghanistan and Pakistan) had encouraged the emergence of Islamist terrorism. Fostering democratic governance, it was thought, would help satisfy and manage the powerful human thirst for political and economic freedom, and would over time undermine the pathologies that feed extremism. Accordingly, the United States in the years after 9/11 launched a project for democratic reform in the greater Middle East. Democracy promotion, long an intermittent goal of U.S. foreign policy, now became the dominant national security strategy of the first decade of the 21st century.[8]

But notwithstanding history's apparent movement toward democracy, seeding and growing it—what the Bush administration labeled a "forward strategy of freedom"—proved extremely difficult. In the Middle East the difficulties were multiplied by sectarian conflict in Iraq and the menace of a nuclear-armed clerical autocracy in Iran. The Iraqi experiment in particular raised fundamental questions, including the very meaning and purpose of democracy, the benefits associated with it, and how and when the benefits can be expected to accrue.

Free and fair elections, even when accompanied by constitutions, it turns out, are necessary but insufficient steps toward a stable democratic society. In Iraq it became clear that elections and a constitution could not by themselves unify the country against an insurgency, insulate it against extremists from outside the country, or reconcile political and theological conflicts between Arab Shiites and Sunnis. In Palestine, free and fair elections were won in 2006 by Hamas, an Islamist, anti-Israeli and anti-American terrorist group that appeared to be unaffected by liberal norms. The Lebanese Shiite party Hezbollah, despite its position in a democratically elected Lebanese government, moved to undermine Lebanese democracy, while acting as a terrorist proxy of Iran and Syria. It seemed that the adoption of democratic procedures was not enough. Elections could produce either extremely fragile or extremely aggressive political systems.

One possible solution to this problem, raised by some democracy experts, was to encourage the development of liberal institutions and economic systems *prior* to the holding of elections. If a nation has no entrepreneurial middle class with an interest in limiting the powers of the state, no habitual commitment to the institutions and virtues of *liberalism*—the rule of law, protections for human rights, civil society—then even free and fair elections are unlikely to produce stable democracies.[9] But as Western history demonstrates, the building of institutions, economic prosperity, and democratic virtues takes time and is far more difficult to accomplish than elections. Although U.S. programs under the Clinton and Bush administration did focus to some extent on civil society and institution building in the greater Middle East, the proper sequencing of liberal institutions and democratic procedures was a luxury denied by the exigencies of history.[10]

A serious complicating factor for U.S. policy was the use, and the continued presence, of American and British military forces in Iraq. Advocates pointed out that the very possibility of democracy in Iraq, and the positive effects of Iraqi elections elsewhere in the region, were the result of the coalition invasion of March 2003, the overthrow of Saddam Hussein, and the removal of his ruthless Baathist regime. A troop presence was clearly necessary for a period to counter the insurgency, support a democratic Iraqi government, forestall a confessional civil war and prevent the use of Iraq as a base for Islamist terrorism.

But military force proved a mixed blessing for the administration's democracy project. U.S. forces can overthrow despots and attempt to provide security (although one criticism of the invasion and its immediate aftermath was the failure of American political and military leaders to make the decision to provide security).[11] By their nature and mission, military forces cannot act as primary agents of democracy's seeding and growth. Despite this intrinsic deficiency, American troops in Iraq demonstrated remarkable adaptability and creativity in the democracy project, developing and implementing, for example, the concept of provincial reconstruction teams to rebuild infrastructure.[12] They also worked hard, and sometimes with success, to encourage the growth of Iraqi civil institutions and to engage its civil society.

In the end, uniformed men and women with weapons were seen more as foreign occupiers than as friends of a democratic political culture. Human rights abuses by a tiny minority of American soldiers also provided a public diplomacy nightmare. Critics in the Middle East, and some at home, pointed to the Abu Ghraib scandal as confirmation of American perfidy and hypocrisy, as well as the moral degeneracy of the "freedom" being peddled by the United States. However inaccurately and unjustly, American forces were too often perceived in the region as belying the stated goal of affording greater liberty, human rights, and prosperity for the nations of the Middle East.

As the difficulties of implanting democracy in Iraq mounted, even neoconservatives were less willing to argue for the use of U.S. military power as the forcing bed of democracy elsewhere.[13] Joseph Nye, a scholar who popularized the term "soft power" for achieving foreign policy aims through persuasion, labeled as "coercive democratization" what he believed to be a fatally flawed policy.[14] And some argued that the administration's democracy goals in Iraq were an afterthought to the primary objective of finding and dismantling weapons of mass destruction—weapons that appear not to have existed when the invasion took place.[15] Democratic foreign policy elder Zbigniew Brzezinski accused the Bush administration of deliberately and falsely depicting a war on terror to promote a culture of fear in the United States.[16]

Despite lingering questions about the use of force and weapons of mass destruction, the problem of what to do about America's long-standing democracy programs remained. Democracy enthusiasts point out that as recently as the 1970s, self-government had been considered out of reach for many nations that, in fact, were to achieve it within the next few years. In those days critics of democracy promotion insisted that "[d]emocracy...was not the natural state of affairs in Central Europe or the Balkans; Catholic (and Orthodox) societies were destined to an autocratic fate; and personal freedom was alien to Asian culture. Some even argued that Third World societies generally needed the firm hand of authoritarianism, as opposed to the messiness of democracy, in order to secure development for their people."[17] History had discredited those critics. Democratic institutions emerged in both Central Europe and the Balkans, and in Catholic countries such as Spain, Chile, and the Philippines. By the late 1990s democracy was developing in several Muslim countries, such as Indonesia and Turkey.

But history did not comfort the growing numbers of skeptics in America. The uncertainties of the freedom agenda in the Middle East threatened to derail it altogether. Some observers, witnessing the growth of Islamist extremism in Western Europe, even questioned whether mature *liberal* democracy (let alone the mere holding of democratic elections) can provide an antidote to Islamist terror.[18] Along with the growing crisis in the Middle East, this troubling thought seemed to give new legs to realism in American foreign policy, that is, the view that we should be less concerned about the internal social and political makeup of a nation than we should its external behavior. If a government adopted nondemocratic policies but kept the lid on extremism and supported American policies when needed, perhaps it was better for the United States to stay out of their internal affairs. Maybe, some realists seemed to be saying, American support for despots wasn't all that bad an idea after all. Just choose your despots more carefully.[19]

But other foreign policy observers strongly disagreed with any suggestion that the United States could or should return to its pre-9/11 policy of support for authoritarian governments in the Muslim world without substantial attention to their internal problems. That policy, even many critics of the administration agreed, had underwritten the development of Islamist extremism by abetting tyranny, blunting economic growth within societies, and reducing the opportunities for the emergence of a middle class and a vigorous civil society and protections for human rights.[20]

For some the problem was not U.S. support for democracy per se but overreaching by the neoconservatives who provided the intellectual framework for the project. According to this critique, perhaps best articulated by Francis Fukuyama, the neocons had abandoned the prudence about sweeping social and political change that once characterized their movement and had in effect been blinded by hubris. The use of force in Iraq without a postwar plan, it was said, demonstrated the arrogance and bankruptcy of their vision for democracy.[21]

For their part, liberal internationalists in the Democratic Party charged that the Bush administration had stumbled because military force was employed unilaterally and with deception. Democracy promotion was a good idea, they argued, but needed embedding in the legitimacy, and the counterbalance to arrogance, afforded by the international community in organizations such as the United Nations.[22] Some liberals emphasized the need for more attention to economic growth as a precursor to democratic stability and a few, harkening to the legacy of Harry Truman and Senator "Scoop" Jackson, called for a more targeted use of military force against Islamist terrorism.[23]

Rediscovering the Value of Religion in Democracy

And so it went. Amid the furious debate about America's democracy project, however, the subject of religion's relationship with democracy remained uneasily on the sidelines of policy debates. Even the omnipresence of Islam in the media, the endless discussions of Islamism in policy think tanks, and the constant debate over what constituted "moderate" Muslims, did not lead to a clear U.S. policy on how to engage Islam or the issue of religion and state in the lands of Islam. Policy makers weren't the only ones averting their eyes. In 2005 the executive editor of the National Endowment for Democracy's *Journal of Democracy* observed that "students of democracy and democratization have paid the whole subject of religion relatively little attention."[24]

Most in the international relations field and the Bush administration bent over backwards in the first years after 9/11 to emphasize that Islam *qua* religion had nothing to do with the problems besetting American foreign policy and that Islam presented no barriers to democracy. Their assurances were intended to parry the charges of Islamist extremists, and of many Muslims in the Middle East, that the U.S. democracy project was designed precisely to destroy Islam. At the same time, the increase of confessional violence in Iraq, Iran's pursuit of nuclear weapons, and the generalized persistence of Islamist extremism in the Muslim world and Western Europe all fed a growing tendency to hold Islam responsible for the West's deepening sense of insecurity.

These two contradictory positions seemed to crowd out serious thought about how American policy might enhance the appeal of liberal democracy by encouraging Muslims to see it as an advantage to their religion, as well as to freedom and prosperity. Books streamed from the presses and conferences were held worldwide to examine the relationship between Islam and democracy. But the assumed political model in these explorations tended to be less secular (religion and state have different but overlapping roles) than secularist (religion is either an obstacle or largely irrelevant to democracy). The question examined was not so much how Islam and democracy could achieve mutual accommodation, but how democracy could emerge without taking Islamic religious beliefs into account or, if one were forced to consider Islam, in spite of it.

At one level it is easy to sympathize with those who don't want to think about religion and its relationship with the institutions and habits of liberal governance. The attacks of September 11, the dictatorship of theologians in Iran, the election of Hamas as the government of the Palestinians—such experiences, they will tell you, suggest the mess that results when religion and politics are mixed. Why make a frustrating, divisive issue such as democracy—whether and how to promote it—even more frustrating and divisive by delving into the religious elements of the issue? Doesn't religion belong in houses of worship rather than in the democratic public square?

—∞—

If you stand high on the top steps of the Lincoln Memorial in Washington, D.C., looking east out over the city, you can see some of the great monuments of the nation's history. With a little imagination and memory you can also detect something of the relationships between religion and democratic freedom as they were understood by America's founding generation and during most of the nation's first two centuries.

In the distance to the south, across the Tidal Basin, you can glimpse the sculptured likeness of the Virginian Thomas Jefferson, a skeptic of organized religion who penned the radical religious truth claim that is the first principle of American democracy.[25] The Creator, he wrote in the Declaration of Independence, made all men equal and endowed each with rights that are "inalienable." Those rights, in other words, belong to each person by virtue of his divinely ordained existence, not because they are granted by the state. Although governments are instituted by men, natural rights are not. Democracy will be secure, Jefferson wrote, only when citizens are convinced that "liberties are the gift of God."[26]

Jefferson's Virginia neighbor and friend, James Madison, wrote in a similar vein that each of us has rights that flow from the duty we owe God, who creates and governs all that is. "This duty," wrote the father of the Constitution "is precedent, both in order of time and degree of obligation, to the claims of Civil Society. Before any man can be considered as a member of Civil Society, he must be considered as a subject of the Governour of the Universe."[27] This was a remarkable affirmation and deepening of Jefferson's religious truth claim.

But, Madison continued, fulfilling one's obligation to God requires freedom of intellect and will and the exclusion of coercion in the civil order. "The Duty which we owe our Creator, and the manner of our discharging it, can be governed only by Reason and Conviction, not by Compulsion or Violence; and therefore all men are equally entitled to the full and free exercise of it according to the dictates of conscience, unpunished and unrestrained by the Magistrate...."[28] Here, then, in man's duty to the God who created him, and in his God-given reason and will lay his natural right to religious freedom.

Rising out of the horizon to the east you can discern the white obelisk, a towering memorial to George Washington, who spoke in his farewell presidential address of religion's importance to the new republic. Invoking no particular tradition, Washington credited the religious enterprise for "dispositions and habits which lead to political prosperity." Religion and morality are, he said, "indispensable supports" of democratic order and "great Pillars of human happiness." "And let us with caution indulge the supposition," the first American president warned, "that morality can be maintained without religion."[29] High on the obelisk's tip, 555 feet above the ground, a metal cap is engraved with the words *Laus Deo,*"Praise be to God."

In the distance beyond the Washington memorial lies Capitol Hill, on which resides the Congress of the United States. In 1789 the first Congress drafted, approved, and sent to the states for ratification the first amendment to the Constitution, which began with these words: "Congress shall make no law respecting an establishment of religion, or prohibiting the free exercise thereof." There is no reference in the two parts of this sentence (known respectively as the "establishment clause" and the "free exercise clause"), or anywhere else in the constitution, to "a wall of separation between church and state." In plain English, that sentence sets out what Congress may not do.

The establishment clause banned two Congressional actions: laws "establishing" a religion at the national level, and laws that interfered with *existing* state establishments. At the time the first amendment was ratified most states had established some form of Protestant Christianity—Congregationalist in the northeast and Anglican/Episcopalian in the south—so most everyone knew what the term meant. State establishments occurred in various guises, and generally included some support for favored clergy and a requirement that state officials believe in God, the Trinity, or some other core Christian doctrine.

The free exercise clause guaranteed religious freedom at the federal level only, but most states had similar guarantees, limited by the provisions of their respective establishments. Madison and Jefferson saw the contradiction and would have applied the ban on establishment to the states had it been politically possible.

As the founders saw it, however, the ban on a national establishment moved them closer to their true goal, the nourishment of the free exercise of religion. The free exercise clause encouraged the religiously informed attributes necessary to democracy as identified by Washington, Madison, and Jefferson, respectively: democratic dispositions and habits, the freedom necessary for man to perform his duty to God, and public affirmation of the transcendent origins of the American proposition. The same week Congress sent the First Amendment to the states for ratification it also passed legislation providing for paid chaplains and requested President Washington to proclaim "a day of public thanksgiving and prayer, to be observed, by acknowledging, with grateful hearts, the many and signal favours of Almighty God."[30]

Gradually during the late 18th and early 19th centuries the various states abandoned their religious establishments and adopted a more thoroughgoing version of the free exercise guarantee. Religious freedom was never perfectly applied, either at the federal or state level. But it was unprecedented in the Western world, let alone elsewhere. Even though anti-Catholic provisions entered some state constitutions with the Blaine amendments late in the 19th century, American Catholic bishops still praised religious freedom in the United States.[31] In the following century the American Catholic experience would have a significant influence on the development of the Roman Catholic doctrine of religious freedom.

Directly behind where you stand, chiseled in the marble surrounding Lincoln's statue, are the searching words of the sixteenth president's Gettysburg Address. At the scene of the great battle Lincoln had reminded a bloodied nation of its unachieved promise and what was at stake in the Civil War. Can a political order endure, he asked, that was conceived in liberty and dedicated to the proposition, articulated in Jefferson's radical religious truth claim, that all men are created equal? In his second inaugural address, as the war raged on, Lincoln again invoked the creator of men and the judge of their actions. "Fondly do we hope, fervently do we pray, that this mighty scourge of war may speedily pass away. Yet, if God wills that it continue...until every drop of blood drawn with the lash shall be paid by another drawn with the sword, as was said three thousand years ago, so still it must be said 'the judgments of the Lord are true and righteous altogether.' With malice toward none, with charity for all, with firmness in the right as God gives us to see the right, let us strive on to finish the work we are in...."[32]

A century later, Martin Luther King stood in front of Lincoln's memorial invoking yet again the failure to achieve the promise but the enduring power of the claim. "I have a dream that one day every valley shall be exalted, every hill and mountain shall be made low...and the glory of the Lord shall be revealed and all flesh shall see it together."

To summarize:

God as creator, governor, and judge of all people
Natural rights in the civil order deriving from man's duty to God
Religion and morality as pillars of human happiness and American democracy
Man as created, obligated, equal in God's eyes, rational, sinful, free

Three decades after King's death, when the Cold War was over but the American culture wars raged, the nation came together to build another series of monuments. Long overdue, the World War Two Memorial was dedicated to "the greatest generation"—the men and women who had suffered and sacrificed their lives to defeat totalitarianism in Europe, Africa, and the Far East and to protect America. From your perch near Lincoln's evocations of God, the memorial lies due east between you and Washington's obelisk, just beyond the reflecting pool. Chiseled in the marble of the World War Two monuments are the words of Roosevelt, Truman, Eisenhower, Marshall, MacArthur, and others who paid tribute to freedom and American sacrifice.

But Jefferson's Creator, Madison's Governour, Lincoln's God, and King's Lord is not there. No reference to the divine appears at the modern memorial. Had Roosevelt's generation abandoned the theistic premises of the founding?

A cursory examination of their speeches and writings reveals that the contrary is true: the leaders of the greatest generation made frequent appeals to God.[33] Something else had happened. By the end of the 20th century the architects and sponsors of the memorial had come to believe that God had nothing to do with the American proposition or the American determination to protect freedom. Or else they believed it was no longer acceptable to say so.

With Lincoln's statue still at your back, look north across Constitution Avenue and you can spy a great, nondescript eyesore of a building whose seventh floor houses the nation's highest foreign policy official. If your eyesight is strong you might glimpse the secretary of state gazing out the window of the State Department toward the memorials, pondering how the American experiment in ordered liberty should inform the nation's foreign policy. To what extent, the secretary might well ask, should the principles of the American proposition inform the project widely understood as critical to the nation's security and well being in the 21st century: employing U.S. diplomacy to encourage the development of stable, peaceful democratic governments around the world?

Democracy and Religion: Is a Happy Marriage Possible?

Leaving aside, for the moment, the American proposition, what can be said about the existing relationships between religion and democracy in the modern world that is of policy relevance? Can religion contribute to the growth of stable democracy while achieving benefits for its adherents and its sacred beliefs? Posing the question this way inevitably raises the vast differences between and within religions, both theologically and in their attitudes toward such matters as human freedom, the role of government, and differentiation—the proper relationship of religion to state. Ample research has shown that some religious traditions, especially Protestant forms of Christianity, are historically associated with the emergence of democracy and its consolidation into mature, stable, peaceful nations.[34] Others, especially Islam, are historically associated with a resistance to democracy's emergence and its consolidation, although, as already noted, these patterns are being challenged.

The largest democracy in the world, India, is the product of Hindu culture and liberal institutions bequeathed by British colonialism. Confucianism, more an ethical system than a religion per se, has had a bivalent effect on democratic growth. South Korea, a Confucian culture with a substantial Christian component, has proven remarkably dynamic in its movement to democracy. China, with a similar cultural background, has not. In the late 20th century, Catholic nations took a remarkable turn toward democracy, but have had difficulty in consolidating it, especially in Latin America. Several Orthodox nations have either embraced democracy (Greece and Greek Cyprus) or adopted its procedures (Russia, Ukraine, Georgia). Russia in particular has had difficulties in consolidation.[35]

Given the considerable theological and historical variations among religions, can anything useful be said about religion and self-governance that could be valid for most, if not all? Columbia University political theorist Alfred Stepan answers this question with a qualified "yes." In his view the "multivocality" present in all the world's religions, including Islam, renders them capable of adaptation to democracy. Stepan argues that Catholics and Protestants "found and mobilized doctrinal elements within their own religions to help them craft practices supportive of tolerance and democracy." Others are capable of similar doctrinal mobilization.[36]

Lawrence Harrison responded to Stepan's political theory by pointing to the empirical data. As late as 2006, only one predominantly Muslim country—Mali—had been ranked as "free" by Freedom House.[37] Moreover, Harrison argued, Stepan failed to distinguish properly between countries grounded in Protestant as opposed to Catholic culture. Some of the latter lacked the attributes such as trust and entrepreneurship that help to consolidate democracy. Harrison acknowledged that in Islam, as in Catholicism, "the progressive cross-current exists, but it has thus far failed to influence the mainstream." Bernard Lewis's hopeful stress on Islam's "equality among believers" as a democratic principle, noted Harrison, had not produced Islamic democracy.[38]

But Harrison does not argue that consolidated, stable democracies are not possible or even unlikely in Islamic or Catholic countries. One purpose of his research and writing, he notes, "is to encourage religious leaders to reflect on the mainstream currents that have led them away from democracy, justice and prosperity; and to explore, in their own cross-currents and the experiences of more advanced societies, the reforms that will lead towards those goals." Religion, in other words, is a major factor in determining whether Islamic and Catholic (and other) societies succeed. "Religious reform that moves away from traditional, progress-resistant values toward the values we associate with modernization may be crucial to accelerated progress in the several lagging regions of the world," especially the Muslim Middle East and Catholic Latin America.[39]

We may draw on the work of both scholars (recognizing that neither is proposing changes in U.S. foreign policy). Stepan, as a theorist, is describing what is possible with respect to religious and political reform. Harrison, as a sociologist, is reporting on what the data show, and concluding from them that democratic change is more likely to take place when it is accompanied by internal religious reform. Our foreign affairs establishment would do well to absorb the argument implicit in both, namely that democracy promotion cannot succeed without taking into account religion as a driver of culture. This means paying attention to the religious doctrines that help determine political attitudes as well as the habits and virtues of religious adherents.

Of course, even if American diplomacy did begin to think seriously about such matters, the questions of what policies to adopt and how to carry them out would remain. We return to that subject in chapters 9 and 10. For present purposes, it will be useful to consider the issues raised by Harrison and Stepan by exploring four areas of democracy's religion-state problem: religious pluralism, the "twin tolerations," social and spiritual capital, and the historic experiences of Protestantism and Catholicism as models of possibility.

Religious Pluralism and the Free Market

Many have argued that the success of the U.S. regime of religious freedom stems from America's religious pluralism. "[P]luralism was the native condition of American society," wrote the American Jesuit John Courtney Murray. "It was not, as in Europe and in England, the result of a disruption or decay of a previously existent religious unity." Later Murray distinguished between mere religious plurality—the presence of differing religious communities—and religious pluralism. The former is usefully seen as a datum of religious demography that could easily yield conflict (as it did in the 17th-century American colonies and has done in 21st-century Iraq). The latter is a political and religious accomplishment that ends conflict. Religious pluralism exists when a variety of religious groups collectively decide to live together, not merely in a concord of toleration, which could quickly break down under stress, but in a joint commitment to the religious freedom of the other. This is what Murray referred to as a condition of "creeds at war, intelligibly," or what Richard John Neuhaus calls religious contention within the bounds of civility, or the civil public square.[40]

Sociologist Rodney Stark argues that religious pluralism is the product of a healthy "religious economy" in which there is a vigorous contention of "current and potential religious adherents, [and] a set of... organizations seeking to attract or retain adherents...." What *distorts* the free market of religion, and harms religious organizations, according to Stark, is "state regulations that either impose a monopoly... or constrain the market by subsidizing a state church and making it difficult for other religious groups to compete." In other words, if religious communities in a democracy will forswear the use of civil authority as a means of achieving religious preference or monopoly, they are moving toward the achievement of pluralism and a religion-state balance (consensual differentiation)[41] that historically has worked to the advantage of all religious groups, including the majority. America's religious economy, its pluralism, and its system of differentiation enable its vigorous system of religious freedom and account for the health of its various religious communities.[42]

As we have already noted, there are difficulties inherent in this understanding of a free market approach to religious freedom.[43] Many traditions evince skepticism of the notion of religion as mere choice—either as one of many "lifestyles" on offer or as one of many paths to God. Michael Sandel's concept of the "encumbered self" helps identify this reluctance to see religious pluralism and competition as inherently a good. Islam and Catholicism probably come closest to the notion that religion is not an individual choice among several equally valid options but an affirmative response to a single transcendent truth.[44] The option is not, in other words, picking this or that religion and encouraging others to pick theirs in the free market. This helps to explain why those two traditions have been resistant to the idea of pluralism, although, as we shall see, the Catholic Church has come to terms with it.

Of all the monotheistic religious traditions, Protestantism is probably most at home with the notion of pluralism, given its emphasis on the primacy of individual conscience. This helps to account both for the native condition of religious plurality in Protestant colonial America and for the achievement of pluralism by the Protestant founding generation. Timothy Shah and Robert Woodberry describe the underlying theology this way: "Because saving faith must be uncoerced and individual, it requires in practice a diversity of independent churches to satisfy the diversity of individual consciences."[45] This refers for the most part to choices within Protestant Christianity rather than outside it. But the emphasis on individual conscience identifies a major dynamic at work within the Protestant-inspired American system of religious freedom. It also helps account for the worldwide success of Protestant cultures in the consolidation of democracy.

The issue of pluralism has important implications for American foreign policy. Preexisting conditions of religious plurality can be a positive factor in a nation's susceptibility to a democratic religion-state balance. Nations with little religious plurality, such as Iran, present particular difficulties for democratic development (although the powerful influence of jurists, theologians, and philosophers in Iranian Shiism can provide a different kind of advantage, and there is also a diversity of views within Shiism). Egypt provides an example of something approaching native plurality. It is arguably the most important and one of the most difficult Arab states to move toward democracy, and the religion-state issue will be critical to success. As it happens, other than Lebanon, Egypt has the largest non-Muslim community of all the Arab states, which lends it a measure of diversity that the others do not have.[46] This is a plus, even if it is far from determinative, in deciding how to proceed. The United States should work harder to persuade Egyptians of the potential for pluralism, and its attendant advantages, present in their native plurality. The same can be said for Iraq.

In sum, there is a practical argument to be made to governments and religious communities that religious pluralism can benefit their adherents and their traditions. As Stark puts it, "religion thrives in a free market, where many religious groups vie for followers and those...[religions] lacking energy or appeal fall by the wayside. By now there is a very large research literature that supports these conclusions."[47] The benefits of a "free market of religions" accrue when plurality has become pluralism, that is, when religious communities accept religious freedom for all.

This is not to suggest that such an argument will be immediately persuasive when addressed to religious groups. Many, such as Muslims in Saudi Arabia, Hindu nationalists in India, or Christian Orthodox in Russia, will instinctively resist. But the case for pluralism should be nested in a broader argument about the advantages of stable and durable democracy to religious communities. Those advantages, history suggests, will not accrue without religious freedom.

For this kind of thinking to be accepted in the Arab world will require more than political development. It will also require internal theological reform. As Stepan suggests, sacred texts that are understood to exclude other religious communities can be reread to accept or even embrace them. But it is also true that the practical tradeoff discussed above can encourage internal reform: accepting religious freedom and pluralism in return for the flourishing of one's own religious community. The tradeoff, it needs be said, does not require the abandonment of truth claims. John Courtney Murray did not abandon the hope that all men would become Catholic. What he rejected was the view that Church monopoly on civil power could fulfill that hope. Nor did he abandon the Catholic claim to be the church left by Jesus Christ for all men, the fullest repository of the truth about God and man. He merely concluded that the claim could only be embraced, and was more likely to be embraced, by men acting freely, uncoerced by any human agent.

There is at work in the logic of religious freedom and pluralism the subtle question of confidence in a religious community's claims: if they are indeed true, and certainly if they are true for all people, why should coercion by the state or private actors be necessary? Why should religious actors and communities fear peaceful competition with other truth claims in a free market, especially if no single religious community has privileged access to political power?

The Concept of "Twin Tolerations"

As noted in chapter 1, much modern liberal philosophy holds, after John Rawls, that democratic society is characterized by a natural proliferation of politically irreconcilable "comprehensive doctrines" about morality, justice, and the common good. In order to prevent the degeneration of democracy into warring factions, Rawls argued, the citizens of democracies must agree to withhold from consequential public policy debates their comprehensive views, the most damaging and divisive of which are the truth claims of religion. In debating issues of major political import, citizens must employ "freestanding" conceptions of political justice to which all might agree.[48]

Although Rawls insisted that he sought to preserve the right of all citizens to hold religious beliefs, and did not seek to privatize them, the import of his argument was to reinforce a broader tendency toward removing religion and religiously informed moral judgments from public democratic argument and legislation.[49] Rawls's theory of political liberalism helped entrench, at least among mainstream academic and media institutions, the belief that a modern, secular democracy cannot permit such judgments to play a public role. The Rawlsian model has clearly had an impact on the intellectual climate of American foreign policy described in chapter 2 and on the hesitancy of the foreign policy establishment to engage religious groups in promoting democracy abroad.

But there is substantial evidence that the Rawlsian understanding of religion and democracy cannot reasonably be expected to succeed in societies with significant religious communities. Alfred Stepan, in an important essay in the *Journal of Democracy* entitled "Religion, Democracy and the Twin Tolerations," argued that historically almost no liberal democracy has "followed the Rawlsian normative map" in dealing with religion, and none in the 21st century is likely to do so.[50]

In an analysis of past and prospective transitions to democracy Stepan concludes that the most fruitful approach to powerful religious communities is neither secularism as understood in modern liberal parlance, nor the strict separation of religion and state, but the achievement of what he calls the "twin tolerations." Democracy, he writes, "is a system of conflict regulation that allows open competition over the values and goals that citizens want to advance." The critical challenge for religious societies is negotiating the democratic boundaries within which this competition can take place.[51]

Achieving the "twin tolerations" requires the negotiation of a democratic covenant between civil and religious authorities. For its part, government permits both private and public religious activity, including activity designed to influence public policy, within very broad, equally applied limits. Religious individuals and communities agree to avoid actions which "impinge negatively on the liberties of other citizens or violate democracy and the law." As already noted, Stepan's analysis of contemporary Confucianism, Islam, and Eastern Orthodoxy suggests that each of these religious traditions, like Christianity, is not "univocal," and that each is capable of achieving the twin tolerations. That achievement, he writes, "normally requires debate within the major religious communities. And proponents of the democratic bargain are often able to win over their fellow believers only by employing arguments that are *not* conceptually freestanding [i.e. the Rawlsian pre-condition] but deeply embedded in their own religious community's comprehensive doctrine."[52]

Stepan provides a useful device for framing American international religious freedom policy. That policy could, inter alia, develop concepts and strategies designed to engage both civil and religious authorities in the pursuit of something like the twin tolerations, that is, a stable politico-religious relationship that can support the emergence of democracy. In societies with large or growing religious communities there are bound to be areas where religion and politics mix. Given the opportunity, those communities will inevitably attempt to influence the societies in which they are situated, the political arrangements under which they live, and the laws and policies of their governments. To expect otherwise—to believe that religious believers can or should be indifferent to the public rules and norms that shape their lives—is no more "realistic" than applying the same expectation to any other group within civil society. Indeed, the very nature of religious conviction can require believers to engage in public policy debates. Bound in conscience to religious and moral truths, such believers do not have the freedom simply to pretend those truths apply only to them or that they have no public implications.

The real question for U.S. democracy promotion strategy, then, is not whether religious belief can be privatized in a liberal democracy. The experience of Western Europe, and France in particular, suggests that privatization is a chimera, achievable only in a homogenous society closed to the outside world, which is to say that it is in practice unachievable in the 21st century. The question for American foreign policy is whether the fruits of belief can at a minimum be accommodated to the democratic common good—whether, in other words, a society is capable of attaining Stepan's twin tolerations.

Religion as Generating Social and Spiritual Capital

A key element of the religion-democracy relationship concerns the compatibility of the practical virtues, attitudes, and habits required and engendered by each. Successful democracies are widely understood to require "social capital," that is, the trust, responsibility, and cooperation that are often acquired by active membership in voluntary associations of civil society.[53] Robert D. Putnam's book Bowling Alone has described in some detail the contributions of religious communities in America to social capital. He notes that "[p]rivatized religion may be morally compelling and psychically fulfilling, but it embodies less social capital" than membership in active religious communities.[54]

Of course, some associations can lead to nondemocratic or anti-democratic beliefs and habits, such as membership in extremist organizations like the Ku Klux Klan or Syria's Baathist party. Another, the Palestinian party Hamas, has won a democratic election but has also amply demonstrated its lack of democratic virtues and habits. In nondemocratic or illiberal societies where religion plays a significant role, the emergence of democracy, and in particular its consolidation into stable democracy, will depend in part on whether the social capital engendered by influential religious traditions is supportive of democratic virtues or not.

Political scientist Corwin Smidt, in a survey of American social capital, has identified several areas in which religious communities make a distinctive contribution to social capital and therefore to the health of American democratic life.[55] Although these categories are not universal, they do reflect characteristics typically exhibited by the entire spectrum of U.S. religious communities, Christian and non-Christian. As such they may have something to tell us about the potential behavior of religious individuals and groups in a pluralistic, democratic regime of religious freedom. At the very least, if Alfred Stepan's analysis is correct, we should not conclude that the social capital generated by religiously motivated individuals and communities in the United States cannot be replicated elsewhere, especially in a system of stable democratic governance.

According to Smidt, U.S. religious social capital is distinctive first of all in its quantity. Citing the work of Putnam, he notes that nearly half of all associational membership, personal philanthropy, and volunteering in the United States occurs in a religious context. Second, Smidt observes, "the social capital generated through religious means may well be more durable than the social capital generated through other means." This is likely true because religious motivations often go beyond the pragmatic calculations that often lead people to civic engagement. "Success, or the lack of it, is not necessarily the standard employed by religious people." Rather, they often remain engaged in a civic enterprise (e.g., soup kitchens or homes for unwed mothers) on noninstrumental grounds, such as faithfulness to one's values or pleasing God. The same calculations, Smidt has found, can increase the range of civic engagement by religious people and lead them to value reciprocity and cooperation for nonmaterial reasons.[56]

When people are motivated by transcendent values and a belief in reward and punishment independent of material gain or self-interest, they can, of course, become fanatics like Osama Bin Laden. But Smidt's point is that they can also become solid citizens whose religiously motivated behavior contributes to democracy by the work they do, the attitudes they bring to their work, and the norms they reflect in the way they live their lives, all of which can serve the common good. This does not mean that religious people are superior human beings, or that all religions yield the same value to democracy. Even within religious traditions in the same country there are variances, and that will certainly be the case across cultures. What it does mean, however, is that in a world of growing religious devotion, the issue of religious social capital is a worthy subject for consideration by anyone seeking to facilitate the growth of democracy.

A similar way to approach the issue of democratic civic behavior and the prospective contributions of religious communities is the emerging concept of "spiritual capital"—the resources that are created when people invest in religion for its own sake rather than as a social institution.[57] Many religious traditions produce social capital like that of other voluntary associations—knowledge, material wealth, trusting relationships, and an appreciation for reciprocity. But research also suggests that religious content itself—both the motivations of the individual adherent and the doctrinal teachings of the tradition—can provide a qualitatively different and even more powerful incentive to actions that are compatible with liberal democracy.

Sociologist Robert D. Woodberry argues that religion can be seen by adherents as both "an investment and a distinct end." Some invest in religion for social returns, including a confirmation of identity, establishing business connections, or gaining power. Others, however, seek something uniquely spiritual for its own sake, such as pleasing God or deepening their relationship to whatever they perceive as the divine. Such people tend to see religion as a resource to meet various challenges (e.g., sickness or political oppression) and as "sources of moral teachings and religious experiences that may motivate, channel, and strengthen people to reach particular ends."[58]

Those ends often include works of charity. In some religious traditions they extend to the international work of relief and development, and reconciliation or peacemaking among people divided along sectarian lines. Some social scientists have concluded from these kinds of activities that the concept of "spiritual capital" can be useful in determining how particular religious communities affect democracy and economic growth precisely because of their religious content and the consequent motivation for working on behalf of others.[59]

An important aspect of the social or spiritual capital issue is whether pro-democracy virtues emerge because of or in spite of religious doctrine. What accounts for the fact of Islamic contributions to democratic habits and virtues in some areas and its absence in others? Part of the answer clearly lies in the influence of other cultural, historic, geographic, and economic forces. In Hindu India, where democracy has rooted despite being sown in some of the most horrific confessional violence imaginable, the legacy of British institutions, including British Protestantism, clearly plays some part. However, the British heritage has not provided the same legacy in Muslim Pakistan.

The social or spiritual capital exhibited by some religions seems to have helped them contribute to democracy more successfully than others—for example Shintoism and Buddhism in Japan, or Protestantism in a variety of nations in Europe, South America, and parts of the former British Empire. Some religious traditions have exhibited social capital to a far lesser extent in one region than in another. A few Roman Catholic villages in China, persecuted and isolated from the outside world, have maintained an insular distrustfulness over time.[60] The opposite has occurred in traditionally Catholic Chile.[61]

Muslim groups have contributed to Indonesian civil society, which, although under siege from Islamist radicals, is stimulating the growth of democracy.[62] By the same token, civil society is almost nonexistent in Muslim Saudi Arabia, where both the domestic climate of opinion and the civic habits of citizens are heavily influenced by one illiberal religious tradition, Sunni Wahhabism. In Shiite-dominated Iran, by contrast, there is a considerable potential for civil society, the result of a long-standing small merchant economy and the theology of Shiism. Iranian civil society is, however, hamstrung by periodic crackdowns from the clerical autocracy.[63]

Some religions appear simply to have been unsuccessful in encouraging social capital in particular countries, such as Orthodox Christianity in Russia and Serbia, Confucianism in China, or Islam in the Arab Middle East (although here, too, there are significant variations). Of course, the authoritarian governments in these countries pose major obstacles to civil society development, as does, to a lesser degree, the Russian government. But it is clear that the religious traditions that have formed these cultures have also posed obstacles to the development of democratic habits and attitudes.[64]

The issue of social/spiritual capital provides another window into the religion-state relationship and religion's potential contribution to democracy. It is in part the role of a regime of religious liberty to encourage the development of religious resources compatible with democracy by enticing religious communities to the experience of influencing and flourishing in democratic states. In this respect, the respective histories of Protestant and Catholic development provide encouraging examples. Both had periods of resistance to liberal democracy, but both have played vital parts in the establishment of particular democratic states. In that process, each tradition saw the flowering of latent principles that helped its adherents develop existing habits and virtues, or produce new ones, that were supportive of liberal governance.

Theology and Reform: The Evolution of Two Christian Traditions

It has become commonplace for observers of Islamic societies to refer to the need for Islamic reform or an Islamic reformation.[65] The question of why reform is needed generally focuses on two problems: the democracy deficit in Islamic nations (which is also associated with the need for economic development) and the emergence of Islamist radicalism. There is, of course, no single template for religious reform, but Muslim scholars read Reformation history and the history of other religious communities.[66] There may be lessons for Muslim reformers, and for those who seek to influence and support Muslim reformers, in the Protestant and Catholic experiences.

It is striking that the vast majority of liberal democracies at the outset of the 21st century had emerged in nations that were grounded in either Protestant or Catholic traditions. It may be, of course, that religious doctrine had little direct influence on liberal norms or that doctrines had to be overcome, ignored, or fundamentally diluted. Many scholars see democracy as primarily the result of geography or economic development or cultural traditions that have little to do with religious teachings.[67] Sociologist Jose Casanova notes that secularists often see the coexistence of religions and democracy as the result of "doctrinal capitulations that make evident...the vacuity of the claims of those religions to possess transcendent revealed truths valid for all times and places...."[68]

What can be said about the contributions of Protestantism and Catholicism to democracy and democratic theory, civil society and social capital, and to the kind of economic development that helps sustain democracy?

The Protestant Model

It is clear from recent empirical studies that Protestantism has been the most effective religious agent of international democratization and modernization.[69] As we have noted, many nonreligious factors affect culture, political development, and the economy. But in terms of democracy and modernization, the performance of countries whose cultures were largely formed by Protestant churches is measurably better than that of those formed by the other major religious traditions.[70]

Data compiled by the Culture Matters Research Project provide compelling evidence of the Protestant-democracy connection. Protestant countries score higher than all others, and significantly higher than most, in both the emergence and the consolidation of democracy.[71] In other words, Protestantism has for some time been associated with liberal, stable democratic systems. This association has not been confined to Western nations but has proven transportable to the third world.[72] In addition, there appears to be a significant correlation between Protestantism and the development of civil society institutions, as well as civil society virtues (social capital) such as trust and ethical behavior. Finally, there has long been a debate about the putative correlation between Protestantism and capitalism. That correlation appears to be borne out by the evidence of per capita GDP in Protestant countries when compared to that of others.[73]

For our purposes the relevant question is how did Protestant religion affect these developments? In some countries that are reflected in the data, such as the Nordic nations, active practice of religion of any kind has been falling for some time. But the cultures of these nations were highly influenced by Protestantism, especially Lutheranism, for centuries.[74] Is there anything in the beliefs and practices of Lutheranism, Calvinism, and the other Protestant traditions that can help explain these rather extraordinary correlations?

The 16th-century Protestant Reformation was not, of course, a democratic event. Martin Luther's writings on Christian liberty presupposed a strong, paternal state. In John Calvin's Geneva, government and church were essentially one in employing the police powers of the state to enforce the doctrines of Calvinism. Disputes over the truths of Protestant and Catholic doctrines, abetted by political and economic forces, loosed almost a century of savage wars in Europe. The 1648 Peace of Westphalia ended those wars and marked the beginning of the modern international order of nation states. It led to a subordination of religion to state rather than any doctrinal or political commit-ment to individual freedom of conscience.[75]

But there was much in Protestantism that would encourage the develop-ment of democracy and religious freedom. Luther had rejected most of the Catholic Church's mediating structures—Petrine primacy, apostolic succes-sion, the clerical hierarchy, and the teaching authority of the pope—and sub-stituted the individual conscience. For Luther, each believer was his own priest and the Bible his sole authority. Luther's doctrine of salvation by faith alone meant, as Woodberry and Shah put it, "that people can acquire saving faith only as they personally and individually appropriate God's word."[76]

The new doctrines of reformed Christianity, soon augmented by the teach-ings of John Calvin, spread rapidly in Germany, northern Europe, England, and Scotland. The notion of individual conscience in matters religious was not yet transformed into universal individual rights, but it would aid in that trans-formation in 18th-century America. Moreover, the absence of a central doc-trinal authority—every man a priest—ensured "an endless ecclesial mitosis," that is, the continuous creation of new Protestant denominations and creeds.[77] Most of the new Protestant groups retained the central doctrines of salvation by faith alone and the sole authority of the Bible. But Protestant individual-ism meant an ever-expanding Protestant religious plurality. That plurality was transformed into genuine religious pluralism in the United States.

Woodberry and Shah point out that Protestantism in one form or another, beginning in the 19th century, began to migrate around the world. Calvinist families and schools produced prominent democratic thinkers, including John Locke, James Madison, and John Adams. Protestantism's native plurality helped spread the voluntary associations that make up civil society. Protestant cultures emphasized mass education and printing (in part reflecting the individual's need to understand the Bible). Their emphasis on individual conscience led them "to tend toward separation and independence from ancient church struc-tures and traditions, as well as political authorities."[78]

Protestants also often took with them economic dynamism. In the early 20th century German sociologist Max Weber had theorized a correlation between certain forms of Protestantism and the worldly virtues necessary to capitalism. Weber believed that Calvinism in particular generated the habits of industriousness and self-discipline that led to capitalist growth.[79] Whether the mechanism identified by Weber was accurate or not, the Culture Matters Research Project appears to have confirmed his conclusions.

Sociologist Peter Berger has argued that the Protestant commitment to free-dom of conscience is uniquely compatible with democracy and its liberal insti-tutions. The doctrine, he notes, resulted in Protestantism's self-understanding as a voluntary association of people who see faith as an individual choice. Berger argues that other religions, if they are to adapt to liberal democracy, must appropriate this model. He attributes the late 20th-century compatibility between Catholicism and democracy to the Church's acceptance of the role of voluntary association within democratic societies, that is, accepting differentiation and forswearing access to civil authority to reinforce a Catholic monopoly.[80] Philip Costopoulos has noted that Islam already exhibits some of the Protestant characteristics, such as individualism and a rejection of hierarchy and mediation, which he takes as a hopeful sign for the compatibility of Islam with democracy.[81]

The influence of Protestantism on American democracy provides a powerful example of the potential for a religion-state compact that is beneficial to both and, ultimately, to all citizens, Protestant or not. American history demonstrates that a religious society can construct a democratic political model that moves beyond mere toleration to a regime of religious liberty, grounded in religious doctrine and empowering democracy itself. Contemplating that history should give pause to anyone seeking to employ the privatization model, especially in countries where religion retains its power to bind consciences and influence public behavior.

The Catholic Experience

During a trip to General Augusto Pinochet's Chile in 1987, Pope John Paul II was asked by a reporter whether he hoped to help bring democracy to Chile. "I am not the evangelizer of democracy," the pope replied. "I am the evangelizer of the Gospel. To the Gospel message, of course, belong all the problems of human rights, and if democracy means human rights then it also belongs to the message of the Church."[82] John Paul was riding, and in many ways leading, what Samuel Huntington has labeled the third wave of democratization. An overwhelming proportion of countries that had become democracies in the 19th and early 20th centuries (the first wave) had been Protestant. The second wave, after World War Two, had been religiously diverse. For the most part, Catholic nations in Europe, Latin America, and East Asia were authoritarian.[83]

Then came the third wave. During a period of fifteen years between 1974 and 1989, some 30 countries shifted from authoritarianism to democracy. Three-quarters of them were Catholic. "The social scientists of the 1950s were right;" Huntington observed. "Catholicism was then an obstacle to democracy. After 1970, however, Catholicism was a force for democracy because of changes within the Catholic Church." Huntington attributes much of the changes to the Second Vatican Council, which met in the mid-1960s, the role of Catholic bishops and priests pressing for democracy from within, support by the Vatican for their activities, and the globe-trotting John Paul II, who managed to visit most of the Catholic countries that adopted democratic institutions.[84]

What accounts for this extraordinary political migration? A comprehensive answer to that question is beyond the scope of this book, but the question itself, and even the outlines of an answer, should be of interest to Muslims and other religious actors interested in the issue of internal reform. This is not to suggest that Islam is similar to Catholicism, either in theology or structure. Sunni Islam in particular has no theological authority comparable to the Catholic magisterium, the teaching authority of the pope in communion with the bishops. Shiite Islam has something closer to a clerical authority, although it is important to recognize that there are no "clerics" in Islam, no ordained priests, ministers, or bishops. But the Catholic experience may still provide useful ideas for reformers. Catholic political practice changed because the doctrine of the church evolved.[85] This did not happen with one Council or one pope, even one so talented and peripetic as John Paul II. The origins of the Church's contributions to democracy go much deeper into its history.

The early and medieval Church provided doctrinal grounds for differentiating between religion and state, both on the basis of the sovereignty of God and on the divine requirement for advancing justice and the common good. Jesus himself recognized the distinction between religious and secular authority and provided a divine warrant for the latter ("Render unto Caesar what is Caesar's and to God what is God's." Matthew 22:21). The apostle Paul taught that secular political authority was "established by God" (Romans 13:1). In the 5th century Pope Gelasius expanded these teachings in a letter to Byzantine Emperor Anastasius that was widely accepted as authoritative during the Middle Ages. God, Pope Gelasius instructed the Emperor, had sanctified two authorities— "the consecrated power of the priesthood and the royal power."[86]

The effects of this dualism on the development of modern European democracy were quite significant. The freedom and authority of the church, *libertas ecclesiae*, limited the power of civil authority from the very beginning of European history. As historian Brian Tierney points out, *libertas ecclesiae*, on the one hand, enabled the church to cooperate with secular authorities in punishing heretics through the inquisitions. But on the other hand, it also laid the groundwork for what would become the modern concept of religious liberty.[87] It did this in part by establishing the political principle that civil authority lacks competence in religious matters, and by providing a separate source of moral authority which commanded the loyalty of citizens.

Catholic doctrine also made important claims about the nature and value of the person, his freedom, and his conscience—the part of the intelligence which aids each person in exercising freedom responsibly. These claims would later be developed and extended as a basis for the Church's support for human rights but they were already embedded in its understanding of God and man. Because they are created in God's image, all persons possess intellect and will. God called each "by name," and, when they rebelled, sent his son to redeem them. The incarnation, life, passion, death, and resurrection of Jesus was an act of redemption and an act of love, signifying man's wretched sinfulness but also his magnificent potential. In the Catholic understanding every person is a repository of sin and of virtue to be developed, both for his own sake and for the sake of his fellow men. Here is where the conscience does its work. Formed by the intellect, the conscience guides the will in choosing good and avoiding evil.

Over the centuries the Church's understanding of conscience and human freedom developed in its historical and political context. Paul had written that "Everything that is not from faith is sin" (Romans 14:23). Standard medieval commentaries interpreted the words "not from faith" to mean "all that is contrary to conscience." Medieval theologians extended this principle by asserting that every person must act in accord with his conscience, so long as he has ensured that it is well formed in the teachings of the Church, and so long as he is certain that his conscience is not leading him to evil.[88]

In the 20th century this teaching on conscience was elaborated by the Catholic Church in its 1965 Declaration on Religious Liberty, which added the concept, not present in medieval Europe, of an immunity from coercion in civil society. During the Middle Ages an erring conscience could lead a person to heretical actions punishable by civil or ecclesiastical authority. The purpose of the inquisitions was to systematize trials of heretics. Brian Tierney observes that such trials can perhaps best be understood by comparing them to the modern notion of treason, a grave crime sometimes punishable by death in modern democracies. In a trial for treason, "a plea of personal sincerity, that the traitor has acted...in accordance with his own conscience, is not a sufficient defense. Medieval people regarded heretics in much the same way."[89]

Modern secularist discourse assumes that the right of individual conscience was achieved in spite of Christianity, and in particular in spite of the Catholic Church. This is not the case.[90] It is quite true that neither the medieval nor the modern Catholic understanding of freedom of conscience is the same thing as the dominant modern conception, that is, radical human autonomy ordered primarily to itself: one is free to do what one wants so long as it does not interfere with the freedom of others. With such an understanding, there is no objective referent, no moral truth for conscience to discern in deciding the right course of action except one's own desires and those of others. This conception of freedom, the Church argues, is grounded in a misunderstanding of the truth about man, namely that his nature (reflected in his conscience) is to seek moral truth.

In one of his major works, the encyclical *Veritatis Spendor* (The Splendor of Truth), Pope John Paul II addressed this point. "Certain currents of modern thought have gone so far as to exalt freedom to such an extent that it becomes an absolute, which would then be the source of values....The individual conscience is accorded the status of a supreme tribunal of moral judgment which hands down categorical and infallible decisions about good and evil....But in this way the inescapable claims of truth disappear, yielding their place to a criterion of sincerity, authenticity and 'being at peace with oneself,' so much so that some have come to adopt a radically subjectivistic conception of moral judgment."[91]

This modern view, as we have seen, was not present in the American founding and has by no means been universally accepted as authoritative in contemporary American democracy.[92] The views of the founding (Protestant) generation were much closer to Catholic doctrine, which has always held that the conscience is properly ordered, in its interior disposition and its public actions, to the moral and religious truths proclaimed by Christianity.[93]

The Church's medieval teaching on conscience, which lacked an immunity from coercion for heretics, nevertheless provided two critical pillars for modern liberal democracy. The first is the conviction that human freedom is ordered to something beyond itself; it is not a free-standing power limited only by its preferences and the contending free choices of others. This idea of ordered freedom is conducive to the virtues required for social capital, spiritual capital, and good citizenship.[94] The second is that the responsible exercise of freedom in civil society requires a moral teacher other than the state. That teacher helps forms a moral consensus among citizens concerning the public good and individual liberties. For Catholics, that teacher is the Church, but in a pluralist society it can be any religious community.[95] Whether Islam can perform that role in a Muslim democracy is a very important question.

The political potential of these ideas was submerged during the 16th- and 17th-century European wars of religion. Moreover, Catholic views of social and political freedom were influenced in a negative sense by the democratic concepts emerging in continental Europe, in particular the anti-Church strains of the French Enlightenment and the French Revolution, both of which viewed Catholicism as part of the detested *ancien regime* and as a barrier to the unbridling of man's rational capacities. In two encyclicals during the 1830s, Pope Gregory XVI condemned the emerging notion of liberalism, including its view of religious freedom. The latter he denounced in no uncertain terms: "this false and absurd maxim, or better this madness, that everyone should have and practice freedom of conscience."[96]

The hostility of the Holy See to 19th-century notions of democracy and religious liberty was driven by Catholicism's self-understanding as the one true church and by the anti-Catholicism of Western European democratic movements. Some of the latter had anti-Church sentiments similar to the French, most notably the German Kulturkampf and the Italian Risorgimento. Liberalism itself was increasingly perceived by Church authorities as an ever growing bundle of anti-Christian ideologies, including Darwinism's implied threat to the distinctiveness of created man, new methods of biblical criticism that challenged the integrity of the scriptures, socialism which threatened traditional teaching on private property, and atheist, revolutionary Marxism.[97]

Institutionally, the Church responded, as George Weigel puts it, by the centralization "of effective authority over virtually all matters, great and small, in the person (and, of course, staff) of the Roman pontiff." As ideas of radical human autonomy developed alongside democratic reform, Rome increasingly viewed "individual freedom of conscience" as a license for indifferentism, subjectivism, and relativism.[98] By removing the teaching authority of the Church from society and politics, the French model seemed, in the minds of Church leaders, to be leading Europe to moral and political disaster.

But the doctrinal basis for religious freedom as the cornerstone of human rights and the democratic rule of law remained embedded in the Catholic tradition. Interestingly, and somewhat ironically, it emerged and blossomed in part as the result of the experience of religious liberty by Catholics living in Protestant-dominated America. As noted earlier, U.S. Catholic bishops were in the late 19th century collectively expressing supreme confidence in their country's brand of religious freedom, despite an earlier surge of anti-Catholicism as Irish immigrants and priests flooded the east coast and despite the adoption by some states of anti-Catholic constitutional provisions.[99]

In the 20th century, that confidence was conveyed to the universal Catholic Church by thinkers such as Jacques Maritain, a French Catholic philosopher reflecting on the American system, and the American Jesuit John Courtney Murray. Their work, combined with the Church's reaction to Nazi and Communist totalitarianism, provided the framework for the articulation of a Catholic doctrine of religious liberty during the Second Vatican Council in 1965. This is the primary teaching of the Council that was transmitted to Catholics throughout the world and contributed to the third wave of democratization.

The document on religious freedom, entitled *Dignitatis Humanae* ("The Dignity of the Human Person"), was explicitly presented as a development, not an overturning, of doctrine. *Dignitatis* taught that all men, because they are created equally in the image and likeness of God, are to be equally immune in civil society from coercion in matters of religious conscience. God made men to know and love him. These human acts of discovery and devotion can only be undertaken freely by each individual in an exercise of conscience, informed by reason and faith, seeking the truth. Moreover, because men exercise their duty toward God in community with others, the immunity from coercion in civil society must extend to all religious communities, within due limits. Perhaps most importantly, *Dignitatis* insisted that governments must not only protect the right of religious freedom, but they also must "favor" the exercise of religion.[100] Here the Declaration came remarkably close to the (largely Protestant) understanding of the right of conscience and its political implications as articulated by America's founders.

Dignitatis ignited a lively discussion within the Catholic Church and even led to schism by a small minority.[101] But it was ultimately embraced by most Catholics, doubtless in part because of their assent to its central message, implicit since the beginning of Christianity: God-made men, equally imaging the Creator and equal in access to redemption through Jesus Christ, deserve a government worthy of their dignity and capable of protecting their free religious quest. For those Catholics living under tyrannical or authoritarian regimes, *Dignitatis* was a call for democratic reform.

By the early 21st century, many of the Catholic democracies of the third wave had not yet consolidated into stable self-governance. But the impetus provided by *Dignitatis Humanae* and its evangelizing pope had made a significant contribution to the moral and political values necessary for successful democracy, both in their emphasis on human dignity and the role of the state in protecting it. Today the religion-state model most known in the Arab world is the French model of *laicite*, filtered through Kemalist Turkey. For the most part, Islamists have controlled the discourse on secularism by identifying it with the French/Turkish model, widely seen in the Arab world as anti-Islam. In its attempts to change this discourse, the United States should provide a different model, one similar to its own, that permits religious values to influence secular politics. In that effort (to which we shall return in chapter 9), American policy makers should keep in mind both the development of the teachings of the Catholic Church and the influence of the American experience, in particular its teachings on religion, state, and human freedom.

Democracy, If You Can Keep It

After the American Constitutional Convention had completed its work, Benjamin Franklin was accosted outside the convention hall by a Philadelphia matron. What, she demanded to know, have you and the other framers achieved? "A republic, madam," he replied. "If you can keep it."[102]

Liberal governance, and especially liberal democracy, is an achievement worthy of any culture or civilization. It is not the cure for all ills, as America's own internal struggles amply demonstrate. It assures neither happiness nor prosperity. But liberal democratic societies create the possibility of human flourishing for their citizens in a way that no other system of government has ever done. Even though the development of liberal democracy has been associated with Christianity, there are in the early 21st century important Muslim democratic experiments ongoing that show the potential for consolidating into stable forms of peaceful, liberal self-government. Even if these experiments fail, it would be the height of folly for Americans to assume that the goal of liberal democracy cannot be achieved in the lands of Islam. The stakes are simply too high.

But how can it be done? And what can American diplomacy do, not only to facilitate the adoption of self-government by citizens in the Muslim world and elsewhere but also to help them keep it? A substantial part of the answer lies in a retooled and more effective policy of advancing regimes of religious freedom. In order to demonstrate how such a policy might work, it will be helpful to explore the origins and development of our existing policy of "promoting religious freedom" around the world. That story will reveal the problems and the promise of a renewed attempt to take religion seriously in a world of faith and freedom.

PART II

Acts

The passage of the 1998 International Religious Freedom (IRF) Act seemed to presage a new chapter in U.S. foreign policy—in effect, the elevation of America's "first freedom" to what many considered its rightful ascendancy in the nation's human rights policy. Now, looking back from the perspective of a decade, the considerable fault lines in the law's conception and implementation have become more apparent.

Driven by bureaucratic and ideological concerns, the State Department has both inadvertently and willfully ignored key parts of the legislative mandate, which was to reduce international religious persecution and to advance religious freedom. For differing reasons, however, neither the Congress, the law's supporters, nor the two administrations under which the IRF policy has operated have called the State Department to account or attempted to alter in any substantial way the narrow approach to implementing the law. As a consequence, the widely trumpeted (and widely feared) International Religious Freedom Act has so far had little long-term effect.

There are signs that this many-sided inertia may be giving way to a grudging appreciation for the broader potential of a realistic policy toward religion. For one thing, sheer frustration at the continuing salience of Islamist terror and a growing awareness of the inevitable role of religious communities in any Middle Eastern political reform have begun to crack into the hardened hull of resistance in American foreign policy circles to religion as a legitimate aspect of culture. For another, the State Department office vested with responsibility for IRF policy has begun to have some measured success in employing the law creatively. But the enormous promise of IRF policy in a world of religiously motivated people and nations remains largely untapped. If it means anything, "promoting religious freedom" still means rescuing people of faith from harm's way.

Part II provides the historical context for the narrow approach that dominates U.S. IRF policy by exploring its conception, birth, and adolescence. It
begins by treating aspects of the debate leading to the IRF Act, with an eye
toward the tactical and strategic maneuvering that facilitated the law's passage
in 1998 but weakened its implementation. It then focuses on the early years
after 1998, highlighting the work of the first two ambassadors at large for international religious freedom, and—between their respective tenures—the almost
two-year "interregnum" during which no ambassador was in place. The years
under consideration, roughly from 1996 to 2006, witnessed not only the IRF
legislation and its implementation but also the corner turning in American
history known as 9/11.

4

⊸∞∞⊷

The Legislative Campaign against Religious Persecution

[Supporters of the new international religious freedom law are] sincere. But they undoubtedly have another object, too: to advance their cause of giving religion a prime role in the American political structure.
—*Anthony Lewis* (*New York Times* columnist)

Although well-intentioned, this bill would create an artificial hierarchy among human rights.... [I]f we are to be effective in defending the values we cherish, we must also take into account the perspectives and values of others.
—Madeline Albright

You're only allowed to sit out one Holocaust each lifetime.
—Michael Horowitz

On successive days in October 1998, just prior to their adjournment for upcoming Congressional elections, the Senate and the House passed, without dissent, the International Religious Freedom (IRF) Act.[1] Their actions ended, in surprisingly abrupt fashion, almost two years of acrimonious debate over whether and how to legislate a U.S. policy against worldwide religious persecution. President Clinton, whose administration had fought vigorously to avoid the constraints of a legal mandate, immediately put out a statement calling the Act "a welcome and responsible addition to our ongoing efforts."[2] He signed it into law on October 27.

Earlier that summer the IRF Act had been declared dead by many observers, including the *New York Times*, which had announced the demise on its front page.[3] In fact disagreements among supporters over both principle and tactics seemed so significant, and the administration's opposition so strong, that few had thought a consensus possible. Business interests within the Republican Party had formed an incongruous alliance with liberal "mainline" Protestant groups such as the National Council of Churches to oppose the Act. The previous spring, the House had passed its own religious persecution law, and its champions much preferred that version, which they considered tougher and more effective than the Senate bill.

Analyzing in detail why the law finally passed in the face of these and other disputes need not occupy us at any length. There was doubtless a confluence of political circumstances that led both legislators and the White House finally to accept it, including upcoming Congressional elections (no one wanted to be labeled "soft on religious persecution"), late concessions that made the statute's language more palatable to the State Department, the president's looming impeachment trial, the single-mindedness of the act's authors (a group of Hill staffers), and the willingness of Republican leaders to ensure a floor vote. A fair assessment would probably include the role of good fortune. One author has used the evocative term "providential" to seal the explanation.[4]

Perhaps the most important long-term explanation for the passage of the IRF Act was the role of the new faith-based human rights coalition that initiated and sustained a campaign lasting almost two years. Without its leaders, in particular two intrepid Washington activists, Michael Horowitz and Nina Shea, and a member of Senator Richard Lugar's staff, John Hanford, there would have been no legal requirement that the United States oppose religious persecution around the world.

What is of greatest importance to our consideration, however, is how the legislative campaign helps explain the implementation of IRF policy in the years after 1998, in particular its narrow focus on persecution and its isolation within the Department of State. Those portentous years spanned the William Clinton and George W. Bush administrations and, as we have seen, the influence or ascendancy of at least three approaches to American foreign policy—liberal internationalism, classical realism, and neoconservatism. The same period witnessed the continuation of the striking international phenomenon that more and more scholars were beginning to track if not fully understand—an increase in religious devotion and practice, and in consequence a deepening relationship between religion and political life, in almost every region of the world.

Perhaps most significantly, the early years of IRFA's implementation were punctuated by the events of September 11, 2001, and what became known as the global War on Terror. The military, intelligence, and law enforcement arm of that war was paralleled by a political strategy to foster democratic institutions in parts of the Muslim world as a long-term antidote to Islamist terrorism. As we have observed, the nation's new IRF policy was not understood by policy makers as related to the War on Terror or even to the Bush administration's freedom agenda. Some of the explanation lies in the secularist assumptions of foreign policy thinkers both outside and inside the State Department. But part of the explanation lies in the nature of the legislative campaign to force the State Department to address the problem of religious persecution.

An examination of that campaign will help us understand why its narrowly humanitarian approach to persecution was not only grudgingly welcomed at the State Department as the least disruptive method of dealing with the issue, but also was considered preferable by many IRF supporters. Once the IRF Act passed, senior officials at Foggy Bottom quickly accepted the movement's premise: "promoting religious freedom" meant denouncing persecutors and achieving prisoner releases. For the most part, it did not mean systematic attention to the structures of persecution. Nor did it mean focusing on religion itself or on the whole range of issues associated with "religious freedom" in its cultural and political sense, especially relationships between religion and state and between religious norms and public policies.

For the State Department, the narrow approach represented business as usual, although intensified by adding a potentially troublesome new bureaucracy and more congressional scrutiny. But the department had dealt with such initiatives before.[5] As we shall see, it was well prepared to ensure this particular project remained ad hoc and subordinate to larger U.S. interests, at least as they were perceived at Foggy Bottom.

In order to understand these political currents and their significance for the future of American national security, we need to explore some of the competing goals and strategies that produced the International Religious Freedom Act of 1998. From the early discussions about a national legislative campaign in 1996 to the May 1997 introduction of the first bill in the House of Representatives to the final debates just prior to the passage of the IRF Act 17 months later, adherents and detractors laid a trail of compromise, betrayal, and faith.[6]

Dueling Laws—Contours of the Legislative Campaign, 1996–1998

The idea for a national political campaign on religious persecution was first widely broached among faith-based activists during a January 1996 conference in Washington, D.C., sponsored by the National Association of Evangelicals. An impressive group of scholars, religious leaders, and politicos, drawn mainly from evangelical Protestant ranks, produced a "Statement of Conscience" that served as the rallying cry (but not always the blueprint) for the later legislative push.[7] After the conference there ensued months of work by a coalition led by Michael Horowitz, a Jewish scholar and activist at Washington's Hudson Institute, and Nina Shea, a Roman Catholic and founder of Freedom House's Center for Religious Freedom.[8] The fruits of their work emerged in May 1997 as the "Freedom from Religious Persecution Act." Drafted by Horowitz, the bill became known as "Wolf-Specter" because of its joint sponsorship by Congressman Frank Wolf (R, Virginia) and Senator Arlen Specter (R, Pennsylvania).

Wolf-Specter went through significant changes before being passed overwhelmingly (375–41) in the House the following May. But the bill was controversial from the beginning, and even the revised version was known to have little chance in the Senate. Driven by a different vision of how the U.S. government should address religious persecution, a group of Hill staffers led by John Hanford produced a bill that afforded policy makers more options. Unlike Wolf-Specter, this bill was conceived largely in secret and was introduced in the Senate in March 1998 as the "International Religious Freedom Act." Sponsored by Senators Don Nickles (R, Oklahoma) and Joseph Lieberman (D, Connecticut), the IRF Act became law in October 1998 after months of bitter wrangling and premature announcements of its death.

Ironically, neither Wolf-Specter nor (despite its title) the International Religious Freedom Act had as a major goal the promotion of religious freedom. Both focused primarily on identifying and reacting to the activities of persecuting governments. The IRF Act paid rhetorical homage to religious freedom but devoted only a brief section (Title V) to the subject. Even here, much of the language was equivocal and nonbinding: "in the allocation of foreign assistance, the United States should make a priority of promoting and developing legal protections and cultural respect for religious freedom." Title V also amended laws on foreign aid, international broadcasting, international exchanges, and Foreign Service awards to incorporate religious freedom as a goal.[9]

Such provisions were helpful and could be used by the State Department to advance religious freedom. But with few exceptions, those elements of the statute have not been employed to encourage regimes of religious freedom. Although IRFA proponents claimed they sought religious freedom, what they really sought was a U.S. effort to reduce religious persecution. As noted, the absence of persecution is a necessary but insufficient condition for religious freedom, which requires a cultural and political framework to nourish and bound the religious rights of individuals and communities.

The IRF Act also required the State Department to issue an annual report on the status of religious freedom in every country worldwide. The report would identify the violators, analyze the violations, and describe what American diplomacy was doing to address them. This report has done more than any other aspect of the law to begin changing the aggressively secularist aspects of U.S. diplomatic culture. But like other elements of the statute, it has not been understood or employed as a policy vehicle to change that culture, alter the long-term behaviors of governments, or promote religious freedom.

In retrospect, at least three major fault lines can be identified in the two-year legislative battle over IRFA, core flaws that would later merge with others to handicap the law's implementation as an anti-persecution policy, let alone as a policy of advancing religious freedom. The first was the early attempt to bypass the State Department altogether and to place a new religious persecution authority in the White House, subject only to the president's direct authority. Although suspicion of Foggy Bottom was understandable, any hope of leapfrogging its influence, and achieving a fundamental shift in U.S. foreign policy in the face of its opposition, was illusory. Unfortunately, that illusion remains to this day influential among some who supported the legislative campaign. It is perhaps most clearly manifested in an agency seen by many as a surrogate for U.S. IRF policy: the U.S. Commission on International Religious Freedom.

The second fault line was the Horowitz coalition's early emphasis on Christians to the apparent detriment of other persecuted religious groups, most notably Muslims. This impulse too was understandable—aiding the persecuted Church was a battle cry among early supporters, and they had good reason to act. Christians are routinely abused in trouble spots around the world, including several Muslim countries. But the seemingly Christian-centered approach to legislation permitted both domestic and international critics to charge that the Christian right was behind the campaign and that they intended to pursue narrowly sectarian purposes such as clearing the way for missionaries. Although the IRF Act as passed was universal in scope, some Clinton administration officials, and many liberal voices, continued this criticism during the Bush presidency.[10]

Third, although the legislative debate elicited complaints from the Clinton administration and the State Department that were predictable and, in some cases, legitimate, it also lifted the veil on more troubling objections to virtually any spotlight on religion within American diplomacy. One particular objection—that religious freedom legislation would create an "artificial hierarchy of human rights," reveals a secularist compunction about religion—especially evangelical Christianity—more properly associated with the Democratic Party and its skepticism about mixing religion and public policy.[11] Secretary of State Madeline Albright and her lieutenants forcefully enunciated that skepticism as they sought to defeat the legislative campaign.

But as we shall see, objections to addressing religion in U.S. foreign policy did not disappear with the Clinton administration in 2001. The George W. Bush team at Foggy Bottom proved every bit as discomfited by broader notions of promoting international religious freedom in U.S. diplomatic efforts as did its predecessor. The State Department's narrowly humanitarian approach to persecution, and its paralysis over addressing the religion-state relationship, was seriously challenged by the events of 9/11. But the IRF issue and its potential contribution to the political dimensions of the War on Terror remained buried at the department until well into the second Bush administration.

Understanding the fault lines revealed in the legislative campaign for IRFA will lay the groundwork for our exploration in later chapters of how the law was to be implemented by America's diplomats at home and abroad.

Foreign Policy without Foggy Bottom

Distrust of the State Department was so strong among the original supporters of Wolf-Specter, and in particular in the mind of the bill's principal author
Michael Horowitz, that it drove many of the key decisions about how to attack
religious persecution in the law.[12] It also ensured that the initial campaign was
designed to force the American government to punish persecutors rather than
promote political and social institutions that might buttress religious freedom.
Horowitz understood quite well the secularist disdain for religion, especially
evangelical Christianity, and the willful rejection by political elites of the religious grounding of American democracy. He believed fervently that such views
were prevalent in the foreign affairs establishment, particularly under the leadership of the Clinton administration.[13]

In the midst of the battle over Wolf-Specter, Horowitz mounted a vigorous
and revealing defense of his vision in a Washington, D.C., speech before the
International Coalition for Religious Freedom. He described in vivid terms a
discussion he had with a senior State Department official that demonstrated
the problem of the secularist elites at Foggy Bottom. He also articulated what
he believed was the real solution to that problem, the "Freedom from Religious
Persecution" bill he had authored:

> [O]ur State Department people just don't get it. I met with a very high
> official of the State Department and he said, "Why are you people work-
> ing so hard on this issue of religious persecution? Don't you understand
> how divisive this is? You know we are working to promote democracy.
> We are working for the right to vote. Don't you understand that when
> we have the right to vote, people will be able to go to church?" . . .
>
> [Y]ou could almost hear him saying, "Give [State] a chance, so that
> people will be able to go to church, or go bowling or do their own
> thing." You could almost hear him add, "not that I would think of
> doing any of those myself, you understand." In his mind, in some
> patronizing way, religion was a form of therapy. . . .
>
> I said, "You don't understand history. Don't you know why we
> have democracy in the West? We don't have the right to go to church
> because we had a right to vote. We have the right to vote and we have
> democracy because of . . . the notion that all men and women are cre-
> ated equal in the eyes of God. . . ."

Horowitz' description of the premises of the U.S. foreign policy establishment contained important truths. His conception of how to resolve that problem, however, helps explain core weaknesses of the Wolf-Specter bill and one

of the key flaws in the IRF Act itself. Referring to persecuting governments, Horowitz asserted that "it is not dialogue that will make those people change their ways. It is the great moral pressure of an aroused America that says, if you want relations with us, you must stop persecuting churches." "America," he assured his audience, "is going to hold the State Department's feet to the fire and change the nature of human rights policy."[14]

Here was the most serious error in the Wolf-Specter conception of how to alter U.S. foreign policy. Horowitz's view of the State Department's recalcitrance and its causes was partly correct, although there were other less ideological problems as well. Nor was he wrong in supposing that that public pressure should play a key role in influencing the department's actions. There is little doubt that the grassroots interest engendered by Horowitz himself played a critical part in the introduction of an IRF bill in the first place.

The crucial flaw in the argument Horowitz put forward, and that many religious freedom supporters accepted, was that the thundering pulpits of an aroused America could have the effect of altering in any sustained way the behaviors of other societies or the entrenched resistance at the State Department to addressing religion in American foreign policy. The analysis itself indicated the unlikelihood of either outcome: suspicion of U.S. motives abroad, or of integrating religion into American foreign policy, could only be exacerbated (as indeed it proved to be) by the fact that passionate Christians and Jews were behind the legislation. In the end, Horowitz simply wrote his religious persecution bill to make punitive actions automatic and to bypass the State Department altogether. Both were tactics doomed to fail.

The centerpiece of the Wolf-Specter bill was the director of the office of religious persecution monitoring. In the original bill and its immediate successor (introduced in May and September 1997, respectively), the director was to be appointed by the president and the monitoring office placed in the president's executive office, rather than at the State Department. The director would have extraordinary powers to punish but very little influence over (or required interest in) addressing the underlying structures of persecution, let alone advancing religious freedom.

Under the bill the director would have the authority to impose punitive sanctions against offending governments without any substantive input from State Department officials or any direction from the president's chief foreign policy official, the secretary of state.[15] The director would by law issue findings that would trigger the withholding of nonhumanitarian U.S. aid from specified persecuting governments. The findings would be made in an annual report to Congress describing the situation in some dozen countries identified in the bill.[16] Should the director find any of the governments of these countries guilty of conducting or countenancing religious persecution, they would be hit with sanctions by the United States.[17]

Only the president himself could waive the sanctions, and even then he was required to explain to Congress, after the sanctions had been publicly announced, why a waiver was necessary to protect American national security. The unprecedented nature of these nearly automatic punishments, which could be employed without vetting in any substantive way by the State Department, ensured opposition from the Clinton administration and especially from Foggy Bottom itself.

Additional opposition to the director's sanctions power came from American businesses and corporations that exported their products to countries subject to sanctions. This factor ensured the early resistance of a number of Republican members of Congress, such as Senators Rod Grams (R-Minnesota) and Chuck Hagel (R-Nebraska).[18] For their part, religious and human rights groups tended to be divided on the subject. Some saw economic sanctions as valuable or indispensable in changing the behavior of governments and cited the success of such measures against the South African government's policy of apartheid. Others saw them as too imprecise and often harmful to the very victims of persecution they were trying to help.[19]

This combination of opponents—the Clinton administration,[20] American exporters, the State Department, some Republican legislators (especially in the Senate), and some in the human rights and faith based communities—proved fatal for Wolf-Specter over the long run. The various objections eventually forced amendments that moved the director and his office out of the White House to the State Department and removed the director's sanctions authority.[21] Once this happened, it meant that the Horowitz coalition had lost on the key aspects of its approach: punishment through sanctions and a White House official with the power to circumvent the State Department. Ultimately, these defeats led Horowitz and many of his supporters to transfer their hopes to another agency outside the State Department: the independent U.S. Commission on International Religious Freedom.

The Genesis of a Proxy

The idea for a separate watchdog agency that would add a level of public scrutiny to the performance of the State Department had modest beginnings. Shortly after the introduction of Wolf-Specter in May 1997, Senate Majority Leader Trent Lott appointed a Republican task force on religious persecution led by Senator James Inhofe of Oklahoma. The task force would examine, as a delicately worded news release from Inhofe's office put it, "some aspects of the Wolf/Specter bill which...may benefit from further discussion and consideration."[22]

In fact, the Wolf-Specter bill had virtually no chance of passing in the Senate. Not only was the Clinton administration working against it and encouraging opposition among Senate Democrats, but Arlen Specter, the Republican sponsor in the Senate, seemed to have little real interest in fighting for the bill. Specter was thought to have sponsored it primarily to burnish his credentials with evangelicals as part of his own reelection campaign.[23] Perhaps most important, Wolf-Specter raised concerns among Republicans who either feared the effects of sanctions on American businesses or opposed its relaxation of immigration restrictions.

Such concerns led Senator Lott to search for a more viable approach, but his solution—the Inhofe task force—never got off the ground. Demonstrating his considerable clout, and that of the evangelicals who supported his campaign, Michael Horowitz apparently engineered the dissolution of the task force less than two months after its establishment.[24] However, two critical factors emerged from Lott's aborted attempt at developing a Senate alternative to Wolf-Specter. First, several Hill staffers long committed to the cause of opposing religious persecution decided that they would invest the time and energy to develop an alternative bill, but this time out of the political limelight and away from the scrutiny and spoiling power of Michael Horowitz.[25]

Second, those staffers, led by John Hanford of Senator Lugar's office, retained a minor but portentous element of the task force's stillborn work: an independent commission. The role of the commission was initially envisioned to be that of a "truth patrol," established for a limited time to ensure that the State Department did not fudge the facts.[26] It reflected the concern of many across the political spectrum that the real story of religious persecution was not being told, either by the mainstream press or by the State Department's annual Human Rights Reports.[27] Under the Inhofe proposal, the commission's function was to be analogous to the U.S. Commission on Civil Rights, holding hearings and developing a database of information available to policy makers.

After the demise of the task force, Hanford and his collaborators on the Hill worked doggedly over the next several months to produce an alternative bill, which was introduced in March 1998 as the Nickles-Lieberman International Religious Freedom Act. Initially Horowitz was outraged, especially given the secrecy that attended the new bill's creation and development, and he went to some lengths to oppose it. Ultimately, however, he abandoned the Wolf-Specter approach to circumventing the State Department and found another vehicle. The Nickles bill had unwittingly provided it: the United States Commission on International Religious Freedom.

During the months before the final passage of the International Religious Freedom Act in October 1998, Horowitz turned his considerable energies to the task of bulking up the commission and diminishing the role of the State Department. He and many of his supporters came to believe that the commission provided the answer to the increasing weight given the department in the IRF Act. As noted, the act put the center of the new policy at the State Department under an ambassador at large. Under the initial draft, the ambassador was to chair the commission. None of this was satisfactory, however, to

those who wanted an international religious freedom policy that was independent of Foggy Bottom.

A great irony of the whole process now emerged. Having abandoned Wolf-
Specter, Horowitz proceeded to lobby vigorously on behalf of the IRF Act's
commission. He helped ensure that it was well funded ($3 million per year),
well-staffed (nine eminent leaders from various religious traditions), completely
independent of the ambassador and the State department (the Ambassador
was made a nonvoting, *ex officio* member), and given a mission considerably
beyond fact-finding.

As successful as Horowitz was, however, his victories fell well short of his
reach. During the month prior to the IRF Act's passage, he also lobbied to eliminate *all* requirements for presidential and State Department action, including
the designation of severe violators, and to replace them with a strengthened
commission.[28] He failed in this attempt, but this extraordinary end-run merely
confirmed that Horowitz and many of the leaders of the legislative campaign
believed exclusively in the efficacy of political pressure from outside. They simply rejected the necessity of integrating the issue into the mission of the agency
most responsible for implementing American foreign policy.

Despite Horowitz's failure to gut the Department's role altogether, the IRF
Act as finally passed did substantially enhance the powers of the commission.
Its mandate now was to raise the profile of the issue, keep pressure on the
Department of State, issue its own separate annual report, and provide separate
policy recommendations on religious freedom to the Congress, the president,
and the secretary of state. As it emerged from the final bill, the commission—
not the Department's office of the IRF ambassador—was seen by many in the
Wolf-Specter campaign, and by many on the Hill, as the centerpiece of the new
U.S. international religious freedom policy.

In the short-term the most significant result of the commission's role
emerged at the State Department. Although officials there were mildly irritated
by the implicit devolution of the department's authority and would occasionally
complain about the commission (especially its statutory right to see classified
information necessary to its work), the latter's high profile helped the department downgrade the position and authority of the IRF ambassador. When he
and his office were tucked away in the existing human rights bureaucracy, his
authority substantially below that normally accorded an ambassador at large,
scarcely a complaint was heard from Capitol Hill, the faith-based community,
or the newly empowered commission.

The commission and its staff have in the years since 1998 drawn some
of the most talented religious leaders, scholars, researchers, and activists in
America. It has in some cases made important contributions to U.S. religious
liberty advocacy, including policy recommendations and an excellent survey
of Islamic law.[29] During the extended period after the first IRF ambassador
left the State Department and the position remained unfilled—a period that

straddled 9/11—commissioners would help prevent the IRF office from being eliminated as a distinct entity.

But the commission has in the years since its establishment also emerged as an untenable proxy for U.S. IRF policy, a government funded quasi-official NGO that by its nature cannot serve the ends its supporters seek. Persecuting governments, their victims, potential allies of U.S. policy, and not a few members of the press and the U.S. Congress are sometimes confused about the commission's role and who is responsible for the official U.S. effort to oppose religious persecution and promote freedom.[30]

The commission's high profile has also had the unfortunate effect of diverting attention from the failures of the State Department, in particular its bureaucratic isolation of the office responsible for carrying out the mandates of the law. This problem is deepened, however unwittingly, by those who do not trust the department and are unwilling to invest the political and financial capital necessary to help integrate IRF into the foreign policy mainstream (an indifference generally acceptable to officials at C Street). Perhaps the commission's greatest failure has been to ignore this foundational problem, whose solution lies both in external policy pressure on the department and, even more important, in changing from within its culture and attitudes about religion.

Freedom for Christians and the Pork Barrel

The Wolf-Specter bill had placed a harsh spotlight on governments practicing the most heinous forms of religious persecution, the victims of which, supporters believed, were largely Christian. The preeminent example was Sudan, where Christians had experienced horrific abuses, including torture, slavery, and forced conversions to Islam.[31] Awareness the breadth and depth of Christian persecution was increasing with the 1996 publication of Nina Shea's *In the Lion's Den* and Paul Marshall's 1997 study of worldwide persecution, *Their Blood Cries Out*.[32] In 1997, the State Department had confirmed the problem in a report on Christians issued at the insistence of Congress.[33]

The Wolf-Specter emphasis on Christians was therefore grounded on compelling evidence. Unfortunately, however, the bill was perceived as downplaying similar evidence about the persecution of non-Christians. Although there were explicit references in the bill to other named religious groups, there was little doubt that Christians were intended to be the centerpiece of the effort.[34] The Christian-centered approach was also fed by a belief that U.S. immigration and foreign policy officials were ignoring the data and were indifferent to the problem.[35] One result was the bill's proposed overhaul of U.S. immigration policy, in particular the mode of determining which asylum seekers could enter and remain in the United States. The bill amended the Immigration and Nationality Act by "lowering the bar" (or, as supporters would have it, "leveling the playing field") for victims of religious persecution, especially Christians.

Supporters knew that people fleeing their countries of origin who actually reached the United States and requested asylum on grounds of religious persecution were sometimes turned away without a full hearing because they were deemed to have failed to meet the legal standard of establishing "a credible fear" of persecution. It was at this point, many believed, that immigration judges and the U.S. Immigration and Naturalization Service would discriminate against Christians. And it was this discrimination that the bill set out to counterbalance.

Under Wolf-Specter, anyone seeking asylum who could claim membership in a "persecuted community" as defined in the bill was considered to have met the credible fear standard if that community had been determined (by the White House director of religious persecution monitoring) to have been subject to persecution during the previous year. Such a person was then automatically granted a full asylum hearing. If the judge in the hearing denied asylum, the applicant was to be given copies of key documents, including any assessments or materials used to determine that the asylum claim was not credible.

Wolf-Specter defined "persecuted communities" as Christians in any of a group of some dozen countries, most of them either Muslim or Communist, such as Sudan, Egypt, Saudi Arabia, China, North Korea, and Cuba. The bill also named two non-Christian persecuted communities—Tibetan Buddhists and Iranian Baha'is—reflecting a kind of pork-barrel approach to identifying victims groups.[36] It permitted the White House director to identify other groups as well, but the default focus was on Christians.

The bill also addressed the issue of "refugees," that is, people who had fled their countries of origin but had not reached the United States. Refugees fleeing persecution, whether religious, political, social, or ethnic, were generally subject to international norms and procedures adjudicated by international offices of the United Nations High Commissioner for Refugees. U.S. embassies and consulates became involved only in a small percentage of cases, but supporters of Wolf-Specter believed that Christians were often short-changed by both the U.N. and U.S. bureaucracies. Accordingly, the bill provided that members of the defined persecuted communities would be deemed to be of "special humanitarian concern" to the United States and to receive resettlement priority as high as that of any other group of refugees.

The evidence of bias against Christian applicants for asylum and refugee status was largely anecdotal,[37] and the Wolf-Specter immigration provisions proved highly controversial. Its pro-Christian emphasis, along with what some believed to be a heightened status for victims of religious persecution, played into the hands of those who charged that the bill established in law an illegitimate "hierarchy of human rights" that favored religious people, especially Christians.

Easing the way for Christian refugees to enter the United States also divided the evangelical community. Although sympathy with their beleaguered co-religionists overseas was a prime motivation for their activism, many evangelicals did not want U.S. law to have the automatic effect of reducing Christian populations abroad, particularly in areas where those populations were already diminishing. This concern centered on the Middle East, where Christianity had been born and had spread in its earliest years. In Israel, Palestine, Egypt, Jordan, Syria, Lebanon, Turkey, Iraq, and Iran, the indigenous Christian populations had long been in decline.

How, some asked, could Christians obey the biblical injunction to be "salt and light" if they were not present in the countries of the religion's birth and adolescence? The same problem was attached to other countries where persecution of Christians was rampant, especially in Sudan, China, Pakistan, and North Korea. Catholics involved in the bill shared this worry, although the Catholic Bishops Conference was far more supportive of amendments to existing U.S. refugee and asylum policy. That policy was, in their view, unjust to all applicants and not just Christians.[38]

There is no question that millions of Christians live under regimes of severe persecution in which they cannot openly practice their faith and in which they are vulnerable to illegal detention, harassment, torture, "disappearance," and murder. Such regimes exist in Sudan, North Korea, Burma, Iran, China, Saudi Arabia, Vietnam, Eritrea, and to a lesser degree in Pakistan, India, Uzbekistan, Egypt, Nigeria, Indonesia, Iraq, Afghanistan, and other countries where governments either sponsor persecution or permit it to take place. In still other nations, such as Jordan, Israel, Russia, and even some in Western Europe, Christian minorities are subject to discrimination of various types.[39]

That their co-religionists in the United States view this situation as a tragedy that has not been effectively addressed by their own government, but should be, is quite understandable. Indeed, one question that nags supporters of U.S. IRF policy to this day is why Christian persecution is not better known among American churches and why there is not more pressure on elected officials. But the data also make it clear that non-Christians are subject to similar depredations, including millions of Muslims who suffer for their peaceful religious beliefs and practices at the hands of Muslim governments and Islamist terrorists or authoritarian governments such as those of China or Uzbekistan. Jews remain vulnerable in various countries, such as China, Iran, and Syria, as do Buddhists, most notably in Tibet at the hands of the Chinese government.

Ironically, the failure to make the Wolf-Specter bill universal in its applicability was inconsistent with the principles established by its early supporters. The January 1996 Statement of Conscience that began the IRF campaign had grappled with this very question. Its final draft had not only identified the persecution of Muslims abroad as a problem for the United States but had also articulated a Christian defense of universal religious liberty.[40] Moreover, it is striking that during the May 1997 House hearings on the original Wolf-Specter bill, several of its supporters testified that it protected the rights of all believers.[41] Although the IRF Act did ultimately embrace universality, the narrower focus on Christians in the original Wolf-Specter bill wounded the coalition's credibility and strengthened the arguments of secular and liberal religious groups that any IRF legislation was manipulated by the Christian right for illegitimate ends. That charge survived Wolf-Specter and endures to this day.

In fact, the narrower approach, accepted early on as a political expedient by Christian religious freedom experts who should have known better, was less a sign of religious "exclusivism" on the part of supporters than of their setting their sights too low. The tactics adopted by coalition leaders tended to sweep aside such principled positions, ultimately to the detriment of the campaign and the goals it sought to pursue.

Later, in the wake of 9/11, some on the Christian right issued intemperate and deliberately offensive public statements about Islam, treating the religion of 1.3 billion people as little more than a perversion and a launching pad for terrorism. These statements exacerbated the already damaging perception in Muslim countries that "international religious freedom" American-style was a Trojan horse for anti-Islamic forces—a view that meshed quite well with the broader understanding of Western democracy and freedom as inherently godless and therefore the enemy of Islam.

Here, precisely on these points, U.S. IRF policy has a vital role to play. If religious freedom is addressed both as a universal human right and in its broader socio-political sense, that is, developing a productive, liberal democratic relationship between the authorities of religion and the state, U.S. policy can help overcome Muslim suspicions. Unfortunately, as the debate over the early bills demonstrated, theological suspicions about Islam among some Christians can supersede the theological commitment to universal religious freedom. So long as these suspicions remain ascendant in their thinking, they are less likely to push the State Department to implement a more effective IRF policy in the Muslim world.

The Department of State and the "Hierarchy of Human Rights" Objection

Whatever the weaknesses of the legislative campaign itself and the IRF Act as passed, an even more foundational question was how the law would be implemented. And here the legislative debate revealed both bureaucratic and ideological barriers that already existed and would later be put to effective use by the Department of State.

The department's operations are organized around regional "bureaus" that manage U.S. relations with countries in particular geographic areas, such as the Middle East, Africa, or East Asia. Headed by assistant secretaries, these regional bureaus are the powerhouses at C Street. They not only control the resources and personnel choices for embassies and consulates, but they also help to mold and implement American policy within their respective countries and regions.

By the late 1970s, both President Carter and Congress concluded that this bureaucratic structure was not providing sufficient emphasis on human rights. Accordingly, Congress established by law a separate bureau of human rights, led by an assistant secretary, and gave it the mandate of integrating the issue into U.S. foreign policy. A key vehicle for its mission was an annual report on the conditions of human rights around the world, which has come to be known as the Human Rights Report.[42]

Although headed by a series of conservative political appointees under the Reagan and elder Bush administrations, the human rights bureau, in my experience, has traditionally been staffed by civil and foreign service officers of a largely secularist bent.[43] Indeed, the field of advocacy for human rights has until quite recently been considered the preserve of the American left, a phenomenon reflected in the discussion of liberal internationalism in chapter 2.[44] Those permanent civil service employees who came to the bureau from the human rights community were generally quite skeptical of the public role of religion, both in America and worldwide.[45]

By 1997 when Wolf-Specter was introduced, the Clinton administration had been in office for almost five years. Its political appointees to senior positions tended to reinforce the secularist tendencies already present at the State Department, especially in the human rights bureau, which the administration had renamed the bureau of "Democracy, Human Rights and Labor." Those tendencies were also present in the bureaus and offices that focused on related matters such as population, refugees, asylum, women's issues, and the environment. Under Clinton the department had decided to sharpen the effectiveness of its own vision of human rights advocacy within U.S. foreign policy by establishing a new under secretary for global affairs to manage all those bureaus that Clintonites saw as part of a seamless garment of rights issues.

Small wonder, then, that for these officials a critical flaw in the Wolf-Specter bill was its establishment of a "hierarchy of human rights." By placing a religious persecution czar at the White House, insulated from State Department's influence, it would seem to grant the issue of religion a bureaucratic status above that of the other human rights Foggy Bottom sought to protect. Officials strongly resisted what they viewed as special and unwarranted treatment for victims of religious persecution, a criticism that was joined by liberal human rights groups, such as Human Rights Watch, and liberal Protestant organizations such as the National Council of Churches. The oldest of the human rights organizations, Amnesty International, had long been associated with the left, and its executive director (describing himself as "left-wingy") questioned the motives of "political and religious conservatives" who were backing the Wolf-Specter bill.[46]

As a result of the opposition generated by these and other views, the key Wolf-Specter amendments to the Immigration and Nationality Act—those designed to level the playing field for religious victims—were ultimately dropped. The successor IRF Act retained some of the original immigration provisions, such as training for American immigration and consular officials on the subject of religious persecution, even though Secretary Albright argued such training was already being done. But the hierarchy charge revealed much about the deep divide over the issue of religion between Wolf-Specter and IRFA supporters, on the one hand, and the bureaucracy at Foggy Bottom, on the other.

There were several major elements of the department's concern over a "hierarchy of human rights." The first, as Secretary Albright put it, was that Wolf-Specter "would create a hierarchy of human rights with the right to be free from torture and murder shoved into second place."[47] This was an odd way to formulate the issue, given that the purpose of the bill was to protect religious victims of torture, not to put torture as a category into second place. Nevertheless, as a matter of principle it certainly did not seem just or appropriate in the nation's asylum and refugee policies to "elevate" victims of religious persecution over victims of other forms of torture or abuse. Few Americans would argue that someone tortured for their religious beliefs was somehow more worthy of their government's help than someone tortured because of their race or gender.

The only reasonable case to be made on this aspect of the hierarchy objection was the one in fact made by Wolf-Specter proponents: in their view, both the Department of State and the Immigration and Naturalization Service (INS) had as a matter of habit tended to undervalue the victims of religious persecution in comparison with other forms. Accordingly, amendments were necessary to force a kind of rebalancing, so that victims of religious persecution would be given treatment equal to others. As one senior staffer at the Catholic Bishops Conference put it, "we labeled this 'affirmative action' in immigration policy in order to attract liberal groups who would otherwise oppose it."[48] But Wolf-Specter proponents ultimately failed to make the case that State and INS discriminated against Christians, a case that was clearly weakened by the perception, however unjustified, that Wolf-Specter discriminated against non-Christians.[49]

Nevertheless, as critics of the administration's hierarchy objection pointed out, the argument was spurious on practical grounds.[50] There were already offices in the State Department that focused on other vulnerable groups, including the senior coordinator for international women's issues and the ambassador at large for war crimes issues. Moreover, the Clinton administration had begun to emphasize what it called the "nontraditional rights," such as a broadened concept of the rights of women and children, and containing the problem of population growth. Given these facts, singling out the Wolf-Specter bill for its inappropriate focus on victims of religious persecution seemed an odd argument to make. To some members of the legislative coalition it merely confirmed the very rationale for their legislative efforts—a State Department (and Clinton administration) bias against religion in general and against Christians in particular.

It is also worth noting that the foundational documents of the United States and those of the United Nations identify, in effect, a hierarchy of rights. This hierarchy has nothing to do with distinctions between victims of torture; the right of all persons to be free of torture is either implied or explicit in these documents. Rather the hierarchy elevates those rights utterly necessary to human dignity, including freedom from torture. The Declaration of Independence asserts that some rights adhere to all human beings, and are inalienable, because they are granted by God and cannot be rescinded by governments. This formulation necessitates a hierarchy. Some rights, such as those identified in the Bill of Rights, were held by the founders to be inalienable, such as the right to free exercise of religion, the right to free speech, the right to freedom from arbitrary arrest or "cruel and unusual punishment."

The International Covenant on Civil and Political Rights (ICCPR), which codifies the Universal Declaration and binds states that are parties to it, recognizes a hierarchy by designating some rights, including religious freedom, as "non-derogable."[51] Other rights granted to individuals, such as the right to subsidized health care or secondary school education, may be crucial to the welfare of a nation, but they cannot be considered "natural rights" as understood by American's founders, or "fundamental" in modern parlance, because they are created by (and thus dispensable by) governments.

The second element of the department's hierarchy objection was more subtle and multilayered, but of greater long-term significance for the new U.S. policy. The essence of the objection was that a separate office and bureaucracy devoted solely to religious issues would unnecessarily expose American foreign policy to the purposes of the religious right. Those purposes were assumed to be illegitimate: the religious right sought to enable conversions to Christianity abroad, and this activity ran counter to department notions of "religious tolerance." Unlike religious freedom, religious tolerance was an essentially negative concept. The idea was to prevent religious conflict by the tolerance of religious difference. Moreover, there was a concern at the State Department that a new religious freedom law and bureaucracy would in effect sanction arguing on the basis of religion for changes in U.S. foreign policy, changes that might clash with the more secular human rights priorities of the Clinton administration. Such a law would create an official, permanent entry point for the religious right into the foreign policy apparatus.[52]

Proselytizing and Religious Tolerance

State's leading spokesman in opposing Wolf-Specter and IRFA was John Shattuck, Assistant Secretary for the Bureau of Democracy, Human Rights, and Democracy.[53] Shattuck had long been associated with the American Civil Liberties Union and was known for effective advocacy across a whole range of civil rights. Shattuck understood religious freedom as "religious tolerance." His views of the meaning and value of that term led him to be suspicious of the motives of the religious right and to fear that their approach would harm U.S. interests.

The two concepts—religious freedom and religious tolerance—can overlap but can also carry entirely separate meanings. "Tolerance" is a term that at its best can mean "respect for views with which I disagree." But the term also can imply putting up with something that is problematic, divisive, or even evil. In early modern Europe, the language of tolerance was used by confessional states (Anglican England, Catholic France) to describe a legal concession to certain Christian minorities. Voltaire's *Treatise on Toleration* approached religion as an evil whose demise must be encouraged by state policy but must be tolerated until that success is achieved. As the term entered modern discourse, it was not understood as the acceptance, much less the embracing, of a good, that is, something that is both natural and necessary for human flourishing. In some contexts, "tolerance" has become a synonym for moral permissiveness and radical individual autonomy.[54]

Religious freedom, on the other hand, can be understood precisely as the embracing and defending of a human good and as a political achievement by the democratic state that protects both religious and nonreligious citizens and promotes the common good. Properly understood and limited, religious freedom encourages among domestic religious communities an emphasis on liberal teachings embedded in doctrine and a deemphasis on illiberal tendencies. It also permits those communities to employ their religious beliefs in democratic debate, on the same basis as other institutions of civil society. Such a regime rejects religious intolerance and forestalls conflict precisely by acknowledging the value of religion as a human good, while privileging no particular religion and inviting all into the public square. Such a regime, as I have argued in chapter 3, has been one of the major achievements of American democracy, present at the founding and, though not unchallenged, still vibrant today.

Assistant Secretary Shattuck had a very different approach to the issue of religion and its role in the common good. In a speech at Harvard Law School after leaving the State Department, he laid out his views:

> The idea of "freedom of religion" is predicated on the existence of more than one religion. But a multiplicity of religions has always meant conflict, and religious conflict often led to war and human

devastation. This was the state of reality for centuries and millennia, and it is hardly a ringing endorsement of religious freedom. Then, in the mid-twentieth century, a new concept emerged in the Universal Declaration of Human Rights that was drafted after the Second World War. This was the idea of *tolerance of religious difference*—an idea that was offered in response to the long and bloody history of religious conflict that had included, in Europe alone, the Crusades, the Islamic conquests, the Inquisition, the Thirty Years War, and most recently the Holocaust.

In short, he summed up, "the modern concept of religious tolerance grew not out of the west, but out of a universal revulsion after World War II to genocide and crimes against humanity—many of which had been committed against or in the name of religion."

Shattuck then outlined contemporary threats to religious tolerance. First was the fanaticism represented not only by Bin Laden but also by Serbian President Slobodan Milosevic and other leaders "who rise to power by fomenting religious intolerance and conflict." The second threat to religious tolerance was closer to home. It consisted of "efforts... by the American religious right to advance a political agenda within the United States government that seeks to promote special religious interests overseas." He was referring to the International Religious Freedom Act and its supporters.[55]

Here was a major element of the objection by the Clinton administration and the Albright State Department to the legislative campaign. As they saw it religious persecution should be vigorously opposed. But religion itself was not seen as a human good to be nourished. Rather, it is more often a source of conflict to be managed via tolerance. Shattuck's argument was that religious tolerance, largely an achievement of the United Nations and the international community, overcame the conflict inherent in religion, represented in modern America by the religious right.

This understanding is at the heart of liberal internationalists' secularist views on religious freedom. It does not acknowledge the American founding as an achievement of religious freedom (certainly not as that term is defined in this book). Secularists assume the founders resolved conflicts over religion by codifying in the First Amendment the toleration of something inherently threatening, namely religion in its public manifestations. This was accomplished by the "separation of Church and State," and by the privatization of religion. These views reject the argument that the American system is an example of Stepan's twin tolerations, that is, a political covenant that trades a ban on establishment for the active involvement of religious individuals and communities in the democratic public square on the same basis as other members of civil society.

Fueling the administration's understanding of religion as a source of conflict were their concerns over evangelical proselytizing overseas. John Shattuck emphasized this problem during a 2007 appearance on a panel at the Pew Forum on Religion and Public Life in Washington, D.C. He posed the question, and the answer, this way:

> What is the role of a government and a government agency in defending the rights of people from our own country to go to another country to work with people in that country who may or may not wish to change their faith? My analysis of this...focuses on the role of government in promoting religious tolerance in order to reduce the prospect that there will be religious conflict. I myself do not believe it is the responsibility or function of the United States government to promote and assist in the work of those who are engaged in missionary work abroad. I recognize it's their right to do that, but I would counsel very much against having a U.S. government agency be involved in activity that could be seen to be or indeed was assisting in that kind of promotion.[56]

In response to Shattuck's remarks, the IRF ambassador emphasized that his office did not support missionaries per se but said that the right of religious freedom itself includes the right to change one's religion. Shattuck replied that he still had concerns about the way U.S. policy is perceived abroad. "I feel very strongly about the way in which, at least in my view, religious freedom is predominantly an issue of religious tolerance. I worry about the connection between our government and those who are indeed engaged in work, entirely legal under the international human rights agenda as you've described, that is appearing to be engaged in changing people's views. That is going to be damaging in the end to our effort to promote what I think is the most important value of religious freedom, which is religious tolerance."[57]

Here we can see the negative view of religion implied in the term tolerance, the idea that its true goal is to prevent conflict. Mr. Shattuck was in particular concerned about "proselytizing that violates a cultural tradition or seeks to persuade people who are members of a close cultural community—indeed, a community of believers—to abandon their beliefs."[58] He does not believe religion to be by definition a negative aspect of human society. But he clearly does not see religion as inherently a human good, a search for truths that, once found, are by their nature to be shared with others. He is correct that the actions of missionaries have violated cultural traditions and have caused members of other belief communities to abandon their beliefs. As we have observed, proselytism can be mercenary, and can exploit ignorance, poverty, and emotional loneliness. This kind of proselytism has indeed created conflict and deserves resolute condemnation.

But if the right of proselytism is understood as intrinsic to the religious enterprise it can also be seen as intrinsic to human dignity. Both the Universal Declaration and the ICCPR recognize the right to change one's religion and to convince others, without coercion, to change theirs.[59] Proselytism can become an activity of peaceful persuasion, a staple of true religious pluralism, that is, creeds in competition within the umbrella of a democratic society committed to civility. This competition rests, above all, on respect for the dignity of the religious other as necessary to the exercise. As such, it can contribute to stable, liberal, and just governance, especially in highly religious societies, and to the achievement of genuine religious pluralism (as it has in America).

This is not to suggest that it is today seen this way by all, or even most, of the Christians or Muslims who seek to persuade others of the truths inherent in their traditions. Some Muslims deny that there is any Koranic warrant to convert non-Muslims to Islam, and very few Muslim societies accept proselytism by non-Muslims. In some Islamic states, the activity of seeking to convert a Muslim, like the activity of apostasy, is a capital offense. John Shattuck is right that proselytizing can create conflict. But his solution seems to be that U.S. religious freedom policy, grounded in a "freedom as tolerance" approach, should not support proselytizing at all.

Wolf-Specter, IRFA, and the Public Square

There was a final dimension of the hierarchy objection, closely related to the others. It is that public manifestations of religion as a rule endanger other rights. When religion or religiously informed moral judgments enter the political sphere, especially when those judgments are derived from theologies such as Christian evangelicalism (a "comprehensive doctrine" in Rawlsian terminology), they are divisive and resistant to democratic compromise. To the extent that religious freedom encourages the entrance of religious communities and their claims into the public square, it must not be permitted any pride of place among human rights. This was a more subtle reason for the State Department's objection to a hierarchy of rights. It reflected the concern that the form of religion represented by the Wolf-Specter and IRFA coalitions—the American religious right—posed a threat to the rights valued by the Clinton administration.

The secretary's most senior human rights official was the under secretary for global affairs—a new position created by the Clinton administration to demonstrate its seriousness about the importance of globalization and the interconnectedness of global issues. The incumbent was Tim Wirth, a Democratic congressman and senator from Colorado during the 1980s. After his departure from the State Department, Wirth became head of the UN Foundation, which focuses on population control and the environment. Wirth was well known at Foggy Bottom for his concerns about the world's population increase. One apocryphal story was that, as under secretary, he displayed a "tree" of colorful condoms on his desk, which remained there (to the delight of some at the department) during a meeting with a somewhat nonplussed envoy from the Holy See.

Such shenanigans were not intended (at least not entirely) to offend the Vatican. To Wirth's mind, the "central switching issue that relates to every-thing else" was the growth of the world's population, which he held to be ulti-mately responsible for many of the world's human rights abuses. In the State Department's press briefing to introduce the 1994 Human Rights Reports, Wirth noted that "[t]he Clinton Administration has recognized the deep impor-tance of...the new non-traditional issues," such as population and the rights of women and children.[60]

These were indeed critical issues to the administration. In prelimi-nary meetings to prepare for the 1994 Cairo International Conference on Population and Development, the State Department supported a wide variety of programs designed to address what they saw as empowering women and children, including abortion rights and sex education. Their primary opposi-tion had come from Roman Catholics and evangelicals who argued that such programs were destructive of the family and the health of children.[61] Clearly the administration's agenda did not accord with traditional religious views.

Here we arrive at the final part of the hierarchy objection. Neither the supporters of Wolf-Specter nor the IRF Act made an explicit argument about religion or religion-based moral judgments in the democratic public square. However, their very presence in that public square highlighted the problem for the administration. There they were, in the halls and on the floor of both Houses of Congress, lobbying the White House, engaging in conferences and in the media. It was quite apparent that the evangelicals and Catholics who were behind the legislative campaign, people such as Charles Colson or Richard John Neuhaus, represented a traditionalist version of Christianity that would very likely contest the administration's vision of human rights. If this kind of religious advocacy got a foothold in the foreign policy establishment, it could mean trouble.

Mission Accomplished, Trouble Ahead

Notwithstanding their fervent disagreements over what the law meant, leaders of the campaign for a law on international religious freedom accomplished a significant feat with the passage of the 1998 IRF Act. Without their efforts the opportunity to integrate this issue more completely into U.S. national security policy would be greatly diminished. And despite its resistance, the Clinton-Albright State Department deserves credit for elevating the issue, however incompletely, within U.S. human rights policy.

But behind the successful story line of the campaign for an IRF law, lurk-ing in the arguments and actions of its supporters and opponents, were all the messy contradictions and tensions we have explored, and others. The IRF Commission, initially an afterthought to the IRF Act, became the central IRF agency for many coalition supporters, diverting attention from Foggy Bottom. The early Wolf-Specter focus on Christians left a lingering perception about the illegitimate Christian-centered goals of the law. At home and abroad fears persisted that IRF Act would have an essentially punitive approach. And some were convinced that the Christian right was not only going to have an office at C Street, but that also the new policy would complicate other human rights priorities.

As we shall see, most of these tensions festered during the first decade of the law's operation and some ended up undermining its effectiveness. The State Department, as the Horowitz coalition had predicted, was to exploit loopholes in the IRF Act to avoid any significant punitive action against anyone, including the severe persecutors it identified. Before many years had passed, the annual act of "designating" these persecutors took on the faint sound of crying wolf. Perhaps most important, for those who feared the potential power and influence of a religion office at Foggy Bottom, headed by a very senior American foreign policy official designated by the IRF Act as the "principal adviser to the President and Secretary of State" on religious freedom, the department proved quite adept at managing that problem.

It is to that story that we now turn.

5

The Lion's Den at
Foggy Bottom

Act I: The Seiple Years (1998–2000)

The acid test of a policy is its ability to obtain domestic support. This has
two aspects: the problem of legitimizing a policy within the government
apparatus...and that of harmonizing it with the national experience.
—Henry Kissinger

Of survival it has been said that the bird is evolution's device for the
perpetuation of the egg. Diplomacy too must sometimes appear to be
the diplomat's invention for the perpetuation of his profession—hence
the legendary diplomat reposting to the condescension of the generals
that they would have no wars to fight were it not for him.
—Geoffrey Jackson

The International Religious Freedom (IRF) Act of 1998 had committed the
United States at least nominally to a policy of reducing religious persecution
and promoting religious freedom throughout the world. Given the Clinton
administration's opposition to religious freedom legislation, however, it was
perhaps unsurprising that neither the State Department nor the White House
showed much interest in elevating the issue within the nation's foreign policy.
Foggy Bottom proved quite successful at ignoring key parts of the new congressional mandate and at managing those charged with its implementation.

The State Department's opposition to Congressional foreign policy initiatives is not unusual in American history, and is partly explained by the natural
tension between the two branches of government with constitutional responsibilities for foreign affairs. What was unusual was the relative indifference
shown by Congress and religious freedom advocates to the department's recalcitrance in implementing critical parts of the law. The lack of concern had

several sources. Some of the evangelicals, Catholics, and Jews who had supported the Wolf-Specter bill were not pleased with various aspects of the IRF Act that replaced it, including the act's emphasis on quiet diplomacy and the possibilities it provided for avoiding any real action.

A few of these supporters were also unhappy with the Clinton administration's first choice for the religious freedom ambassador established under the law, a man whom many evangelicals knew, Robert A. Seiple. Although Seiple was a prominent evangelical himself, some suspected that he was too "soft" and insufficiently willing to denounce and punish persecuting governments. Some evangelicals turned their attention to another human rights issue, trafficking in persons, and never quite regained their enthusiasm for pressing the issue of religious persecution within the U.S. Department of State.

Indeed, as we have noted, many of the original Wolf-Specter supporters (including some who were admirers of Robert Seiple) ignored the State Department because they considered it either irrelevant or an obstacle to be circumvented and instead focused their attentions on the IRF Commission. This allegiance had the effect of diverting political energy away from the State Department and toward an important but ancillary element of the foreign policy apparatus established by the IRF Act. As a result, there was little scrutiny and virtually no criticism of the department's internal treatment of the new religious freedom office, either by Congress or by the coalition that had produced the law.

But congressional inertia also had to do with confusion and ambivalence over the meaning and reach of the new policy. Even though it explicitly required the United States to "promote religious freedom" internationally, few were willing to see this goal as more than one of condemning and punishing persecutors and rescuing their victims. For many supporters of the legislation, its humanitarian dimension was always the central goal. Fellow believers were suffering, and the job was to relieve that suffering as quickly as possible. Ironically, the humanitarian approach was quickly seen within the State Department as the most felicitous. Unlike more policy-oriented advocacy for religious freedom, the focus on persecution turned out to be the least disruptive and most easily isolated.

Those who had this narrow view of the new policy, both inside and outside the department, instinctively adopted modest standards of success. For example, they looked to the accuracy and completeness of the descriptions of persecution in the State Department's new *Annual Report on International Religious Freedom*, rather than to policy actions based on the reported facts. A typical discussion point in Washington was whether senior State Department officials (including the IRF ambassador) had "raised the issue" of prisoners and abuses with foreign governments. To paraphrase the lead actor in a former television series about the White House, only at the Department of State can "raising the issue" be confused with "solving the problem."

With such standards U.S. religious freedom policy was judged more by its motion, and its short-term alleviation of suffering, than by its effect on the structures of persecution. Such criteria had little or nothing to do with long-term success in implanting religious freedom as a cultural and political norm. The result of such modest expectations was a sense of movement that was misleading. Even though the State Department was skirting aspects of the law, it quickly succeeded in identifying the facts of persecution in the *Annual Report,* which was widely praised for its identification of problems (if not their resolution). This partial success of the report added to congressional complacence.

However, a few on the Hill and in the religious freedom community, including some on the new commission, understood the test that lay ahead. If the United States was to be truly successful in attacking persecution and promoting religious freedom abroad, there would have to be a shift in culture at Foggy Bottom. It would not be enough simply to issue annual reports, provide lists of the worst persecuting governments, and spring Christians and others out of prison from time to time. Full implementation of the law would require the rooting and the development of its core institution at the State Department: the office of international religious freedom with a powerful senior official at its head, one who would seize and employ all the authority at his or her disposal.

Mr. Seiple Comes to Washington

He seemed a perfect choice to help rebalance the Clinton administration's moral ledger, which was increasingly in the red, and to mount a new foreign policy initiative.[1] Robert Seiple was a former marine officer who had flown 300 combat missions in Vietnam, an ex-athletics director and college president, and an evangelical Christian with a reputation for integrity. During the debate over Wolf-Specter and IRFA he was the president of World Vision, a huge and influential evangelical Christian relief and development agency. When challenged by State Department interviewers about World Vision's policy of hiring only Christians, Seiple stood his ground. During his tenure, he said, 30 employees had died helping people in need, and not just Christians. World Vision staff had to be sure of their own faith if they were going to risk their lives. And, he added, the organization's hiring practices were perfectly legal. He made no apologies.

It was the spring of 1998. In March Senator Nickles had introduced his IRF bill and supporters of Wolf-Specter were increasingly concerned about the fate of their own bill. In April Robert Seiple received a telephone call at his Seattle World Vision office from Julia Taft, the State Department's assistant secretary for population, refugees, and migration. The two knew each other from the intersection of their work in the field of relief and development, and both happened to be Republicans—an unusual phenomenon among political appointees at the State Department under the Clinton administration. On that day, however, Taft informed Seiple candidly that the department was urgently looking for a person with high visibility and credibility in the evangelical community, someone whose appointment as a "senior advisor" on international religious freedom might help the administration fend off the bills that were wending their way through Congress.

Seiple had been with World Vision for over a decade, and he recently had given notice that he would not renew his five-year contract. He was looking for another challenge, and Taft's call was intriguing. Seiple's own beliefs, which he would often refer to as a "theology that touches the ground," obliged him to fight not only for the persecuted church but also for those outside the church who were suffering. As president of World Vision he had traveled to the world's centers of war, disease, and famine.

As he visited the killing fields of Bosnia or Rwanda or the starving children of Sudan, Seiple sought not only to comfort and sustain the victims but also to assess the causes of their travail. For him the answers lay both in the relief and development techniques of modern organizations such as World Vision and in the forgiveness and reconciliation that were at the core of his brand of Christianity. Indeed, he believed that every legitimate religion was at some level grounded in those virtues, which, if sustained and practiced collectively, would have prevented many of the catastrophes he had witnessed.

Seiple was a powerful speaker, and storytelling was at the center of his art. For Christian audiences and those sympathetic to Christianity, he could draw at will from an enormous reservoir of biblical imagery, delivered in the cadences and tones of an evangelical preacher. Once, during the second year of his tenure at the State Department, he shocked Clinton staffers by assuring a gathering of Christian leaders at the White House that "the tomb is empty, and the gates of hell will not prevail against his church."[2]

But most people in the Clinton administration understood that for Seiple such beliefs were not a hindrance to his work. They formed his motivating premise and accounted for his consistency and effectiveness. For the more secular or non-Christian audiences that were the norm for his position as ambassador, he would employ the same passionate tones in stories that illustrated what he saw as his life's work: inducing reconciliation and forgiveness among factions, especially those motivated by religion.

One of his favorite stories centered on a Lebanese Maronite named Mary, paralyzed by a Muslim soldier who had shot her after she refused to recant her religion. The point of the narrative, which Seiple told to international and domestic audiences alike, was not the soldier's hatred, or even what could be construed as Islamic extremism. The story line was Mary's forgiveness of the man who had destroyed her physical well-being. Seiple visited the young woman in her home near Beirut, where she labored with a watercolor brush held between her teeth to produce her "paintings of forgiveness," one of which he proudly displayed in his office. When he stood before the State Department press corps announcing the issuance of the first *Annual Report on International Religious Freedom,* Seiple told the story of Mary and dedicated the report to her.

Such narratives helped the new ambassador articulate the importance of employing religious motivations to forgive, to "live with our deepest differences," and to reconcile people of radically differing religious views. His own religious motivations had led him to put his theology "on the ground" during much of his adult life. Having fought in Vietnam, Seiple yearned to participate in the healing of that troubled country. In 1988 he had returned to Hanoi as head of World Vision to negotiate a deal to provide artificial limbs for those who had lost arms and legs in the war.[3] He would later travel to Vietnam as ambassador at large for international religious freedom to continue that process.

After Julia Taft's phone call, Seiple had given considerable thought to whether the position at the State Department would permit him to put some of his passion to work on behalf of religious freedom. But weeks passed and he heard nothing more from Washington. Suddenly things began to move quickly. In May, Assistant Secretary for Democracy, Human Rights, and Labor John Shattuck called Seiple to say that he should come immediately to Washington for an interview, but he added confidentially, the job of senior advisor was his if he wanted it. During the interview, Seiple feared that his answers to the question about World Vision's hiring practices would prove an obstacle for the liberal Clinton administration, but Shattuck's assurances had turned out to be correct. The job was his for the taking.

Why the sudden turnaround? It is unsurprising that the State Department could not make up its collective mind about who should fill a position whose religious mandate was viewed with suspicion. As it turns out, the department did not make the decision at all. A pastor who was a spiritual counselor to President Clinton, now in the midst of the Lewinski scandal, had learned of the State Department's interest in Seiple, whom the pastor also knew well. When he suggested to Clinton that Bob Seiple might provide a boost to his administration, the president agreed with alacrity. It was Clinton's own intervention that got the State Department off the dime and offered Bob Seiple the job the administration hoped would stave off the legislation currently under consideration in Congress.

On June 18, 1998, President Clinton introduced Seiple as the new senior advisor for international religious freedom to a gathering of government officials, religious leaders, and members of Congress in the Roosevelt room of the White House. Among those present were Secretary Albright and Assistant Secretary John Shattuck. Three prominent religious leaders who had just returned from an administration-sponsored trip to China were also in attendance.[4] Clinton spoke about his commitment to religious freedom but pointedly warned against the bills being discussed in Congress. "America," he told the audience, "is not strengthened in fighting for religious liberty or in fighting against religious persecution by laws that are so rigid a President's hands are tied."[5]

For Seiple it was a bracing moment. As he approached the podium to speak, he knew that the challenge before him was enormous. He knew that the administration saw him, at least in part, as a means to parry evangelical hostility toward the president and as someone whose appointment would diffuse the drive toward legislation. But Seiple had no intention of playing a passive or ineffective role at State. He had encountered and overcome daunting challenges before. He had seen the bloated bodies of genocide victims floating in Rwandan rivers and held children dying of starvation in Sudan. As head of World Vision he had moved mountains to help the victims of such disasters. He had led a huge international agency and he knew how to get things done.

Most important, he believed in himself. He had successfully applied his own brand of problem solving as combat pilot, athletics director, college president, and head of World Vision: know your target and the rules; maintain a confident optimism; refuse to be distracted by personal attacks or the biases of those who oppose you; surround yourself with capable people whom you trust and give them authority; and, most important of all, trust in God. Seiple was supremely confident that his mode of operation would permit him to succeed at the State Department. When Madeleine Albright told Bob's wife, Margaret Ann, that the secretary of state would be seeing more of her husband than she would, he was skeptical but grateful for the secretary's words of commitment.

Ironically, the Clinton administration's hope that Bob Seiple's appointment would help reduce evangelical ire toward the president proved to be off the mark. For one thing, the president made little effort to associate himself with the work of the new office. For another, as Bob Seiple himself anticipated, the evangelical community was split over his appointment because they were not of one mind over the role of the State Department and the proper methodology for dealing with religious persecution or advancing religious liberty as part of the nation's foreign policy.

The Lions at Foggy Bottom

What he hadn't anticipated were the obstacles that would be presented by the State Department bureaucracy and its culture. Seiple proved adept at cultivating relationships with senior officials at the department, especially the secretary herself, her advisors, and the under secretaries and assistant secretaries who were ostensibly his peers. Many were suspicious of the new policy and some created long-term problems for its implementation. But they also tended to like and respect Bob Seiple, whom most saw as a peer and a colleague with experience and gravitas, endearing in manner and a straight shooter on policy matters, even if a novice in foreign affairs.

Seiple prided himself on a personal guideline for action, "truth without surprise." That meant he would seek to inform people in advance of an action he intended to take. For foreign governments, it meant he would travel to discuss their religious freedom problems in private before they were criticized publicly in the *Annual Report*. Within the department it meant he was a team player. He would do what he thought was right, but would never knowingly upstage or embarrass his colleagues. Such characteristics made him a good choice as the first ambassador at large for international religious freedom.

But as he was soon to learn, the challenge at Foggy Bottom was more than one of building relationships with Secretary Albright and the senior political appointees who ran the department, as valuable as those relationships were. The State Department is one of the nation's oldest executive branch agencies, dating from 1789. Its staid and steady bureaucratic culture is built around practices designed to induce that most prized of diplomatic virtues, policy consensus, especially among the powerful regional bureaus that compete for resources and policy weight. It was difficult enough for new offices and functions to emerge from this culture, but Seiple represented a troublesome new policy imposed from the outside. Many perceived his office to be the result either of congressional meddling, political blackmail by the Christian right, or both.

When Seiple showed up for his first day of work in August 1998, there were a number of positive signs. Clinton had told the White House audience that the senior advisor's job would be "to make sure that religious liberty concerns get high and close attention in our foreign policy." Seiple knew that in order to succeed he would have to have access to key policy makers in the department and at the White House. Julia Taft had told him it was critical that he attend the high-level "D meetings" at the department.

"D" stood for "deputy secretary," and the man who held that title was Strobe Talbott, the number two official in the department and an expert on the former Soviet Union. On three mornings each week, Talbott gathered in his office the department's highest-level officials, including the under secretaries and assistant secretaries, to provide guidance, receive information, and ensure that Albright was properly informed of their activities. Typically, Talbott would begin the meeting by giving his own impressions of pending issues, and then go around the room to ask questions or see whether others had anything to add.

Taft pointed out to Seiple, quite accurately, that this gathering was where he would see senior officials on a regular basis. If he was to have an impact on policy at a high level, he must be in this meeting. This made good sense, and Seiple had made attendance at the meetings one of his conditions for accepting the job. The department agreed but it was to prove a mixed blessing. On the one hand, it was here that he met and developed the relationships that would prove vital to his tenure. It was in these meetings that he came to know senior officials such as Karl Inderfurth, assistant secretary for South Asian affairs, and key advisors to the secretary, such as Jim O'Brien and Wendy Sherman, who would become his advocates in the secretary's inner circle.

On the other hand, it was also in the Talbott meeting that the new ambassador discovered a stark and unpleasant reality: no one at the State Department had given the slightest consideration to what it meant to ensure, as the president had put it, "that religious liberty concerns get high and close attention in our foreign policy." Worse, no one was concerned enough to find out. It was true that Albright had instructed U.S. posts to increase their reporting on religious freedom and that she had cultivated the advisory committee on religious freedom established by Warren Christopher.

But these actions were, like the Seiple appointment itself, primarily a means to avoid any serious change in U.S. policy and certainly to avoid any substantive elevation of religious freedom itself. State was consumed with the day-to-day management of its various bilateral relationships, and that process simply could not accommodate the addition of the troublesome topic of religion. In his entire two years at the State Department, Seiple was later to write, neither Talbott nor any other official asked him a question about religious freedom during the D meetings, much less raise its implications for U.S. foreign policy.[6]

In the early months, however, the D meetings were the least of the new senior advisor's problems. Seiple's office was housed in John Shattuck's bureau of democracy, human rights, and labor. The location of the office in this bureau made sense at a certain level—religious freedom was, after all, a human right— but the decision was eventually to provide a source of constant tension and one of the key obstacles to the integration of religious freedom into the foreign policy of the United States. For the department, the placement of Seiple under Shattuck was designed to ensure proper management of the religious freedom issue and to avoid the problem of a "hierarchy of human rights."[7] Months after the passage of the International Religious Freedom Act, Bob Seiple's official job description listed him as "Ambassador at Large" but described his job as "Special Advisor on International Religious Freedom issues in the Bureau of Democracy, Human Rights and Labor, and...subject to the broad direction and overall policy guidance from the Assistant Secretary for DRL."

Under the IRF Act, however, the very purpose of a new office and a new ambassador was to extract religious freedom from its position of relative obscurity at the department and give it new energy and authority. But Seiple saw the question of location as a typical Washington bureaucratic turf fight, a dispute he disdained and for which he had no stomach. He decided not to resist his placement under the human rights bureau. It was an understandable calculation for a new official trying not to frighten the natives. But for the long term, it was a decision that would invite trouble.

Not long after Seiple arrived at the State Department, John Shattuck was on his way out, having been appointed by President Clinton as U.S. ambassador to Czechoslovakia. His replacement was another powerful advocate for human rights, Harold Hongju Koh, a Yale law professor who brought to the job a quick mind and an engaging personality. The Koh-Seiple relationship was a critical one to both men. From the day of his arrival at the department, Koh was faced with the presence of a senior official in his bureau whose lines of authority were not entirely clear. For whom did Seiple work? Did he report to Koh or the secretary or someone in between? What responsibility did Koh have for religious freedom, and what authority over the new policy?

The answers to these questions remained uncertain during the balance of the Clinton administration and, as we shall see, were unresolved by the time Seiple's successor took his place under the Bush administration. It was a textbook example of Foggy Bottom's near effortless ability to stifle the baby's growth without actually strangling him in the crib. No one outside the department complained about this ambiguous arrangement, least of all the members of the Horowitz campaign, for whom the position of the ambassador was a distraction from the focus on the IRF Commission.

Ultimately, neither Congress nor the commission were to pressure the State Department successfully to resolve the problem of the ambassador's status and authority, in part because some believed Bob Seiple would get the job done wherever he was situated, but in part because others distrusted him, or did not like the way the IRF Act had turned out. Even as the isolation of the ambassador's office within the human rights bureau became more and more evident in the years ahead, it was met with general indifference by those who might under different circumstances have taken action.

For Seiple, the blurred lines of authority became consequential only when it affected his capacity to do his job, which he saw in the beginning as one of raising the profile of religious persecution within the State Department and with the countries that practiced persecution. The department bureaucracy's labyrinthine ways began to encroach when it became clear that the "senior advisor to the secretary of state" (as he was styled in the months before he became ambassador) could not even send her a memorandum without the approval of others. This obstacle remained in place even after he was confirmed by the Senate as ambassador at large and as principal advisor to the secretary of state and the president on matters of religious freedom.

Because he was situated in a bureau headed by an assistant secretary, Seiple was instructed that he could not send his written views directly to Albright but must send them through Shattuck (and later Koh). Once again Seiple did not fight what he considered to be an absurd bureaucratic hiccup.[8] His reasoning was that he "did not mind Harold reading" his memos. This seemed a reasonable solution so long as Koh did not object or hold up Seiple's work. And, in fact, the relationship between the two men was strong enough that this arrangement did not present a serious problem.

But—like the placement of the office of international religious freedom in the human rights bureau—the bureaucratic precedent was to raise long-term obstacles for promoting religious freedom. It was not until 2005 that Seiple's successor as ambassador, John Hanford, was to win the right from the outgoing Colin Powell regime to communicate directly in writing to the secretary of state. It was a right that remained fragile at best under Powell's successor, Condoleezza Rice. The logic was not complicated: there was simply no reason that an official, no matter how senior under the enacting legislation, should have direct and regular access to a busy secretary of state if that official's portfolio had little to do with the major issues of American foreign policy.

An IRF Staff, or Else

Notwithstanding his confidence in himself, by December 1998, barely four months into the job, Bob Seiple was deeply frustrated. His staff consisted of a secretary and a part-time official, Alexandra Arriaga, who worked for Harold Koh but was on loan to Seiple. Arriaga was a primary mover behind the secretary's advisory committee on religious freedom. She was a smart and effective human rights advocate, but Seiple knew that he could not integrate the issue into U.S. foreign policy without a permanent staff, one that was substantially larger and worked exclusively for him.

For one thing, he was an aggressive traveler and saw a major part of his job as that of visiting the countries where persecution was rampant. He wanted to meet and understand the victims, size up the respective political and cultural environments, meet with NGOs and human rights and religious leaders, and—most important—begin developing fruitful relationships with high-level government officials with whom he could negotiate changes in policy. But such trips required careful planning and preparation, and the office would have to function during his absences. None of this was feasible without an effective staff.

Of more immediate concern was the fact that by the summer Seiple had to produce a huge and detailed report. The IRF Act, passed in October 1998, had required that the first *Annual Report on International Religious Freedom*, covering every country in the world, be presented to Congress by September 1999. A staff was already in place for doing the leg work—the reports office of the human rights bureau had for years produced the department's human rights reports. They knew how to take the drafts prepared by American embassies around the world, compile them, and edit them into a single report with a chapter for each country.

But the new religious freedom report would require more than collating and editing embassy drafts. There would inevitably be conflicts over wording and judgment, particularly since, under the law, the descriptions of religious persecution would form the basis for findings against countries who were "particularly severe violators" of religious freedom and against whom the imposition of sanctions would be considered. This was serious business, and Seiple could not simply hand the job over to Harold Koh's reports staff without any supervision or input from his own office. It was imperative that he quickly develop a permanent staff that was dedicated exclusively to the mission of promoting international religious freedom. But after four months on the job, he had no permanent staff and none on the horizon.

In December, Seiple went to Koh and told him that he was thinking of resigning. "I have no intention," he told the assistant secretary, "of presiding over a disaster." Soon the prospects of a permanent religious freedom staff began to emerge and Seiple was able to settle in to begin the job that the law had mandated him to do. Gradually, he turned the day-to-day operations over to his office and began to travel to the countries where the problems were. Within the next 18 months, he or his staff would visit some 40 countries, most of them the world's worst violators of religious freedom. Despite the prodigious obstacles that lay in his path, he began to lay the tracks for a potentially significant change in U.S. foreign policy—the systematic and effective engagement by American diplomacy of religion as a matter of U.S. national interests.

Evangelical and Catholic Fire

Some in the Christian community were suspicious of the Seiple appointment. As the IRF Act wended its way through Congress, they feared that he would be used by the administration to kill the sanctions provisions of the legislation. Some believed that he would be buried at the State Department in a high-profile but powerless position. In fact, Seiple was outspoken against the indiscriminate use of sanctions. He was known to favor "promotion, not punishment" as the best means of effective change. He was also a strong advocate for the use of prudence by Christian missionaries abroad. Although he acknowledged their right and their biblical responsibility to evangelize, he liked to point out that Jesus had given the Great Commandment ("love one another as I have loved you") before giving the Great Commission ("Go and make disciples of all nations").

Seiple's criticisms of ill-informed and culturally clueless American missionaries could be searing. He told the eminent evangelical magazine *Christianity Today* that Western missionaries who descended on Russia after the fall of the Soviet Union were like "the great Oklahoma land rush; everybody threw their Bibles in the back of their Conestoga wagons and came running." In his view, the callous actions of missionaries constituted "an assault on Russia" and reflected insensitivity to the Russian Orthodox Church. As a result, he said, the Orthodox Church partnered with the Russian government to pass laws restricting religious freedom, and it would take years to undo the damage.[9] Doubtless some in the evangelical community were offended by such views.

Seiple had also alienated some Christian leaders by refusing to sign letters in support of the Wolf-Specter bill, which he considered too blunt an instrument to be effective. He knew most of the participants of the campaign for Wolf-Specter led by Michael Horowitz. In 1996 he had signed a declaration of Christian leaders, on the subject of the American judiciary's usurpation of power, drafted by Wolf-Specter supporters Charles Colson and Father Richard John Neuhaus.[10] After his appointment at the State Department, Seiple met several times with Michael Horowitz, encounters that were not pleasant and established for both men the fact that they did not look at the world through the same window.

For Horowitz, Seiple represented the worst of all worlds. In a series of articles debating Seiple's two-year performance at the State Department, Horowitz later poured scorn on what he labeled as the envoy's "passive and risk averse approach to dealing with hard-core religious persecutors," an approach that he believed to be the natural mode of operation at the department.[11] For Seiple, Horowitz was the consummate showman, concerned as much for his own profile as for his product. Seiple had absolutely no use for the table-banging, bludgeon-brandishing methods employed by Horowitz, which he had put into the legislation he was supporting. Nor did he believe the issue should be politicized; a Republican who shared the general disdain for President Clinton's immoral behavior, he rejected any thought of using religious freedom as a partisan political issue.

As recounted in chapter 4, Horowitz and many of his supporters had abandoned Wolf-Specter during the summer of 1998, at about the time that Bob Seiple assumed his duties at the department. They had turned their attentions to strengthening the independent IRF Commission, which they had come to view as the one retrievable element of their campaign against religious persecution. Consequently, they saw the commission as the core of the International Religious Freedom Act.

In an extraordinary ploy to weaken the role to be played by Seiple and the Department of State in the Nickles bill, Horowitz in September persuaded a group of powerful evangelical leaders, including Colson, former Senator Bill Armstrong, Gary Bauer, and James Dobson, to send a letter to Senator Joseph Lieberman, a cosponsor of the bill. The letter urged that most of the functions assigned to the ambassador and the State Department in the IRF Act be transferred to the commission, in effect removing the need for an ambassador at large.[12] This was, of course, the very position that Seiple (now at the State Department as special advisor to the secretary) would assume as the head of the office of international religious freedom created by the IRF Act. The advice was rejected, but the letter was a telling example of the campaign's distrust of the Department of State and, among some, of Seiple himself.

The coalition's concerns about Seiple were typified in the reaction to an op-ed he published in December. The incident revealed much about the problems Seiple faced inside and outside the department. As originally drafted, the piece was a blunt indictment of those who persecuted on the basis of religion and an eloquent statement of Seiple's philosophy. It was vintage Seiple: tell the truth, give hope to the oppressed, emphasize forgiveness and reconciliation, and find ways to induce governments to value religious freedom. But few public documents emerge from Foggy Bottom as originally drafted, and certainly not an op-ed on the subject of religion. By the time the draft had been reworked by officials in the human rights bureau and elsewhere in the department, it had been considerably changed. It now asserted that the president and secretary of state had ensured that religious freedom was "a central element" of American foreign policy. It also implied that sanctions were in disfavor ("This Herculean objective will never be advanced as a result of unilateral measures by a single state....").[13]

Seiple did not like particularly like the revised edition, but he accepted it. When the op-ed appeared on Christmas Eve in the *Washington Times*, he received several critical letters from coalition supporters, alerted by Michael Horowitz. One, from Richard John Neuhaus, said the language of the piece "will surely be read by many as trade talk for business as usual." "[M]any people," the influential Catholic intellectual added, "went along with compromises and accommodations [in the law] because of their great confidence in your leadership."[14]

Blazing a Trail Outside Washington

Notwithstanding the difficulties emerging from inside and outside the State Department, by the spring of 1999 U.S. IRF policy was beginning to show signs of life. In May, Bob Seiple was sworn in as the first ambassador at large for international religious freedom. Gathering this time in the Roosevelt Room of the State Department was a huge crowd of supporters from Congress, the human rights community, and a wide variety of religious groups, including Christians, Muslims and others.

Secretary Madeline Albright was away and could not attend the ceremony. Her joking prediction to Margaret Ann Seiple the previous June—that Albright would see more of Bob than his wife would—had not materialized. In fact, Seiple had not met with the secretary at all during the ensuing year. But Albright was soon to play a vital role in Seiple's tenure. Later that summer she would review his recommendations on which countries should be designated for the first time under the law as "countries of particular concern" for particularly severe violations of religious freedom.

Before he made those recommendations, Seiple was determined to visit as many of the candidate countries as possible. His office staff, although still small, was at least growing and extremely capable. Perhaps most important, they worked for Seiple, not the assistant secretary for democracy, human rights, and labor. Seiple's deputy was a talented young foreign service officer named Henry Ensher, a Middle East hand who had already assisted his boss in arranging trips to China and Bosnia and had accompanied him to Saudi Arabia, Egypt, and Israel.

Ensher was on loan from the Bureau of Near Eastern Affairs for six months until a permanent replacement could be found. In addition, Jeremy Gunn, a lawyer, author, and powerful religious freedom advocate, had been detailed to Seiple's office by the U.S. Institute of Peace. And Seiple had convinced the Department of Defense to detail a chaplain to him for two years, a U.S. Navy Serbian Orthodox priest, Milan Sturgis. These three were to provide staffing until a permanent staff could be recruited and brought on board.

These officers and their successors could not help noticing that the ambassador was an aggressive traveler who eschewed easy schedules and comfortable meals. In what became affectionately known by his staff as "combat travel," Seiple's trips were frequent and the pace was sometimes brutal. Between January and July, he made five separate trips to China and Indonesia, Russia, Uzbekistan and Kazakstan, Vietnam and Laos, and finally Austria, Belgium, Germany, and France. He disliked the delays that often attended checked baggage, so he would manage a week or ten-day trip out of a single carry-on bag. Remarkably, he would emerge each morning from his hotel room clean, pressed, and ready for action. His staff sometimes wondered whether they were working for an American diplomat or a U.S. marine with a suit that refused to wrinkle.

This initial round of trips was designed to convince foreign governments that America's new policy was a serious matter and must be taken seriously by persecuting governments. Seiple wanted to convey to his interlocutors that he had the authority to recommend U.S. sanctions against their respective governments and would do so if necessary. But he also wanted them to know that they could trust his word and should work with him. No matter how despicable their policies, it did little good for their victims or for U.S. policy if foreign officials refused to meet with the ambassador or to discuss potential changes in policy.

As already noted, this approach was something that some members of the campaign for Wolf-Specter did not accept. They favored punishment, or the threat of it. But, Seiple reasoned, simply punishing persecuting governments could worsen the plight of the victims by triggering more abuse. Sanctions could also cut off any possibility of negotiated changes in policy that might prevent future abuses and secure long-term protections for religious freedom. Seiple believed that a combination of carrots and sticks might help him negotiate changes, and he was glad to have the threat of sanctions as a means of getting the attention of persecuting governments. But if governments would not talk to him, he was convinced, sanctions would do little good and could deepen the problem he wanted to resolve.

In January 1999 he traveled to Beijing, where he met with religious leaders and key government actors, including the head of the Religious Affairs Bureau, Ye Xiaowen. Ye was an ex–military official who had the reputation of being a committed atheist in charge of religion in China. (Seiple wryly labeled him "O Ye of little faith.") Ye was a serious infighter in the Communist party who had positioned himself as gatekeeper to changes in China's religion policy. He made it clear in his meetings with Seiple that change would be painfully slow, if it was to occur at all. Indeed, his central message was that there were no serious religious problems in China, and that no one was in prison for his or her religious beliefs or practices.

Struck by the recalcitrance of Ye and other Chinese officials, Seiple returned to Washington and began seriously to contemplate the possibility of recommending that Secretary Albright designate China as a "country of particular concern" under the new law.[15] He knew that some countries would not be difficult to designate, such as Sudan, which had occasioned much passion in the Christian and human rights communities, and which Seiple often called "the poster child of religious persecution." Others were not likely to be challenged at the State Department either—such as Iraq, where Shiite religious leaders were routinely tortured and murdered by Saddam Hussein, or Iran, where the Baha'i were subject to terrible persecution. These were the obvious candidates, and Seiple did not anticipate significant resistance within the department to their designation.

China, however, was another matter. President Clinton had made improving the U.S.-China relationship a centerpiece of his foreign policy. He was fighting for (and later won in Congress) the designation of China as a country with "most favored nation" (MFN) trade status with the United States. This action decreased the statutory requirement for human rights scrutiny but was defended by the president and his advisers as good for human rights. U.S. exporters, keenly aware of the huge market that China presented, naturally favored the change. The human rights community, including religious rights advocates, were split on the matter, which is why the administration's policy ultimately passed in Congress.

Opponents of permanent MFN status for China, which included many in the Wolf-Specter coalition, believed the concession to be unconscionable and that it would communicate to Beijing that the United States was abandoning human rights in favor of business. Others, however, argued that increased U.S.-China trade would benefit human rights in the long run, as would admitting China to the World Trade Organization. According to this argument, participation in the WTO would require adherence to international rules of conduct with labor and business and would help habituate the Chinese to international human rights standards. Over the longer term, the growth of capitalism and an entrepreneurial class would help destroy the vestiges of Communism that continued to fuel human rights abuses.

Whatever the rights and wrongs of the Clinton policy, one thing was certain: the East Asian and Pacific bureau of the State Department, and their counterparts on the staff of the National Security Council, would fiercely resist the designation of China as a country of particular concern under the new religious freedom law. From their point of view, a public, unilateral condemnation of China by the United States would seriously complicate the administration's policy of strategic partnership with Beijing. Even worse would be the imposition of economic sanctions, permitted (although not required) under the International Religious Freedom Act. Far better to continue working behind the scenes on human rights issues as they arose and to seek multilateral cooperation for a China resolution in the United Nations Human Rights Committee.

The Battle over China

The International Religious Freedom Act had established a high standard for designation as a country of particular concern: a government must have been guilty during the previous 12 months of causing or tolerating "systematic, ongoing and egregious" violations of religious freedom, such as rape, torture, forced conversions, or the deprivation of fundamental liberties on the basis of religion. Once a country had been designated by the secretary of state, she would then need to choose from a menu of "actions" to take against that country, a menu that included everything from a waiver of all action to the imposition of serious economic sanctions.[16]

Seiple was careful in his assessment of whether a given government met the legal standard. He argued before Congress that the "spirit of the law" required him to consider the *impact* of designation on the victims of persecution. The chairman of the House subcommittee on human rights, Chris Smith (R, New Jersey), among others, rejected this interpretation and insisted that the designation process should simply constitute a finding of fact. Considerations of the impact on victims, he argued, must come after designation when the State Department is deciding what actions are to be taken. Those considerations should not be part of the designation decision itself, which should rely exclusively on the question of whether a government met the standard established by the law.

Seiple's broader interpretation of the designation process would later lead him to resist adding countries to the CPC list that he believed were making progress. For example, in 2000 he employed the threat of designating Uzbekistan to win the release by that government of a significant number of religious prisoners, a move that brought both praise and criticism from human rights and faith-based groups. But when it came to China, Seiple was convinced by his trip that the combination of Beijing's resistance to changing its policies and the dismal status of the victims warranted designation.

He knew that unrecognized Protestant "house church" leaders and underground Catholic priests were routinely rounded up and imprisoned, sometimes for months or longer. Some were abused and tortured. The year before Seiple had traveled to China, a Catholic bishop, Su Zhimin, had disappeared after celebrating mass during a visit from Congressman Smith. In Tibet, Buddhists who publicly revered the Dalai Lama risked imprisonment and worse. In Xinjiang province, peaceful Uighur Muslims were subject to similar abuse because of suspicions of insurrection. Seiple concluded from his discussions with Ye Xiaowen and other Chinese officials that there was little chance of significant movement on religious prisoners, much less on more systemic changes. He decided to get China's attention by fighting within the State Department for its designation as a CPC.

By this time (summer 1999) I had replaced Henry Ensher as Seiple's deputy. As we began to discuss the prospect of designating China, Seiple and I were struck by the resistance we encountered from State Department and NSC officials charged with managing the overall U.S.- China relationship. New to the issue, I had mildly hoped that the facts of Chinese persecution would speak for themselves, and that the discussion would center on what action if any should follow in the wake of designation. Instead, we discovered that State Department and NSC China officials were prepared to argue the issue on its legal merits and to fight hard against designating China.

One argument was, incongruously, that the level of persecution simply did not meet the high legal bar of "systematic, ongoing and egregious persecution." Last-minute disputes over the China chapter of the *Annual Report on International Religious Freedom* revealed part of this tactic. One evening I found myself in the office of a deputy assistant secretary of the Bureau of East Asian and Pacific Affairs addressing the bureau's insistence that we use the word "harassment" rather than "torture" for what was visited on disfavored Chinese religious leaders. In the precincts of Foggy Bottom, words, like ideas, have consequences, especially when statutory imperatives are involved.

But the central argument employed by the bureau and its China desk was one we would hear often at the department, and not just from our China experts: the persecution that undeniably existed in China was not fundamentally religious in nature but was, in fact, political. Tibetan Buddhists, Uighur Muslims, and Chinese Christians were opposed by the government not because of their religion, but because they represented a political threat to the Communist regime. Accordingly, there was no legal basis for designating China a country of particular concern under the religious freedom statute.

This argument rested, like many good legal arguments, on a half truth. (As we shall see, I was to hear another version of this argument from a high official in the department after Seiple's departure.) There was little question that Chinese officials feared the political effects of religious devotion. But neither Tibetan culture nor the actions of Tibetan dissidents can be understood apart from the religion that is Tibet's defining characteristic. The fact that Chinese authorities believe their country's unity threatened by the devotion of Tibetans to an exiled religious leader with political significance, the Dalai Lama, does not diminish the character of their abuse of Tibetans.

That there are nonreligious factors contributing to acts of persecution, not only political but ethnic and economic, does not change the fundamental nature of the acts themselves. When people are abused by their government because their peaceful religious beliefs and practices have political consequences and are considered politically threatening, that is religious persecution. Part of the problem at work here was the inability of diplomats to accept that there are legitimate political manifestations of religious belief. To this day, such attitudes pose an obstacle to American diplomacy's engagement with a world of public faith.

The issue is more complex, but still essentially the same, for Chinese Uighur Muslims. Ethnic Chinese Hui Muslims are controlled but generally free of persecution and live in various locations around the country. The Uighurs, however, are concentrated and isolated in northwest China, just across the border from India, Pakistan, and various central Asian republics. As a result, the Uighurs are carefully watched by Chinese authorities, who suspect them of insurrectionist and terrorist activities. And in fact there have been Uighurs involved in terrorism, including a few in transnational Islamist terror.

U.S. IRF policy does not, of course, provide any warrant for violence, much less terrorism. But we have seen over and over again—in places such as China, Uzbekistan, and even France—that pious Muslims are wrongly stigmatized as potential terrorists because of the presence of extremists in their midst. In China and Uzbekistan, this has resulted in the abuse of innocents. All the more important that the United States, especially as part of its own war against religion-based terror, stand with those who are wrongfully punished. This means not only standing for their right not to be tortured and abused, but also their right as religious people to have an impact on the rules and laws under which they live.

The State Department's China experts made a similar argument that the government's abuse of Chinese Christians, especially Catholics, was more political than religious. They pointed out, quite correctly, that Christianity in general was growing rapidly in China and had done so since the 1960s and 1970s, when it was almost destroyed during the horrors of the Cultural Revolution. Clearly it was Christianity's rapid and sustained growth that discomfited the Chinese government; it feared any movement it could not control. This anxiety was to become jarringly clear when a Chinese health movement with spiritual overtones, Falun Gong, seemed suddenly to pop up from nowhere in the late 1990s, commanding the allegiances of millions. The government's reaction was vicious and immediate. Thousands were imprisoned and hundreds were tortured, some to death.

By contrast, the State Department's China experts noted, the various official organizations set up to manage Christian groups—the Protestant "Three Self Movement" and the Catholic "Patriotic Association"—were not inherently persecutory. Like the other arguments, this one contained a grain of truth. Millions of Chinese Protestants and Catholics did in fact worship in peace within the officially sanctioned religious organizations. The problem was, of course, that millions more refused to acknowledge or join the official organizations, and thus became "house church" Protestants or "underground" Catholics. It was these Christians, and especially their clergy, that were all too frequently the victims of persecution.

In fact, however, the actions of these unofficial "dissident" Christians rested on perfectly clear and nonthreatening theological grounds. Protestant denominations worldwide have historically resisted government management of their affairs while remaining loyal citizens. Chinese Protestants were not in any way involved in anti-government activities, except to resist government control over their religious affairs. But Chinese officials feared Protestantism because they could not understand its theologically decentralized character. They did not know how to determine who was in charge.

Catholics, on the other hand, often rejected the authority of the Catholic Patriotic Association because they could not accept Beijing's appointment of bishops without papal approval. Chinese officials feared Roman Catholicism because it was manifestly a western import and because its leader (Pope John Paul II) had played a personal role in the destruction of Communism in Eastern Europe.

During the summer of 1999 these and other arguments were placed before Secretary Madeline Albright so that she might review the candidates for the U.S. government's first designations of countries of particular concern under the IRF Act. Because this was the first review, Albright was quite concerned about the implications of the designations, especially China. At the outset of the discussions, one of Albright's aides told Seiple that he had a 10 percent chance of convincing her to designate Beijing.

Outside the department, virtually no one expected that China would be on the list. Steven McFarland, executive director of the U.S. Commission on International Religious Freedom, told the Associated Press that the commission had "already drafted a press release objecting to [State's] failure to single out China."[17] He added that he hoped it would not have to be used, but his expectations were typical of those who were skeptical of the administration's willingness to use the law in what it viewed as a critical relationship. Pariah states with which the United States had no serious relations, such as Sudan, Iran, Iraq, and Burma, were all expected to be named, but not China.

As it happened, Albright was to make a long trip in early September that would conclude in New Zealand. There she would meet with Asian leaders, including the Chinese. During the first Washington meeting on designations, which occurred in August, she expressed exasperation that she was being asked to make such an important decision so quickly. Seiple understood her dilemma and decided not to pressure her. Wait until you return, he told her, and we will revisit the issue.

While Albright traveled, Seiple worked hard to overcome the resistance he knew existed within the building and at the National Security Council. Lacking any natural allies at the Clinton White House, he drew on his growing relationship with the first chairman of the Commission on International Religious Freedom, Rabbi David Saperstein. Saperstein was well known and respected in liberal Democratic circles and had supported both the Wolf-Specter and Nickles bills. He contacted National Security Advisor Sandy Berger to tell him how important the China designation would be as a sign of the administration's seriousness about religious freedom.

At the same time, Seiple sent Albright a memo while she was traveling—duly channeled through Assistant Secretary Harold Koh—that presented the arguments for designating China and others. Others in the building provided a fierce counter argument that China's designation would harm U.S. interests and that China's behavior did not meet the standards established in the law. When Albright returned, she convened another meeting and announced her decision. It was a clear victory for Seiple: China would be on the list. Other designees were Iran, Iraq, Sudan, and Burma. Two regimes not recognized as governments by the United States were identified as well: those of Slobodan Milosevic in Serbia and the Taliban of Afghanistan. Laura Bryant, staffer for Congressman Bob Clement (D, Tennessee) and a primary drafter of the International Religious Freedom Act, later told Seiple that she was stunned that he had won the battle over China.

Reinforcements Arrive

I joined Bob Seiple's staff in June 1999, just in time to participate in the process of designating countries of particular concern and of putting together the first *Annual Report on International Religious Freedom*. During the previous year I had been only dimly aware of Seiple's appointment and of the battle that was raging in Congress over IRF legislation. In perusing the positions available for the summer of 1999, my eye stopped on a phrase I had never seen on a State Department job list: "religion." Ambassador Seiple was looking for a replacement for Henry Ensher as his deputy in the office of international religious freedom. After looking into Seiple's background, which I found intriguing, I went for an interview. I wondered whether his West Coast evangelical sensibilities would jibe with my own southern-fed Roman Catholicism.

As I strolled down the rear corridor of the State Department's seventh floor to meet Ambassador Seiple in his office, it was pretty clear that if he wanted me and I took the job, it would be unlike any other I had encountered in my sixteen-year foreign service career. This office, unavoidably, would have to involve itself explicitly and directly in the religious motivations and purposes of individuals and groups, as well as of governments that were both allies and adversaries of the United States.

Seiple's deputy would be required to make the case that religion, as well as religious freedom, actually warranted a distinct niche in U.S. foreign policy. I knew that many of my colleagues, whether out of secularist sensitivities or just good sense, would avoid the job for these very reasons. Many would consider it a move that, to put it mildly, would not be a "career enhancer." I decided I would accept this risk, which I knew was a real one. But I was also intrigued by the opportunity to do something really new in the foreign service. And the truth is that I relished the chance to observe and develop the policy implications of religious liberty.

As I entered Bob Seiple's office, it quickly became clear that I needn't have been concerned about our compatibility. I was sporting a modest beard that matched my gray hair, and when we shook hands, Seiple greeted me spontaneously with some risky words. "Robert E. Lee!" he exclaimed with a gleeful smile that I was to come to know well. It occurred to me afterward that either he had done his homework and knew that I was a proud southerner or he was capable of an off-the-cuff political incorrectness that might get him into trouble in the politically correct precincts of Foggy Bottom.

I have never asked him about this, but either explanation is plausible. Seiple is a man of considerable learning who works hard to prepare for important tasks. But he also possesses an impish delight in personal humor, which, despite its risks in the professional world, he regularly employs with remarkable effectiveness. In his final meeting with Madeline Albright, he imparted a colorful warning about the new IRF Commission, which was just completing its first year of operation: "Date them," he told a laughing secretary of state, "and let them take you home, but don't let them kiss you."

The U.S. Commission on International Religious Freedom

Seiple's warning about the commission reflected more than a bold sense of humor. He had succeeded in developing a relationship of trust and candor with the commission's first chairman, Rabbi David Saperstein. That relationship had helped reduce White House opposition to Seiple's recommendation that China be designated a country of particular concern and helped ensure that the relationships between Commission staff and Seiple's staff were strong and largely productive.

But by the end of his tenure at State, Seiple had become extremely wary of the commission's role in America's new international religious freedom policy. Two years later, having observed its work in the interim, he would publicly call for its dismantlement by Congress.[18] In retrospect, such a position may seem harsh until it is viewed against the appropriate standards: the commission's purpose and its performance.

Designed to last for four years as an external check on the State Department's well-known ability to bury congressional initiatives it didn't like, the commission substantially failed to carry out this mission. Although it did increase the pressure on the Clinton and Bush administrations on a number of religious freedom issues and had considerable impact in a few, such as Sudan and Iraq, its work did little to alter what had been always been, and remained, the department's ad hoc approach to the issue of religious persecution and its desire to avoid altogether the systematic promotion of religious freedom.

Rather than work to change that pattern, which would have required a sustained advocacy aimed at rooting the new policy into the culture of Foggy Bottom, the commission decided that the standard of success for America's new international religious freedom policy was less the performance of the State Department, or its new office of international religious freedom, than the performance of the commission itself. It and its supporters were so convinced of the commission's importance that they secured the repeal of the four-year sunset clause. The U.S. commission became, for all intents and purposes, a permanent institution.[19]

In its earlier drafts, the IRF Act had placed the ambassador at large in the commission chair, but the final version made him a nonvoting, ex officio member with little official influence. The goal was to ensure the commission's independence from the State Department, but also to ensure that the ambassador and the commission talked to each other. Independence from the State Department, however, was sealed less by this device than by the direct annual appropriation from Congress. This funding mechanism took a while to set in place; the IRF Act only provided for an authorization to fund, rather than an actual appropriation. But the chairman of the Appropriations Subcommittee over State Department spending was Frank Wolf (of Wolf-Specter). Although Mr. Wolf did not in the beginning seek funding for the IRF Office in the State Department, he ensured that the commission received an annual appropriation of $3 million.[20] (Later he would be directly responsible for a significant increase in IRF office staffing.)

As noted, Bob Seiple soured on the role of the U.S. Commission on International Religious Freedom. My own concerns about that institution, expressed in the previous chapter, are largely different from Bob Seiple's concerns. He did not like the commission's "watchdog role" and its habit of "cursing the darkness." He wanted the commission to work in tandem with the State Department and not to criticize it openly. He resented the lack of trust such criticism implied (and his successor has shared those concerns).

Seiple's view of the commission tends to confirm that he never quite accepted the need to transform the department's bureaucratic culture. A man of fierce independence, he never perceived the commission as anything other than another agency that ought to be helping the overall mission, not critiquing it. He believed that any shortcomings that existed at the State Department were his charge, not the commission's. Unfortunately, that approach—combined with the overall indifference of the Bush administration to the position of ambassador at large—left his successor in the lurch.

Assessing the Seiple Years: The Camel's Nose

The ultimate assessment of Bob Seiple's two years (1998–2000) as the first ambassador at large for international religious freedom must await the emergence of a more complete understanding of the policy's fate. If the United States manages to integrate religious freedom more successfully into its foreign policy, Seiple will deserve a considerable amount of the credit. But it is reasonable to make some preliminary observations now, a decade after the passage of the IRF Act and the beginning of his two-year tenure at the State Department.

In many ways, Seiple was a brilliant choice by the Clinton administration for the first ambassador at large. His record of exceptional personal accomplishment also reflected a life lived for others. A family man with a reputation for integrity, he was a proud Republican and a devout Christian. Small wonder that President Clinton himself, under siege in the Lewinski scandal, wanted this man on his team.

The problem was that there was to be no religious freedom "team" at the Clinton White House or at the Albright State Department, except for Seiple and his staff. The new ambassador quickly learned that he was being set loose to fend for himself, nested deep in the department's bureaucracy, where he had little authority and few resources. Typically, he took this not as a slight on him or the issue he championed, but as a challenge to be addressed as best he could.

Other than his early threat to resign if he did not get a dedicated staff (a reasonable place to draw the line by any standard), he made the decision not to complain. When no one asked him questions or evinced any interest in religious freedom for its own sake in the regular senior staff meetings convened by Deputy Secretary of State Talbott, Seiple did not seek to change the dynamic in those meetings or to intrude upon the agenda set by the department's senior leadership. His decision to remain in the background both enabled and handicapped the work of the religious freedom office in its first two years.

If Bob Seiple saw himself as the vanguard of a new and potentially effective element of American foreign policy, he concluded after several months that he could not successfully pursue his mandate by altering structures at the State Department. Lacking the authority or the resources to transform the department's culture, he took his mission where he thought he could do the most good, that is, outside the United States. During his two years as ambassador at large, he spent almost as much time away from his office as in it. He and his staff traveled widely and encountered directly the worst abusers of human freedom in the world. It was here, in the governmental laboratories of discrimination and abuse, that he made his mark and where his legacy remains.

It is one of this book's arguments that "success" in American international religious freedom policy cannot primarily be measured by case work. As anyone who has worked in this field can attest, the freeing of a prisoner or the saving of a family from persecution can be the single most gratifying element of the IRF mission. That kind of success serves to remind that there are real people at the end of national policies, flesh-and-blood human beings whose lives and well-being are, or ought to be, precious to those of us who grind the wheels of bureaucracies. But saving individuals cannot be the core of our international religious freedom policy. It does little or nothing to change the behavior of governments or the cultures that sustain persecution. It does little or nothing to create the conditions for durable democracy or carry the fight against religion-based terrorism.

Seiple understood these arguments but did not wholly accept them. His training and instincts led him to focus on getting prisoners out of jail, which he did with remarkable success. Hundreds of Christians, Muslims, Buddhists, Hoa Hao (Vietnamese), and others were freed from terrible conditions as a direct result of his personal interventions in places such as Uzbekistan, Vietnam, Laos, and Saudi Arabia. These people were freed for a single reason: Bob Seiple was persistent, trusted, and respected by the government officials he convinced to act.

Contrary to the criticisms of his detractors, Ambassador Seiple was not an easy touch. I was present at a meeting between him and the Laotian Ambassador at the State Department in which Seiple described with bluntness the sanctions that could result if the Laotian Government failed to prevent the forced conversions that were occurring in some provinces and to release religious prisoners from jail. The ambassador went to work within his own government channels. Within weeks, prisoners were freed. Over the next few years, the numbers of forced conversions began to decrease, although they periodically returned with the change of local and national officials.

This problem—the fragility of positive changes that occur because of short-term relationships as opposed to cultural and political acceptance of change—returns us to what is perhaps the central obstacle to be overcome in U.S. religious freedom policy. Persecution can and does occur at the whim of tyrants, local or national, but it often is the result of deeper cultural practices, resentments, and institutions. Changing the structures of persecution is long-term work. It is not secured merely by the convincing of ambassadors or even of national leaders. A society must be convinced that institutions of religious liberty are consistent with its worldview, and governments must conclude that the religious beliefs and practices of all citizens must be protected and nourished.

Again, Bob Seiple understood these arguments. Indeed, his work since leaving the State Department in September 2000 has amply demonstrated, in places such as Laos and Vietnam, his own determination to build new structures from the bottom up.[21] If his work at the department can be criticized, it is that he did not plant the bureaucratic seeds that might have grown more rapidly under his successors. He might, for example, have made the case that the IRF office should be directly under the Secretary of State, as the law seemed to require, or that his position should not be viewed as subordinate to that of the assistant secretary of democracy, human rights, and labor. He simply did not see it that way.

Nor did his background or temperament dispose him to fight the internal battles such initiatives would have required. His utter disdain for the backbiting, often dishonest culture of Washington, D.C., a culture not absent from Foggy Bottom, was part of his charm and his personal effectiveness. That disdain, in part, led him to decide that two years as ambassador was enough for any sane person, and that after the second *Annual Report on International Religious Freedom* was released in September 2000, he would kick the dust from his heels and leave the nation's capital.

One further legacy merits mention. In 1998 Ambassador Seiple created a regular confab of American Muslims, which he called "the Islamic Roundtable." This was almost three years before the events of 9/11, but Seiple knew that the religion and culture of Islam would play an enormous role in the success or failure of American international religious freedom advocacy. He wanted to learn more about the religion and to reach out to Muslims of good will who, he felt, should know of his efforts. He developed strong relationships with a number of Muslims, including Laila al Marayati of the IRF Commission and Sheikh Hisham Kabbani of the Islamic Supreme Council of America.

These two Muslim leaders were very different in the way that they practiced their religion and in their political views. Dr. Al Marayati was a physician, mother, and powerful spokeswoman for Muslim women. She would later travel with a commission delegation to Saudi Arabia, the sole woman on the trip and the only Muslim. Sheikh Kabbani was a Sufi who moved comfortably in conservative Washington circles because of his biting criticism of some American Muslims who he said were soft on terrorism. Both liked Seiple and listened carefully to what he had to say. He was what he appeared to be—a man of deep religious convictions who respected them for who they were.

In the wake of 9/11, which occurred a year after Seiple's departure, the Islamic Roundtable emerged as the only regular venue at the State Department where Muslims and American foreign policy officials could meet. As such, it was one of his most important legacies. But like other opportunities, this one was only minimally exploited by the Colin Powell State Department. In the end, its association with the office of international religious freedom was too problematic. That factor, combined with the priorities of the next ambassador, permitted the Roundtable to fade into oblivion, an opportunity missed by an institution whose short-sightedness on matters of religion seemed to have few limits.

6

⁂

Interregnum (2000–2002)

The methodology of foreign policy...is that we must be gardeners and not mechanics....We must [act]...gently and patiently, not trying to force growth by mechanical means, not tearing up the plants by the roots when they fail to behave as we wish them to. The forces of nature will generally be on the side of him who understands them best and respects them most scrupulously.
                                        —George F. Kennan, 1954

A diplomat is someone who can tell you to go to hell in such a way that you actually look forward to the trip.
                                        —Caskie Stinnett, 1960[1]

The Bush-Gore presidential election of 2000 was by all accounts a wrenching experience for the nation. The drama of uncertainty, centered in the Florida recounts and the ultimate recourse to the courts, riveted the country's attention until George W. Bush was finally declared president-elect on December 12, 2000, almost five weeks later than the norm. The delay left the Bush team just over a month to prepare for the transfer of power, scant time to sift through thousands of résumés for the political appointments to be filled by the incoming president. Both campaigns had been focused on winning the election, and it was perhaps understandable that some of the administration's political appointments were late in coming.

What happened with the naming of Bob Seiple's replacement as the ambassador at large for international religious freedom, however, conveyed an unexpected and troubling signal from the new president's team. It has become a staple of American punditry that George W. Bush has drawn upon his religious

161

convictions more than any other president in modern history. The stories are legion and generally well known. Asked during the 2000 presidential campaign about his "favorite philosopher," Bush said that it was Jesus who "changed my heart." One of his earliest actions as president was the faith-based initiative, which sought to remove what he believed were unconstitutional obstacles to the use of public monies by religion-based charitable organizations.

Later, when asked whether he had consulted his father, former president George H. W. Bush, about plans for invading Iraq, the president responded that he had consulted his heavenly father. Such public religiosity occasioned disdain from Bush's opponents, including many in the press. One memorable reaction was that of Ron Reagan, son of the late president, whose public eulogy at his father's funeral included a bitter criticism of George Bush for using God as a "mandate" for engaging in an unjust war in Iraq.[2]

Few would disagree that President Bush was genuinely motivated by his religious beliefs and that they had a discernible impact on his behavior as president. The deep division among Americans about the propriety of his motivations is in part explained by the development in recent decades of the concept of a wall of separation between church and state. As we have noted, that wall has become, for many, a constitutional barrier against the effects of religiously grounded judgments about the common good.

Although President Bush may have evoked his faith more consistently than other modern chief executives, scholars of American religion and of the presidency have pointed out that his employment of the language of faith is not unusual among American presidents in general, especially during wartime. According to this view, Bush stands well within the traditions of American history in his choice of words and actions.[3]

Unfortunately for us in the office of international religious freedom, we were soon to learn that the new president's strong religious views had few if any policy implications for the position established by law as "principal advisor to the president" on international religious freedom. As events were to show, the White House not only failed to treat the job as a senior policy position once it was filled, but deemed it so unimportant that it was left vacant for a solid year beyond the norm for even less senior State Department positions. This indifference on the part of a Republican administration thought to have a serious interest in advancing religious freedom simply reinforced Foggy Bottom's long-established habit of resisting unwanted congressional mandates.

The Bush team took over on January 20, 2001. By late spring or early summer most of the senior State Department officials—assistant secretaries and higher—had been nominated, confirmed by the Senate, and had assumed their jobs, including the new Assistant Secretary for Democracy, Human Rights, and Labor (DRL) Lorne Craner. But the IRF ambassador's nomination did not emerge from the White House until the end of September, more than a year after Seiple's departure. Had the nominee been confirmed immediately by the

Senate, his arrival at the State Department would still have been late in the day but not excessively so. As it happened, however, the new ambassador (John Hanford) did not assume his position until May 2002, at which point the position had been vacant for almost 20 months.

In the next chapter we explore the reasons for this unfortunate delay and the effects it had on the new, still fragile, American religious freedom policy. As we will see, although there were several unrelated factors involved in the delay, they could have been overcome had the policy of advancing religious freedom been taken seriously by the new administration. The ambassador's appointment and the function it represented were simply not viewed as important enough to treat as significant to the conduct of U.S. foreign policy, let alone to the protection of U.S. national security.

At Seiple's departure there were five of us remaining in the office of international religious freedom. I had no way of knowing that the next 20 months would be the most difficult, and the most exhilarating, period of my career. Before Seiple's replacement arrived, we would encounter various obstacles, including an attempt to absorb the ambassador's position into the DRL assistant secretary's portfolio. When that gambit failed, we found ourselves engaged in a constant struggle to prevent the office from becoming a minor cog in the wheels of the DRL bureau, an organization of dedicated individuals who, despite their determined efforts and the justice of their cause, had long constituted the least influential bureau in the Department of State.

In the end the IRF office, and the IRF function, survived, in part as a result of the work of a handful of people in the department, on the IRF Commission, and on the Hill. Our "enemy" at Foggy Bottom, let it be said, was not so much hostility to our mission as indifference to, or confusion about, the policy value of religious freedom. There were those, to be sure, who continued to resent the IRF Act and the office as an imposition of the religious right or even the vanguard of American theocracy. Such views were sometimes disproportionately influential, but they still constituted a minority. A more common attitude was that religious freedom is a human right like all others and, as such, merits no more policy effort than other human rights, and less than some. The latter view stemmed from a sense that religion causes more problems than other human endeavors. In this context promoting religious freedom means, as much as anything else, protecting people from religion.

As it turned out, indifference and confusion proved every bit as corrosive as outright opposition.

The Albright Regime Departs

When the Supreme Court's December 12 decision (*Bush v. Gore*) made it clear that George W. Bush was the new president of the United States, an audible groan could be heard within the department's DRL bureau. Conversations during the Florida recounts reflected a sense of outrage among many that the Republicans were stealing the election. A grim joke circulated, not entirely in jest, that the bureau should call for a UN investigation of human rights abuses in Florida.

Farewells to the Clinton political appointees in DRL that December were sad and heartfelt, as if a team were being tragically dismantled prior to having accomplished its mission. Most of the departures were indeed an occasion for sadness, even among those few of us who were frustrated by the Clinton team's resistance to a broader and more effective religious freedom advocacy. Since Bob Seiple's resignation the previous September I had served as interim head of the IRF office. During the remaining months of the Albright regime I had grown closer to the bureau's leadership, especially Assistant Secretary Harold Koh. Despite real differences between us it was difficult not to like and respect Koh, an eloquent defender of human rights and a very decent man.[4]

Koh's departure left a veteran foreign service officer, Michael Parmly, in charge of the human rights bureau during the transition from the Clinton to Bush administrations. Until Koh's replacement arrived, Parmly served as acting assistant secretary and by mutual agreement my own supervisor, given the absence of any other discernible chain of command. For those five months, from January through May of 2001, we had a close and largely cooperative relationship, both of us awaiting new bosses and hoping that the Bush administration would do well by our respective foreign policy mandates. Parmly readily approved our travel plans for the office staff and supported my trip to Egypt and Saudi Arabia in January (chapter 8). When I made a rather harrowing two-week trip to China (chapter 10), despite the opposition of the Chinese government, Mike Parmly was extremely helpful. Upon my return he sent my trip report around the building and, after I had briefed staffers and members of Congress about the trip, repeated the findings in testimony before the Congressional Human Rights Caucus.

Neither Parmly nor I, of course, had any way of knowing that his new assistant secretary, Lorne Craner, would take office in early June whereas my own tenure as acting head of U.S. IRF policy would continue for another year. That year proved to be one of dramatic change in international affairs and of America's perception of her place in the world. During that interregnum the nation would not only experience a new president, secretary of state and a new Republican team at Foggy Bottom, but also would endure the attacks of September 11, 2001. Unfortunately, from inside the department, we also witnessed a widening gap between the promise and the implementation of America's international religious freedom policy.

As the election campaign heated up in the fall of 2000, my own expectations had been high. No matter which party won the election, I thought, the future of the religious freedom office seemed secure. Ambassador Seiple had for some time planned to depart his position after two years on the job, leaving me to head the office during the fall and in the early months of the new administration while a new ambassador at large was nominated and confirmed by the Senate.

Seiple and I expected that the victors, whether Democrat or Republican, would move quickly on that score. Both George Bush and Al Gore were said to be personally interested in religious freedom. Gore's running mate, Senator Joe Lieberman, had been a co-sponsor of the 1998 IRF Act and had during his debate with Republican vice presidential candidate Dick Cheney cited that law as one of his most important accomplishments as a Senator. Even amid the rancor of the fall recounts and Supreme Court decision, I remained optimistic about U.S. international religious freedom policy and relished the opportunity to lead the office until its new captain emerged.

Because I expected that any interregnum in the IRF function would last no more than a few months and the new ambassador would be in place by the spring, my initial goals were modest. I sought to maintain the profile of the office at home and abroad and to maintain key relationships on the Hill and with the U.S. Commission on International Religious Freedom. Within the department, however, Seiple's experience strongly suggested that maintaining the status quo would be a challenge even for a few months. My job would be that of ensuring the autonomy of the office and the position of ambassador at large and to be prepared for his or her arrival. Determined that our new boss would hit the ground running, we prepared a conceptual schedule of ambassadorial activities for the first eight months on the job. Despite the difficulties he had encountered, Bob Seiple had laid the groundwork for expanding America's ambitious new international religious freedom policy. My task was to ensure that the ground remained in place and was well maintained for his successor.

Our staff's travel schedule for the months after Seiple's departure was intentionally heavy. We considered it vital for key governments around the world to understand that U.S. religious freedom policy did not stop with that departure or with the change of administrations. Accordingly, we planned the aforementioned visits to the Middle East and China, as well as to Vietnam, a country which, along with Saudi Arabia, remained a lively candidate for designation as a "country of particular concern" (CPC) under the IRF Act. We also scheduled a trip to the Vatican, Austria, and Belgium in order to gauge the breadth of the problems of religious intolerance we had already discerned in Paris and feared were brewing elsewhere in Western Europe. Other members of the staff traveled to Pakistan, Tibet, Indonesia, Russia, Azerbaijan, Georgia, Belarus, Uzbekistan, and Nigeria.

As important as these trips abroad were, we also realized that it was vital to maintain and increase the support of the American public for U.S. policy. It had now been over two years since the passage of the IRF Act. Many who were involved in the legislative campaign had lost touch with the office, and I was convinced that the vast majority of the American people had no idea we even existed. Accordingly, we gave talks at college campuses, academic conferences, military schools, civic organizations, and the like, all over America. We also tried to continue Ambassador Seiple's American Islamic Roundtable and to extend it to American Buddhists and Hindus, with plans for Jews, Orthodox, and other religious communities. What I learned in these encounters, as we shall see, was almost as valuable as my discussions with the victims and the perpetrators in overseas dens of persecution.

A New Assistant Secretary Arrives

"It will take about two weeks to size each of you up. Once I make up my mind about someone, it will take a good deal to change it." As I listened to Lorne Craner in his first meeting with all the office directors of the DRL bureau, I was worried. The announcement of Craner as the new assistant secretary had been a surprise. Few of the civil or foreign service officers in the bureau knew him, but I was to get to know him quickly. He had been president of the International Republican Institute (IRI), the Republican counterpart to the Democrat's National Democratic Institute, both funded in part by the National Endowment for Democracy. I learned that Craner had developed a reputation at IRI as a tough and effective manager, someone who knew how to develop and implement programs to encourage the institutions of democracy abroad.

It was a fair assessment, confirmed by Craner's performance at his first "BPP" session with the new Deputy Secretary of State Richard Armitage. "Bureau program plans" were Foggy Bottom's strategic planning documents. They told the senior managers of the department what an assistant secretary or ambassador at large intended to do over the next several years and what resources he needed to do it. Under the Albright regime, Harold Koh's presentations were truly inspiring and supported by clever and informative power point slides. Under the Powell regime, Armitage was the manager, the chief of staff. A barrel-chested, gruff-sounding man, Armitage would not have liked Harold's "dog and pony show." He wanted the bottom line quickly and often would interrupt his briefer when he believed that line was fading from view.

Lorne Craner fit this requirement perfectly. He, too, liked the bottom line, and he seemed to speak the deputy secretary's language. In place of Koh's eloquent human rights appeals, Craner spoke of programs and the dollars needed to fund them. He was a master of his brief and only got into trouble when he strayed into ambiguous issues, which neither he nor Armitage particularly relished. Both were smart managers with the air of people who needed to move to the next task.

It was early May 2001 when Craner came to the bureau for an informal meeting with office directors and described his tendency to make fast judgments about his employees. My own instincts were to form quick impressions of people as well, but my experience had taught me to look again. The business of managing people was more properly understood as leading, which I viewed as a function of clarity and inspiration. Let your people know where you want them to go, that you respect them, and that you will give them the authority to do their jobs. If that doesn't work, then you make changes.

What worried me about Craner's expression of management style, however, was not its divergence from my own. It was that his expectations were bound to clash with what I saw as my job. Unlike the other directors in that room, I did not work for Lorne Craner on a permanent basis. I was a placeholder for the ambassador at large, who would be senior in rank to Craner when he arrived, and would, I hoped, work out an arrangement that clarified his lines of authority under the secretary of state as the IRF Act had intended. As noted in the last chapter, Bob Seiple had made the decision not to waste his limited capital fighting that battle and had been enough of a heavyweight in the building, and in his relationship with Harold Koh, that the damage was limited or at least not apparent. Circumstances were soon to make the damage quite apparent.

By June when Craner was sworn in, I was beginning to wonder whether there was a serious problem delaying the nomination of the new ambassador. I had heard disturbing rumors that IRF supporters were wrangling over who the nominee should be. Meanwhile, the new Powell team was almost complete. Personal and professional relationships among senior officials were already being formed. My concerns about the ambassador's position peaked when I heard about the "double-hatting" proposal.

After arriving at C Street, Powell's seventh-floor management team had concluded, with considerable justification, that there were too many senior officials with access to the secretary of state. Under Secretary Albright there had been a whole platoon of senior advisors, counselors, and ambassadors at large on issues from women's rights to war crimes to counter terrorism to the states of the former Soviet Union. Powell's military background, and that of his closest advisors, led him to employ a more hierarchical approach to decision making. If all these officials had direct access to him, they reasoned, it would not only make demands on his time for the officials themselves but would also channel pressure from their "constituents"—those within the department and outside it who supported their missions—directly to the secretary.

Albright had dealt with this problem in part by not chairing regular meetings with all senior officials, a job she relegated to the deputy secretary of state (as related in chapter 5). Powell decided to reverse this approach: he would pare down the number of senior officials but would chair the senior meetings himself. While all of this made sense from the secretary's point of view, it was distinctly bad news for the still fragile IRF office. Sure enough, as time passed with no official candidate for ambassador in sight, rumors began to circulate that the seventh floor was considering a plan to "double hat" the new assistant secretary for democracy, human rights and labor as IRF ambassador.

To the Powell handlers, the idea of absorbing the ambassador's work into that of the DRL assistant secretary's was not a question of animosity toward religious freedom but merely good management of the secretary's time. In their minds, what could be more draining than the prospect of those who were perceived as domestic constituents of the IRF Act (e.g., evangelical Christians and human rights activists) knocking on the Secretary's door to demand action? I also feared that the management decision now under consideration was also a reflection of the low priority accorded by Secretary Powell's team to the new office and its function. "Double hatting" was a euphemism for keeping religion out of his hair and returning to the status quo ante by placing religious freedom entirely under the human rights bureau where it had always been.

Fortunately, two forces came to our aid: the U.S. Commission on International Religious Freedom and the U.S. Congress. The former made it clear to the White House and the department its opposition to double-hatting. Members of Congress let the White House know that they had not passed the IRF Act only to see it ignored by the new administration, at least not in the virtual abolition of the ambassador's position.[5] Later, in Congressional testimony, when asked about the double-hatting scheme, Powell demurred and said that he was still looking for a new ambassador for religious freedom. Some on the Hill later noted the irony that the IRF Act, thought to be the work of American evangelicals, had been signed by President Clinton only to face the prospect of its virtual elimination under Bush, a man many believed was beholden to the religious right.

As I saw it, all this raised the stakes of my position as placeholder for the next ambassador. Under the circumstances, I felt it imperative that Lorne Craner understand from the outset the tentative nature of our bureaucratic relationship. I had been a team player throughout my career and had no desire to buck his authority or embarrass him in any way. Indeed, I began to conclude that his programmatic approach was bringing new and needed discipline to the bureau's work. I let him know that I would defer to him so long as he agreed that nothing should be locked in stone regarding the office's relationship to the rest of the bureau or the secretary or other long-term decisions about the office's status. Such decisions had to await the arrival of the new ambassador. In retrospect, I am convinced that this attitude was the correct one, but as the months went by without a new ambassador, it contributed to growing tensions between me and DRL's "front office," consisting of Lorne Craner and Michael Parmly.

The trouble began when Craner asked all office directors for their "BPP" numbers for the coming year. What, he wanted to know, did we need in the way of personnel increases? I sat down with Paul Martin, who was serving as my deputy in the office, to decide how best to present our case. In the previous

year I had argued for moving toward a total of seventeen permanent staff positions. We had gotten to three permanent positions and two loaners. Paul and
I decided to ask Craner to support us for five new positions over the next two
years. When we made the presentation to him, he listened politely and indicated he understood the case. But when the office directors reassembled the
following week, he made it clear that he expected everyone to cut their requests.
He had no intention of going to the deputy secretary with an unrealistically
high number of personnel requests.

I was in a quandary. I understood Craner's point, but here was the first of
the inevitable hurdles I would have to face with any new assistant secretary.
I did not want him to go to Deputy Secretary Armitage with a request for "x"
number of positions for the DRL bureau, some subset of which were for the
religious freedom office. I wanted him to present his own numbers, and then
say that, as a separate matter, this is what the office of the ambassador at large
says it needs. I was perfectly prepared to defend the request but never got the
chance. The IRF office would remain staffed at very low levels until several
years later, when the new ambassador sought and, after much resistance from
within the department, achieved the help of Congress in increasing its size.

As a later member of the DRL front office told me, Lorne Craner saw the
dilemma I presented as "authority versus responsibility." So long as the office
of international religious freedom was housed in DRL, he was responsible for
it and had to have authority over it. He was going to run the religious freedom
operation as he saw fit until someone over him told him otherwise. Had I been
in his position, I cannot say that my view would have been different.

The Value of the International Religious Freedom Report

Perhaps the most consequential effect of the IRF Act has been its requirement
that the State Department produce an annual report that provides the status of
religious freedom in each country worldwide and describes what the United
States is doing in countries where violations are taking place. The report—
containing a chapter on almost 200 nations—is transmitted to Congress
each September and made public. Despite some shortcomings, the report has
done more than any other factor to institutionalize thinking about religion in
American diplomacy.

The reason is not difficult to fathom. The reporting requirement means
that as a practical matter, at least one foreign service officer in each of our
embassies or consulates around the world must pay serious attention to the
subject of religion. These men and women, usually junior grade officers who
have human rights as part of their portfolios, are required each spring to author
the first draft of the IRF report on their respective countries. In order to accomplish this in a professional way, during the year they must make contacts within

the government and civil society, and with the various religious communities and victims of religious persecution, on the subject of religion. For the most part, these drafts have been excellent descriptions of the problems that beset countries around the world, so much so that the *Annual Report on International Religious Freedom* is widely considered the best of its genre.

Embassy drafts are sent to the State Department early in the summer, where they are collated and edited, sent to the regional and other relevant bureaus and offices for comment, and then finalized by the reports staff. This process takes months and sometimes yields heated exchanges over a word, sentence, or concept. Disagreements often occur between the country desk (responsible for the entire range of U.S. interests in a given country) and the office of international religious freedom. I related in the previous chapter my discussion with the East Asian bureau over their contention that the word "torture" should be replaced by the word "harassment" in the China chapter of the IRF report. In discussions with officials at our Saudi desk, I encountered honest but fierce dissent over whether a child, raised as a Christian in America but abducted to Saudi Arabia by its father and raised as a Muslim, could be said to have been "forcibly converted" to Islam as contemplated in the IRF Act. Such debates may appear to some cynical, to others superfluous. In reality, they are a sign of seriousness and the fact that there is now an office within the U.S. government whose job is to drive the debate and to ensure that the reports are the result of reasoned discourse.

Weaknesses of the IRF Report

It is somewhat ironic but hardly surprising that some of the State Department's opposition to Wolf-Specter and the IRF Act revolved around the requirement for an annual IRF report in both those bills. This is a good example of the nonideological, resource-driven concerns that any government agency has and that Foggy Bottom has in spades. Despite the fact that American diplomats constitute in many ways the forward base of American security, the State Department's operations budget is a tiny fraction of the defense and intelligence budgets. In this case, critics in the department reasoned, State already had a human rights report, which included religious freedom. Why produce a separate report that would be redundant? In the end, the State Department had been so convinced in the summer of 1998 that the IRF Act would die that it did not make plans for producing the first annual IRF report the following year.[6] And unfortunately, the IRF Act failed to authorize funding for the new reporting requirement.

When I arrived in the office in June 1999, the reports staff was scrambling to make up for lost time. Many decisions made that summer in producing the first *Annual Report* were done on the fly and by instinct. The law required an executive summary for the problem countries and I spent many hours debating with irate desk officers which of their countries would have the ignominious fate of being included. The "countries of particular concern" (CPCs), that is, the very worst persecutors, were obviously going to be included—countries such as Sudan and Iran. But even their inclusion generated controversy. The IRF report was going to be issued prior to the secretary's actual decision on the CPCs. Few desk officers were eager to concede their country's guilt prematurely.

Ambassador Seiple and I agreed that that all the worst persecutors would have to be in the executive summary. But we also wanted to identify other violators of religious freedom, even if their policies did not amount to systematic "persecution" in the sense of bodily harm. If nothing else, we wanted to use the summary as an indicator of future problems as well as a way to identify those countries that are, or might be, on the CPC list. Accordingly, we established three categories designed to capture persecutory behavior, even if it did not meet the CPC standards.[7] This included, first, totalitarian regimes; second, states whose policies were manifestly hostile to minority or nonapproved religions; and, third, a slightly less severe category, states that neglected the problems of discrimination or persecution. The government of India, among others, had been accused of that kind of neglect in its failure to move resolutely against Hindu extremists.

Moving down the scale of severity, we added a fourth category: governments that passed discriminatory legislation or had policies that disadvantaged certain religions. Russia's 1997 religion law was the model for this group. Fifth, and most controversially within the Department of State and at the Quai d'Orsay in Paris, we added a category designed to highlight a problem we thought widely ignored and that both Seiple and I had encountered in our travels: religious discrimination in Western Europe. To the outrage of some in the bureau of European and Canadian Affairs, we included the category "Stigmatization of Certain Religions by Wrongfully Associating Them with Dangerous 'Cults' or 'Sects.'" Unfortunately, this section has not survived the strong views of some at the department, and others across the Atlantic, that it is arrogant and counterproductive to criticize our European allies on their treatment of religion.

The biggest shortcoming of the IRF Report was that the IRF ambassador did not actually control it. Because the IRF office was housed in the DRL bureau, and because the IRF Act provided no funding for a separate report, it had to be produced by the existing DRL reports staff, which worked for the DRL assistant secretary not the ambassador (who was, in any case, viewed as subordinate to the assistant secretary). This not only made the assistant secretary the ultimate arbiter of the report, it discouraged the ambassador from using it to drive broader policy. The potential for this use of the report lay particularly in the section describing U.S. actions in each country. As the IRF Commission pointed out, those sections tended to be drafted as mere catalogues of embassy meetings and events that seemed unconnected to U.S. policy. They should have been used as actual records of U.S. efforts to advance religious freedom, records that could be used to measure the effectiveness of American IRF policy.

For their part, DRL assistant secretaries understandably saw the report as a drain on their personnel resources. Assistant Secretary Craner certainly viewed it that way and ultimately succeeded (to my delight) in getting it passed entirely to the IRF office. Craner's initial effort, however, was to reduce the IRF report to an addendum to the human rights report. Even though that failed, the very fact that it was broached demonstrated the department's resource-driven attitude, and its policy indifference, to the "promotion of religious freedom."

As already noted, there were perfectly sound management reasons for Craner's effort—why have two reports, one covering all human rights and one devoted only to religion? Why burden his staff with doing the Human Rights report in January, with its section on religious freedom, and another in September devoted entirely to religious freedom? DRL's reports staff consisted of some ten permanent officers, headed by a director. When it was time to begin working and editing embassy drafts for either report, those officers would be temporarily augmented by another ten or so. Many of the latter were retired foreign service officers who had expertise in the countries for which they were responsible. Others were interns, usually very bright college or graduate students. This twice annual increase and decrease in the reports staff seemed to Craner, and to the permanent members of his reports staff, no way to run a railroad.

However, folding IRF back into the Human Rights Report would have been a return to the status quo ante, a gambit that demonstrated precisely why the leaders of the IRF legislative campaign did not trust the State Department. To them, a separate report was needed in order to avoid having religious liberty issues buried in a larger document and largely ignored. This view, reflected among religious freedom advocates from both parties on the Hill, ensured that the IRF report would remain separate and independent. As it turned out, Craner's attempts led ultimately to a showdown within the department that offered a real opportunity to the IRF office. By 2005, Ambassador Hanford's office was fully in charge of the IRF report for the first time, and it was well on the way to having sufficient personnel and hiring authority to produce it. As we will see, however, its potential as a policy instrument remains largely unfilled.

What Is "Religious Persecution"?

There was another internal conflict over the IRF report that demonstrated both the department's confusion about the international role of religion and, given the marginality of the issue, its relative indifference to how the conflict was resolved. Not long after his arrival, Assistant Secretary Craner made clear his discomfort over the broad standard we were using in the report to identify those guilty of "religious persecution." The ongoing dissent over that phrase, which came to a head shortly after Ambassador Hanford's arrival on the scene, is worth recounting.

Defining religious persecution too broadly can cheapen its meaning and the effectiveness of policy action. Simply because the victim of abuse is religious does not mean he has been the subject of religious persecution. If a Muslim cleric is tortured or a Protestant pastor murdered, the key explanatory datum is the motive of the perpetrator. Did he commit the act either because of his religion or that of his victim, in part or in whole? If the explanation falls entirely on nonreligious factors, such as greed or ethnic rivalry, then the bill of particulars against the perpetrator should omit religion. To do otherwise would be to reduce the power of the term "religious persecution" and to lessen the credibility of the reporter. During my years in the office of international religious freedom I came to know which of the religious advocacy groups were scrupulous about accuracy in such matters (the American Baha'is are a good example) and which ones were prone to overstating the role of religion to garner our attention. These latter groups proved the danger of exaggeration, which included the likelihood that we would discount or ignore their reports and their advice.

However, if the term "religious persecution" is defined too narrowly other problems ensue. I often encountered in the human rights community and the State Department analysts who were oddly reluctant to impute religious motives to human rights abusers, such as the Islamist regime in Sudan, when it was clearly warranted. The slavery practiced by Sudanese government-supported militias, this argument went, was a hideous example of long-standing tribal practices that were best explained in economic and ethnic terms. The problem was, however, that newly taken slaves were often forcibly converted to Islam, an action that unambiguously put this worst of human rights depredations squarely into the category of religious persecution, along with the other categories.[8] To omit religion in such a case did a disservice to the victims and the nature of the crime, not to mention the determination of how the United States might attempt to address the problem.

This issue was of such fundamental importance that I had focused several paragraphs on it in the introduction to the first IRF report (1999). Using the Serbian dictator Slobodan Milosevic as an example, I posed the question of whether his crimes against the people of Kosovo did or did not constitute religious persecution. Led by Milosevic, Serbia's Orthodox troops had carried out a campaign of murder, rape, and torture against the largely Muslim population of Kososo. What, if anything, did religion have to do with it?

Noting that people of good will could disagree over the definitional issue, the introduction continued: "many would argue that the predominant causes of the Serb campaign were political... nationalist... and ethnic... [and that] religion played an insignificant role in the conflict." This was in fact the position taken by some in the department's European bureau. I added that, from this point of view, it was significant that non-Muslim Kosovars were also targeted by the Serbs. Furthermore, "[s]ome would add that religion does not play a significant role in the culture and identity of Kosovar Albanians."[9] People who held this view would not label the Serb campaign religious persecution. Milosevic's bill of particulars would, of course, include human rights abuses of the worst kind—but religious persecution would not be one of them.

On the other hand, the introduction noted, "others argue that the ethnicity of Kosovar Albanians is inextricably bound to their Muslim heritage, both in their own minds and, more important, in the minds of their Serb tormentors. According to this view, any historical explanation of the 1999 Serb campaign that omitted religion as a significant factor would be inaccurate and misleading." The Serbs viewed Kosovo as "the cradle of Orthodoxy: neither the methodical nature of their effort to drive Kosovar Albanians from Kosovo, nor its ferocity can be understood without reference to" the religion of both sides. I added that the destruction of mosques by Serbs and of churches by returning Kosovars provided further evidence that religion played a significant role in the conflict.

Serbia was not the only case where religion was one of many factors motivating human rights abusers. The introduction also mentioned Sudan and Tibet, where putatively nonreligious factors such as ethnicity and separatism were major parts of the equation. The concluding sentence was the source of Lorne Craner's concern: "In cases of persecution *where religion is but one explanatory factor among many,* recognizing that people of good will can assign differing values to the role of religion, we generally have noted that the persecution occurred in part on the basis of religion. Such wording reflects a judgment that the factor of religion is distinctive enough to warrant its inclusion in the report (emphasis added)." In short, we had adopted a "significance" standard. If religion was a significant element in explaining persecution, we called it religious persecution.[10]

As he observed the operation of the IRF reports Craner came to a very different view. He believed that the significance standard we were employing was too broad. This came to a head in a dispute over wording for the 2002 IRF report. Craner argued that religious persecution should be defined as a human rights abuse in which religion was a "primary" factor. He said he was concerned that under our current standard, the Israeli-Palestinian dispute could be categorized as religious when, in his view, it was anything but religious. IRF Ambassador Hanford (who had by then taken office) rebutted this argument by citing our language from the 1999 report, and warning that a number of cases—for example Vietnam's abuses of Protestants in the Central Highlands, which had clear economic and political dimensions—might be classified as "other than religious" if we applied Craner's narrower standard. Hanford did not add that in the hands of skeptics, that standard could be used to keep the office of international religious freedom out of their hair. He did note that it would not be a good thing for the Bush administration to be seen as backtracking from a more stringent standard used under the Clinton administration.

In the end Craner did not entirely carry the day. Had his narrower definition prevailed, the State Department would have had yet another excuse to marginalize its attention to religion. But as it was the "compromise" definition approved by senior Department officials was revealing. The new standard read: "Although acts of violence against religious minorities may have several causes—for example, ethnicity or a perceived security threat—multicausality does not necessarily diminish the significance of religion."[11] This word fix did not change much (in State Department parlance we labeled it "changing 'happy' to 'glad'"). In fact, it was not intended to alter the definition. It was a Solomonic split-the-difference solution intended to avoid further dispute between Craner and Hanford.[12] That was considered of far more significance than the issue itself.

Flying the Flag at Home

As I bided my time within the department, hoping the Bush administration would nominate Bob Seiple's replacement soon, I knew it was vital that we continue the initiatives begun by Seiple to raise the profile of our new policy among the American people. Part of that job involved talking to the usual suspects, namely think tanks, human rights organizations, college faculties and students, gatherings of faith-based groups, and the like. I encouraged each member of our office to hit the road within the United States, as well as overseas. All of them were eager to do so. As we fanned out across the country, we were struck by the fact that so few people knew about our office or even that their government had adopted a policy of advancing religious freedom.[13]

This was in a sense hardly surprising. The American people are well known for their attention to local and state matters, as well as a tendency to focus on foreign affairs only when the nation is at war or some vital interest is at stake. Our job, as I saw it, was to make the case that fundamental American interests were involved in our religious freedom policy. It could not simply be a matter of rescuing our co-religionists abroad, although that would always be a major part of our policy and an entirely justifiable reason for supporting it. As a national policy, however, we had to promote religious freedom for all people, not just Christians and Jews. Our reason for doing so could not be that of aggressive secularism, namely that religion was one among many life-style choices that deserved protection. That understanding of the issue had contributed to the subordination of religious freedom in our State Department's human rights advocacy.

As I told audiences at college campuses and conferences, we should understand religious freedom as our founders had understood it, the enervating core of those natural rights granted to every human being by God. Without religious liberty protected by governments and honored by societies, no person can live a truly human life. Without it, especially in the non-Western world where the practice of religion is widespread and growing, stable self-government is simply impossible. And without the spread of stable and durable democracy, how can we hope to live in a world in which governments respect the rule of law, their own citizens, and other nations? U.S. policy should be aimed at helping other nations and cultures evoke the principles of human dignity that are at the base of religious freedom. Those principles are at least implicit in most religious traditions, even if they are dormant in some. The United States needs to find ways to encourage the translation of those principles into political institutions.

Now among some of our elite college faculties, such thoughts are held to exceed the bounds of settled orthodoxy when uttered by private citizens (which is why they are seldom uttered in the presence of the generation—my generation—now in charge of higher education in our country). Coming from the lips of an American official, however, these ideas can produce consternation bordering on apoplexy. During a conference in Connecticut, one professor from a highly regarded institution of higher learning opined that the entire international religious freedom policy of the United States might be an unconstitutional establishment of religion.[14] Another professor from another important university said that, listening to Tom Farr, she felt like she was in church.[15] That was not, I am confident, intended as a compliment.

There are clearly religious undertones to the understanding of religious freedom adduced here (although one might have difficulty finding a church where that view is expounded from the pulpit). This understanding derives in significant part from the Roman Catholic declaration on religious freedom and from the religion clauses of the First Amendment as they were understood by the founding generation (chapter 3). The two are entirely consistent. They represent an approach to human dignity, human rights, and democracy that derives from the collective American religious experience—Protestant, Jewish and, ultimately, Catholic in inspiration, but also confirmed by the lives and fortunes of American Mormons, Jehovah's Witnesses, Seventh Day Adventists, Christian Scientists, Muslims, Hindus, Buddhists, and members of other religions, as well as agnostics and atheists. Many of the latter two groups would contest the point, but it is my contention that there is no sound basis for religious freedom, including the freedom to reject religion, without reference to the religious nature of humanity. As related in chapter 1, there is ample evidence of man's innate desire to determine whether there is a transcendent reality and, if so, the implications for living a good life.

Can Religion Be a "Good"?

My own views on this subject were not fully developed when I entered the office of international religious freedom and I doubtless profited from some of my encounters with State Department colleagues who disagreed with my approach. From the beginning I sought to find a reasoned way for the United States to acknowledge the religious element of human nature and to incorporate it into our foreign policy. These efforts sometimes produced exasperation among the defenders of secularist orthodoxy in the department, especially those who had the responsibility to approve what I wrote for publication.

In one exchange an assistant to the Under Secretary for Global Affairs, after reading my draft introduction to the first IRF report, remarked with irritation that I was engaging in "special pleading for religion." He was right. On another occasion I drafted an op-ed entitled "Why Religious Freedom?" which we hoped to place in a major newspaper. The draft contained the statement that the United States "look[s] forward to the day when every government recognizes the value of religion." A colleague in DRL responded: "*We cannot say that.* [his emphasis] We are not promoting the value of religion, but the value of religious freedom." That op-ed never saw the light of day.

Such views reflected a reading of the first amendment that was typical at Foggy Bottom, namely that the founders' concept of religious freedom was designed in large part to protect America from the divisive effects of religion itself. In a passage of Ambassador Seiple's testimony for one of his appearances before the House International Relations Committee, I had drafted a sentence that referred to religion (the human quest for transcendence) as "a good." When I sent it around for clearance, I received a firm rebuke from a staffer who worked for the under secretary for political affairs. That passage must come out, she said, because it failed to acknowledge "the constitutional rights of all citizens, including the right to say and believe that religion is bad and should not be practiced." The right to make that argument is fully protected under the free speech clause of the First Amendment. But preceding the protections for free speech in the First Amendment are the two religion clauses which were designed to guarantee the free exercise of religion.[16] That guarantee is rendered nonsense if the premise is that religion is bad for citizens.

In the introduction to the first IRF report I somehow managed to get department consensus on a rather oblique argument about the value of religion, namely that the achievement of fundamental human rights for all people would be furthered by religious freedom if it encompassed a *religious* understanding of universal human dignity. I began by noting that the State Department's human rights report of the previous year had marked the fiftieth anniversary of the 1948 Universal Declaration of Human Rights. The report had argued that democracy was the best way to fulfill the Declaration's promise of a world in which "all human beings are born free and equal in dignity and human rights." In the 1990s, the report observed, the number of democracies in the world had almost doubled, but still human rights abuses multiplied.

"The lesson," I wrote, "is clear:...[by itself] freedom is no guarantee of human dignity. Respect for the intrinsic value of the human person requires the soil of liberty to grow and flourish, but the source of that value lies elsewhere." There was, of course, "more than one understanding of the source of human dignity," and all religions did not agree on the issue. But, I continued, "many of the world's religions share common assumptions about human nature and human dignity." Those assumptions were captured in the Universal Declaration's assertion that "'all human beings are endowed with reason and conscience.'... Reason and conscience direct us to the source of that endowment, an orientation typically expressed in religion."[17]

Written two years before the attacks of 9/11 and almost five years before the U.S. invasion of Iraq, these ideas seem in retrospect to have greater salience than I realized at the time. For the United States to promote "religious freedom" in the secularist sense dominant at Foggy Bottom, that is, as the right to practice an activity that is inherently dangerous and therefore needs "tolerance" or privatization, is grounded in a misunderstanding of human nature. As we explore in chapters 8 and 9, the antidote to religious extremism in the 21st century is not democracy's privatization of religion but democracy's wise and prudent *involvement* of religion in the public square.

If the American experience in Iraq has taught us anything, it ought to be that religion is too powerful and too important to be privatized. It should have taught us that political freedom alone, even if organized around sound democratic procedures and a solid democratic constitution, cannot resolve the tensions inherent in the relationship between religion and state. In order for democracy to succeed in societies where a religious tradition or traditions influence political culture, those traditions must reconcile themselves to, if not embrace, the central requirement of liberal democracy: respect for human dignity. Those in the U.S. foreign policy establishment who insist that this cannot be done, or that it is unconstitutional or inappropriate for U.S. officials to be involved in such matters, are unduly limiting our capacity to defend ourselves.

There was another factor at work in the State Department's understanding of religion and religious freedom: the often misused concept of "pluralism." As we have seen, to those who view religion as inherently divisive, religious pluralism represents a dispersion of destructive passion—a helpful companion to the privatization of religion. There are faint echoes of this view in the American founding: in Federalist Paper number 10 James Madison emphasized the value to democracy of a proliferation of interest groups, including religious groups. A wide diversity of such interests in civil society would discourage the accumulation of too much political power and influence by any single entity. This idea was tied to the concept of democratic checks and balances, itself an extension of the Protestant emphasis on original sin.

But Madison's understanding was quite different from the views of modern skeptics in whose hands religious pluralism becomes a warrant for relativism and indifferentism. In their reading religious freedom is grounded in the principle that there can be no single religious truth, that absolute truth claims lead inevitably to intolerance, and that pluralism is the only protection against religious tyranny. It is one thing to avoid concentrations of political power in the hands of any one religious group (which was a central goal of the nonestablishment clause). It is quite another to insist on the deracination of religion itself as a defense of liberty. This was not what Madison, or the other founders, had in mind.

Seeking the Help of American Religious Communities

Given the importance of the participation of religious communities in a democracy, it seemed to me entirely reasonable to reach out to American religious groups that had not been involved in the legislative campaign that produced the IRF Act. As noted in chapter 4, Tibetan Buddhists had been tangentially involved as a designated religious community under the original Wolf-Specter bill, as had Baha'is. But for the most part, American Buddhists, Hindus, Orthodox Christians, Muslims, and others did not participate in the debate over the law.

Accordingly, we set out to establish regular meetings of American Buddhists and Hindus, respectively, and had plans for other groups. Our initial meetings brought Washington-based Buddhists and Hindus to the department, where they reacted enthusiastically to our idea of regular gatherings, which would in future include their co-religionists from around the country. We told them that we wanted to learn more about their traditions and the varieties of belief and practice that typified both. Equally important, we invited their ideas on how best to promote religious freedom in the countries where their traditions were dominant or influential.

In the end, however, these meetings went the way of the Islamic Roundtable, which had been instituted by Ambassador Seiple. There was simply too little interest in the department for such religion-based initiatives, either because they were thought to rest on shaky constitutional grounds or because they had little relevance to IRF policy as it was being practiced. As we shall see in the next chapter, Ambassador Seiple's successor focused almost entirely on persecution, and he viewed such gatherings as marginal to the goal of attacking persecution.

During the interregnum, however, I gave a high priority to continuing the outreach program to Muslims begun by Ambassador Seiple and to expanding that program to the other groups. We set out to reenergize the Islamic Roundtable, which we renamed the American Muslim Roundtable.

We contacted Muslim leaders who had attended the meetings under Seiple, such as Laila al Marayati, who had been among the first appointees to the U.S. Commission on International Religious Freedom and a member of the commission's delegation to Saudi Arabia. Our association with these and other Muslim leaders developed at several levels. Most important were the individual meetings, conferences, and planning sessions, several of which took place at American University under the auspices of Professor Abdul Aziz Said.

It was at these events that I began to comprehend both the complexity and the unity that flows from this huge and growing religion. Although Islam was born in the Arabian deserts and exported by Arab tribes, Arabs today constitute only 20 percent of Muslims worldwide. India, a Hindu-majority nation, has a huge Muslim minority (about 100 million people). Ex-Pakistani diplomat and Professor Akbar Ahmed, who had written a biography of Pakistan's first president, Mohammed Ali Jinnah, tutored us on the tribal nature of Pakistani and Afghan society, as well as Jinnah's secular vision for Pakistani democracy. Ghanan Professor Sulleyman Nyang, of Howard University, introduced us to African Islam. Islam has long been present in sub-Saharan Africa and is growing rapidly in some areas, as it is in the "post-religious" societies of Western Europe.

Notwithstanding appearances, Muslims do not all see the world in the same way. Hearing the views of Professor Seyyid Hossein Nasr (George Washington University), an Iranian Shiite who has written authoritatively on Muslim philosophy and theology, is very different from listening to the Sunni African expressions of Sudanese Professor Abdul an-Naim (Emory University), or the sharp political-religious opinions of an American convert such as Ibrahim Hooper of the Council on American-Islamic Relations. One of my closest confidants during these months was another American convert to Islam, Alex Kronemer, who came to work in the human rights bureau. Alex's Jewish father had set him on the path to Judaism until, when he was quite young, his parents were divorced. His Christian mother then raised him in a Lutheran church. His later encounters with religious intolerance turned Alex away from religion for many years until he met an Egyptian woman while in college at American University, whom he would later marry and who was instrumental in his conversion to Islam. Alex told me that in Islam he had found "a way of integrating his two religious halves."

Kronemer had a marvelous capacity to explain his religious beliefs and how they applied to his life. A man of engaging intellect and empathy, he was able to personalize for me the value of a religion that sometimes seemed inscrutable and forbidding. I wanted Alex to serve as my permanent deputy in the office of international religious freedom, but he was lured away from the department by the opportunity to film and produce a documentary on the life of the Prophet Mohammed, which was shown on PBS a little over a year after 9/11.

Like adherents of other religions, some Muslims are Muslim in name only and have been thoroughly secularized by their life in the West. Observant Muslims (perhaps like observant Christians in an analogous situation) do not particularly like to speak of "secular Islam," but the phenomenon exists. I was warned of it in a meeting with Grand Sheikh Seyed Tantawi of Al Azhar in Cairo, although his concerns also extended to observant Muslims he feared had been corrupted by living in the West. Be careful, he told me, where you learn your Islam. It was a well-meaning but thoroughly unrealistic suggestion, much like a Calvinist warning a Muslim to take care where he gets his Protestantism. Islam, like Protestantism, is rarely understandable in monolithic terms.

Madison Avenue and the Muslim World

I experienced firsthand the potentially confusing effects of Islamic diversity in State Department meetings immediately after 9/11, when the office of the under secretary for public diplomacy began a somewhat frantic search for Muslims who could explain (preferably quickly and in short sentences) what in the world was the problem. Among the participants in these meetings were highly respected American Christian and Jewish scholars of Islam, as well as—initially at least—members of our Roundtable.

Others included controversial but important critics of Islam, such as Daniel Pipes, and secular Muslim feminists. (The State Department is nothing if not multicultural in its search for answers.) A particularly interesting, if perplexing, meeting centered around one of the feminists, an Afghan woman whose prescription for our coming engagement in her country was to get rid of the imams and the mosques. When I suggested that religious freedom provided an alternative strategy, she protested that, as a Muslim, she had nothing against Islam per se, and to prove it produced a photo of herself, cigarette and cocktail in hand, with her arm around a distinctly uncomfortable looking Muslim cleric.

The department did not accept her proposal. In their wisdom, the State Department's public diplomacy experts decided that they would attempt win Muslim hearts and minds with two venerable American institutions: Madison Avenue and television. The idea was that networks throughout the Muslim world would carry American-made TV spots demonstrating how religiously active and professionally successful Muslims were in the United States. These propaganda moments were actually done quite well and were in many ways representative of the American Muslim experience. Perhaps understandably, given the goal of the campaign, they did not explore the fear that many American Muslims felt in the wake of 9/11, a fear deepened by unexplained arrests and even a few murders of U.S. Muslims. Madison Avenue does not do unexplained arrests, much less homicides, well.

Ultimately, the department's public diplomacy campaign failed to increase support for American policy in the Muslim world. For one thing, the absence of balance in the TV spots made them appear manipulative. Perhaps it would have been wiser to include some of the problems that ensued for American Muslims after 9/11, and the ways that they were resolved within the American system of justice. Also, Muslims in the test audiences abroad may have perceived that they were being conned because of the medium as well as the message. Although Muslim teenagers may take their fashions, and refine their sins, from American MTV popular culture, their parents do not appear to be happy about this phenomenon. At the very least, they seem unprepared to change their negative attitudes about America (many of which derive from television), much less alter their religiously motivated behavior, based on TV spots. Madison Avenue public diplomacy was dropped after a few months trial and the expenditure of several million dollars.

A Family in Harm's Way

As we saw in chapter 4, one of the most difficult dilemmas for American Christians was the question of asylum in the United States for their co-religionists overseas. Early drafts of the Wolf-Specter legislation would have made it easier for any individual Christian in a country where Christians as a group were designated as a "persecuted community" to gain asylum in the United States. Critics charged that this would privilege Christians to the detriment of other victims, to which advocates plausibly replied that the provision was merely intended to balance past and ongoing discriminatory practices.

But among Christian advocates for a new law there were additional problems: was it justifiable to privilege a Christian for asylum in America because his *community* was endangered, regardless of whether the applicant himself was being persecuted? Would this not have the effect of encouraging individuals to flee to America whether or not their individual cases warranted such an extreme action? Many of these people lived in regions where Christianity was born and established itself in the early centuries—especially the Middle East. Did American Christians really want to set up mechanisms that would encourage the demographic tragedy already under way, namely the flight of ancient Christian populations from the places of Christianity's birth?

For most in the legislative movement the answer was clear. The United States must, on a case by case basis, do justice to anyone with good reason to flee their countries because of human rights abuses. Moreover, if Christians were being treated unfairly by those who adjudicated asylum and refugee cases, this was an outrage. Ultimately, the IRF Act made an attempt to address this issue by requiring the training of U.S. refugee and asylum officials on religious persecution. But the terrible quandaries faced by persecuted Christians fleeing their countries of origin remained acute, and the IRF Act, I was soon to discover, had little immediate impact on the problem.

I had been on the job for just a few months when I began to receive telephone calls and faxes from Hill staffers and Christian groups about what I will call here the "Karimi case."[18] The Karimis were an extended Iranian family of eight members (including a teenager, a young girl, and a mentally handicapped woman) situated in a dangerous refugee camp in Van, Turkey. While in Iran, members of the family had converted over the course of several years from Islam to Christianity.

According to my sources, the lives of the Christian Karimis in Iran had become increasingly dangerous. They worshiped covertly but some were arrested, imprisoned, and tortured. Some were fired from their jobs. The children were harassed at school and one was expelled. Labeled "apostates," they feared for their lives. In 1999 they fled Iran over the mountains to Turkey and, so they hoped, safety. Thus began their encounter with the world described during the campaign for religious persecution legislation as unjust and anti-Christian—the world of refugee and asylum adjudication.

The existence of the United Nations High Commissioner for Refugees is one of the success stories of the international community. Designed to regularize the processing of those who flee their countries because of a well-founded fear of persecution, the UNHCR has offices all over the globe. Their job is to determine whether people qualify as refugees and, if so, to help place them safely in other countries. Millions of people owe their lives or well-being to this system. In Turkey, there were by the late 1990s four offices, and some 70 permanent staffers, supplemented by five nongovernmental organizations under contract. The contractors would do preliminary screening of refugees and assist them in traveling to formal UNHCR interviews.

Twice the Karimi family had endured an 18-hour bus ride from their refugee camp in Van to Ankara for UNHCR interviews. They had been rejected each time. UN employees had concluded that family members were not what they said they were—converts to Christianity—and that they therefore did not have a well-founded fear of persecution in Iran. When contacted by American NGOs about the case, our office had queried the UNHCR through its Washington office, asking for details. These were soon forthcoming and were presented in a way that seemed plausible. Members of the family had been interviewed separately and had given conflicting versions of their conversions, especially the circumstances of their respective baptisms. Their knowledge of Christianity was poor, a factor that UN interviewers weighed heavily. Anyone risking their lives to be Christian in Iran, the UN reasoned, would have a secure knowledge of the object of their devotion.

These explanations were given to us by the UNHCR openly and without reservation. The interviewers, we were assured, were fair and thorough and fully realized the stakes. But as I began to process the information provided by the UNHCR, I became increasingly troubled. Much of the evidence for the conclusion that the Karimis' knowledge of Christianity was poor had come from the applicants' inability to answer questions about the structure of the Bible. But UNHCR interviewers themselves had noted that the applicants had not had access to a Bible in their native Farsi. They had learned of the scriptures from hearing it translated from an English Bible and were generally familiar with the main stories of the four Gospels and the Book of Acts. Was it not conceivable, I wondered, that they could have been drawn to Christianity by hearing those stories read to them?

But there was another problem. Each of the applicants apparently told the interviewers that during the baptism ceremony they had not been asked to repeat any words or phrases. If true, this absence of any creedal or liturgical response was troubling. Although I was no expert on all the forms that Christian baptisms could take, it did seem likely that most if not all of them required some verbal affirmation on the part of adults. Still, it remained conceivable, to me at least, that there had been a language barrier that explained the silence or some other factor, such as fear of discovery.

I was face-to-face with a nightmare. I had been in the foreign service long enough to know that heartbreaking humanitarian cases appeared with regularity and, unless there were an official with the power to do something, diplomats had little leverage. But here we were dealing with a UN agency that had appeared to act with thoroughness and openness. In their dealings with us, there was little sign of bias or indifference. I knew that reversing their decision would be well nigh impossible, but my instincts told me that there was something missing in these stories. The thought that innocent people, including children and a handicapped woman, might have been victimized by their incapacity to communicate, or by an excessively academic approach to determining whether they were Christians, haunted me. I argued to Bob Seiple that we should ask the U.S. Immigration and Naturalization Service to get involved. He agreed.

Later that summer the INS sent its own officials to Turkey to interview the Karimi family. They concluded that six of the eight applicants were indeed Christians and entitled to refugee status in the United States. But now another nightmare emerged. In its wisdom, the INS concluded that the teenager had failed to make the case that he had converted to Christianity, and that the handicapped woman could not have converted because she lacked sufficient understanding to make such a choice. In short, the United States had decided to override the UNHCR decision and give refuge to most of the Karimi family.

Incredibly, however, it had also determined to abandon a teenager (whose mother and father were not in the group) and a severely retarded woman to their fate in a Turkish refugee camp, from which they would almost certainly be forcibly repatriated to Iran. Whether they were Christians or not, these two were now officially the relatives of Iranian Muslim apostates. Although I was gratified at INS cooperation in the case, I was stunned and outraged at the bureaucratic lunacy that could yield such a decision. By this time, Ambassador Seiple had departed the State Department so I began to lobby senior INS officials to reverse the 6/8 decision on humanitarian grounds. After several letters and phone calls in which I laid out the case, they agreed. By early 2001, all the Karimis reached the United States, where, I am told by a close relative, they reside to this day as faithful Christians.

I took from this experience two lessons. First, nothing can be more personally gratifying than helping someone flee injustice and achieve freedom. Although many others played a part in this saga, I was satisfied that my own efforts, and the scores of hours involved, had been justified by the outcome. This was the kind of activity that makes one want to get up and go to work each day, and to smile even in the midst of bureaucratic inanities.

But the second lesson was even more important: there are Karimis all over the world, millions of them, people who are at risk of their lives and well-being because of the way they search for and worship God. Even with the best of intentions and bureaucratic savvy the United States is not in a position to rescue them all, or even a significant portion of them. Our IRF policy can certainly help the victims of religious persecution and give them hope by publicizing their plight and pressuring their governments to stop the abuse. We can, and should, act to rescue one soul when it is possible, let alone a family. But over the long term something else is required. That something, I was increasingly convinced, was the systematic advancement of the idea that religious freedom can benefit every society and every people.

Back to the Future

The obstacles to achieving this objective, I was soon to learn, had only begun to show themselves. My goal during the interregnum had been to maintain the autonomy of the office and the official status of the ambassador at large for international religious freedom. As I awaited the nomination, confirmation, and arrival of the new ambassador, events were to conspire against that goal. It is to that story that we now turn.

7

⌒⦿⌒

The Lion's Den

Act II (2002–2006)

The diplomat is neither a preacher of penitence, nor a judge in a criminal case, nor a philosopher. His sole and exclusive interest must be the
real and downright interest of his country.
—Heinrich von Bulow

The Story behind the Appointment of the Second
IRF Ambassador

As the Bush team took over in January 2001, the morale of our small office
had been high, as were my own expectations. We knew that the new president
cared personally about religious freedom and that there had been considerable discussion in Republican circles about candidates for the new ambassador at large. I strongly suspected that the nominee would be political. For one
thing, my sense was that there were few senior diplomats willing to take the
job or interested enough in the issue to do it well. Moreover, the evangelicals, Catholics, and Jews who had supported the IRF Act were, with important
exceptions, Republicans and I assumed that they would have their respective
candidates. So although there were a few professional diplomats I would have
been delighted to have as Ambassador, I felt reasonably sure that my new boss
would come from outside Foggy Bottom.

I had no inside information about White House thinking, but I paid attention to the rumors. And they were intriguing. One of the earliest names I heard
bandied about was that of former Indiana Republican Senator Dan Coats, who
had retired from the Senate in 1998. As he departed the Congress, Coats had
played a pivotal role in ensuring that the IRF Act came up for a vote, an action

187

that suggested that he was personally invested in the law. But soon his name began to be floated for secretary of defense, and it was clear that he was moving at another level in administration thinking. Ultimately Coats was named as U.S. ambassador to Germany, where he served with distinction.[1]

Another name that emerged was Elliott Abrams, who had held, among other positions, that of assistant secretary for human rights in the Reagan administration's State Department. Later, while president of the Ethics and Public Policy Center in Washington, D.C., he had been appointed to the first U.S. Commission on International Religious Freedom. When the Bush administration took over, Abrams was chairman of the commission. He knew the State Department well and had the vision to be a power player. He was certainly capable of overcoming the bureaucratic and policy obstacles that had emerged under Seiple's tenure and were growing during the interregnum. Abrams would have been a logical choice for the job had it not been for the difficulties he would inevitably have faced during Senate confirmation.[2] As it turned out, he was named senior director for human rights and international operations at the National Security Council, and still in a position to assist in rooting the new religious freedom policy.

A third name was broached by a group of influential Catholics led by Deal Hudson, the publisher and editor of *Crisis* magazine and the White House liaison to the Catholic community. Hudson had expressed interest in various positions at the State Department,[3] but his real passion lay with domestic policy. His initial idea for ambassador at large, John Klink, struck me as a good one. At Hudson's behest I spoke at some length with Klink. He had a savvy intelligence and a realistic understanding of the obstacles he would face at State, as well as the will to address them successfully. But in the end John Klink was not put forward for the IRF position.

The other name floating out there was John Hanford, the Senate staffer who had been the principal architect of the International Religious Freedom Act. After I arrived on the job in the summer of 1999, Hanford was one of the first people I went to see in order to understand the policy that I was now defending and to know who were the key players on the Hill. I found him gracious and informative. We quickly became friends, aided by our common devotion to religious freedom and to the fact that we were both southerners. The discovery that we had attended the University of North Carolina at the same time led to much conversation, which, any Tar Heel will understand, necessarily included the revered subjects of Dean Smith and Andy Griffith. Hanford had been a Morehouse Scholar at Carolina, the university's top merit scholarship. For some 14 years prior to his nomination as ambassador, he had led congressional efforts against religious persecution and had directed a Congressional Fellows Program dedicated solely to this issue.

Late in the spring of 2000 Hanford had learned of Bob Seiple's intent to resign as ambassador at large after two years on the job. He came to me to ask if

I would support his attempt to get Bob to stay on. I said it appeared that Seiple had his mind made up and was unlikely to change his plans, but that I certainly supported any attempt to keep him. Not long after that meeting, I received a call from Hanford that was revealing of the way the man works and of why he had been successful as a staffer for so many years. He had put together thirteen reasons why Seiple should remain, and he read them to me. I was impressed. I was also amazed that he had spent so much time and energy on this project, but, as I was to learn, Hanford takes such commitments quite seriously, and he was now personally committed to getting Bob Seiple to stay.

When Hanford presented the thirteen points to Seiple, he too was impressed and, I suspect, not a little touched. Others had urged him to stay as well, but no one had invested in the effort like John Hanford. As I had suspected he would, Seiple thanked Hanford for his confidence but said that he had made up his mind. His plan was to start his own religious freedom NGO, and he intended to move ahead on that project as soon as his departed the State Department in September. The finality of Seiple's decision freed Hanford to think of other candidates, including himself. Doubtless those who supported his work on the Hill encouraged him to consider the job.

John Hanford clearly had experience and knowledge on the issue of religious freedom. But it was not his way to take such a decision, or any other important decision, quickly or lightly. He spent weeks querying his closest confidants about the prospects of his being nominated, including members of the new White House team and his aunt, Elizabeth Dole, who had been elected to the Senate as a Republican from North Carolina. I learned of Hanford's thinking when he came to me to ask what I thought of his "throwing my hat into the ring." Frankly, my first thought was to be skeptical. The names that were surfacing for the ambassador's position were typically more senior people whose professional status would provide a much needed weight to our mission, which was struggling to maintain its place at the State Department.

And yet I knew firsthand of Hanford's grasp of the issues and of his bull-dog-like concentration on achieving his goal once he was engaged. Although I was not enough of a Washington insider to estimate what his chances were, he seemed to me to be a long shot, given the other names out there. But I respected his abilities, and told him that in my view he should move ahead. I also took the opportunity to begin warning him of the obstacles that would lay in his path at the State Department should he succeed. It was the first of many conversations that would take place over the ensuing months.

By the spring of 2001, the White House had made a tentative decision on the new ambassador at large. How seriously the names mentioned were considered, I do not know for sure, but I suspect that each was in the mix in the early months of the administration. Traditionally, when the White House wants to float a name informally prior to announcing it, that name will appear in Al Kammen's *Washington Post* column, "In the Loop." On May 2, that column contained the putative nominee. It was John Hanford.[4]

I was surprised but gratified—for the moment. Lorne Craner would soon be confirmed by the Senate as the new assistant secretary for democracy, human Rights, and labor. As recounted in the previous chapter, we had our first informal meeting with him on May 3. After that meeting, my concerns about the independence of the office began to mount, and I hoped that the new ambassador would be on board soon. But it was not to be. John Hanford would not be sworn in as ambassador at large for another full year, a year in which the status of the office became increasingly fragile. When Hanford finally arrived in May 2002, the obstacles he faced had grown to a serious level.

The Campaign against John Hanford

The responsibility for the prolonged and unnecessary vacancy in the ambassador's position lay in several places. First was the White House. After floating Hanford's name in the spring, the administration was subjected to an anti-Hanford campaign from a few vocal Bush supporters that, in all prudence, it was obliged to consider as a domestic political matter. But the White House apparently made the decision simply to put the nomination to the side and let things sort themselves out. As a result, administration officials who knew full well of the State Department's resistance to the new religious freedom policy, and should have known of the vital importance of getting an ambassador on board quickly, abdicated their responsibility. They did not formally announce the "intent to nominate" Hanford until September. A narrow vision of the ambassador's mission, that is, that of denouncing persecution rather than promoting religious freedom, may also have reduced the sense of urgency attached to filling the position.

Second, many of the evangelicals, Catholics, and other groups who had supported the International Religious Freedom Act knew of the campaign against Hanford, and some were against it. But they failed to speak out, or at least to speak out in an effective way. Had they done so, in particular had they let the White House know of their displeasure, it is likely that the personnel managers there would have moved more resolutely. But once Hanford's name had been floated, there was apparently no significant pressure to resolve the disagreement over his candidacy quickly in order to protect the position and the office.

Third, there was little or no effort on the part of the commission to move the White House to bring the dispute to a close. It is difficult to assign motives to the commissioners. It is, however, a reasonable inference from their silence on the Hanford nomination, and their silence once he took office, that they simply did not perceive support for the ambassador's status within the State

Department as part of their job. I believe this to have been, and to continue to be, a serious misreading of the commission's responsibilities to U.S. international religious freedom policy.

Fourth, with the notable exception of Representative Chris Smith, a fierce and consistent supporter of religious freedom who pressed the White House to move ahead on Hanford, other supporters in Congress apparently did little to urge a quick decision once the campaign against him had begun.[5] Like many of the NGOs and others who had supported the new law, they appear to have been hesitant to act in the face of the opposition to Hanford. Once his nomination actually went forward, the Senate found itself dealing with the effects of 9/11. But even accounting for the delays that 9/11 produced in the system, the Hanford nomination was given too little priority in the Senate, which did not hold his hearings until December.

Fifth, John Hanford himself bears some responsibility for prolonging the vacancy. The campaign against him was a bitter one, and he had to work hard to overcome it, which he ultimately did. Once the Senate hearing took place, Hanford was easily confirmed, but it was to be another four months before he took office. There were personal reasons for this further delay, but John knew full well the problems that were mounting within the State Department.

Finally, and most important, the campaign against John Hanford bears the most responsibility for the prolonged vacancy in the job. Without that effort to prevent his taking the ambassadorship, it seems clear that Hanford would have been nominated, confirmed and on board well before September 11, and possibly as early as the same month (June) that Lorne Craner officially joined the department. That campaign was led by Michael Horowitz.

John Hanford had made a number of enemies during the months when his team was drafting what became the International Religious Freedom Act. Horowitz's dominance of the Wolf-Specter coalition, and his aggressive attitude to any opposition, had convinced the Hanford team to do its work in secret. This did not sit well with many who had worked since 1997 on the legislation. Although in retrospect the secrecy is in part understandable, it unnecessarily alienated some who might well have become more enthusiastic supporters of the ambassador and the State Department office created by the bill. Yet it is also reasonable to conclude that those who were somehow offended by being excluded from the team's work, or otherwise felt slighted in the final weeks of negotiations in the summer and fall of 1998, should have been able to transcend their personal feelings on behalf of a cause that many had supported for years.

After the Hanford name was floated by the White House, I had a number of conversations with influential people who I had reason to believe were hesitant about his candidacy. My purpose was not so much to lobby for John as it was to communicate my growing concern about the vacancy of the ambassador's position. I spoke to one veteran in the field who had respect for Hanford as a Christian and for his passion about religious persecution but who feared he was not the right man for the job of ambassador at large. This person feared that Hanford lacked the gravitas needed to overcome the opposition that existed in the State Department and that his emphasis on individual cases of persecution was too narrow. I responded that problems at the State Department were merely getting worse the longer the position went unfilled. It seemed to me that under the circumstances it was important to get behind the president's choice. To delay his arrival much longer would harm our common effort to advance religious freedom.

I also went to see the new chairman of the commission, Michael Young, dean of the George Washington University School of Law. Young was not part of the push to prevent the Hanford nomination, but I knew that he had concerns. Early during the commission's first year, Hanford, while working for Senator Lugar, had made an ill-fated attempt to limit the commission's funding, fearing that it would become too powerful and, ultimately, a permanent fixture. That fear, of course, was later borne out. At the time, however, Young disagreed strongly with Hanford's actions. I made the same pitch to Young that I had earlier: please support the president's choice. I need an ambassador at the State Department. Young responded that his views of Hanford would depend on his actions when he came into the job. Neither of us knew at the time that many months remained before that would occur. In the interim, however, Michael Young made a direct request within the department that Hanford be placed, as he believed the law required, directly under the secretary of state. As we shall see, this request was not granted.

During the summer of 2001, I heard from the man who apparently was the alternative being urged on the White House by Michael Horowitz and others. His name was David Aikman, who had for years been a correspondent for *Time* magazine, and the author of an outstanding book on champions of freedom during the 20th century.[6] I had met Aikman the previous year at a conference on religious freedom in China, a subject on which he was one of the world's leading experts.[7] At the time I invited him to the State Department to meet our staff and to give his views on various issues. All of us were impressed. Urbane, intelligent, friendly, Aikman seemed to me a very good man, although I had given no thought of his becoming ambassador. For one thing, he had no government experience. When he called me to say he was being put forward as a candidate, I went to meet him at the Old Ebbit Grill near the White House.

Aikman said that he knew of Hanford's candidacy, and that he personally thought very highly of John. But, he said, he had been approached by Horowitz and wanted my views of the job and what he might do to prepare in the event he was chosen. In a long conversation, I described the position to him, the mission of the office, and many of the problems that the new ambassador would face. I told him we had given John Hanford a blueprint of what the new ambassador would need to do in his first eight months and that I would provide it to him as well.

The dimensions of the problem became clear to me, however, only when I met Michael Horowitz face to face for the first time. It was on June 4, during a reception in the State Department's splendid eighth-floor Roosevelt Room after Lorne Craner's swearing in as assistant secretary. I had spoken on the phone several times in the past with Horowitz, most notably during the Karimi case described in the last chapter. As usual, he had played the role of outside catalyst in that case, sending faxes and making phone calls on behalf of the Karimis. I admired Horowitz's persistence, but he clearly had doubts about anyone unwise enough to work in the U.S. foreign service, even someone who, like me, was occasionally on his team. During one memorable telephone call, when I told him that I was working the Karimi case hard but behind the scenes, he told me, "You're just too damned nice to get this done." Later, after all but two of the Karimi family had been cleared to come to America, he faxed me what for him was high praise for a foreign service officer: "We're 6/8 of the way home! Keep working!"

I spied Horowitz in the Roosevelt Room and went up to introduce myself. He was quite friendly and we chatted briefly. He then grabbed my arm and, pulling me close, said in mock confidence: "Don't worry. We're going to make sure that John Hanford doesn't get the job." I made a feeble attempt to dissuade him, and he listened but then walked away.

Hanford Arrives, the Lions Roar

The secretary of state's conference room is on the seventh floor of the department, directly across the hall from the secretary's own suite of offices. Like the Roosevelt Room above it and the adjacent Treaty Room, this particular conference space is an oasis of rich fabrics, deeply polished mahogany antiques, and magnificent oil paintings. Here, I imagined, was where John Hanford would attend his first senior staff meeting after being sworn in by Deputy Secretary of State Richard Armitage. It was an event that I had eagerly anticipated for almost two years. Our office's leader would be presented to other senior officials at the Department of State as the president's and secretary's principal advisor on religious freedom.

But I also had reasons to be concerned. The earlier attempt to "double hat" the ambassador's position, combined with the administration's attitude of relative indifference to the filling of that position, made me worry that something might go wrong. But, I told myself, the Clinton administration had included Hanford's predecessor, Bob Seiple, in its senior staff meetings. Surely a Republican administration would do no less.

When John Hanford arrived for the swearing in, however, my worst fears were confirmed. After he left Armitage's office the new ambassador at large for international religious freedom was escorted to the secretary's morning staff meeting and introduced to the department's senior officials. On the way, he was pointedly informed: you may remain for this particular meeting, but it will be your last.

It was May 2002. Bob Seiple had resigned almost 20 months ago. Since his departure, I had served as the head of the office of international religious freedom, working to retain its autonomy while waiting for the Bush administration to fill the ambassador's position. The profile of the office within the department had continued to diminish as the Powell regime consolidated itself and became accustomed to dealing with Assistant Secretary Craner as the senior official with authority over issues of religious freedom. Now, on his first official day on the job, John Hanford was in effect being given his walking papers as "ambassador at large." Notwithstanding that title, and his having been confirmed by the Senate, he was to be treated as a "special interest" appointment, not a senior member of the department. There was simply no need for someone heading the religious freedom office to be in the regular senior staff meeting with the secretary.

There is nothing magic about senior staff meetings at the Department of State. Policy matters are seldom decided there. They are often employed as opportunities to update the secretary on issues of the moment from around the world or to hear the secretary's priorities for the day. Major policy decisions are typically handled in a measured fashion at the State Department. Often those decisions involve weeks or months of meetings within the department and among other agencies and the drafting of options and information papers, all leading to decision memoranda for the secretary or the president.

What the senior staff meetings do convey, however, is who is senior and who is not. From the first day he stepped into the State Department, it was clear to the other ambassadors at large, the under secretaries, and the assistant secretaries (who are the key policy officials at Foggy Bottom) that John Hanford was not a peer. Even though ambassadors at large were by department regulations senior to assistant secretaries, this official was going to be handled differently. Whatever Hanford's title, it was immediately made clear to all that he did not in fact work as "principal advisor to the president and secretary of state" as the IRF Act said he did. He worked in the bureau of democracy, human rights, and labor, and his de facto supervisor was the DRL assistant secretary, Lorne Craner.

I had prepared Hanford for the possibility that this would happen. He chose, perhaps understandably under the circumstances, not to challenge his downgrading, deciding instead to work slowly within the department to establish relationships and build confidence in him. This might have worked had the downgrading decision been based on him alone. Whether people respected John Hanford within the department was less important than the fact that the Powell team had no intention of upgrading the issue of religious freedom.

Toward the end of Powell's tenure, after more than two years on the job, Hanford made a plea for inclusion in the senior meetings. He was turned down. This occurred in spite of a remarkably accurate, and what should have been an alarming, judgment by the State Department's inspector general (IG), which in 2003 conducted a months-long, routine investigation of the DRL bureau. Most of the findings and recommendations were unremarkable. But its findings concerning the IRF office were stunning.

The State Department investigators concluded that America's international religious freedom policy was not working: "The current structure that places the congressionally mandated office of the Ambassador at Large for International Religious Freedom within DRL is at odds with the Department's organizational guidelines and has proved to be unworkable." This was a reference to the fact that ambassadors at large are senior to assistant secretaries, but that the IRF ambassador had, since the inception of the position, been subordinate to an assistant secretary. "As a consequence, *the purposes for which the religious freedom function was created are not being adequately served*" [emphasis added].[8] When this judgment was sent to Congress, I was hopeful that it would lead to pressure on the department. There was some interest,[9] but in the end the IG report was ignored by the Congress, the White House, and the State Department.

In the summer of 2008, six years into Ambassador Hanford's tenure and during the last months of the Bush administration, the State Department's public listing of "senior officials" included scores of positions, from senior advisers and coordinators to special envoys and special representatives. Their portfolios ranged from empowerment of women to commercial and business affairs. There was even a "special envoy for the Organization of the Islamic Conference." But the official designated by the IRF Act to lead the nation's policy on international religious freedom was still not on the list.[10]

In retrospect, it seems ironic that the ambassador's position under Hanford's predecessor, Bob Seiple, had been treated as more substantive by the Clinton-Albright team than by the Republicans under Colin Powell or Condoleeza Rice. Part of Seiple's relative success in that regard was doubtless due to his solid relationship with Secretary Albright and with Harold Koh, the assistant secretary who had preceded Lorne Craner. Hanford did not have the advantage of either relationship. Moreover, by one particular action Craner had made it clear, before the two men had ever met, that he had little regard for Hanford's authority and that he intended to retain control over Hanford's office. The incident was to demonstrate how difficult the new ambassador's job was going to be.

In the fall of 2001, after he had been formally nominated by the president, John Hanford asked me to stay in the job as his deputy and director of the office for an additional year, beginning the following summer (when my current tenure would end). After a period of some reflection I accepted, and informed the DRL front office. Within days, Assistant Secretary Craner moved to prevent this from happening by formally offering the position to another foreign service officer who was at the time in an overseas post. In one sense Craner's action was understandable. As related in chapter 6, he and I had clashed and he preferred to work with someone else. But there was only one circumstance under which he might believe my position was his to grant: that John Hanford was his subordinate, and there was no need to consult him.

Thus began a rocky relationship that ensured Hanford's first year was a difficult one. He spent weeks within the building fighting to ensure that other senior officials would support him in what seemed to be a simple proposition: the man who by law was the head of the office of international religious freedom, as well as the president's principal IRF advisor, had the authority to choose his own staff, and particularly his own deputy. In the end, Hanford won this skirmish. I was to remain as director until my departure in the fall of 2003. But his welcome to Foggy Bottom could hardly have been less propitious.

Another Struggle over China

As recounted in chapter 5, Bob Seiple had in 1999 won the initial battle within the department over whether to designate China as a "country of particular concern" (CPC) for particularly severe violations of religious freedom. By 2002, however, it was reasonably clear that the designation was having little if any effect on the Chinese. For one thing, it had proven to be a toothless, rhetorical denunciation. As the IRF Act permitted them to do, the Clinton and Bush administrations followed the designation with the "action" of reaffirming an existing human rights sanction, in this case the one that had been imposed in the wake of the 1989 Tiananmen Square massacres. That restriction forbade the export of U.S. crime control and detection equipment to the Chinese. Even among those who opposed punitive sanctions as a policy instrument, this double use of an empty punishment seemed a cynical ploy. "All this has done," as one skeptic put it, "is force the Chinese to buy their barbed wire and tear gas from the French."[11]

Initially the Chinese, although untouched by the "sanction," were quite irritated by the CPC designation itself. China is famously sensitive to the issue of "face" in the international community. Throughout the 1990s its officials fought vigorously (and successfully) in the U.N. Commission on Human Rights to defeat U.S.-sponsored resolutions condemning Beijing's human rights abuses. But as the CPC designations, duly accompanied by a reaffirmation of the ban on crime control equipment, recurred year after year, even the Chinese began to yawn. Any hope that the IRF "stick" might change that government's behavior, a dubious proposition in any case, dissipated when it became clear that neither the Clinton nor Bush administrations were serious about employing pressure. Indeed, one could argue that repeated China designations have set back the cause of religious freedom in that country by debasing the CPC coinage.

To give credit where it is due, both presidents Clinton and Bush pressed their Chinese counterparts on religious persecution. Both presidents spoke privately with President Jiang Zemin about their own faith. Their overt religious views very likely stimulated Jiang's policy interest in religion and contributed to the intensity of his involvement in a Chinese National Work Conference on Religion later in late 2001. The following year Bush devoted fully one-third of a major Beijing speech to the issue. As valuable as this and other presidential efforts are with the Chinese, significant policy shifts by a Chinese government are usually slow in coming. Any outside government, even the United States, seeking to influence those shifts must devote time, resources, and policy planning to the effort. Consistency in addressing any internal issue, let alone the internal issue of religion, is an utter necessity.

John Hanford began his tenure as ambassador at large with a determination to have an impact on Chinese religion policy. Unfortunately, just before his arrival in May, we missed a golden opportunity to ensure greater U.S. attention to religion in China and to lay the groundwork for Hanford's influence on our policy. It was one of those events which almost made me despair of continuing to fight for IRF within Foggy Bottom.

President Bush was going to China in February, and I knew that he was going to give a speech with a significant religious freedom message. Hanford had been confirmed as ambassador at large in January. As far as I was concerned, it was a "no-brainer" that the President's principal adviser on religious freedom should be on a trip in which this was to be a major presidential theme. I floated the idea in the department and at the staff of the National Security Council (NSC), but there was little interest. Typically, the NSC staff was unwilling to get involved in decisions they thought rested within the State Department. As I had learned from long experience, the next step was to get sympathetic people outside the department but with influence at the White House and the National Security Council staff to lobby for Hanford's inclusion on the trip.

One former official with years of experience in China tried to help and copied me on a private e-mail to an influential head of an NGO whose support we sought. The e-mail is worth quoting at some length:

> Tom is right; the President himself is the #1 advocate of religious freedom with the Chinese, and it WILL be high on the agenda....His sense is that he is "getting through" to Jiang Zemin with the idea that religion can be a POSITIVE force in China. BUT the job of putting together the strategy/talking points has been delegated to State. That means EAP [China desk], DRL and IRF have to slug it out.

When I suggested to [a named senior NSC official] that an efficient way to send a message was to take the new IRF Ambassador along, he said, "That's up to State Dept. politics."

My heart sank at the grim accuracy of that judgment, and of what followed.

The secularists in the two former, larger, more influential and better staffed offices, if left to themselves, will...conclude that [other named State Department officials] are (more than) enough to take along on the trip.

THEREFORE, [the former official warmed to the theme]. . our issues won't be STAFFED OUT, fleshed out, or symbolized by John's presence unless the issue of IRF gets highlighted TO BUSH by OTHERS outside State....Let me just mention/warn you that whoever is on the trip/in the conversations will be the people setting the agenda for OTHER top visits to and from China this year. IRF will be playing "catch up" for quite a while if John is NOT included.

John Hanford did not accompany the president on his February trip to China. The NSC official was quite correct that State Department politics would decide who went. No one in the Bush administration saw the need to override politics as usual at Foggy Bottom. And the e-mail turned out to be correct in its final prediction.

Nevertheless, Hanford came to the job the following May determined to have an impact in China. During his first six months on the job, he and I traveled to Beijing twice, as well as Nanjing and Shanghai. At the time, we believed his instructions were sufficiently broad that he had the opportunity to build a structural relationship on the issue of religion that might well have a significant policy effect over the long-term. However, it proved impossible for him to garner the kind of sustained attention from Foggy Bottom that would have been necessary for his proposals to take root. Partly as a result of lost opportunities, the United States government has had little impact on the issue of religion and religious freedom in China. The stakes on this issue are high for the Chinese, their neighbors, the international community, and the United States. There are indeed opportunities to influence the Chinese on the issue of religion, especially in the areas of law and social science, but we must be willing to seize them.

Our plane set down in Beijing in August 2002 for the first visit, barely three months after John Hanford had assumed his position as ambassador at large. The IRF staff had researched a long list of issues and had drawn heavily on the lessons learned during my two-week sojourn in China the previous year (see chapter 10). We had prepared a series of recommendations for Li Baodong, the director general of the North America office at the Ministry of Foreign Affairs and the major Chinese interlocutor with the United States on issues of security and human rights. Hanford had met Li earlier that summer in Washington, D.C., and both wanted to use this trip as a means of preparing for an upcoming meeting between President Bush and the new Chinese president, Hu Jintao. Hanford would also meet with Ye Xiaowen, director of China's State Administration for Religious Affairs (Bob Seiple's "O Ye of little faith"), and Li Dezhou, vice minister of the United Front Work Department, the party agency that exercised overall supervision over Ye and the problem of religion in China.

Our recommendations included a number of perennials that had been publicly discussed for years. The Chinese had seen them before, had routinely rejected them, and their responses on this visit were no different. For example, we requested access by an international agency to the Panchen Lama, the child named by the Dalai Lama as the reincarnation of the deceased tenth Panchen Lama. The Panchen is the second most revered religious figure in Tibet. The Chinese had subsequently named their own successor and were keeping under house arrest the young man identified by the Dalai Lama, denying any access to him by outside observers. The Chinese action was roughly equivalent to the affront to Catholics represented in Napoleon's arrest and persecution of Pope Pius VII. The Chinese did not respond to Hanford's request, and the young man remains under house arrest to this day, to the distress of Tibetans everywhere.[12]

Like others before and after him, Hanford also urged resumption of the Sino-Vatican dialogue, which had been interrupted in January 2000 by one of the periodic series of illicit Chinese "official" ordinations of Catholic bishops, followed later that year by the Vatican's controversial canonization of Chinese martyrs on the anniversary of the Chinese Communist revolution. The choice of date in particular had infuriated the Chinese, who believed that the slight was intentional. By the time of our visit, however, the relationship appeared to have stabilized a bit, and we suggested that the Chinese invite Pope John Paul II, or at least a high-level Vatican delegation, to Beijing. The United States, we said, would be willing to facilitate the dialogue.

For the Chinese, the Catholic issue had several dimensions, including the Vatican's continued recognition of Taiwan rather than Beijing as the capital of China. But the Vatican had long since made it clear that it would recognize Beijing in return for an agreement over the critical issue of bishops—their appointments and ordinations, the fates of the "underground" bishops (and priests), and the fate of those "official" bishops, like Fu Tieshan of Beijing, who openly defied the Vatican.[13] The Chinese authorities fear all religion, but they notoriously feared this "foreign import" of Roman Catholicism, especially given the role of its leader in bringing down communism in Western Europe.

We believed that an agreement between China and the Vatican would lead to greater religious freedom for Catholic bishops, priests, nuns, and laypeople.

We further suggested that the Chinese government issue invitations to the U.N. Special Rapporteur on Religious Freedom and the U.S. Commission on International Religious Freedom, respectively, to visit the country. Both suggestions were ultimately accepted.[14] And, as always, we provided a list of religious prisoners languishing in Chinese jails with the request that they be released.

Prisoner releases were important, not only for the freed individuals and their families, but also for the publicity that it brought to the problem of religious persecution. We had met with John Kamm, founder and president of the Dui Hua Foundation and one of the West's leading expert on Chinese prisoners.[15] Over the years Kamm had gained approval from the Chinese to compile a database of Chinese prisoners from official sources. He had ingeniously used this information to convince the central authorities that Chinese laws in some cases were being abused by local officials, in gaining consideration for legal or regulatory changes, and in securing the release of prisoners. Kamm provided us with a list of religious prisoners that represented all the religious groups, including the Falun Gong. His method of approaching the Chinese via the path of law has proven one of the most promising structural, long-term methods of dealing with religious persecution *and* religious freedom, although one that the United States has largely failed to exploit.

There were a few unusual, though not unprecedented, requests as well, such as official Chinese recognition of the Jewish religion. I had already observed the difficulties experienced by Jews in Shanghai, and ensured that Ambassador Hanford visited the historic but "official" Jewish synagogue in that city, where no religious services were permitted except under the most unusual circumstances. Just before our departure, we had learned that Israel had cancelled a planned Albert Einstein exhibit in China because the government insisted on deleting references to Einstein's Jewish background. Although there were few if any native Chinese Jews, there were plenty of Jewish expatriates in the country, many of whom had trouble practicing their religion. When Hanford raised this issue with Ye Xiaowen, Ye denied that the Einstein exhibit had been cancelled on the grounds that Einstein was a Jew. In a "some-of-my-best-friends" argument, he noted that, after all, Karl Marx had been a Jew. Ye said that Jews were not part of the Chinese nation and didn't need recognition.

Ambassador Hanford made an unusual but very important request on a problem he believed could be solved. He asked that China publicly support the right of parents to teach religion to their children, and that all Chinese religious communities be freed to engage in the teaching of minors. He was criticized when he returned to Washington noting the assurances of Ye Xiaowen and others that there were in fact *no* prohibitions on the teaching of religion to children.[16] That turned out to be a half truth—the constitution can be read not to prohibit such teaching—but in the provinces it is routinely interpreted to do precisely that.

The most promising of the items on our list, however, had to do with Chinese registration laws and the establishment of a permanent working group to act as a counterpart to the office of the ambassador at large for international religious freedom. We knew that the Chinese were struggling to decide what to do with their laws on religion, especially their registration laws. A National Work Conference on Religious Affairs in December 2001 had generated considerable discussion in China about religion, much of it unfortunately focused on tightening up the existing system of registering, controlling, and managing religious communities. The conference had been addressed by President Jiang Zemin, who told the assembled apparatchiks that religion "may outlast the party and the state." Such a statement from a Mao successor a mere 25 years after the Cultural Revolution was remarkable. Jiang urged the participants, according to the *South China Morning Post,* to find ways to "make socialism and religion adapt to each other."[17]

Hanford later described these proposals in testimony before a subcommittee of the House International Relations Committee.[18] He noted that the very requirement for registration of religious groups often would criminalize normal religious behavior. If registration had to be retained, at least registration standards should be made transparent and rationalized across the country. At a minimum, this would work against the abuse of regulations by local officials who used them arbitrarily to advance their own interests. The result was very often religious persecution. He told both Ye Xiaowen and Li Baodong that if the Chinese wished, our office would provide specialists on international law, religion, and registration to explain the experiences accumulated in other countries and to make recommendations.

There are at least two schools of thought on how to maximize the chances of Chinese acceptance of U.S. proposals on religion. One, employed by Ambassador Hanford and many others, was designed to exploit the Chinese desire to manage the U.S. relationship. "America management" was an important issue for the Chinese government, given our commercial and other ties and given their desire to maintain China's growing status in the international community. The United States, among all nations, was most willing to take actions at the United Nations or other multilateral forums to embarrass China by condemning its human rights abuses. For all those reasons, Chinese officials often had instructions to work with us and respond where they could to our requests. The occasions when they did not have such instructions, of course, were those periods when the relationship was in the tank, such as after the inadvertent U.S. 1999 bombing of the Chinese embassy in Belgrade. But it made good sense to take advantage of this dynamic, which we most often did by getting prisoners out of jail or getting China to invite UN human rights officials to the country.

Ambassador Hanford added to this approach an ingenious twist, which he used to good effect in many of his meetings. He described how the U.S.

political system worked on issues of religious persecution. When American church groups read of their co-religionists in China being put in jail or abused, they would put enormous pressure on elected members of Congress and the White House to punish China. Our system was such, he told the Chinese, that elected officials who wanted to keep their jobs would have to respond. It was very important, therefore, that the Chinese pay serious attention to the cases that he was bringing to their attention. This was a nice touch because it did not directly insult Chinese officials for religious persecution but fit their under-standing of "political systems" driving government policy.

The weakness of this approach, of course, was its short-term nature. Although Chinese officials might (and sometimes did) accede to short-term requests, they were not about to consider structural changes or major policy shifts on religion in order to manage their bilateral relationship with the United States. Taking this reality into account, the second school of thought is that U.S. policy could have an impact on such changes by making both short- and long-term proposals that are seen, or have the potential to be seen, by the Chinese government as directly in its interests, and by establishing a perma-nent mechanism for making the case for long-term change. In the broad area of human rights, the annual U.S.-China dialogue was seen by some as fulfilling such a role.[19]

The Chinese seemed interested in Hanford's discussion of registration problems, a reaction that I chalked up to the internal debate triggered by the National Work Conference a few months earlier. But Hanford did not want this discussion to become merely one more set of talking points that the Americans always brought to Beijing. He knew that his suggestions might be passed up the chain within the government or they might not. Like other suggestions and requests given to the Chinese during visits such as this one, or in the more formal U.S.-China human rights dialogues, they might generate an immediate rebuttal, a delayed rebuttal, or simply be ignored and pass into oblivion.

Accordingly, Hanford proposed a permanent bilateral interagency working group on religion that would follow through on both short-term problems and long-term structures such as Chinese religion law. The working group would be headed by Hanford and Li and would meet formally several times each year. Its membership would move substantially beyond the Chinese Ministry of Foreign Affairs, however, and would include representatives of such organizations as the United Front Work Department, the State Administration of Religious Affairs at the national and, as appropriate, the provincial levels, representa-tives from state security agencies, and from Chinese academic institutions, especially the Chinese Academy of Social Sciences. Each of these agencies and institutions would be replicated on the U.S. side. Ongoing talks and prepara-tions for the regular meetings would be led by designated representatives at the U.S. and Chinese embassies, the Chinese Ministry of Foreign Affairs, and the State Department's office of international religious freedom.

Li was intrigued by this proposal, although he naturally had concerns about its acceptance at higher levels of the party. In the ensuing months, however, it also became clear that Li was willing to follow through if the proposal were pressed by other senior American officials. In the end, however, this did not happen. Our attempts to include a reference to this recommendation for Deputy Secretary Armitage's visit to Beijing later that year, and for President Bush in his upcoming meeting with the new Chinese Premier, were nixed within the department. The case for a permanent Sino-American working group on religion, given all the truly urgent issues of our bilateral relationship, was simply not high enough on the State Department's list of priorities.

Had this idea been embraced by the United States—especially after being shown some interest by the Chinese—it is entirely possible that our influence over China's religion policy would have been institutionalized and increased over time. But the proposal was permitted to lapse. It was buried in that undistinguished graveyard of episodic American talking points, perhaps to be resurrected at a later date by U.S. officials, perhaps not.

Using the IRF Act Creatively

Although the issue of religion in China remained virtually intractable throughout his tenure, Ambassador Hanford learned from his experiences there and put that knowledge to work in another communist country nearby, Vietnam. After our August 2002 meetings in China he had traveled on to Hanoi, where he began a series of negotiations to which he returned again and again over the next several years. The Vietnamese government was almost as fearful of religion as were the Chinese, and in some ways looked to Beijing as a model. And yet Vietnam's history was quite different from China's. Not only was Hanoi struggling to recover from what we in America call the Vietnam War and its aftermath, but also it had in some ways a better relationship with Christians. Lacking China's concerns about Taiwan, Hanoi had begun to work with the Vatican on the appointment of bishops and even on the expansion of seminary training. It had established Vietnamese versions of China's "patriotic" churches that were less restrictive for some Protestant groups. Even Vietnamese Muslims appeared to have some freedom of worship, which I had discovered in a visit to a Hanoi mosque during a trip there in October 2001.

But Vietnam was still a haven for religious persecution. Leaders of indigenous Hoa Hao and Buddhists were constantly under observation and the threat of arrest. In remote provinces, especially the Central Highlands and the north, Protestant evangelicals were subjected to arrests, forced renunciations, and the demolition of their churches. Even Hanoi's approximately 200,000 Catholics were served by only four priests as late as 2001. American religious groups who were admitted to Vietnam remained under close scrutiny by authorities, as I had learned in Hanoi in conversations with Adventists, Mennonites, and representatives of the Assemblies of God.

Like their counterparts the world over, these men and women hoped to win the confidence of local authorities by avoiding any association with the U.S. government (rejecting any U.S. funding, for example) and by doing good works rather than proselytizing (which was forbidden). One told me that local believers did not always understand why he could not talk about religion with them even as he assisted them with medicine or learning to read. He would explain to them that the time was not right but that he had hope that would change. An elderly married couple described how they had worked for years teaching remote villagers how to dig holes deep in the ground to keep diabetes medicine cool and safe from spoilage. The villagers were, of course, grateful, but the old couple was in constant danger of arrest.

From the beginning of his tenure as ambassador, John Hanford went to work in Vietnam with a vengeance. In trips to the country from 2002 through 2006 he and his staff designed and implemented a plan that has begun to pay dividends, although it is not without its problems or its critics. During the first two years, he characteristically built relationships inside Vietnam and expanded his knowledge of facts on the ground. By 2004 he had developed a bill of particulars so overwhelming against the Vietnamese government that, against predictable resistance within the State Department, he convinced Secretary Powell to designate Vietnam as a country of particular concern. But this was merely the first step in his plan. Hanford had assured the Vietnamese privately that they need not remain on the list, particularly during the consideration of Vietnam by the Congress for most favored nation trading status, if they were willing to take some bold steps.

The IRF Act contained a provision never employed until now, even though the act stipulated it as a "primary objective" for dealing with countries of particular concern. After designating a country as a CPC, the State Department was authorized to negotiate a binding agreement with that country as a means of removing them from the list. Working for months with American diplomats and the Hanoi government, Hanford negotiated such an agreement in May 2005. Although it has not been made public, the document's general provisions are reasonably clear. It pledges the national government to pass laws against forced renunciations and to ease restrictions on unregistered religious groups. Later that summer, because such steps had not yet been taken, Hanford ensured Vietnam remained on the CPC list despite the agreement.

But by late 2006, Hanoi had taken some major steps that led Hanford and the Department to remove Vietnam from the CPC category. This was something entirely new. Heretofore, the only nations who were removed from the list had been those whose tyrannical governments had been overthrown by U.S. military action—Serbia, Afghanistan, and Iraq. Now, for the first time, the IRF Act had been used as it had been intended—to leverage governments to cooperate with the United States, in this case also exploiting the Vietnamese desire for most favored nation status.

Hanford described his reasoning in his announcement of the action: "Four years ago, when I was appointed Ambassador at Large, tens of thousands of people, entire villages in some cases, were being rounded up and pressured to renounce their faith. Today there are laws against forced renunciations and reports of this disturbing practice are very isolated. When I first traveled to Vietnam," he continued, "there were dozens of individuals imprisoned for their religious beliefs. Today all of those people have been released...[including] Buddhists, Catholics, Protestants and Hoa Hao, some of whom had been in jail for many years....When we designated Vietnam a CPC, only three Christian groups were able to practice in the country legally....and hundreds of churches were shut down." Now hundreds of churches had been reopened, formerly outlawed religious communities were being recognized (including Buddhist groups and the Baha'is), seminaries were opening, and pastors were being trained.[20]

His decision was severely criticized by a few religious freedom groups, including the IRF Commission, which expressed its "strong disappointment," and cited countervailing evidence of continued persecution within Vietnam.[21] By the spring of the following year, Hanford publicly insisted that the agreement was holding, although, in fact, it is too soon to tell whether it will have any long-term effect.[22] It is entirely possible that it was merely a ploy by Hanoi to win most favored nation status from the United States. If so, the agreement itself would still constitute a positive step. But should the Vietnamese change their calculus, their anti-persecution policies could easily be reversed. Should they do that, there is little historical reason for them to believe the State Department would make them pay for reneging on the agreement.

But whatever the future holds for religious groups in Vietnam, John Hanford and the officers of the office of international religious freedom had accomplished something unprecedented. Applying his attention to that country over four years, he exploited both the movement of history and the provisions of a law he had helped write to ease the suffering of substantial numbers of human beings of all faiths. And, as the head of one of Washington's leading religious freedom NGOs told me, Hanford's use of the IRF Act had provided a very useful tool in pressing for change from the inside in other countries, such as Uzbekistan, which was put on the CPC list in 2006.[23]

The Saudi Conundrum

Chapter 8 explores the sources of Wahhabi extremism in Saudi Arabia, which, it is now widely acknowledged, has been exported around the world with catastrophic consequences. For the present, it is important to understand how Ambassador Hanford, his colleagues in the IRF office, and the Saudi experts in the State Department managed to exploit the new winds that began to blow in Arabia after the 9/11 attacks and, in particular, after Al Qaeda made a successful 2003 attack in Riyadh itself. These events led the ruling house of Saud to begin questioning its 200-year political compact with Wahhabism, a virulent theology and clerical establishment that had provided much of the theological warrant for Bin Ladenism.

Although Hanford traveled to Saudi Arabia, he did much of his relationship building in Washington with the influential Saudi Ambassador and member of the royal family, Prince Bandar, as well as Bandar's successors. When I left the office in late 2003, we had begun to focus on concrete proposals that might fit into and encourage the new thinking now taking place in Riyadh. Drawing on my January 2001 trip there, I provided before leaving a few thoughts on how the United States might exploit the shifting zeitgeist in U.S.-Saudi relations. During the next two years Ambassador Hanford took his time to circle around the issue, sending his staff to Saudi Arabia and doing research on the status of religious groups and religious persecution in the kingdom. He also focused on the bigoted literature used in Saudi classrooms and exported around the world for use in Saudi-financed mosques, including in the United States.[24] By 2004 he was able to add Saudi Arabia to the CPC list for the first time, aided in his battle inside the State Department by increasing demands for the designation from the IRF Commission and the Hill.[25]

By 2005, the Bush administration had decided to engage in a "strategic dialogue" with the Saudis across a whole range of issues. The centerpiece was security cooperation against the scourge of Al Qaeda. But the Saudis were not willing to address the question of Islam directly, either in the form of Wahhabi contributions to extremism in Saudi Arabia (let alone elsewhere) or the inevitable role of Islam in any long-term solution to Saudi difficulties. Nor was the State Department interested in doing so. What it was willing to do was piggyback on the work already commenced by the office of international religious freedom on the questions of "intolerant literature and extremist ideology" and on the fate of non-Muslims and disfavored Muslims within the kingdom. This effort was undertaken by the Partnership, Education, Exchange, and Human Development Working Group.[26]

The result of the dialogue on religion appeared in July 2006. Unlike the Vietnam agreement, this did not constitute a binding contract between the United States and Saudi Arabia and was not officially published. But it led to an informal document that noted "the Saudi Arabian government has confirmed that it is pursuing and will continue to pursue the policies outlined below." Those policies were categorized under four headings: "Halt the Dissemination of Intolerant Literature and Extremist Ideology with Saudi Arabia and around the World"; "Protect the Right to Private Worship and the Right to Possess and Use Personal Religious Materials"; "Curb Harassment of Religious Practice"; and "Empower the [Saudi] Human Rights Commission."

Once again, John Hanford had managed to use the IRF Act creatively, taking what the Saudis, the State Department, and the movement of history would give him and turning it into a positive force. If the informal Saudi pledges were in fact carried out, the beneficiaries would not only be religious minorities in the kingdom, but also the victims of Islamist extremism around the world.

The Hanford Legacy

If it is too soon to judge the legacy of Bob Seiple (1998–2000) as ambassador at large for international religious freedom with any finality, it is certainly premature to make any but the most tentative judgments about the tenure of John Hanford (2002–present), who remains in the job at this writing. But six years of work at Foggy Bottom have yielded sufficient fruit to measure his performance against the arguments of this book, one of which is that U.S. IRF policy should broaden its focus to the political relationships between religion and state, both to increase the effectiveness of its anti-persecution efforts and to employ religious freedom in the quest for stable self government around the world.

John Hanford, it needs to be said, would disagree, at least in part, with being measured against this standard. He has never seen his mission as ambassador, or the mandate of the IRF Act, as entirely consistent with the broader IRF foreign policy objectives advocated in this book. In May 2007, this point was highlighted when Hanford and I appeared together in Washington, D.C., at a conference sponsored by the Pew Forum on Religion and Public Life. Joining us on the panel was John Shattuck, head of the John F. Kennedy Library and former assistant secretary of state for democracy, human rights, and labor under the Clinton administration. Shattuck had been the Department of State's leading spokesman against the need for IRF legislation.

The Pew Forum conference was entitled, "International Religious Freedom: Religion and International Diplomacy," and it posed the following questions to the panelists: Has the State Department interpreted the international religious freedom policy too narrowly over the past decade by focusing on individual cases of religious persecution? Does the country need new legislation to mandate a high-level understanding of religion among State Department officials? Does a robust international religious freedom policy truly advance U.S. national interests?

Ambassador Hanford began with a defense of his policy, followed by a critique from Shattuck and me.[27] He then responded. Let John Hanford speak for himself:

> I certainly won't argue the issue [U.S. IRF policy] has had its challenges in being mainstreamed over time. That's true of any issue, but

there's something about religion and the way many people react to it....An awful lot of progress has been made in mainstreaming the religious freedom issue in the State Department, and the way you do that...is...by earning the trust day after day after day as you work with all the different people and bureaus over time, and they realize you are helping to advance the goals of the U.S. government in advancing democracy, fighting terrorism, and promoting stability and security around the world and for our nation. We've made a great deal of progress in doing that through our work.

After addressing Shattuck's comments that some saw the IRF Act as a front for American missionaries, as codifying an illegitimate hierarchy of human rights, and as mostly a vehicle of punishment,[28] Hanford turned to my critique:

Turning to some of Tom's...suggestions, the focus of the International Religious Freedom Act is diplomacy on behalf of religious freedom. If you look at the act, you can see that really is the focus. It *is* promoting religious freedom, and we do that, but after you've had a warm fuzzy discussion with the Communist government, where they'll point to their constitution and say, "Look, our constitution guarantees religious freedom," the only way you can really get down to brass tacks is to talk about the violations and how those need to be addressed, and how people need to be released from prison or torture chambers. [emphasis added]

...I would say the return on investment for our little office in terms of the promotion of freedom and human rights around the world has been significant compared to much of the work of our government. I'm not sure Tom is saying the whole agenda he's laying out—which is a very ambitious one—should be imposed on the Religious Freedom Office....

I agree there is a vast, untapped potential. My concern is that [our] efforts go into advancing religious freedom in a country, not just in understanding religion writ large or a broad sense of tolerance, though we fight hard for that....I call this...the thousand-step problem. There are three steps that have to happen. First you have to have believers on the ground that cry out, "We need help." Secondly, someone issues a press release and brings this to people's attention. Thirdly, people jump up and down and say, "Somebody needs to do something about this."

I would argue our office does step two and three better than anyone in the world. We publicize the problems. We jump up and down all the time, but the State Department is saying, "Somebody needs to do something about this," and we try to lead in doing that. But those steps are easy. The hard part is the other 997 steps of working with the government day in and day out, argument after argument, to get people out of prison, to get laws changed, to travel there, to build relationships, to win them over.

What I want to defend is my office's mandate to do that work, because if we're required to do a lot of other things that are much more amorphous, we will lose the ability to do that, and we'll be watered down to doing nothing more than issuing this report and occasionally piping up about problems. We need to stick with our efforts on fighting the core problem, and that is the right of people to simply believe what they want to believe.

...The most appropriate issue for a government to talk to another government about when it comes to religion is the religious freedom issue. I'm all for talking more broadly about the importance of religion, and I agree fully about the importance of religion to stability and to a democratic society, and I make these points, and I have those discussions, and I'm in an interfaith dialogue with Muslim ambassadors, but, boy, is that slow, amorphous work.

When I sit down with the foreign minister and talk about basic human rights their government had signed onto in U.N. documents, they don't fault me for that. They occasionally do say, "Why do you Americans care so much about religious freedom?" I have to explain it's a part of our heritage. But that is the best vantage point for me to argue for these basic rights. That's where a government belongs at the table. That's what we should be leveraging: our diplomatic channels, our open doors of dialogue with these governments. That's where we get the greatest rate of return on our efforts.

Ambassador Hanford was right that I am not arguing that the entire burden of the broader policy toward religion advocated in this book should be borne by the office of international religious freedom. However, that office is currently the sole agency in the U.S. government's foreign affairs establishment with the mission of engaging religion in the international order. If the policy of the United States is to change, it stands to reason that the change must begin, or at least be supported, in that office.

His comments make clear that John Hanford does not see it that way. Although he acknowledges the need to help "advance the goals of the U.S. government in advancing democracy, fighting terrorism, and promoting stability and security around the world and for our nation," his own goals and especially his methodology have led him in a different direction. The "997 steps" that he has taken, especially in Vietnam and Saudi Arabia, have been vintage Hanford: the slow but remorseless building of a case and carrying out a plan whose primary objectives are "to get people out of prison, to get laws changed,...[to fight] the core problem, and that is the right of people to simply believe what they want to believe."

That approach was also evident in his work to free Abdul Rahman from the fate of execution for apostasy at the hands of an Afghan court. Hanford declared the freeing of Rahman a victory for religious freedom.[29] In the context of the way he (and, for the most part, the Department of State) understands his job, it was a victory. But if religious liberty is understood as the achievement of a stable democratic covenant between religion and state, then the flight of Rahman suggested a failure of U.S policy, not a success. A regime of religious freedom would not only reject state coercion for apostasy, it would protect and ultimately encourage public religious expression and debate, including about the issue of government involvement in apostasy or blasphemy. In Afghanistan, the protection of public religious expression is utterly necessary if mainstream, moderate Muslims are to overcome the extremist *shari'a* views now held by members of the government, and especially in the courts. In that country, as in so many others, religion must become part of the solution to the challenge of democracy and the threat of Islamist extremism.

It seems a reasonable inference from the evidence that John Hanford does not see his job as addressing these issues. It is not that he is unconcerned about the structures of persecution, as the foregoing discussions of his work in China, Vietnam, and Saudi Arabia have shown. Perhaps that work will pay dividends for American national security over the long-term. Moreover, his efforts and those of his colleagues in the office of international religious freedom have resulted in the freeing of prisoners in other countries as well. In Central Asia, for example, there remain lively possibilities that their work will produce the kinds of progress seen in Vietnam.

But his approach to the structural issues has generally involved one-on-one diplomacy, as he puts it, "working with the government day in and day out, argument after argument, to get people out of prison, to get laws changed, to travel there, to build relationships, to win them over." He sees a clear distinction between "talking more broadly about the importance of religion," which is "slow, amorphous work," and what he sees as the primary content of his job: working with governments to reduce persecution. But the evidence suggests that, despite his undoubted devotion and single-mindedness, his methodology has had little long-term impact.

In fact, that slow amorphous work is far more likely to reduce persecution over the longer term, and to advance religious freedom, than is one-on-one diplomacy, which is better suited to addressing individual cases. The Sino-American interagency working group on religion, which Hanford himself proposed, would have provided a venue for regularizing discussions and instituting programs designed to demystify and rationalize Chinese views of religious communities. This is the kind of institutional framework that could be established in a number of countries, supervised by the talented staff of the office of international religious freedom in cooperation with our embassies overseas and our country desks in the Department of State. An institutional approach could involve larger numbers of foreign government agencies and private actors. It would also broaden the implementation of U.S. IRF policy beyond one ambassador and one office.

Ambassador Hanford's preference for private diplomacy, and his tendency to focus on persecution, have also led him to resist getting himself or his office involved in broader policy matters that should involve religion, but often don't. The IRF office does not participate in formulating U.S. policy for key countries such as China, Russia, Egypt, or Saudi Arabia; democracy promotion strategies; funding nongovernmental projects on law and civil society in key countries; or decisions on foreign aid. In the end, he does not see these issues as directly relevant to his mission. For similar reasons he has not wanted the IRF office involved in planning NGO grant programs and in granting funds to NGOs who seek to address issues of religious freedom. In the absence of his voice at the State Department, not surprisingly no one else has taken a leadership role. The result is an almost complete lack of State Department funding for NGO activity in advancing religious freedom, however defined.[30]

Two additional legacies merit emphasis. During John Hanford's tenure, with assistance from members of Congress such as Frank Wolf (R, Virginia) and Chris Smith (R, New Jersey), and often against the resistance of State Department officials, the staff of the IRF office has grown from a handful of officials to approximately 25. Many of these men and women are highly accomplished and utterly dedicated to the cause of opposing religious persecution and of advancing religious freedom. As Hanford puts it, "we have almost more Ph.D.s per capita than any other office, more lawyers than any office but the legal office, and probably more seminary grads. I like to say we can out-think, out-sue and out-pray any other office at the State Department. But," he adds quite sensibly, "we're still a tiny office taking on the whole world's religious freedom problems."[31]

Unfortunately, the proportion of foreign service officers (FSOs) in the IRF staff remains quite low. While brilliant and creative minds from outside the diplomatic service are attracted to this issue of growing importance to our nation, few FSOs see it that way. It is perceived by most of them—even those who are interested in religion as a policy issue—as a dead-end for their careers. It would be difficult to make the case that they are wrong.

This situation can only change with policy decisions from a president and a secretary of state that are designed to mainstream the issue of religion in American foreign policy. Those changes will involve more than the IRF office and its ambassador, and must especially target the regional bureaus at the State

Department. In chapter 9 we will elaborate the steps that might be taken in this regard, but they include the systematic training of FSOs about religion and international affairs, the adoption of a religion subspecialty under the political and economic career paths that most diplomats are assigned or achieve, and incentives involving promotions and awards.

Perhaps most important, the issue of religion and the U.S. policy of promoting religious freedom will need to be integrated, as Ambassador Hanford put it at the Pew Forum, into U.S. strategies for "advancing democracy, fighting terrorism, and promoting stability and security around the world and for our nation." Despite his argument that this goal has to some extent been achieved, the evidence suggests that very little integration has actually taken place. Truly integrating those critical national security issues into our IRF policy, and vice versa, would very likely increase the numbers of Foreign Service Officers willing to cast their lot with the office of international religious freedom or engage in other foreign affairs activities that involve religion.

Second, the IRF ambassador and his office now have full authority over the annual IRF report. This is potentially one of the most important changes that have occurred under Hanford's stewardship at the State Department. The report has long been seen as the most comprehensive of its kind in cataloguing the violations of religious freedom that occur around the world. That is a critically important accomplishment by itself, one that, as both Bob Seiple and John Hanford have emphasized, helps give hope to the persecuted by shining a light on their fate. Former prisoners of conscience such as Natan Sharansky, who languished in the Soviet gulag for years, have made it abundantly clear how important it was for them—for their morale and their capacity for hope—that the United States spoke out openly and honestly about their torment.[32]

But the IRF report has a greater role to play in a broad effort against persecution and the advancement of political regimes of religious freedom. It can become more than a catalogue, however accurate, of the outrages perpetrated by some men against others. It can be used as a policy tool to undermine the structures of persecution and advance the structures of freedom. This can be done by employing the sections on U.S. actions in each country chapter as more than a disjointed catalogue of embassy efforts and visits by U.S. officials (who always "raise the issue" of persecution). Those activities, as important as they are, are rarely part of any broader U.S. strategy. Too often they are not tied to the abuses and restrictions described elsewhere in the chapter.

The explanation for this disjointedness is clear: there is no overarching U.S. policy to address the problems themselves, let alone encourage the institutions that can overcome them or connect them to larger American interests. The *Annual Report on International Religious Freedom,* in short, should become a major policy tool for engaging—not merely describing—a world of faith.

PART III

Particulars

Many obstacles and opportunities face American diplomacy as it engages a world increasingly influenced by public manifestations of faith. Both problems and possibilities, of course, exist in every region and every culture. But two challenges loom above the others: those presented by the lands of Islam in the greater Middle East and those presented by China. In both, U.S. policy makers and diplomats remain largely ignorant or confused about the effects of religious doctrines, communities, actors, and political theologies. But the stakes are too high for our religious myopia to remain untreated. We now turn to the task of discerning the politico-religious landscape in these two areas and exploring how we might address them more fruitfully in furthering American interests.

That U.S. foreign policy has at its heart the defense of American interests should shock no one. Doubtless, however, many abroad (and some at home) will see such a statement as chauvinistic and retrograde, a throwback to less enlightened times. To that canard I can only plead anti-utopianism or, better said, realism properly understood. Just as human beings are religious by nature, so too do nation states appear to be in the nature of things. What has changed in recent years is the increase in quantity and power of transnational actors and trends. But nations, societies, and governments remain the primary objects of diplomacy. Even Al Qaeda cannot do its wicked work without the cooperation, the acquiescence, or the stupidity of governments. Until nation states fade we must continue to work in and through them to counter the evil that men do, and to encourage the better angels of their nature. More to the point, we must continue to love our own nation, serving it, and honoring those who have sacrificed their lives or well-being in foreign fields, with the best national security strategies we can muster.

Our journey of discernment begins at the heart of Islam, Saudi Arabia, where a pernicious political theology called Wahhabism has reigned virtually unchallenged for over a century. The implications of Wahhabism for the Saudis themselves have been serious enough, but those implications have also spilled out into much of the Muslim world and beyond. Most important, the strains of Wahhabism exported from the desert kingdom have melded with other versions of Islamist radicalism to nourish and empower Bin Ladenism and similar Islamist extremist movements. These trends are broadly understood within the U.S. foreign policy establishment, but—as my trip into the desert kingdom (chapter 8) demonstrated—the options for engaging them are severely limited by the religion-avoidance syndrome that continues to dominate U.S. policy.

The problems presented by Saudi Arabia and Wahhabi political theology can only be successfully resolved over the long term by the development of stable Islamic self-government in the desert kingdom and elsewhere in the greater Middle East. To date, American efforts to promote democracy have been thin. They have largely ignored the important role of religion in the cultural underpinnings that must exist if democracy is to be peaceful, stable, and enduring. The United States has an opportunity to recalibrate and strengthen its efforts by engaging the religious communities and actors that will be vital to success or to failure. We explore that opportunity in chapter 9.

From the Middle East we turn to the Far East and the ancient state of China. The move is jarring in a sense: having departed from lands suffused with religion we now find ourselves in an officially atheist state whose recent history includes an attempt to destroy religion altogether and replace it with a Maoist form of Marxism. To its credit, China's current generation of leaders has largely understood the tragedy and futility of the Cultural Revolution. Unfortunately, China's government has replaced a policy of eliminating religion with one of management by suppression. It is trying to ride the dragon of China's exploding religious devotion by applying the iron hand of socialist bureaucracy. It is French *laicite* on steroids. The Chinese system results in periodic bouts of persecution, occasionally deadly. It is unlikely to succeed over the long term.

America's interests are, as always, both humanitarian and strategic. The human suffering occasioned by Chinese persecution is sometimes quite serious, and U.S. diplomats from time to time heroically succeed in reducing it, springing a fortunate handful of believers from prison or inducing the central authorities to sanction a provincial official. The strategic dimension of the problem, however, is virtually unnoticed in American foreign policy circles. Unless the Chinese can abandon their policy of religious repression and learn to tap the enormous resources represented in Chinese religious communities, the trajectory of China's religious demography will lead to large scale instability. It is in American interests to help the Chinese avoid this problem, and chapter 10 explores how that daunting challenge might be met.

In short, in the lands of Islam and in China, religious realism and religious freedom rightly understood offer a new and better way to protect the fundamental security interests of the American people. To those vital issues we now turn.

8

———— ∞ ————

Seeking the Heart of Islam

Muslims are drawn to Mecca like filings to a magnet, attracted by the
integrative power of a journey to the heartland.... Simply to set foot
there may answer years of longing.
— Michael Wolfe

Religious freedom does not exist in Saudi Arabia.
— U.S. Department of State

It was early January 2001 when our plane set down at King Khaled International
Airport in Riyadh, Saudi Arabia. No one on that flight could have known that in
barely eight months the United States would be attacked by other commercial
aircraft controlled by terrorists, most of them born here in the desert kingdom. With the benefit of hindsight it is not difficult to identify the warning
signs then present in Saudi Arabia and elsewhere in the Muslim world. In the
months and years after September 11, 2001, Americans learned that a handful
of officials in the CIA, FBI, and the White House had isolated bits of information that indicated a pending Al Qaeda attack on the United States. Their failure to communicate with each other, and their consequent inability to draw the
inferences that now seem so agonizingly clear, is well established.[1]

If too few American officials were alert to short-term indicators, even fewer
were paying attention to the ideological seedbed of the attacks—the malevolent
and dehumanizing theology that dominated this modern Arab nation where
Islam had appeared some 14 centuries ago. As I deplaned in Riyadh, religious
persecution was on my mind, not religion-based terrorism or the relationship
between the two. I had been acting head of the State Department's office of
international religious freedom (IRF) for four months and expected to hear

soon of the incoming Bush administration's nominee to replace Bob Seiple as the IRF ambassador at large.

For the time being, however, I wanted to get a firsthand look at the Saudi approach to religion. My experiences since Seiple's departure, including the preparations for this trip, had increased my concern that U.S. IRF policy was not working as it should. Its focus on persecution and prisoner releases was helping to obscure a strong diplomatic distaste for understanding religion as a policy matter. As it turned out, the trip would increase my conviction that the U.S. policy of "promoting religious freedom" needed a much broader application. The attacks on the American homeland later that year led me to begin thinking of IRF policy as a means of pursuing the struggle against terrorism.

Unfortunately, years after the attacks of 9/11, American foreign policy continues to resist any such role for its policy of advancing religious freedom. There is no systematic approach to what ought to be a central task of U.S. national security strategy, namely, understanding the religious wellsprings of Islamist extremism and its origins in places such as Saudi Arabia. There is too little thought given to supporting religious actors capable of altering the climate of opinion that nurtures the terrorists, their extremist religious views, and the export of those views.

To be sure, there are nonreligious factors contributing to the rise of Islamist terrorism, including political and economic grievances, social alienation, and modern technology. Nor is Saudi Arabia the only nation that has contributed to the brutal theology that gave us 9/11, and it is by no means the only country with a part to play in altering or containing it. Egypt, in particular, was the birthplace of two of the most important 20th-century precursors of contemporary Islamist extremism, Hassan al-Banna, the founder of the Muslim Brotherhood, and Sayyid Qutb, whose writings have inspired generations of young Muslims to the murder of innocents.

The teachings of Mawlana Maududi, the founder of the political party Jamaat-al-Islam in India and Pakistan, have likewise influenced many radicals and terrorists, including the Taliban. These and others have fed the terrorist movements that derive from the Sunni tradition. Moreover, there are Shia variations of Islamist extremism, especially that of Ayatollah Ruhollah Khomeini and his spiritual progeny in Iran and Iraq, which threaten vital American interests in the Middle East.

But no soil has proven more fertile to the growth of national, regional, and transnational Islamist terrorism than the place where Islam was born.

—◦◦◦—

There are, it seems, at least two Saudi Arabias. One is symbolized by the Saudi town of Mecca. For virtually all 1.3 billion Muslims worldwide Mecca is the geographic and spiritual center of Islam. It is situated in the middle of a narrow tract of barren desert surrounded by mountains along the west coast of Arabia— a region called the Hijaz. It was here in the late 6th century that Mohammed was born into a tribal, polytheistic, divided society, and where he grew to man- hood. Muslims believe that in 610, when Mohammed was 40, he began to receive from the archangel Gabriel an extended revelation that, when written down, became the Koran. During the ensuing 22 years of Mohammed's life, the revelations developed and the religion of Islam was born. Meccans resisted the new monotheistic religion, and in 622 Mohammed and his small band of followers were forced into exile. Moving north to Medina, the Muslims gained adherents and in 629 returned in force to Mecca, which quickly capitulated.

Mecca had for centuries been the site of a cube-shaped building called the Ka'ba, which was surrounded by the structures and idols of countless Middle Eastern religions. Mohammed cleared the area of its idols and declared the Ka'ba the Muslim House of God. Three months before his death in 632 he led tens of thousands of Muslims on what has become known as the Farewell Hajj. He designated a pilgrim route around the Ka'ba and between Mecca and the surrounding desert, fashioning existing rites into a Muslim ritual that is still performed today. At the climax of the Farewell Hajj, Mohammed "deliv- ered the last verses of the Koran, completing the foundation of the Muslim religion, making the Hajj and the sacred book its capstones."[2] Islam was now complete.

For almost 14 centuries the Hajj, or annual pilgrimage to Mecca, has been a primary religious obligation for Muslims. One of the five pillars of Islam, it is required at least once in the lifetime of every Muslim able to undertake the journey. Its significance within Islam is difficult to overstate. Indeed, the term "religious obligation" is insufficient to capture the longing for the journey and the meaning of its destination. Today over two million Muslims from 125 coun- tries perform the Hajj each year, the largest annual gathering of people for a religious purpose on earth. Michael Wolfe, an American convert to Islam who has written about his own experience of the Hajj and edited a compendium of accounts by other travelers to Mecca, puts it this way:

> Muslims are drawn to Mecca like filings to a magnet, attracted by the integrative power of a journey to the heartland. More than a city, Mecca is a principal part of speech in a sacred language and the direction Muslims pray in throughout their lives. Simply to set foot there may answer years of longing. Mohammed's story takes on new meaning in Mecca too, as that of an exemplary human being who, when he went to make the Hajj, made it over in the spirit of Islam....[The Hajj has become for millions] a reminder of how life ought to be lived....[3]

There is another Saudi Arabia. It is in many ways symbolized by Riyadh, the capital of the modern kingdom and the seat of its government. Riyadh is situated some 500 miles northeast of Mecca in the center of the Arabian desert region known as the Najd. The Najd was the birthplace of Muhammad bin Abd al-Wahhab and spawned what is certainly the most consequential theological interpretation of Islam inside the kingdom and arguably its most destructive interpretation elsewhere in the Muslim world. Among its other distinctions, Riyadh is the birthplace of Wahhab's most famous progeny, Osama Bin Laden. Which of the two Saudi Arabias will be dominant over the early decades of the 21st century will have much to say about Islam and considerable influence on the fundamental interests and security of the American people.

Osama Bin Laden and the terrorist movement he came to embody have become global phenomena, their momentum detached from the sands of Arabia. Indeed, during the 1990s, the government of Saudi Arabia declared him persona non grata in his own country and has in more recent years waged a ferocious campaign within the country against his organization, Al Qaeda. But neither Bin Laden nor Al Qaeda can be fully understood apart from the ideas and institutions prevalent in the country where he was raised and educated. Unless those ideas and institutions are substantially altered or contained, they will continue to inspire recruits for Bin Ladenism long after he is gone, not only in Saudi Arabia, but also in Muslim communities throughout the world. The glue of his movement is not Bin Laden, nor a drive to power, wealth, or blind hatred. It is the devastating conviction, spawned and nourished in this desert kingdom centuries after the death of Mohammed, that God demands violence and coercion in carrying out his will. And, despite its pledge to cease official support for the export of these ideas, the Saudi government has not yet demonstrated its will, or even its ability, to achieve that goal.[4]

The Bin Laden family's roots run deep into the kingdom and its capital city. Osama's father, Mohammed Bin Laden, built Riyadh's first concrete building and his engineering and construction firm was a mainstay of the city's remarkable growth. Once a provincial town of mud buildings, modern Riyadh is replete with marble palaces and mosques, many of them built or financed by the Saudi Binladen Group.[5]

Mohammed Bin Laden had been very close to the Saudi royal family. In 1958, when King Saud's corrupt and extravagant rule had virtually bankrupted the government, Mohammed quietly loaned enough money to Crown Prince Faisal to bale the king out. Later the Bin Laden firm was given contracts to renovate the Grand Mosque in Mecca and the Prophet Mohammed's mosque in Medina for a total cost of more than $18 billion. There was a dark irony in all this. Osama's spiritual forebears, the Wahhabis, had for two centuries also been intimately allied with the House of Saud. They had long ago not only plundered the treasury of the Prophet's Mosque but had also destroyed the surrounding structures and gravestones as affronts to *tawhid,* the Koranic doctrine that God alone must be the subject of human veneration and worship.[6]

Osama was steeped in the Wahhabi theology that dominated his home-land. In due course he expanded its toxic premises, turning them against the House of Saud and into a transnational terrorist movement.[7] In the 1980s he led a group of Arab fighters to Afghanistan, where they joined the Afghan jihad, funded and armed by the United States, against the atheist Soviet occupation. It was there in 1988 that Bin Laden formed Al Qaeda. He was soon joined by the Egyptian doctor who had also studied in Saudi Arabia and who would provide much of the intellectual firepower for the terrorist movement, Ayman al-Zawahiri. Zawahiri's spiritual and intellectual mentor was fellow Egyptian Sayyid Qutb, a man who had been radicalized by a 16-month sojourn in America and by his torture in Egyptian prisons under the regime of Gamal Abd al-Nasser.[8]

During the 1950s and 1960s many of Qutb's peers and students, members of the Muslim Brotherhood, fled to Saudi Arabia to avoid persecution by Nasser's regime. While at Jeddah's King Abdul Aziz University in the 1970s, Bin Laden joined the Muslim Brothers. It was here that he read the loci classici of modern Sunni extremism, Qutb's *Milestones* and *In the Shade of the Koran*. As he read, Osama attended lectures by Qutb's younger brother, Mohammed.[9] Thus did Sayyid Qutb's teachings mix and find sustenance in the felicitous theological soil prepared by Wahhabism.

After the 1989 Soviet withdrawal from Afghanistan, Osama Bin Laden returned to Saudi Arabia convinced that he and his Arab jihadists had defeated the great atheist power. But his satisfaction soon turned to rage with the arrival of U.S. forces on Saudi soil in the wake of Saddam Hussein's invasion of Kuwait. Although small numbers of American forces had long been stationed in the kingdom, their mission was now openly and, to Bin Laden, shame-fully revealed—to "protect" his Muslim homeland against another Muslim country, Iraq.

Initially Bin Laden was simply angry that Saudi Arabia could not protect itself, and he offered to raise a private army to repel the Iraqis. When the government refused his offer, he concluded that the problem lay with the House of Saud and, preeminently, with their patron the United States. Like Soviet forces, Bin Laden observed, American troops had invaded Muslim lands. Unlike the Soviets, the Americans had been *invited* by Muslim rulers into the very heart of Islam. As he saw it, the presence of the troops not only desecrated the birth-place of the Prophet and Islam's holiest sites, but they did so at the behest of the Saudi King. Drawing on and extending Wahhabi teachings, and those of Sayyid Qutb, he concluded that the king's actions constituted heresy and necessitated jihad against the Saudi government. As for U.S. troops, Bin Laden decided their arrival in the kingdom was a modern continuation of the infidel crusades, which had in fact never ended.[10] Bin Laden and his fellow terrorists concluded that a "defensive jihad" was the long overdue response required of every Muslim the world over.

Virtually unknown to U.S. intelligence at the time, Bin Laden moved in 1992 to Sudan, where he began to finance minor terrorist operations under the protection of Hasan al-Turabi's radical Islamist regime. Turabi was the head of the Sudanese Muslim Brotherhood. In 1994 the Saudi government revoked Bin Laden's passport and two years later he returned to Afghanistan, where he engineered a series of attacks against the United States. In 1998 Al Qaeda suicide bombers hit U.S. embassies in Kenya and Tanzania, killing hundreds of innocent people, many of them Muslims. In October 2000, three months before my arrival in Riyadh, Al Qaeda launched another mission, this time at the southern tip of the Arabian peninsula. A suicide crew on a small boat laden with explosives struck the USS *Cole* in the Gulf of Aden. Seventeen American sailors died.

By the late 1990s American intelligence officials were belatedly paying attention to Bin Laden and Al Qaeda, although it is now clear that, despite the embassy bombings and the attack on the USS *Cole*, neither they nor U.S. policy makers understood the nature of the threat or the danger it posed. As we touched down at Riyadh airport, Osama Bin Laden was residing in Kandahar, Afghanistan, under the protection of the Taliban, finalizing his plans to attack the World Trade Center, the Pentagon, and the U.S. Capitol. An exile from his own country, he and his brand of Islamist extremism were soon to become Saudi Arabia's most infamous legacy.

The arrivals terminal at King Khaled airport was, like much of the city itself, modern in aspect, with clean, sleek lines. As we entered the building we were at first struck by the natural light from large glass panels on walls and ceilings high above the floor. Then we encountered the long black lines of separated, burqua'ed women waiting to go through passport control. We witnessed a similar segregation in the restaurants, where dining rooms were set apart for women and children. There was a troubling naturalness to this system, as if it reflected a rightly ordered distinction between the dignity of men and that of women and children. It was vaguely reminiscent of my native Georgia, where black citizens were not present as diners in the restaurants of my youth, and where—to my childish eyes—the movement of black Americans to the rear of public buses was simply part of the social landscape.

But there were other, darker places in the cities of Saudi Arabia. Situated among the buildings and streets were public squares similar to those in cities around the world, where one might expect to find statues and fountains surrounded by pigeons and children at play. The public squares of Saudi cities are used to punish criminals according to Wahhabi prescriptions. The idea is to render justice and, in a Wahhabi rendering of *shari'a*, to teach about God's purposes. Thieves are dismembered. Murderers, rapists, apostates, and drug dealers are beheaded, sometimes with appalling inefficiency and cruelty. Asked whether the beheadings were difficult, the kingdom's chief executioner scoffed. They are in fact quite natural and easy to carry out, he replied.

A father of seven, his son is being trained to the profession which, he said, is "God's work."[11]

Preparing for Riyadh

"Religious freedom does not exist in Saudi Arabia." The State Department's first *Annual Report on International Religious Freedom* (1999) made what was at the time considered a rather unusual, even plucky assessment.[12] Distinctly undiplomatic in its bluntness, the judgment earned plaudits for telling the hard truth at Foggy Bottom. In fact, it and the report were understated. There was then and is now in Saudi Arabia nothing even approaching religious freedom—no differentiation between religion and state, no right of individuals or communities to worship, manifest religious beliefs, raise children in the faith, train clergy, propose religion-based arguments (other than Wahhabi) to influence public policy, or any of the other elements of a true regime of religious liberty.

In the early years after the passage of the 1998 International Religious Freedom Act (IRFA) the mandate to "advance religious freedom" was pursued in Saudi Arabia and elsewhere in the Middle East much as it was in China or Vietnam. The goal was to denounce, and where possible reduce, religious persecution as a humanitarian imperative. As a result IRFA policy was isolated from broader U.S. foreign affairs and national security interests. It was manifestly not seen as a means to further the post-9/11 strategy adopted by the Bush administration in the greater Middle East, namely to encourage the development of liberal, stable self-government as the way to "drain the swamps" of Islamist radicalism and hatred. The president's "forward strategy of freedom" was unconnected to the U.S. policy of advancing religious freedom, and vice versa.

In the years prior to 9/11, IRF Ambassador Seiple (1998–2000) followed the lead of State Department lawyers in construing the IRF statute narrowly. Designations of "countries of particular concern" (CPC) were understood to be based solely on "systematic, ongoing and egregious" persecutory activities during the 12 months preceding the finding.[13] This meant that during a given year there must have been a pattern of bodily harm incidents such as torture or imprisonment without charge for designation to be warranted. Judicial executions, including beheadings, were not considered germane unless the crime was overtly religious in nature, such as apostasy, and there had been a pattern of such proceedings.

In short, because these kinds of incidents occurred in Saudi Arabia only sporadically or not at all during the respective periods in question, they did not meet the law's requirement that they be "systematic and ongoing." As we shall see, I began to question this interpretation after Seiple's departure and ultimately concluded that Saudi Arabia should be designated as a CPC. My internal arguments at the department did not persuade, however, and Saudi Arabia was not put on the list during designations while I was head of the office of international religious freedom (2001). Nor did it occur during the first two years under Ambassador John Hanford (2002 and 2003). Saudi Arabia was finally designated in 2004 under Hanford and Secretary of State Colin Powell.

Under Seiple's tenure the office defended the narrow reasoning because it was considered a plausible rendering of the statutory language. Moreover, like most others in the foreign policy establishment, we discerned little substantial connection between Saudi religious policy and broader American interests. At the time the problem seemed primarily humanitarian in nature. But even in that context there was more to the narrower position than legal hair splitting. We wanted to use the law to effect real change in persecutory behavior and not simply as a means of "nailing the bad guys" without any substantive reform as a result. As recounted in chapter 5, Seiple had decided to push for China's designation only after his discussions with Chinese officials convinced him that they would continue to ignore our arguments for reform, and that putting them on the list might lead to actual changes in Chinese behavior.

But Seiple felt differently about Saudi Arabia. He believed that his advocacy had already made a difference in Saudi policy and that listing the kingdom as a severe violator would be counterproductive. During his 1999 trip to Riyadh, officials told him that the Saudi government protected non-Muslim worship so long as it was "private." Seiple recognized the fragility of this policy; even if carried out assiduously, it did not constitute anything like religious freedom, and could in fact generate persecution of those who failed to remain "private." Moreover, that term could be defined in ways advantageous to the government. But he decided that this was the kind of small official step that could form the basis for official Saudi movement away from persecution.

Accordingly, Seiple requested and obtained Saudi agreement to an action that seemed significant, even remarkable, at the time. The government made a *public* declaration within the kingdom that private non-Muslim worship would be permitted. A Saudi official repeated this affirmation at the United Nations Human Rights Commission meeting in Geneva. We believed such moves by a country so fiercely committed to coercive management of religion constituted progress worth building upon. Unfortunately, "building upon" the Seiple initiative, and on my own discussions in the kingdom, would have to wait until the aftermath of 9/11 and a slow, unsteady shift in the U.S. worldview about Saudi Arabia.

The Baha'i Lesson

My view of the Saudi problem began to change in late 2000 after Seiple left and my tenure as temporary head of the office began. Like others I became

convinced that Saudi support for Wahhabism was an American national security problem only when it became clear how much that brand of Islam had
contributed to the theological context of Islamist terrorism. However, there
were two other milestones in the progression of my thinking. One was my trip
to Saudi Arabia. But the first was my encounter with a modest but eloquent
Baha'i gentleman.

In the fall of 2000 I had been asked to brief the watchdog agency created
by the IRF Act—the U.S. Commission on International Religious Freedom—
regarding the latest round of CPC designations. The 2000 CPC list replicated
that of the previous year—Burma, China, Iran, Iraq, and Sudan, plus the
Serbian regime of Slobodan Milosevic and the Afghan regime of the Taliban.[14]
The commissioners present at my briefing included several outspoken critics of
our failure to include Saudi Arabia on the list, including Nina Shea of Freedom
House and Elliott Abrams (the prominent neoconservative who would later be
rumored as a candidate for IRF ambassador at large). Both made their objections clear and I was not surprised by what they had to say. What stopped me
cold was the intervention of Commissioner Firuz Kazemzedeh, a professor
emeritus at Yale University and an American Baha'i.

In some Muslim countries Baha'is live in supreme danger because they
are viewed as apostates from Islam, a crime meriting death under one interpretation of *shari'a* (an interpretation that prevails in some democratic, as well
as theocratic regimes, as we have seen in Afghanistan).[15] Although their freedom is at risk throughout much of the Muslim world, their homes of greatest
peril tend to be Iran, where they are subject to periodic imprisonment, torture,
and execution, and Wahhabi-dominated Saudi Arabia. On this particular day
I had just completed my legal analysis of why Saudi Arabia did not make the
cut for the CPC list, and was conscious of the exasperation this argument had
produced among the commissioners and their staff. I resisted their arguments,
confident in my legal interpretation of the IRF Act.

Then Professor Kazemzedeh, who had not yet spoken during the meeting,
leaned forward across the table and affixed me with his genial countenance.
"The International Religious Freedom Act establishes as one of its criteria for
CPC designation [he was now reading from the statute] 'the systematic, ongoing, and egregious violations of religious freedom, including…flagrant denial
of the right to life, liberty, or the security of persons.' I am, Mr. Farr, a Baha'i.
In Saudi Arabia I may not exist. Is that or is it not a systematic, ongoing, and
egregious denial of life, liberty, and security?"

Kazemzedeh was, of course, right. My narrow legal analysis, while technically defensible, had sidestepped both the humanitarian and political core of
the matter. A regime of religious freedom must be grounded in the political
recognition and protection of human dignity. If the United States was going
to advance religious freedom in Saudi Arabia, it could not base its judgments
or its policy steps on a mechanical calculus of persecutory actions during the

past 12 months. It had to take into account the theological and anthropological pathologies that drove Saudi policies.

Commissioner Nina Shea made the same argument in a slightly different way. The relative absence of "bodily harm" incidents in any 12-month period, she pointedly noted, was the result of ruthless and effective deterrence by the Saudi government, such as public beheadings or torture in Saudi prisons. Non-Muslim religious minorities understood the potentially brutal implications of their being caught practicing their respective rites and duties privately, let alone openly. Fear of those implications led non-Muslims either to hold surreptitious, underground worship services or to forego any religious gatherings at all. There was absolutely no question of their articulating religiously informed moral arguments against Wahhabi policies, such as the dismemberment or beheading of criminals or the legal subordination of women and girls.

The Kazemzedeh encounter was on my mind as I prepared to travel to Saudi Arabia. The kingdom has some 22 million residents, 17 million of whom are Saudi citizens. By Wahhabi interpretation of Islamic doctrine, all Saudi citizens are Muslims de jure and de facto. In truth, a few Saudi citizens have over time converted to other religions, such as Christianity, but they practice those faiths at enormous risk to themselves and their families, even in private. As noted, apostasy is a capital crime in the kingdom, as is attempting to convert someone from Islam to another religion.

We were occasionally visited in Washington by Christian missionaries who worked covertly in Saudi Arabia, and we were amazed at their willingness to live with such danger. Once, at the end of a meeting in Ambassador Seiple's office on the seventh floor of the State Department, an Australian Pentacostal missionary to Saudi Arabia asked if he might pray. He did so with such fervor and volume that a group of alarmed colleagues—unaccustomed to praying of any kind at Foggy Bottom, let alone Pentacostal praying—gathered outside the door thinking the ambassador and his staff were being assaulted. I wondered how this missionary, so obviously and energetically committed to his faith, could survive in a country like Saudi Arabia.

In such meetings we would counsel missionaries to know and respect the cultures in which they evangelized. This was especially difficult in Saudi Arabia, where their very existence (like that of the Baha'is) was forbidden. Still, they persevered, occasionally tossing common sense to the winds. During the late 1990s, a group of Filipino Christians decided to try and convert the kingdom prior to the end of the millennium and managed to smuggle in thousands of Bibles. They walked through the residential streets of Riyadh, tossing the Bibles over walls into the gardens of Muslim homeowners. Picked up by the Mutawa'in (religion and morals police), they were thrown into jail, but through the intervention of the United States were deported, apparently unharmed. This was the kind of intervention expected of America's policy to "advance religious freedom."

Wahhab: His Ancestors and His Progeny

Abu Hajer al-Iraqi was a former Iraqi military officer who had participated in the Arab jihad against the Soviets in Afghanistan. In the mid-1990s he joined Bin Laden in Sudan and, despite having no theological training, had become the head of Al Qaeda's "fatwa committee." In this capacity Abu Hajer produced fatwas that authorized Al Qaeda attacks on American troops and on the United States. His reasoning, which explicitly justified the murder of innocents,[16] was filtered through the work of an 18th-century theologian named Muhammad bin Abd al-Wahhab, the father of Wahhabism. But the logic of modern Islamist terrorism had received its prototypic articulation centuries earlier by one of Wahhab's spiritual ancestors. It was occasioned by Islam's first large-scale defeat at the hands of infidels.[17]

Sweeping out of the Asian steppes in the 13th century, the Mongols—descendants of Genghis Khan—savaged Baghdad and destroyed the Abassid caliphate, for half a millennium the seat of Islamic civilization. These Mongols eventually converted to Islam but were still seen by some as a threat to the religion itself and to the community (umma). An influential jurist of the conservative Sunni Hanbali school named Taqi al-Din ibn Taymiyya (1263–1328) concluded that even the converted Mongols were actually infidels. They did not fully accept shari'a and retained elements of their native laws. Accordingly, ibn Taymiyya wrote that the Mongol rulers had to be killed in a defensive jihad. Those Muslims who supported them must be killed as well. Should bystanders be caught up in the conflict, their fate would be sorted out in the next life: innocents would go to heaven, others to hell. The Muslim duty was to wage jihad in defense of Islam.[18]

In Islam's classical age, jihad was a core principle of Islamic theology and it remains so today.[19] It is an idea with a considerable history, one which is at the heart of a fierce debate within contemporary Islam. All Muslims believe that jihad means striving to do God's purposes. The contemporary question, of course, is what precisely God's purposes are and how are they to be fulfilled by Muslims. Some believe that the striving includes the use of violence against non-Muslims, heretics, and apostates in order to subdue them. Other Muslims argue that the extremists have co-opted and distorted the concept for their own purposes. If jihad is indeed a central tenet of Islam, those who seek a "moderate" Islam should surely support this argument. Simply to equate jihad with terrorism is not only inaccurate but self-defeating as a premise of foreign policy.

It is all the more critical, to Islam and the world, that mainstream Muslims embrace their solemn, urgent obligation to retrieve the concept of jihad from the terrorists, and not simply insist (as some do) that its use by radicals has no plausible connection to classical Islam.[20] That very plausibility helps explain why young Muslim men and women are attracted to extremism. They may have experienced injustice or hate the West or have grievances against their rulers, but those hatreds and grievances are transformed into extremism by the conviction that God has prescribed a remedy, in this world and the next, through the religious obligation called jihad.

In the early centuries of Islam, the idea of jihad proved a remarkably effective stimulus to the conquering of non-Muslim territories.[21] Before he died in 632, Mohammed had subdued most of the Arabian peninsula. By the end of the 7th century Arab Islamic rule had spread by the sword to all of Arabia, Palestine, Syria, Mesopotamia (Iraq), Persia (Iran), and west to Egypt and parts of Libya. By the middle of the 8th century, Arab Muslim armies had swept west across north Africa and north over the straits of Gibraltar into Spain, ultimately crossing the Pyrenees into Gaul (France). This westward path into the infant European civilization was blocked by the Frankish king Charles Martel at the battle of Poitiers in 732, after which Muslim forces withdrew into Spain. They remained there as part of an important Islamic civilization centered on Cordoba (and later, Granada) until finally expelled by the Spanish *reconquista* in 1492.

In 661, Arab Muslim armies conquered Kabul (Afghanistan), opening the way to central Asia, India, and the Far East, where Islam would take root in subsequent centuries. Eventually the religion made its way to China, where it resides today among ethnic Hui Chinese as a minority and as the dominant religion of the ethnic Uighurs in the northwest province of Xingjiang. Islam also spread to Indonesia, today the largest Muslim country in the world. It remains the central religious and cultural influence in North Africa and parts of sub-Saharan Africa, the Arab Middle East, Iran, central Asia, and Pakistan. Such spiritual tenacity cannot be explained by military conquest alone. In particular, scores of millions of southeast Asians converted to Islam freely, embracing what they saw as its Koranic message of compassion and mercy.

As articulated in the Koran and the sayings of the prophet (hadith), jihad has two meanings for Muslims, one an interior struggle for virtue and self-control in obedience to God, the other an explicitly military conquest of non-Muslim territory in obedience to God. The former holds great promise for liberal governance,[22] the latter poses serious obstacles. Part of the problem is that in the rapid spread of Islam during the early centuries the military meaning of jihad was dominant. It was employed by "the overwhelming majority of early authorities, citing the relevant passages in the Qur'an, the commentaries, and the traditions of the prophet...."[23]

Strictly speaking, the military goal of jihad was not the conversion of non-Muslims by coercive means. In an October 2006 letter to Pope Benedict XVI, 38 leading Muslim jurists from around the world addressed this issue. They rejected the suggestion, which they inferred from the Pope's speech at Regensburg, Germany, the previous month, that Islam was spread by the sword, and that jihad was a vehicle to force non-Muslims to accept Islam. The conquests of the early centuries, the jurists told the Pope, were "political in nature," and most conversions came through "preaching and missionary activity." To force others to believe is contrary to the explicit Koranic doctrine, "There is no compulsion in religion" (2:252). To coerce belief, they wrote, "is not pleasing to God...God is not pleased by blood."[24]

The element of truth in this statement is important, as is the reasoned dialogue that it appears to entail. Although there were clearly abuses, the early jihads were understood by Arab conquerors as defending the rule of Islam, and of God, and extending it. In that sense jihad was similar to the methods of some rulers in Medieval Europe, for whom the use of military force to gain and control territory was done in God's name. Charlemagne's conquering of the pagan Saxons is an early medieval example of this.

Under the Muslim conquests, Christians, Jews, Persian Zoroastrians, and later Hindus became *dhimmis* who were protected in theory by strict rules and permitted to remain in their own traditions. They were subject to significant disabilities, in particular the requirement to pay a tax (the *jizya*). The consequences of refusal or default were dire. But dhimmis retained a degree of autonomy in their personal affairs. They were, Bernard Lewis notes, what we would call second-class citizens. But we should also acknowledge, he writes, that "second-class citizenship, established by law and revelation and recognized by public opinion, was far better than the total lack of citizenship that was the fate of non-Christians and even of some deviant Christians in the West."[25]

Here lies the point for those who would help Islam root out its own 21st century heresies of extremism and terrorism, as practiced by Wahhabis, Bin Ladenists, and others. The military uses of jihad have no legitimate modern application. The conquering of lands and the establishment of dhimmis, while understandable in a medieval context, need redefinition by modern Muslims in order to accord with contemporary views of human dignity and freedom, both of which are present, if dormant, in Islamic traditions.

Offensive jihad of the type practiced by Mohammed and his successors has no place in the 21st century. Within Islamic jurisprudence, offensive jihad requires a legitimate Islamic ruler, such as the Sunni Caliph, to apply the rules that attach to its use. That ruler no longer exists, which is why some Sunni extremists seek its restoration. As for defensive jihad, it can be declared by lesser authorities under emergency circumstances, which is why self-styled authorities such as Abu Hajer and Bin Laden—drawing on traditions like that of ibn Taymiyya—have been able to exploit the concept. But surely in the modern world it is self-evident that permitting anyone to declare themselves an authority in such a vital matter is to render the concept of jihad, and the use of the fatwa that declares it, nonsense. Bat Ye'or, one of the major historians (and critics) of jihad and the dhimmi system notes, "a number of contemporary and Muslim theologians and intellectuals want to break away from the prison of jihad....There is profound intellectual and spiritual ferment in the Islamic world today."[26]

Unfortunately for Islam and the world, the doctrine of defensive jihad has become a weapon in the hands of radicals with grievances, real or imagined, in great part through the agency of Saudi Wahhabism. Muhammed bin abd al-Wahhab (1703–1793) was born under Ottoman suzerainty in the eastern Arabian region of Najd. Although the Najd was a remote area of Bedouin Arabia, Wahhab himself was well traveled in the Arab world. He visited, among other places, Basra, which is where he probably encountered Shiism. He may have visited Baghdad and even Persia, although these travels are questioned by scholars of Wahhabism. What is certain is that Wahhab spent years of study in Medina and Mecca. It was in Medina that he encountered, and was drawn to, the works of ibn Taymiyya.[27]

For our purposes Wahhab and his spiritual descendants raise two major problems that render the use of jihad lethal, both to its victims and to Islam itself. The first is the doctrine of *tawhid* and its implications for Islamist extremism. The second is the political-theological marriage of Wahhabism with a tribal family of the Najd that in the 20th century would become the ruling family of Saudi Arabia.

The concept of *tawhid* is quite literally the core of all Islamic belief. *Tawhid* means the oneness and unity of God, which is most clearly reflected in the first pillar of Islam, the Muslim testament of faith (*shahada*) that there is no God but God and that Mohammed is his messenger. All Muslims believe in "one God, who has no partners or equals, and who was not begotten and who begets no other."[28] The implications of this strict monotheism for Islamic belief and practice are difficult to overestimate.

In the most positive sense, *tawhid* places a premium on pleasing God through prayer and grateful obedience. It can both validate and intensify the internal jihad and the achievement of virtue. In addition, for some Muslim traditions, pleasing God requires the application of reason to understand God and God's purposes. In this focus on God's will Islamic monotheism illuminates a question central to distinguishing between moderates and extremists, namely, what does God require from human beings? Who are they and how are they to act in obedience to God?[29] For all Muslims the answers to these questions are to be found in the Koran and the Sunna.

Of the two, the Koran is preeminent. Muslims believe that the Koran was recorded verbatim by Mohammed from God through the agency of the angel Gabriel. Muslims accept the Koran as the literal word of God; it cannot be changed. All agree on its substantial integrity and inalterability. Indeed, the Koran in important ways occupies a more elevated status in Islam than does the Bible within Christianity. The role of the Koran is not strictly analogous to even a literalist view of the Bible, as Western observers sometimes assume.

It is perhaps more similar to the Christian understanding of Christ himself—uncreated, eternal, and divine.[30]

After Muhammad's death in 632, his sayings were collected in the hadith, which were in subsequent centuries augmented by broader narratives of his conduct and that of his companions. Together the hadith and the narratives constitute the Sunna of the Prophet, which most Muslims consider as the second most authoritative source in Islam. Unlike the Koran, however, the texts of the Sunna are not agreed but are scattered among several authoritative compilations.[31]

Belief in the inalterability of these sacred texts has not relieved Muslims of the interpretive task—that of correctly understanding God's word. The way that Muslims around the world interpret the Koran and Sunna is utterly central to their beliefs concerning who God is and what God requires of them in every aspect of their lives. There is no central interpretive authority in Islam, but those jurists who are accepted as authorities on Koranic exegesis do have, at least potentially, a substantive authoritative role in the lives of Muslims, especially in Shiite Islam. The texts, especially the Koran, have natural and powerful implications for political norms in any Islamic state, including a democracy.

For moderates, the task of interpretation has become more difficult in modern times because of what Khaled Abou El Fadl calls "a vacuum in religious authority" caused by the "disintegration of the traditional institutions of Islamic learning and authority." The classical schools of Islam had provided disciplined methodology to Koranic exegesis and to defining the *shari'a*, which Muslims consider Islamic law. Today, Abou El Fadl notes, the state has coopted the role of the jurists for the first time in Muslim history. Saudi Arabian theocracy, he argues, is a novelty in Islamic history.[32]

But the novelty has deep roots. Through Taymiyya and Wahhab the doctrine of *tawhid* became a rationale for anti-humanist irrationalism, the Koran an instruction manual for extremists, and the Sunna a guide to terror. If God alone has sovereignty in the affairs of men, there is no room for human freedom or dignity. If God's desires for mankind are explicit and without ambiguity in the Koran and Sunna, there is no need for human agency in discerning his purposes. What God needs is enforcers. The *shari'a*, which has come down to the 21st century as God's law, is the instruction manual.

Wahhab, drawing on Taymiyya, taught that any deference to the classical juristic traditions or any application of human reason to religious texts or problems constituted the sin of "ascribing partners to God" and thus heretical transgressions of *tawhid* deserving of death. The same reasoning made heretics out of anyone producing music, art, or nonreligious poetry, venerating saints or praying for their intercession with God, or even placing tombstones on family graves. Leaping over the traditions reflected in dhimmitude, Wahhab was "rabidly hostile" toward Christians and Jews, let alone polytheists. But he reserved his greatest hostility for the ever-widening circle of Muslims branded as heretics and apostates under his definition of orthodoxy. A focus of his animus was the Shiites, whom he may have encountered in Basra but who also lived in various parts of Arabia. In the hands of Wahhab and his descendants, the very essence of Islam became the vehicle for dividing Muslims, for institutionalizing jihad as religious violence against anyone outside his narrow band, and for redefining Islam as radicalism.[33]

Wahhab's ideas, according to some scholars of Islam, would very likely have received little attention in the Muslim world had they not been given political sanction and, in the late 20th century, substantial funding by the government of Saudi Arabia.[34] The Wahhab-Saudi alliance was sealed in the 18th century and it continued through the establishment of the kingdom of Saudi Arabia in 1932. In the years between the end of World War I and the founding of Saudi Arabia, the Saud ruler and future king ibn Saud sought to spread his dominance from the Najd to the Hijaz, the area of western Arabia where Mecca and Medina are located.

In his war against rival tribes and Islamic communities, Saud authorized in effect a Wahhabi jihad. According to Hamid Algar, there were 400,000 killed or wounded, massacres in the cities of Ta'if, Burayda, and al-Huda, public executions of 40,000 people, and 350,000 amputations. The Shiites of Arabia suffered particular cruelties.[35] Virtually all the victims of Wahhabism in these years were Muslims. And Islam itself.

Women and Children: Wahhab and Foggy Bottom

As I prepared for my trip to Saudi Arabia, one issue that had gained public attention in the United States was the Saudi treatment of women and children. In some ways the Koran is progressive in its understanding of women in God's plan. For example, it permits the inference of equality in inheritance laws and within the family. Although there are certainly countervailing passages, such as those interpreted as permitting the beating of wives and the reduced value of women's testimony in courts, modern Islamic feminist movements have a substantial textual basis on which to rest their claims of equality for women.[36] Not surprisingly, however, these texts and traditions are virtually ignored in Wahhabi-dominated Saudi Arabia. Women and girls are revered in the kingdom, but, as I was to learn, it is a reverence bereft of any sense of personhood. In fact, women are often reduced to instruments in the Wahhabi political theology.

The issue that had drawn the attention of the public was the abduction and forced conversion of American children who had been raised as Christians. Typically the problem began when a Saudi man married an American, sired children in the United States, allowed them to be raised as Christians, and then divorced the mother. The father then took the children to Saudi Arabia, where they are by law, as issue of a Saudi man, not only Saudi citizens but also Muslims. In some cases American courts had given custody of the children to the mother, and the Saudi father simply abducted the children.[37]

The Saudi constitution is the Koran. Saudi *shari'a* law is viewed as the codification of Koranic doctrine. It does not recognize the authority of U.S. courts, and the kingdom is not a party to the international Hague convention on child abductions. When females become adults they are virtually without legal rights deriving from their status as human beings. Such rights as they have usually flow from their relationship to fathers or husbands. Again, while this reduced status can plausibly be grounded in the Koran and the Sunna, the reverse is also true. In Indonesia, Turkey, Senegal, and other Muslim states, the legal status of women is commensurate with that of men.

But Saudi treatment of abducted female children had outraged many in the United States who were aware of the ordeals endured by "left-behind" American mothers. Some of these women have spent a lifetime (and most of their resources) trying to rescue their children from Saudi Arabia. A few have even charged that the State Department and the American embassy in Riyadh have been cruelly inattentive, or even hostile, to their pleas for help. At the time I traveled to Saudi Arabia in early 2001, the case that had done more than any other to raise this issue in the public mind was that of Pat Roush.

Roush's two daughters, ages seven and nine, had been abducted by their Saudi father and taken to Saudi Arabia in the mid-1980s. Although baptized and raised in the United States as Christians, they had in the Wahhabi kingdom automatically been assumed to be Muslim. Their distraught but determined mother had spent two decades lobbying members of Congress, presidents, American ambassadors, and Saudi officials. Some tried to help, but the girls— now adults, the eldest married and with a child—remained in Saudi Arabia.[38]

Pat Roush's story is in many ways an American tragedy, a tale of personal sacrifice and suffering that any person of good will can understand. Although Roush did not succeed in the quest to retrieve her daughters, her lobbying did lead Congress to include in the 1998 International Religious Freedom Act a requirement that the State Department's annual report record any instance of the abduction of a minor American citizen from the United States, his or her forced conversion, and the refusal of a government to permit the child's return.

In the State Department, however, this aspect of the IRF Act was—like the law itself—largely considered the result of special pleading by the Christian right. I had many exchanges about the Roush case and similar issues with my colleagues on the Saudi desk, in the office responsible for child custody cases and others. Some insisted that these events could not be considered abductions or forced conversions in any legal or moral sense. They argued that the Saudi government was not a party to international law and there was no legally binding reason for them to honor the decisions of U.S. courts, especially when rulings contradicted Saudi law. Furthermore, they noted, it was not unusual for a divorced parent to change the religion of minor children in the United States. All of this, some U.S. officials argued, amounted to disputes over child custody, disputes in which the United States should involve itself only very carefully, if at all.

There was, in fact, a substantial grain of truth to this argument. Similar disputes occurred when divorced American parents took children to western European countries and the courts there refused to order that the children be returned to the United States. Even within the United States the religious practices of minor children followed that of the divorced parent with custody, and this sometimes involved a change of religion—for example, children raised as Jews taken by a divorced father or mother and baptized as Christians. Moreover, it certainly was not the case that State Department officials simply did not care about the fate of the "left behind" mothers or their children.

But there was something else at work here, something that eluded the analysis at C Street. The Saudi cases amounted to more than what had become an unfortunate norm in the West—the wrangling of separated and divorced parents over child custody. In retrospect it seems clear that these cases were also indicators of the perverse theology that fed Islamist extremism. I am not suggesting that State Department officials should have seen it this way; few had that kind of insight, and I was not one of them. I am suggesting that attitudes at the department reflected an unfortunate tendency to instrumentalize and ignore religious practice as something with occasional (largely negative) humanitarian results but no rightful claim as a policy matter with implications for broader American interests.

In fact, the welcoming into the kingdom of abducted children who are presumed in law to be Muslim *because their fathers are Saudis* provides a window into the harsh reality of Wahhabi jurisprudence and public theology. It is not only that the religion of the father is imputed to the child as a matter of blood transfer, as it were. It is also the utter absence of any sense of personhood and dignity intrinsic to the child or her mother. Born of Saudi fathers, they are quite simply Muslims, regardless of how they were raised or how they were formed elsewhere, or what their non-Muslim mothers intended. They are instruments, not persons. And the role of the state is to enforce that understanding.

The terrible potential of this theological lacuna was revealed to the world in 2001 when *Mutawwa'in* prevented Saudi schoolgirls from fleeing a burning building because they were not properly covered. As a result, 14-year-old girls died either by being burned or through asphyxiation.[39] This is an issue of women's rights and also an indicator of a severe deficiency in Islamic humanism. Thirteen centuries into its existence in the land of its birth, Saudi Islam has yet to come to terms with its impoverished theological anthropology, the greatest single barrier to democracy and stability in the kingdom.

It is worth noting that the Roman Catholic Church, as recently as the 19th century, struggled unsuccessfully with an analogous problem. In the 1860s a Jewish child named Edgaro Mortara lived with his parents in the Italian Papal States. Ill and thought to be dying, the five-year-old Edgaro was secretly baptized by a Catholic employee of his parents. When the baptism was discovered by civil and religious authorities, Edgaro was forcibly taken from his mother's arms, raised as a Catholic, and became a priest. The church's theological reasoning at the time was clear—baptism is a sanctifying grace, a necessary and sufficient condition of initiation into the body of Christ. Today the sanctioning of such an action by Church authorities is unthinkable, not because the doctrine of baptism has changed, but because the Church has altered its understanding of the role of civil authority and coercion in matters of religion.[40] This is the kind of evolution that will be necessary in the birthplace of Islam, and in other Muslim countries, if they are to join the ranks of Islamic democracies that are stable and enduring.

To the Heart of Islam

In deciding what to discuss with Saudi officials in Riyadh, I faced a dilemma. Most American human rights officials on such trips carry with them lists of prisoners or other victims for whom they advocate in some fashion. There is a pressing humanitarian need for such advocacy, and the Karimi case had given me firsthand experience of the gratification that can result.[41] I also knew, however, that this kind of advocacy did little for future victims. It neither addressed the structures of persecution nor advanced religious freedom. I decided to raise an issue that went to the heart of the Saudi political theology: the treatment of non-Muslims living and working in the kingdom.

Of the seven million "guest workers" who live in the country, many are Hindus and Christians. These people run the oil wells and refineries, man construction crews, drive trucks, and serve as domestic servants in Saudi households. As the Seiple agreement with the Saudis revealed and the Hanford agreement later confirmed, the most forward-leaning view of "religious tolerance" for noncitizens in the kingdom is that they may worship in private. Non-Muslims may not worship publicly lest they offend the collective Islamic sensibility. There is no question whatever of non-Muslims, or for that matter non-Wahhabi Saudi Muslims, carrying their religious beliefs into the policy arena.

In practice, Saudi policy has meant that non-Muslims may worship alone or in tiny groups so long as they are not discovered. Many Christians in fact succeed in such underground activity, often without incident, but they are always at risk of discovery. I heard from Saudi officials, and, unfortunately, from some U.S. officials who agreed, that these expatriates were in Saudi

Arabia voluntarily and knew what they were getting into. In effect, their work contracts signed away any right to religious freedom.

In March of 2001 there was little enthusiasm in Washington or at the American embassy in Riyadh for pressing the Saudis further than Ambassador Seiple had done. But I decided to test the waters. After arriving in Riyadh my first meetings were with non-Muslim representatives of various nationalities and faiths, including Protestants, Catholics, Jehovahs Witnesses, and Mormans. Later I would meet with foreign embassy representatives whose fellow citizens living in the kingdom were Hindus and Buddhists.

Not surprisingly, most of the non-Muslims were quite concerned that I do nothing to draw direct attention to them. They were careful to emphasize that their missions did not involve proselytism, an activity that was forbidden in the kingdom on pain of death. Proselytism is, of course, a highly charged issue throughout the Muslim world, as well as in Russia, China, and India. As noted in the Introduction, the right to persuade others of the truths of one's beliefs lies at the very core of religious freedom. It is vital not only as a personal right but also, even more important, as a means of accommodating religious expression within the democratic public square. The substitution of peaceful persuasion for external jihad offers one means for Islamists to develop their religious obligation (*da'wa*) to spread Islam in the modern world.[42]

But these men and women lived and worked in Saudi Arabia primarily to serve the various expatriates of their respective faiths. In my travels to promote religious freedom, I frequently heard similar pleas from their counterparts in other authoritarian countries, such as Egypt, Vietnam, and China. They were inevitably people of enormous faith who had dedicated their lives to serving their co-religionists abroad. They were living what they saw as a carefully balanced accommodation with the authorities, and they feared drawing the spotlight to themselves and their colleagues in faith.

In Saudi Arabia many of these people had become accustomed to living like criminals, which they certainly were under Saudi *shari'a*. They moved their places of worship periodically so that local Saudis would not become suspicious and alert the *Mutawwa'in*. The official Saudi position on acceptable "private" worship was driven in part by a saying attributed to the Prophet Mohammed on his deathbed, namely that there should not be two religions in Arabia. This had led Omar, the second caliph after Mohammed, to force the resettlement of ancient Arabian Jewish and Christian communities into areas outside Arabia.[43] Although the validity of this particular hadith was questioned by some Muslim jurists over the centuries, it became a cornerstone of modern Saudi Wahhabi doctrine. It led the Saudis not only to ban the construction of churches, synagogues, or other non-Muslim religious buildings in the kingdom, but also to tell non-Muslim "private" worshipers that any gatherings must remain small and inconspicuous. They must not occur regularly at a particular location, lest a church or other non-Muslim place of worship de facto be established.

Some of the representatives told me that the police had tried to infiltrate their groups with spies. All of their worship services were vulnerable to raids, but Catholics and Orthodox Christians had an added burden. They needed regular access to an ordained priest in order to receive the sacraments of the Eucharist and confession, both indispensable to their religious lives. But priests were few and far between in Saudi Arabia and the tiny few who managed to get into the kingdom were spread quite thin.

Accurate statistics were hard to come by, but we estimated that there were between 500 thousand and one million Catholics in Saudi Arabia,[44] many of them Filipino house servants or manual laborers from South Asia. These people had no access to the handful of priests in the country. Even if they lived in Riyadh near the western embassies where masses were held, they could not simply show up and walk in. As I learned while attending one of those masses, Saudi security agents routinely surveyed the people who entered.

Unfortunately, the embassies of the expatriate Catholics and Protestants seemed to care little about the problem. In my meetings with representatives from foreign embassies in Riyadh it was clear they had more pressing concerns. In particular they did not want to disturb the flow of Saudi currency into their countries, money that came from their citizens working in the kingdom. Their indifference, I discovered, was not reserved exclusively for Christians. They had no intention of working to protect the religious rights of their fellow Hindus, Buddhists, or others.

There was another religious minority subject to even worse repression in Saudi Arabia, and that was the Shiite community, which lived primarily in the eastern parts of the country. Saudi Shiites were viewed with suspicion and condescension by Saudi authorities and especially by the Wahhabi clerical establishment. These suspicions flow first from their theological differences but also from the putative ties between Saudi Shia and their Iranian co-religionists across the Persian Gulf. Iranian Shiites have always been viewed from Wahhabi Riyadh as infidels and rebels, but the divide deepened after the 1979 Khomeini revolution. The problem became even more explosive when the Shiite-Sunni sectarian conflict in Iraq threatened to spill over into neighboring countries.

As a consequence of such factors Saudi Shiites often live tenuous lives and are severely restricted in the kinds of religious activities they can pursue. For example the government routinely forbids the foundational ceremonies of Shiite Islam—the annual Muharram rituals consisting of passion plays and processions of repentance commemorating the 7th-century martyrdom of Husayn in Karbala.[45] Saudi Shiite leaders are often subject to abuse, including imprisonment, torture, and even death. Unlike the non-Muslim minorities, Saudi Shiite representatives made a strong case to me for persistent and open U.S. intervention on their behalf. One Washington-based Shiite activist brought his Saudi father to visit me at the department, and both described the harrowing life lived by their family in the kingdom.

A fundamental principle in the office of international religious freedom was "do no harm." I had no thought of doing anything that would endanger the lives or well-being of the religious minorities in Saudi Arabia, Muslim or non-Muslim. But the fears of the latter group about "shaking things up" and drawing attention to themselves raised the question of what America's religious freedom objectives could realistically be in such a theologically and politically rigid nation.

Saudi Arabia in the past has helped provide America with more or less stable access to oil, as well as general support for our various strategic interests in the region. In the years after 9/11, the Saudis provided vital intelligence about Islamist extremists. As noted, American troops had been stationed on Saudi territory after the first Gulf War, and the Saudi government is important to our interests in the Israeli-Palestinian conflict. The traditional view in the foreign policy establishment was that the United States must support the Saudi royal family and Saudi government lest dissent in the kingdom lead to a revolution and the emergence of Wahhabi, anti-American tyrants.

This attitude, combined with the qualms of Christians and other non-Muslims on the ground, had the effect of restricting our approaches in Riyadh to occasional humanitarian cases. U.S. interventions occurred so rarely that they sometimes worked quite well. As with the Filipino Pentacostals, a few high-level telephone calls would usually do the trick. Even the Roush case had occasioned some grudging movement on the parts of senior Saudi officials acting in response to personal pleas from senior American officials. But the failure of the Roush appeals amounted to much more than the occasional setback in ad hoc diplomacy. As noted, the Saudis in the end refused to return the children to their mother because of a fierce and cruel rigidity in their understanding of human dignity and the relationship between civil authority and religious obligation.

After meeting with various religious groups I traveled to the offices of four agencies of the Saudi government. The first was an obligatory and proforma session with the America desk of the Saudi Ministry of Foreign Affairs. America desk officers the world over are selected for their skills in "America management," and—at least in the business of discussing religion—such meetings were often unproductive. This was no exception. Next came the Majlis Al-Shura, a consultative body of Saudi tribal and religious leaders, the closest thing the Saudis have to a national representative institution.

The most telling encounters, however, were with the Ministry of Islamic Affairs, whose job is to ensure religious conformity in the kingdom, and the

Ministry of the Interior, which is responsible for internal order, including the often futile attempt to manage the *Mutawwa'in*. The warrant of these policemen of religion and morals is believed to derive from the Koran and the hadith, as interpreted by Wahhabi jurists.

In each of the meetings, to the distinct discomfort of the American embassy officials who accompanied me, I made the same three "suggestions." I decided to use that term instead of "proposals" because the latter are considered more formal. I had no instructions from Washington to say what I was going to say so I avoided the more official wording. I suspected that my suggestions would be rejected but was careful to preface them with arguments that might at least help get them a hearing and lay the groundwork for future development.

First, I assured my interlocutors of my respect for Islam and the kingdom's central role in that religion. I was not there to request changes in Saudi religious policy but to seek clarification and understanding of existing policies. Second, I spoke as a religious person, a Christian who shared with many Saudis the belief that religious obligations have an impact on all of life. As I spoke about this, some of my Saudi hosts were clearly intrigued. As for my American embassy colleagues, I could sense their growing nervousness.

Next came an attempt to sketch out the problem candidly but without unnecessary offense. I expressed appreciation for the stated Saudi policy of protecting private non-Muslim worship, which had been publicly announced in the wake of Ambassador Seiple's visit three years ago. What, I asked, might a reasonable and objective person infer from that stated policy? One got the feeling from the way it was implemented that the government had in mind by "private worship" a solitary person reading and praying in a bedroom. While this kind of worship was indeed practiced in many religions, most religious people worshiped in groups, praying, chanting, singing, or hearing a sermon. Some, such as Roman Catholics and Eastern Orthodox Christians—of which there were hundreds of thousands in their country—also needed access to an ordained priest.

Surely, I argued, regular peaceful gatherings of such people ought to be considered "private worship" under the government's implied definition. But a reasonable observer might conclude that the government's policy was being ignored by the *Mutawwa'in*. I noted we had information that they continued to infiltrate private worship groups who posed no threat whatsoever to the kingdom or to Saudi citizens. This point in my presentation raised the temperature a bit at the Ministry of the Interior, where a representative of the *Mutawwa'in* may well have been present, albeit unannounced to me. I got the distinct feeling from one Saudi official's countenance that he would have shot me had a weapon been available (although he might have had to wrestle my embassy colleagues for the privilege). Saudi citizens, I asserted, had apparently not gotten the word about the policy because they had not ceased reporting private worship services to the *Mutawwa'in* when they discovered them.

—⁂—

The stage was now set for my three "suggestions," each of which was, I argued, consistent with a reasonable interpretation of stated Saudi policy. First, the Saudi government might procure a series of buildings in Riyadh and elsewhere in the kingdom wherever there were non-Muslims. Under the control of a new ministry, this building would be rented out to religious groups for their use. It would have no exterior or interior religious symbols affixed. Such items would be brought by each group, used only inside the building and taken away at the end of services. The *Mutawwa'in* would be instructed to leave the worshippers alone, and private Saudi citizens would understand that religious activities occurred there under the protection of the Saudi government. Non-Muslims could use the building with impunity, no longer having to sneak about like criminals. My interlocutors listened, their faces betraying increasing concern.

Second, the government should explicitly and publicly criminalize the practice by the *Mutawwa'in* or anyone else of infiltrating and raiding non-Muslim worship services, whether in government buildings or private homes. Such a practice was entirely inconsistent with the avowed policy of permitting private worship. Third, significant numbers of Roman Catholic and Orthodox priests should be allowed to enter Saudi Arabia so that the hundreds of thousands of Catholic and Orthodox Christians living in the kingdom could receive the sacraments necessary to their religious practice.

These suggestions did not, to put it mildly, please my hosts. To the first, they responded that the Prophet Mohammed had banned churches from the Arabian peninsula. As noted, this particular hadith is not universally accepted as authentic by Muslim scholars inside or outside Saudi Arabia. I continued: the issue was not only churches, but also Hindu and Buddhist temples and venues for other religious ceremonies. This argument, of course, went beyond even mainstream Islamic tolerance for "peoples of the book," a Koranic concept that included monotheistic Christians and Jews and sometimes others, but not (at least in the kingdom) Hindus and Buddhists.[46] At this point during the meeting at the Ministry of the Interior, Saudi officials appeared suddenly to be called away to some other emergency, and the meeting ended abruptly.

My goal had been to air some of the principles that would have to be addressed theologically as well as politically by the Saudis. The "suggestions" were intended to form the basis for a dialogue on the practical consequences of a system, driven by an understanding of religious obligation that was manifestly corrupting of human dignity and freedom. I had consciously avoided such a moral condemnation, however, and stuck to a critique of publicly stated Saudi policy. I allowed myself to imagine that a dialogue on this basis, if pursued quietly and persistently with the Saudis over the course of the next months and years by U.S. officials at all levels, might have a positive effect on other indigenous forces for reform, religious or not.

Given what I had already experienced in the startup of America's new religious freedom policy, I knew that the pursuit of this goal was a long shot, both for the Saudis and the Department of State. A few months later, a delegation of American religious leaders from the U.S. IRF Commission repeated some of these same suggestions. But, like Ambassador John Hanford's later proposal of a U.S.-China working group on religion, these ideas were not followed up by the State Department. Even after it became clear that most of the planners and attackers of 9/11 were Saudis, the U.S.-Saudi dialogue on religion remained largely ad hoc and fruitless until 2006.

In that year, as discussed in the previous chapter, Ambassador Hanford and the department concluded with the Saudis an interesting and potentially groundbreaking agreement on religion, one that drew upon and expanded the matters raised by Ambassador Seiple in 1998 and discussed during my trip and that of the commission in 2001. Under the terms of the 2006 agreement, which is not binding on either party, the Saudis pledged to cease official support for the export of intolerant materials outside the kingdom and to take steps to reduce the impact of these teachings domestically. Unfortunately, the potential of the 2006 agreement appeared increasingly to be limited, both by a lack of clarity over Saudi follow-through and by the downturn in the American military-democracy project in Iraq. The latter made the Bush administration even more hesitant to push the Saudis over something so sensitive as religion in the kingdom.

As the second Bush term neared its end, it seemed clear to administration supporters and critics alike that the United States could not afford to rile the Saudis at a time when their support would almost surely be needed to calm the confessional hatreds in Iraq and its neighboring states. In one of the worst-case scenarios, Saudi support would be critical if the Middle East were to erupt in a regional Shiite-Sunni religious war.

Thus was the primary "lesson" of 9/11 shunted to the side. The birthplace of Islam, of Wahhabism, and its stepchild Bin Ladenism was left to evolve on its own. Although there were a few hopeful signs of political and theological movement in the desert kingdom, there was among American officials no sense of urgency about encouraging that movement. The belief that U.S. support for despots in the Middle East had helped spawn Islamist transnational terrorism, and that its long-term antidote was stable self-government, was swamped by the season of "realism" that once again descended on American foreign policy.

9

∞∞∞

Islam and the American Opportunity

[I]t would be nice to think that someone is arguing with the terrorists and with the readers of Sayyid Qutb.... But the enemies of these people speak of... United Nations resolutions, of unilateralism, of multilateralism, of weapons inspectors, of coercion and non-coercion. This is no answer to the terrorists.

The terrorists speak insanely of deep things. The antiterrorists had better speak sanely of equally deep things. But who will speak of the sacred and the secular, of the physical world and the spiritual world? Who will defend liberal ideas against the enemies of liberal ideas?
—Paul Berman[1]

He is a moderate Muslim: He prays only once a day.
—Western journalist referring to a British Muslim mayor[2]

Understanding the Enemy and the Antidote

In the early 21st century few threats to fundamental U.S. interests surpass those presented by Islamist extremism. The danger is multifaceted. It has national, regional, and transnational variants. Most vexingly, it draws—however unjust and distorted the connection—from certain understandings of Islam. Indeed this is the common thread: each radical movement is motivated by a sense of powerful religious obligation grounded in particular readings of Islam's sacred sources. This threat cannot be defeated by military force alone, even when combined with state-to-state diplomacy and the largely secularist freedom agenda promoted by the United States in recent years.

Over the long term, Islamist radicalism in its various forms—terrorism fueled by jihad, extremist *shari'a,* clerical despotism—can only be defeated by durable, peaceful Islamic democracies. Such democracies must derive from, and be supported by, their respective cultures, especially the particular expressions of Islam that have molded them. Recent developments in Turkey and Indonesia suggest that Islamic parties and communities competing in the democratic public square, bargaining on the basis of their political and religious interests, can reduce the appeal of extremism and can encourage reformist thinking within Islamic establishments.[3] If democratic bargaining and theological reform can yield democratic political theologies, religious and political actors can achieve something like the "twin tolerations" discussed in chapter 3. In this way democratic political Islam can denude extremism of its power.

If the United States is to encourage the twin tolerations in the lands of Islam and elsewhere, it must alter the way it thinks about religion and democracy. Policy makers and diplomats must learn how to enable religious and political leaders capable of deriving liberal norms from the texts and traditions of Islam. Much will be required to achieve these goals. Within the U.S. foreign policy establishment, both intellectual and structural shifts will be necessary. In the Muslim world, it will require both political-constitutional changes and theological evolution. The United States will need to realign its policies to encourage such developments, a point to which we shall return at the end of this chapter.

⊷

The spectrum of Islamist radicalism is broad and complex, with multiple cross currents and contradictions. It includes extremist Shiite groups, such as Lebanon's Hezbollah and Iraq's Mahdi militia. Each operates in a particular political context, but each also receives funding and some measure of theological energy from Iran's version of Shiite extremism—Khomeinist clerical autocracy.[4] The policies of the Iranian government and the Islamist extremists it supports implicate vital American interests in Iraq, Lebanon, Syria, Israel, and across the broader Middle East. By the same token, Sunni extremist groups such as Hamas and the Taliban threaten U.S. allies and security interests in the region. These derive their religious warrant from the teachings of Sunni radicals such as Hassan al Banna, Sayyid Qutb, or Maylana Mawdudi.[5]

As a rule, Shiite and Sunni extremists despise each other as heretics worthy of slaughter. Some scholars argue that the growing Shiite-Sunni enmity in the Middle East, triggered by American military intervention in Iraq and Afghanistan, could rival the devastating impact of the 16th- and 17th-century European wars of religion.[6] At a minimum, rising tensions between these two major Islamic sects are likely to dominate developments in the greater Middle East for years.[7] Shiite Iran has been freed to pursue its interests more aggressively by the removal of the Sunni Baathist Iraqi regime and army from its western border and its replacement by a Shiite-dominated Iraqi government. To Iran's east, a threatening Sunni Taliban government has been replaced by a far less threatening (at least in a physical sense) democratic Afghan government.

The Shiite revival and Iran's growing assertiveness have alarmed the Sunni Arab governments of Saudi Arabia, Egypt, and Jordan. Concern over the growth of what Jordan's King Abdullah called "a Shiite crescent" from Beirut to Tehran[8] could lead Sunni states to develop their own nuclear weapons capabilities. Certainly Sunni Arab governments are likely to continue some level of support for Sunni extremist groups as a means of parrying Iranian, and Iraqi Shiite, influence.

Despite their deep enmity, however, Shiite and Sunni radicals have shown themselves capable of cooperation against infidels, especially Israel and the United States, whose sins supersede the extremists' internal hatreds. Iran, for example, has supported the Sunni terrorist group Hamas, an anti-Israel Palestinian spin-off of the Muslim Brotherhood. There is also evidence that Iran has supported Sunni insurgents in Iraq,[9] which demonstrates Tehran's desire to keep the United States bogged down and weakened. It also suggests that Tehran seeks to prevent the emergence of a stable form of Shiite Iraqi self-government grounded in the relatively democratic teachings of Grand Ayatollah Ali al-Sistani. That kind of Muslim democracy could undermine the more authoritarian system established in Iran by Grand Ayatollah Ruhollah Khomeini.

Pan-Islamist cooperation against U.S. interests, and against Israel, can be stimulated by Sunni extremists as well. As we have seen, Sunni Wahhabi progeny such as Al Qaeda have provided a broad Islamic theological rationale for terrorist attacks against the enemy, including any innocents that may inhabit its lands. Although Sunni rather than Shiite extremists have dominated the transnational terrorist movements, it would be imprudent to assume that Sunni-Shiite conflicts in the Middle East, or even the mutual loathing of their radical wings, will preclude their cooperation against U.S. interests, either abroad or in the American homeland.

Of most immediate consequence to American national security, however, are the Sunni Salafist and Wahhabi theologies that have fueled the likes of Al Qaeda and continue to be nourished in and exported from Pakistan, Afghanistan, Egypt, and Saudi Arabia. Much of the funding still emanates from the Saudis (despite the Saudi government's efforts to cease any "official" assistance). These theologies and the groups they sustain not only work against American policies in Iraq and the Middle East but also pose a direct and potentially lethal danger to the American homeland.[10] Most experts agree that should Islamist terrorists procure a weapon of mass destruction—chemical, biological, or nuclear—and the means to place it on American soil, they will use it.

The central goal of transnational Islamist terrorists is to establish through jihad the sovereignty of God, represented in *shari'a* law, as they understand those core Islamic principles, either in particular regions of the world or worldwide. Some wish to restore the Islamic Caliphate abolished by Kemal Ataturk in 1923. Their goals require them to kill Americans, destroy American institutions, and attack the ideas that sustain them. For Americans, there is no withdrawing from or "negotiating down" this threat—no "isolationism" to which America can safely return, no system of treaties or state alliances that can defeat it. At best those alliances can delay the terrorists; at worst they can return us to the false and dangerous sense of security that facilitated the attacks of September 11, 2001. We must defeat this enemy, root and branch. To fall short means failing our children, our country, and the democratic system that, despite its weaknesses, remains the best example of self-governance in history.

The lead U.S. strategy must remain the targeted use of military force, supported by intelligence and law enforcement activities. Although it complicates the long-term goal of facilitating stable self-government in the Middle East, the United States must remain militarily engaged, not only against the terrorists wherever they are but preeminently also in the broader Middle East. Our forces must be employed to forestall the disintegration of that region into a chaotic training base for variants of Islamist extremism. The defeat or withdrawal of American forces would confirm one of the motivating beliefs of the terrorists—derived from U.S. retreats in Vietnam, Lebanon, and Somalia and from our failure to respond to the Al Qaeda attacks of the 1990s—that America is morally corrupt and weak, that it is incapable of understanding what is at stake, and that it lacks the stomach for a sustained battle.

But military action alone, however effective, will not be sufficient to overcome the scourge of Islamist extremism or terror. Indeed, tactical military successes can pose a danger to American interests if they encourage the belief that radical Islam can be defeated like Nazism. If we are to limit the threat of radical Islam the United States must make its democracy promotion efforts more effective. It must alter the traditional approaches of neocons and liberals to the democracy project, and resist the neorealist call for a return to reliance on state-to-state diplomacy. It must help Muslims build the social and political institutions that will kill the radical ideas that, left to themselves, will ensure an endless supply of radicals bent on attacking America.

The American Weakness

Notwithstanding a few encouraging signs in recent years (to which we shall return), the United States has for the most part failed to understand the religious dimensions of the threat, or to incorporate religion into its counter-terrorist strategies, especially democracy promotion. A host of factors have converged to keep religion off the policy table, including a kind of religion-avoidance syndrome, an inordinate fear of political Islam, a default "realism" that refuses to incorporate religion into strategy, and a tendency to project Western secularist preferences into the minds of Muslim reformers. U.S. policies have often been grounded in the belief that the only effective antidotes to Islamist extremism are either democracies that relegate Islam to the private sphere or authoritarian governments that control religion, such as Egypt and Saudi Arabia. Such policies have proven at best ineffective. At worst, they have nourished the very forces they were intended to destroy: Islamist extremism and terrorism.

As we saw in chapter 2, it is not only the skeptics of the American freedom agenda who have a tendency to circumvent the thorny issue of religion. A telling example is former British Prime Minister Tony Blair, a staunch defender of democracy promotion in the Middle East. In a 2007 *Foreign Affairs* article, Blair insisted that Islamist extremism "may have started with religious doctrine," but during the late 20th century was transformed into an "ideology," that is, something formed around political ideas and entirely separate from Islam. So urgent is Blair's need to detach from Islam in discussing extremism that he descends into a form of political correctness.

The Koran, he writes, is "a reforming book, trying to return Judaism and Christianity to their origins, much as reformers attempted to do with the Christian church centuries later. The Koran is inclusive. It extols science and knowledge and abhors superstition. It is practical and far ahead of its time in attitudes toward marriage, women, and governance." There are important truths in this statement, but its purpose is not to describe the Koran or analyze the role of Islam. Its objective is to remove them from the policy discussion. The message is the same as that of the American 9/11 Commission: religion may be present as a factor in the explanations of historians and sociologists, but it has little or nothing to do with the policy problems that face us.[11]

It is true that Islamist extremists may have any number of motives that are not overtly religious. Such motives often should be seen in a religious context, but in official U.S. circles they rarely are. A 2006 U.S. National Intelligence Estimate (NIE) on Islamist terrorism was typical in this respect (even though it employs a religious term to describe the terrorists). The NIE asserted that four elements were "fueling the spread of the jihadist movement." Those elements are "entrenched grievances," Iraq, the slow pace of reform in Muslim nations, and anti-U.S. sentiment. Among the grievances identified by the NIE were "corruption, injustice, and fear of Western domination, leading to anger, humiliation and a sense of powerlessness."[12] Nowhere does the analysis appear to describe or incorporate the religious doctrine of jihad in understanding the actions of "jihadists," much less in countering those actions.

Each of the factors cited in the NIE is relevant to understanding the terrorists and fashioning a strategy to kill or capture them. What the NIE fails to identify, however, is the set of religious ideas that form the ultimate, transformative motive by which legitimate grievances become lethal threats. The terrorists doubtless are angry and humiliated. They perceive corruption and injustice in their own societies because those pathologies are rampant. American policy should be more effective at countering such problems and in encouraging reform that alleviates the grievances that nourish terrorism. But that policy cannot afford to ignore the religious ideas that motivate the terrorists.

U.S. analysis of Islamic ideas should, of course, be cautious and respectful. Mere mortals must take care when they engage in critical exegesis of someone else's religion. One reason is simple justice—the profound respect due another's most sacred beliefs, not because those beliefs are necessarily true, but because they are central to the dignity of the person who holds them. Another is prudence about the unfamiliar. One must be cautious in drawing conclusions about another belief system, especially when those conclusions form the basis for policy. But neither these nor other prudential considerations justify ignorance in devising U.S. national security policy.

The United States cannot ignore the religious content of the ideas whose triumph is the final goal of the terrorists. It must recognize the "hydra effect" that these ideas, and their plausible connection to Islam, impart. In Greek mythology, the hydra had nine heads; decapitating one merely produced nine more. Killing the human agents of radical Islam will not kill the ideas that recruit or sustain them. Although the deaths of people such as Bin Laden, Ayman al Zawahiri, or other terrorist leaders can affect the morale of their cadres, killing the leaders will not remove the reasons for others to take their place. To Islamist terrorists death is the door to paradise and the reward promised by God for their actions to "defend" Islam. The victory of their ideas will mean neither reform nor justice but the enslavement or destruction of all who resist, including the American people.

Foreign affairs scholar, Mary Habeck, has noted the irony: "The consistent need to find explanations other than religious ones for the [terrorist] attacks says, in fact, more about the West than it does the jihadis. Western scholars have generally failed to take religion seriously. Secularists, whether liberals or socialists, grant true explanatory power to political, social, or economic factors, but discount the plain sense of religious statements made by the jihadis themselves."[13] Preeminent among those statements was the February 1998 declaration made by Osama Bin Laden, discussed in chapter 1 (and dismissed by some realists as a nihilist sexual fantasy).[14]

Misunderstanding Political Islam and Islamism

Confusion and disarray over terms like "political Islam" and "Islamism" have afflicted U.S. actions in the Muslim world for some time. In a 2000 study of U.S. policy toward Islamism sponsored by the Council on Foreign Relations,

Robert Satloff observed that "U.S. officials are profoundly reluctant to view (or have great difficulty in assimilating) the organic connection between religion and state that exists in many other societies." At the same time, he noted, this "deep reticence to engage in any religiously tinged policy debates" often leads to an incongruous willingness to accept without challenge "virtually all religious claims [in other societies] with official status."[15]

U.S. policy toward political Islam, Satloff argued, had been inconsistent throughout the 1990s, especially in Iran, Algeria, and Turkey. Islamism was not always seen as clearly and inherently inimical to U.S. interests, so U.S. policies tended to vacillate. By the end of the 1990s, however, Washington had developed a policy toward Islamism that was "reasonably coherent and beneficial to U.S. interests. Namely, the United States recognizes that Islamist political movements almost invariably pose threats to key U.S. interests and, often, to the stability and security of U.S. allies."[16]

Like others, Satloff defines Islamism as "the pursuit of political power with the aim of establishing regimes based on *shari'a* law." He then identifies what he sees as the intellectual or ideological core of the threat posed by Islamism: "the challenges posed by Islamism and Islamist movements [are]...the basic claim that religion (indeed, a certain religion, and a certain interpretation of that religion, no less) is the chief determinant of right and wrong...." Religion as the basis of morality, in other words, is at the root of the drive to establish *shari'a* regimes. The truth claims of Islam, he correctly notes, are "both alien and unnerving to American policymakers."[17]

The Clinton administration, Satloff argues, had in the end produced clear policies towards Islamism. For Islamist states such as Iran and Sudan there was now "a strategy of containment, whose objectives range from retribution to resource denial to behavioral change." To counter Islamist movements, U.S. strategy now emphasized counter-terrorism, economic assistance, and "gradual political reform in host countries." The purpose of political reform was not to engage Islamists, but to promote "individual liberties and then elections." However, the United States must leave "operational decisions on the pace and content of political reform to its partner governments."[18]

This study, appearing in the year prior to 9/11, reveals a great deal about mainstream American foreign affairs thinking at the time. The study was prescient in identifying the aversion to thinking in religious categories that dominated U.S. diplomacy in the 1990s, but in the end its own analysis was limited by a similar incapacity. Its premises were those of classical realism and, to some extent, of liberal internationalism. The United States must not involve itself too deeply in the internal affairs of its "partner governments," most of them authoritarian and repressive, each of which must be left free to decide "the pace and content of political reform." The very purpose of political reform was to marginalize the Islamists and the *shari'a* regimes that they were assumed to seek.

Moreover, the problem with *shari'a* was not its arbitrary nature, the fact that it is for extremists a blank check. The problem with *shari'a* is its *religious* nature: it is grounded in Islam's claims about right and wrong, and is therefore ipso facto illegitimate. There is no attempt to determine whether Islamists or their views of *shari'a* are fixed, no concern for the relationship between religion and state except that they be kept separate. In short, Islamism was understood entirely in modern secularist political categories.

The policies reflected in such thinking did not anticipate the rage that led to 9/11. Unfortunately, however, the post-9/11 freedom agenda has also failed to amend the secularist principles reflected in the study. Our foreign policy in all its aspects—private and public diplomacy, foreign aid, democracy, and civil society programs—simply has not addressed forthrightly or consistently the religious content of whatever is meant by terms such as Islamism, political Islam, or "moderate" Muslims.[19]

There is a more fruitful way of approaching Islam and Islamism as a policy matter. In his book *The Future of Political Islam,* Graham E. Fuller defines an Islamist as "one who believes that Islam as a body of faith has something important to say about how politics and society should be ordered in the contemporary Muslim world and who seeks to implement this idea in some fashion."[20] Here the terms "political Islam" and "Islamism" begin as neutral analytical categories. Judgments about Islamists can be based on their words and actions rather than on the labels themselves.

The advantage of this approach is that it avoids the misleading premise that Islamism is the root of the problem—that any connection between Islam and politics is unacceptable. That approach ignores the human reality that serious religious adherents, like serious nonreligious people, quite naturally want to influence the moral and political norms under which they live and order their lives, and to bring to bear on those norms their most fundamental beliefs. What is unnatural and unrealistic is to write off anyone who sees connections between their religious beliefs and political life as dangerous or extremist. This is as true of Muslims as it is of Christians, Jews, Hindus, or anyone else.

The Continuing "Realist" Temptation to Ignore Religion

In late 2006, a bipartisan panel of eminent Americans presented a much-awaited report on U.S. policy in Iraq and the Middle East. Named the Iraq Study Group (ISG), the panel made a series of recommendations designed to strengthen the Iraqi government and permit a drawdown of American troops. ISG also made significant recommendations for diplomacy, including, in effect, the abandonment of neoconservative unilateralism, muting the goal of democracy promotion, and returning to realist and internationalist orientations as a way to get the United States out of Iraq.[21]

The report called for state-to-state negotiations in which the United States would attempt to convince Iraq's neighbors, especially Syria, Iran, and Saudi Arabia, that it was in their national interests to cooperate in stabilizing Iraq. The report also called upon the UN secretary general to appoint a special envoy to Iraq, and for an international support group that would include key regional actors and permanent members of the UN Security Council.[22] As one veteran foreign affairs journalist put it approvingly, "[t]his report asks the world to help us find our way back home."[23]

The treatment of Islam in the report is of a piece with the realist thinking described in chapter 2. The analysis relies on realist understandings of power, including the drive to power of religious groups. It assumes the centrality of national interests in understanding and attempting to solve, or mitigate, the problems of Iraq and the looming Shiite-Sunni conflict. It makes an innovative attempt to internationalize the religious aspects of the problem, which it labels "sectarian" rather than religious. The study is laced with acknowledgments that sectarian conflict is a major problem in the Middle East. Indeed, the word "sectarian" appears over and over again, a usage that serves both as a synonym for "religion as problem" and a way to avoid serious analysis of how religious actors and ideas might contribute to reconciliation and stabilization.[24]

A good example is the report's brief treatment of the most important religious leader in Iraq (and arguably in the Shiite world), Grand Ayatollah Sistani. Sistani appears in a section entitled, "Sectarian Viewpoints." The lead-in is almost apologetic: "Because Iraqi leaders view issues through a sectarian prism, we will summarize the differing perspectives of Iraq's main sectarian groups." Sistani is described as one of the most "vital power brokers" in Iraq, but, the report notes, he refuses to talk directly to U.S. officials. It observes that "Sistani's influence may be waning, as his words have not succeeded in preventing intra-Shia violence or retaliation against Sunnis."[25] The analysis makes no effort to explain the nature or source of Sistani's influence, why it might be helpful, why it is waning, or why the United States has not succeeded in opening a direct channel to him. The report recommends that the United States "make efforts to engage all parties in Iraq," including Sistani, and that the administration "consider appointing a high-level American Shia Muslim to serve as emissary to him." It also recommends finding ways to talk to another "sectarian leader," Moqtada al-Sadr.[26]

At this point the report comes as close as it dares to religion. "The very focus on sectarian identity that endangers Iraq," it observes, "also presents opportunities...." How should the United States grasp those opportunities? It should encourage "dialogue between sectarian communities" as part of the new diplomatic offensive.[27] That offensive should include "the holding of a conference or meeting in Baghdad of the Organization of the Islamic Conference or the Arab League or both, to assist the Iraq government in promoting national reconciliation."[28] The Saudi government could contribute by using "their Islamic credentials to help reconcile differences between Iraqi factions and build broader support within the Islamic world for a stabilization agreement, as their recent hosting of a meeting of Islamic religious leaders in Mecca suggests."[29]

Each of these recommendations has merit, and the ISG should be commended for addressing religion, however obliquely. Unfortunately, the report's emphasis on the traditional avenues of diplomacy subordinates, if not abandons, the only long-term solution to the religion-based turmoil in the Middle East—stable Muslim democracies. The logic of the recommendations, and the habits of analysis they represent, ensure that the report ignores the role that Islamic teachings, filtered through Muslim leaders, might play. There is no direct acknowledgment that Sistani's brand of Muslim democracy constitutes the only viable hope for long-term political stability in Iraq, or that Sistaniism in power might provide a powerful stimulus to Shiite democrats in Iran. The appeal to the Organization of the Islamic Conference, a pan-Islamic organization with almost 60 member nations, does suggest a desire to involve existing Muslim institutions. But this may reflect a pass-the-buck multilateralism more than anything else. Although the recommendation merits consideration, the OIC has historically proven singularly ineffective in engaging inter-Muslim problems.[30] It should not be employed as a way for American diplomacy to avoid grappling with Islamic factions and ideas.

The most unfortunate but revealing aspect of the report's analysis is the notion that Saudi Arabia's "Islamic credentials" can play a positive role in Iraq or the Middle East over the long term. The only credentials on offer in the kingdom are Wahhabi, and they represent the problem, not the solution. It is true that the Saudi government might block financial and personnel support for Sunni extremists in Iraq and elsewhere in the Middle East. In traditional realist fashion, the report seeks to address that problem with a trade-off of Saudi and Iranian national interests. In return for Iranian forbearance in supporting Shiite extremists, the Saudis might cease support of Sunni radicals.

That, certainly, is a short-term compact worth exploring, in the same way that it makes sense to continue pressing Saudi Arabia to cease support for Wahhabism. But the notion that the current governments in Tehran or in Riyadh are going to solve the problem of extremism is hardly an example of "realism" in any commonsense meaning of the term. Saudi and Iranian state action might stop extremist groups in certain tactical situations. But neither government has the incentive or the capacity to do so permanently.

As they attempt to make sense of these problems, American foreign policy thinkers seem increasingly aware that traditional habits of analysis are insufficient. This awareness was on display in 2007, when three elder statesmen of American foreign policy—Henry Kissinger, Zbigniew Brzezinski, and Brent Scowcroft—came together to muse about dramatic changes in the international system. "The world is much more restless," observed Brzezinski. "It's stirring. It has aspirations which are not easily satisfied." Scowcroft agreed:

"It's a world where most of the big problems spill over national boundaries, and there are new kinds of actors and we're feeling our way as to how to deal with them." Kissinger, the doyen of modern realism, seemed to proclaim its demise: "The international system is in a period of change like we haven't seen for several hundred years...We are used to dealing with problems that have a solution...[but] we're at the beginning of a long period of adjustment."[31] Later Kissinger went even further. The Westphalian system based on nation states, he said, is "collapsing."[32]

As we move toward the second decade of the 21st century, the old frameworks of realism and internationalism are unlikely to constitute the sole or even primary orientation for a successful American diplomacy. The forces of what Bernard Lewis once labeled "Muslim rage" have severely complicated state-to-state relations in the Middle East.[33] While Iran, for example, clearly is pursuing a nationalist foreign policy, that is, with objectives that appear to fit traditional categories of national interest, Tehran's Khomeinist worldview introduces a religious element that can (and has) complicated our ability to understand their methods and their intended destination.[34]

The hard reality is that while expedients such as those recommended by the Iraq Study Group may well be necessary in the short term, there is only one long-term solution to the problems now afflicting the Middle East. Only governments and societies that accept the principles that make democracies last—civil liberties and human rights—can counter the religious, social, economic, and political pathologies that are nourishing Islamist extremism and terrorism. Although the United States needs allies outside the Middle East to assist in its efforts to encourage stable self-government, it must lead the effort, not revert to the kind of multilateral discourse that takes a glacial pace toward oblivion. U.S. policy must employ all the tools at its disposal, military and diplomatic, in a new strategy of encouraging regimes of ordered liberty in the Muslim world.

Rand and the Secularist Temptation

Secularist premises are not limited to those who are skeptical that U.S. programs can engage Islam. The RAND Corporation has for years produced influential foreign policy studies. It has been particularly forward looking on U.S. policy and Islam, producing in recent years a series of penetrating analyses on that subject.[35] Two of these studies, one in 2003 and a follow-on in 2007, argue forcefully that American policy makers insufficiently understand the threat of Islamist extremism and have failed to construct successful strategies to combat it. They strongly advocate engaging moderate Muslims and supporting moderate Islamic institutions in the development of democracy.

Both studies provide valuable insights into the weaknesses of U.S. strategy and generate useful programmatic recommendations (to which we shall return). Both assume that "moderate" Muslims, labeled modernists and liberals, are for the most part Muslims who can either banish Islamic teachings from politics (privatization) or ignore the most problematic teachings in order to render them harmless. This approach appeals to views from across the spectrum of American foreign policy thinking. But the studies also reveal the dangers of failing to take Islam seriously enough.

In 2003, Rand scholar Cheryl Benard made one of the first sustained arguments for U.S. engagement with Islamic groups in order to foster Muslim democracies. Benard explicitly rejected the term "Islamist" because of its imprecision. Too often, she observed, it was "used...to describe either the fundamentalists or the traditionalists."[36] In her typology, the fundamentalists are extremists who threaten America. By contrast, traditionalists are either literalists or reformers who favor "cautious adaptation to change, being flexible on the letter of the law to conserve the spirit of the law."[37] But, she writes, "[m]odern democracy rests on the values of the Enlightenment; traditionalism opposes these values and sees them as a source of corruption and evil." Traditionalism requires *shari'a,* and most traditionalists will support some form of extremist punishments, discrimination against women, or other extremist versions of Islamic law.[38] U.S. policy should support the traditionalists only to isolate the fundamentalists.

On the other end of the spectrum are the "secularists," who seek the privatization of Islam. They are, asserts Benard, America's "most natural allies," given that "Western democracies are premised on the separation of church and state." But even secular Muslims can be anti-American and are often thought to be unrepresentative of Muslims, although, the study notes, the success of Turkey's laicist system suggests secular Muslims may not be as unrepresentative as they appear.[39] Ultimately, however, the study recommends only selective engagement with secularists because they may not be sufficiently representative of Muslim societies.

Finally, Benard argues that U.S. democracy policy should give priority support to Islamic "modernists," whose "vision matches our own." The advantage of modernists is that they, like their Christian counterparts in the West, "selectively ignore" religious doctrines and sacred texts, thereby emphasizing the "true message" of the religion and appropriately consigning the literal text to "history and legend." She identifies the prominent American Muslim intellectual, Khaled Abou El Fadl, as one who adopts this approach. As Benard puts it, when "the literal text of the Koran or hadith conflict with contemporary values," Abou El Fadl teaches that "in the final analysis, Islamic theology requires that a person abide by the dictates of his or her conscience."[40]

In 2007, four Rand scholars (including Benard) published a follow-on study in a book entitled *Building Moderate Muslim Networks.* It argues that radical Islam's clear advantages in funding and organization must be countered by an American-backed program to construct networks of Muslim moderates outside the Middle East. The networks would then channel "modern and mainstream interpretations of Islam back into the Middle East from Muslims elsewhere." Islamists, such as Egypt's Muslim Brotherhood, should not be engaged or supported because they "seek to establish some version of an Islamic state, or at least the recognition of the *shari'a* as the basis of law."[41]

In the interim between 2003 and 2007, Rand scholars had investigated more thoroughly the phenomenon of Muslim secularism. The 2007 study devotes an entire chapter to the subject. Noting that "authoritarian secularists" such as Iraqi Baathists subordinated religion to the purposes of the party or the state, the study identifies a "liberal secularist" as one who views the state "as the neutral administrator of daily life and governance" and who "treats religion as a personal matter or, in some instances, as a communal matter, but one that must be kept discrete from the political realm." Repeating the claim from the 2003 study that liberal secularists were "among the [Muslim groups] most compatible with Western political and social values," Rand scholars now elevated liberal secularists to the role of potential partners in U.S. network building.[42]

Rand's rethinking of Muslim secularism was occasioned by their discovery that this most Western-like of Muslim groups is in fact much closer to the norm in Islamic history, and in contemporary life, than most of us thought. "Historically and intellectually," the authors now concluded, "the role of secularism in the Islamic tradition is considerably more significant than analysts and policy-makers generally believe. Further, secularism in today's Muslim world seems to be in an incipient period of growth, with an evolving group of leaders and an expanding network." Supported by "like-minded liberals in the West" Muslim secularists are building on "the deep strands of rationalist and humanist thought present historically in Islamic thinking and philosophy, and on the secularist movements of the last century." Some historians, the study notes, argue that secularism actually came from Islam to the West in the "rationalism, critical thinking and scientific inquiry" of medieval Islamic philosophy.[43]

There is in the Rand studies much of value, including the identification of a rationalist tradition within Islam and solid recommendations on systematizing America's engagement with Muslim moderates. The United States should indeed support "expanding networks" of democracy-supporting Muslims, whatever their views of the relationship between Islam and politics, provided that they can be successful in attracting wide support from other Muslims. But the studies also reveal the danger of projecting Western secularist premises into the minds of Muslims. Although Rand scholars see themselves countering a presumption *against* secularists in U.S. foreign policy, both studies in fact reinforce the de facto separationist approach to Muslim democratic development already embedded in U.S. policy.

First, the Muslim "modernists" portrayed in both studies as the best hope for Islamic democracy are more a product of wishful thinking than a realistic account of reformers who are likely to influence large numbers of Muslims. A careful reading of Khaled Abou El Fadl makes it abundantly clear that he does not seek to instrumentalize Islamic texts and traditions in the way suggested. To the contrary, he staunchly defends Islamic teachings that appear most troublesome to Rand and to U.S. policy makers, such as *shari'a* and jihad, and has been attacked for that very position by other Muslims and by American conservatives.[44] Moreover, Abou El Fadl's defense of freedom of conscience should not be taken to imply that conscience supersedes the moral or spiritual norms reflected in Islamic doctrine. His point in the quoted passage was not that Muslims should employ freedom of conscience to follow "contemporary values." He sees the human faculty of conscience as a means of attaining, not circumventing, Islamic religious truths.[45] The same could be said of traditional Christian understandings of conscience.[46]

Second, the study's analysis reflects the modern secularist view that religion must be separate from politics because it is at base irrational. Medieval Islamic rationalist philosophy is seen in a positive light not because it represents a rational approach to Islam but because it is seen as a pre-modern version of the secularism that excludes religion from discourse over public policy. In effect, Rawlsian concepts of secularism are employed to reinvent both Muslim and Western history.[47]

Third, the Rand analysis reflects a central flaw in much contemporary thinking about religion and politics, and of U.S. policy toward Islamism: the assumption that the fundamentals of religion are at the end of the day little more than opinion rather than received truth. As such, religious dogma is considered malleable and up for barter when other human imperatives beckon. At some level this premise undoubtedly holds true. Few religious adherents are eager to suffer unnecessarily for their religious beliefs if they can see alternatives. As we have noted, nonreligious developments can affect the way religious doctrine develops, especially the institutions and procedures of democratic governance. Economic growth, a robust civil society, and democratic institutions not only can counter the alienation felt by Muslims in many countries of the broader Middle East, but also can serve to confirm the validity of doctrine that fosters human freedom.

But a purely instrumentalist understanding of how to engage Islamism can also lead to serious policy mistakes. It is dangerous to assume that the identification of Muslims willing to ignore (as the 2003 Rand study puts it) the most troublesome Islamic doctrines can produce stable liberal political systems. U.S. policy cannot safely disregard the sacredness and irreducibility of some religious teachings, including the most difficult, such as jihad, *tawhid*, and *shari'a*. It is in this sense that many, perhaps most, Muslims are examples of what Michael Sandel has labeled the "encumbered self."[48] Muslim actors outside the West may not see themselves as picking and choosing among Islamic doctrines, discarding those judged infelicitous by modernists. The danger is that strategies such as those recommended in the Rand studies will lead the United States further afield from mainstream Islam, which is where the answer lies. In the end we must identify ways to influence those Muslim leaders who are committed to Islam's central tenets, not those we fancy will abandon them.

To be sure there is some validity in Rand's argument about secularism. Networks of secular Muslims are organizing, especially in the context of America's own regime of religious freedom. For example, Muslims held in 2007 a Summit on Secular Islam in Florida, and after its proceedings declared, "there is a noble future for Islam as a personal faith, not a political doctrine." If "political doctrine" means an Islamic state, rule by the clerics, or *shari'a* courts that impose cruel punishments and demean Muslim women, then U.S. foreign policy should vigorously support these self-styled secularists.

But "secularism" as used by foreign policy analysts appears to mean much more. It includes the view that Islam is at its core incompatible with democracy and that, for democracy's protection, it must be privatized or fundamentally altered if not abandoned altogether. This is a view widely accepted among conservatives in the United States, including the Christian right, which tends to accept Samuel Huntington's view that the problem for America is not extremist Islam but Islam itself.

In the end, American policy makers should avoid placing their bets on the basis of labels. The skepticism of Islam qua religion, combined with skepticism of all religion, will inevitably move our policy in the direction suggested in the Rand study—assuming that the good ("moderate") Muslims are those who can cordon Islam outside the public square and restrict it to a peaceful set of private rituals that have nothing to do with politics. This is good work if you can get it, which is to say that American policy should support moderates so defined to the extent that they have a real chance to move particular Islamic societies in the direction of liberal self-government. But the evidence suggests this category of Islam is a long horse. Our goal should not be to empower "secularists" and to privatize religion, but to find those Muslims, whether we label them Islamists, modernists, secularists, or traditionalists, who are capable of creating and sustaining self-government that provides for the well-being of all its citizens.

Indeed, as we have seen, history suggests that religious dogma can be interpreted within a religious community to meet the challenges of modernity if dogma is seen to have been misunderstood, corrupted, or insufficiently developed. The Roman Catholic Church's embracing of religious freedom as an immunity from coercion in civil society was the result of theology and history working together, not the result of calls from outside the Church for it to "modernize," much less for it to ignore or set aside its basic truth claims. If Islamic democracies are to develop, this pattern of internal reform is more likely to be the cause. Accordingly, if American policy makers wish to encourage the development of an Islamic political philosophy of freedom, true "realism" suggests it should side with the stakeholders, not those calling for abandonment of the core.

The premises of the Rand studies are sorely deficient as the basis for promoting stable democracy in the Muslim world. An American religious freedom policy that either follows the course of rigid separationism or simply tries to ignore Islam as a faith is a recipe for failure. Such policies are more likely to increase the religion-based hatred for America and enhance the terrorism it has generated. If it is to succeed, American diplomacy must change the conversation about "political Islam." It must open the door to Muslim liberal democracy not by marginalizing Islam, but by inviting it in.

The Default Preference for Authoritarianism

As noted in chapter 3, the United States has promoted democracy in various spots around the globe for well over two decades. But until the surprise attacks of September 11, 2001, it did so only sporadically in Muslim nations and rarely in the Middle East. The Bush administration's post-9/11 democracy initiative in that region constituted a major departure from the foreign policy of the preceding half century.

Since the end of World War Two, American administrations had routinely supported or accommodated secular, anti-democratic regimes in Muslim countries, such as that of Gamal Abd al-Nasser, Anwar Sadat, and Hosni Mubarak in Egypt, the Shah in Iran, Hafiz al-Assad and his son, Bashir, in Syria, and Saddam Hussein in Iraq. Successive administrations have been loyal allies of the House of Saud—a royal family whose rule has been anti-democratic, suppressed all non-Wahhabi forms of religious expression, and supported the global diffusion of Wahhabi political theology. However inadvertently, that policy laid the theological groundwork for transnational terrorism.

Each of these regimes, although different in other ways, has had in common the systematic repression of human rights. Each has limited or denied the fundamental elements of liberal governance, such as equality under the law, an independent judiciary, a free press, economic freedom, and the liberty of association that limits the reach and corruptibility of the state. These regimes have restricted or forbade the religious freedom of both individuals and communities, including Muslim and non-Muslim groups. Governments in Iran, Iraq, Syria, and Egypt, mirroring to a certain extent the French-inspired approach of Kemal Ataturk and his successors in Turkey, have perceived "political Islam" as a threat to their authority. Each has in some way imposed a command-based secularism, an authoritarian separation of religion from political life, or, in the cases of Iran and Saudi Arabia, exploited and manipulated Islam to increase or consolidate power.

U.S. support for such regimes was to a significant degree based on fears of Islamist extremism, fears that certainly had an empirical basis. The 1979 overthrow of the Shah constituted a revolution in the classical sense, sharing characteristics with both the French and Russian revolutions.[49] But there was a new element in Iran, an augur of the religious resurgence that Western scholars and policy makers would be slow in crediting. The Iranian revolution put in place a regime whose *raison d'être* was reflected in Ayatollah Khomeini's Shiite political theology. Moving forthrightly away from traditional Shiite quietism, Khomeni put clerics in charge of the state. The result was an "Islamic Republic" ruled by Islamist jurists, a virtual dictatorship of the theologians.[50]

Less than two years after the Shiite revolution, Sunni Islamists assassinated Nasser's successor, Anwar Sadat. The next two decades produced growing numbers of Shiite and Sunni extremist groups whose goals and methods were grounded in their views of religious obligation. As serious problems multiplied in the Middle East—the Iran-Iraq war, economic stagnation, government corruption, mass illiteracy, human rights abuses, and assaults on women's rights—the relative dearth of civil society institutions increased the political importance of mosques, the one place where gatherings of religious citizens legally and routinely took place. As it developed during these years, political Islam was dominated by extremists. Both they and more secular liberal opponents of Middle Eastern despots were either controlled by governments or ruthlessly suppressed.

The United States was already hesitant to press for reform of friendly authoritarian regimes in Cairo, Riyadh, and Amman, which American officials took to describing as "moderate" Muslim states. During the 1980s and 1990s, U.S. administrations became even more fearful of empowering political Islam. There were compelling reasons, including America's ever expanding need for oil and its desire to protect the only functioning democracy in the Middle East, Israel. The achievement of both these goals would be endangered, it was thought, if American pressure for political reform destabilized existing authoritarian regimes and brought Islamists to power.[51]

In short, partner governments in the Middle East were valued precisely for their ruthless effectiveness in suppressing political Islam. This led to startling inconsistencies, both at the level of strategic policy and in the promotion of human rights. During the 1980–1988 Iran-Iraq war, the United States remained officially neutral while providing arms to Saddam Hussein and ignoring his development of chemical and biological weapons, largely as a means to curb the Khomeinist Shiite revolution. In retrospect, it is clear that this strategy failed over the long term. It certainly did not restrain the rooting and development of Khomeinism within Iran or its potential for radicalizing Shiites in Iraq.

Of course, U.S. support of Saddam during his war with Khomeini's Iran was also designed, under classical realist assumptions, to maintain a balance of power in the Middle East. The nature of Hussein's own Baathist party, on the one hand, which like Assad's had modeled its methods on Nazi and Soviet methods, was well understood by the United States, including its routine, savage suppression of Iraqi Kurds and Shiites. But because it was secular, the Iraqi regime was considered at least predictable and stable. Khomeini, on the other hand, was a dangerous religious zealot and Iran was now in effect an Islamist theocracy, by definition a greater danger to American interests.

In neither case, however, did American policy makers believe it useful to mount a program of democracy promotion. For the most part even the secular efforts of the National Endowment for Democracy were not considered appropriate for Iraq or Iran, let alone the engagement of Iraqi or Iranian Muslim actors or communities. U.S. interest in Iraqi opposition movements tended to focus on secular exiles such as Ahmed Chalabi. The twin premises of American policy were that Middle Eastern Islam was not culturally ready for democracy, and that political Islam would lead inevitably to extremism.

U.S. human rights policy also reflected these assumptions. In 1982 the Reagan administration joined the international community in roundly condemning the massacre by an Israeli-backed Lebanese Christian militia of 800 Palestinians, including women and children, in two refugee camps. Earlier the same year Syrian President Assad's military forces had destroyed the town of Hama in southern Syria, killing somewhere between 10,000 and 25,000 men, women, and children. The town's crime had been to harbor members of the Muslim Brotherhood, a Sunni Islamist movement that challenged the authority of Assad's Baathist party. Neither the United States nor any other Western nation registered a serious complaint about the Hama massacre, and Assad continued to be courted by American secretaries of state and presidents for the next two decades.[52] In 2006, as noted, the Iraq Study Group recommended that the United States negotiate with Syria in seeking to reduce its support for Islamist extremists in Iraq and Lebanon.

Today, in the post-9/11 world, many American observers remain convinced that the threat posed by Iran's clerical regime, coupled with its pursuit of nuclear weapons, its support of Islamist terrorist groups in Lebanon and Palestine, and its backing of Shiite radical elements in Iraq, confirms the wisdom of U.S. support for rigid secularism in the Middle East. As noted, this preference for secularists has been reinforced by the empowerment of extremists such as Hamas through democratic elections elsewhere in the region. Some conclude that our democracy programs should be significantly scaled back, or abandoned altogether.[53] Others who believe the United States should continue its support for democratic reform in the Muslim world argue that "separation of mosque and state" is the best means of dealing with political Islam and the threat of extremism. They point to the model of Turkey, where democracy developed over the course of the 20th century. Islam, they argue, was successfully forced to the sidelines in Turkey, and the United States must help keep it there.

The American Opportunity

Polls show that democracy is extremely popular among Muslim publics around the world.[54] This is understandable—the desire to throw off the shackles of tyranny and to hold elections is quite natural, particularly given the abundance of contemporary evidence that democracy is achievable. It is less clear what elections would produce in the key countries of the greater Middle East whose cultures are a continuing source of Islamist radicalism, especially Saudi Arabia, Egypt, Pakistan, and Iran.

In Iraq, democratic procedures, even as bolstered by the military successes of 2007 and 2008, have not secured a stable democracy. In the worst case, Iraq could become a central Middle Eastern battle ground for rival nationalisms and religious sects. Parts of the country could also become a recruiting and training station for Al Qaeda. Afghanistan has shown considerable promise as a democratic nation. But the threat from the Taliban and Al Qaeda, operating with relative impunity from the border between eastern Afghanistan and northwest Pakistan, remains high. Over the long term, the fate of democracy in Afghanistan and Pakistan will depend in part on whether they can eliminate the extremist *shari'a* orientation of schools, courts, and jurists and develop among Muslim communities and political parties a democratic political theology.

The fate of these countries and their neighbors over the next two decades will have enormous implications for American security interests. The movement of history suggests that authoritarian regimes, such as those in Egypt and Saudi Arabia, will not remain in place indefinitely, and are likely to be displaced by either violent or peaceful means. Continued U.S. support for those regimes could prolong their hold on power but would almost certainly increase the appeal of Islamist extremism. The policy dilemma in each will be whether U.S. pressure for democratic reform will empower extremists or undermine them. There will continue to be demands to stick with the devils we know.

The Bush administration's confidence in its "forward strategy of freedom" was shaken by the vicissitudes of the Middle East and by its own policy mistakes. The difficulties of consolidating democracy in Iraq, the strategic threat of Iran, the electoral victories of Islamist radicals in the Levant, and the need for cooperation by Saudi, Egyptian, and Pakistani governments against their own domestic extremists and those on their borders are factors that led the United States to curb its democracy agenda in the very nations where stable democracy would bolster American national security.

America's democracy strategy, in tandem with its policy of advancing religious liberty, should be recalibrated and retargeted toward democratic political Islam. This will require greater knowledge of Islam and Islamism in its varieties across the region, a new openness by the United States to the liberal possibilities of political Islam, and the development of guidelines to discern which groups can be enticed to democratic norms, such as the equality of women, the development of Islamic social/spiritual capital, and the critical value of religious freedom, especially the forswearing of coercion in matters of religion. It will require a new awareness by American diplomacy of religious actors who can achieve the difficult interpretative and leadership tasks necessary to the project. Above all, it will require communicating to Muslims of all stripes that democracy is not hostile to religion and does not require its removal from political life. The trade-offs between religion and democracy—the twin tolerations—can lead to the flourishing of both.

As noted earlier, there are a few hopeful signs that the United States is beginning to overcome its fear of political Islam and to acknowledge that Islamism in some form will continue to influence the political arrangements in most Muslim countries where extremist interpretations of Islam are readily available. Some of the progress is the result of practical necessity. In implementing HIV and tuberculosis programs funded by the U.S. Agency for International Development (USAID) in Bangladesh, for example, it has become clear that the opposition of local religious authorities will reduce the effectiveness of the programs. Accordingly, it has been necessary to engage those authorities on theological as well as practical grounds in order to achieve religious sanction for health programs. The results have been quite positive.[55]

Other U.S. funded programs have begun to discern the principle at work here, namely that in Muslim societies Islamic teachings will influence success or failure. This has had an impact on U.S. democracy programs in both South and East Asia, such as those funded by the National Endowment for Democracy, the State Department's Human Rights and Democracy Fund, and the Democracy and Governance division of USAID. Programs in Pakistan designed to develop political leaders and political parties inevitably encounter Islamists and Islamist groups, and cannot possibly communicate with them without understanding their religious motivations and goals. The American embassy has begun to encourage Pakistani authorities to study the relationship between religious schools and state authorities in America as a possible model for madrassah reform.[56]

For years these kinds of efforts have been blocked by strict separationist interpretations of the U.S. constitution, which have led to fears of entanglement with religion. Those fears have by no means disappeared. A 2007 study by the Center for Strategic and International Studies identified the problem. Among their findings: "Some officials said they believe that the Establishment Clause categorically limits government activities related to religion, while many others said they were not sure of the specific ways the clause should shape their actions and decisions.... Some government officials said they are sensitive about approaching religion because they fear being personally attacked—via litigation or public opprobrium—for possibly violating the Establishment Clause. Although usually unclear on the legal parameters of this engagement, government officials are often certain of the political risks involved."[57]

These perceived legal obstacles are heightened by others. USAID and State Department officials are understandably hesitant to be responsible for providing funding or support to Islamic groups if there is a chance it would be employed for extremist purposes. This is a perennial risk of engagement with Islam. But the stakes are sufficiently high to warrant the risk, which can be abetted by the development of guidelines for and the accumulation of experience in engaging Islamic groups. Unfortunately, there is as yet no uniform or consistent U.S. policy on these matters.

A new American religious realism can help stem the flow of future terrorists by facilitating the growth of liberal systems that integrate Islamist parties rather than alienate them. Existing Muslim democracies provide evidence that that this can work. Large Muslim majorities in Indonesia, Malaysia, Bangladesh and Turkey have rejected the imposition of extremist *shari'a* laws.[58] The prospects of living in a country in which economic, educational and professional opportunities exist in the context of liberal Islamic norms are far more likely to destroy Islamist extremism than the secular democracy often represented in U.S. and Western European programs.

An oft-cited example of secularism succeeding in the Muslim world during the 20th century is the Turkish Republic. The founder of the Republic, Mustafa Kemal, known as Ataturk, drew on the secularist French model in imposing a Turkish version of *laicite*, in effect banishing religion from public life. Some American foreign affairs thinkers have seen this Frenchification of Turkish Islam as a model for the Muslim world.[59] Others have concluded that the Ataturkist experiment with modernization and privatization of Islam has failed and is being replaced in the 21st century by militant, anti-secular Islam.[60]

But both views are very likely based on a misreading of the role of Kemal, Islam and Islamist communities in Turkey. The Turkish journalist Mustafa Akyol has written of Kemal's true legacy, which is not a healthy secular democracy but a static Turkish nationalism grounded in Kemalism, itself an ersatz religion. "The vacuum created by absent religion," argues Akyol, "was replaced by a new public faith based on Turkishness and the cult of personality created around its hero, Mustafa Kemal Ataturk. 'Let the Ka'aba be for the Arabs,' wrote poet Kamelettin Kamu, 'for us, Cankaya is enough.' That new shrine was Ataturk's residence."[61]

Kemalism endures in 21st-century Turkey but it no longer dominates. For several years Turkish elections have been won by an Islamist political party, the Justice and Development Party (AKP), which has formed the government since 2002 and styles itself after the Christian Democratic parties of post–World War Two Europe. The AKP-led government has presented problems for the United States, voting, for example, to deny use of American bases in Turkey to invade Iraq. Nor has its record in office been unblemished. Although it swept into power with strong democratic and anti-corruption credentials,

AKP's prime minister, Recep Tayyip Erdogan, has been accused of authoritarianism and corruption, including attempts to suppress opposition media and using his office for personal monetary gain.[62] In late 2008 a constitutional crisis loomed when Turkey's top court overturned a law seen as emblematic of the government's Islamism. Passed by the AKP-dominated Parliament, the law allowed universities to grant women the right to wear headscarves. Using that law as an example, Turkey's chief prosecutor requested the court to disband the AKP (an action not without precedence in Turkey; in the 1990s the constitutional court banned an AKP precursor party).

Whatever the fate of the AKP itself, the experiment of a democratic Islamist party in power is an important one for the region and for the United States. It may well be that such abuses of power as have occurred under the AKP are well within the norm for Turkish politics. Moreover, Turkey has experienced significant economic growth under AKP's tenure, and its government has not presided over significant regression in religious freedom as many expected.[63] Indeed, Akyol observes that today it is the Kemalists, the Turkish secularists, who pose the main obstacle to religious freedom for Christians in Turkey, not the democratic Islamist government.[64]

Traditional diplomacy will continue to play an important role in bilateral or multilateral negotiations when they are appropriate. There clearly are circumstances when it makes sense to press Syria over its support for Hezbollah or Iran over its backing for radicals in Iraq, or Tehran's quest for nuclear weapons. In both cases, negotiations would likely be effective only if backed with credible threats of consequences, including the use of force, should the regimes not cooperate. Traditional diplomacy will also have its place in gaining intelligence cooperation from governments in the region.

But a fundamental, long-term change in U.S. policy toward Islam is required. For better or worse, the forces of electoral democracy have been loosed in the Middle East and are unlikely to disappear. The question for American policy makers is not whether we can underwrite the "stable" cooperative autocrats. The question is which Muslims will win the battle over democracy, extremists or Islamist parties that will sustain liberal democracies as they evolve. The former are likely to ride democratic elections to power and proceed to destroy any hope of liberal democracy in the short term. It is the forces of democratic political Islam, not secular autocrats or secularist reformers, that we must find ways to support, so that they will determine the future of politics and of extremism in the Middle East.

Although there has been discussion within the U.S. government over whether and how to engage Islamist parties that may be open to democracy, such as Egypt's Muslim Brotherhood and its more liberal spin-off, Hizb al-Wasat, that debate has yielded no major policy changes.[65] The default separationist position—that we must avoid such groups and support secularists or "modernists"—has largely prevailed in our private and public diplomacy and in our democracy program spending. But if durable democracy is to root itself in Muslim countries and not regress into either secular or theocratic authoritarian regimes, American diplomacy must begin systematically to engage and support those practitioners of political Islam who are open to liberal democratic institutions and norms.

There is, of course, no magic formula for achieving this goal. Nor are the views of the United States likely to be easily embraced by Muslims. Many will continue to see any official U.S. involvement in Islamic conversations as a Trojan horse designed to undermine Islam. Our European allies (and some in the United States) are sure to ridicule any such effort as at best a waste of time and at worst a spur to extremism. Indeed the argument is sometimes heard that "adding religion to the mix in the Middle East" needlessly complicates an already complex situation. But that argument is like saying "adding gasoline to the mix" needlessly complicates the running of the internal combustion engine. It may be volatile, but to ignore its role is to ensure failure. Conceding both the volatility and the importance of religion in the Muslim world, let us explore some of the fundamental principles that ought to underlay U.S. policy and then outline a few concrete steps that might be taken to adjust our policy.

Although these principles and the steps they yield are focused on Muslim-majority lands, many of them are transferable to other countries and other religions. They certainly implicate the work of the office of international religious freedom at the Department of State, which is the only agency of the U.S. government currently with the job of engaging religion. But these principles and steps should be adopted across the whole of the U.S. foreign policy establishment. Should that happen, it would represent a corner turning in America's engagement with a world of faith and freedom.

General Principles

Religion is normative, not epiphenomenal, in human affairs, and has inevitable public consequences. Drawing on religious norms, religious actors can affect democracy in many ways, for good and ill.

For most people and most faith traditions, religious belief has natural and powerful implications for society and politics. Virtually all religious traditions have a political theology, or a set of doctrines that influence political views.[66] For that reason, a state-imposed privatization of religious belief and practice, or the cordoning of religion and religiously informed moral norms outside the democratic public square, does not accord with human nature and is unlikely to succeed except through repression. Where religion is embedded in culture it will influence political life in one way or another.

> *Authoritarianism, whether secularist or theocratic, increases Islamist extremism. Only stable, consolidated, religion-friendly democracies can contain or destroy extremism. Durable Islamic democracies are more likely to emerge when Muslims see democracy as a means of flourishing religiously, as well as politically, socially, and economically.*

For American policy makers, the Turkish lesson is not that the Muslim world should imitate French secularist institutions, but that it should find ways to encourage a compact between Islamic communities and liberalism. The central criterion for stable democracy in a religious culture is not the marginalization and control of religion but its normalization within democratic society. This process can be encouraged by achieving a sustainable covenant between religion and state that both nurtures and limits the role of religiously informed expression. The challenge for American foreign policy is to find ways to help Muslims succeed in achieving such a covenant.

> *Prudence, not paralysis, should be a critical part of our efforts to promote democracy. Stable democracy is as much an achievement of culture as it is the result of bargaining among elites. It is unlikely to be imposed from without, either by force of arms or clever diplomacy. There is no certainty that all Islamic cultures can achieve the kind of reform that will underpin stable self-government. But acknowledging these realities should strengthen our capacity and determination to influence political reform in Muslim nations, not weaken it or—worse—cause us to abandon the project.*

As we have seen, some conservative American foreign policy thinkers have succumbed to a form of utopianism. Lured by the hopeful examples of post-war Germany and Japan, and even more by what appeared in the 1990s to be the "natural" emergence of democracy in Russia and other states of the former Soviet Union, some intellectuals have tended to sacralize the democratic state as both inevitable and a cure-all for the human condition. This view, accompanied by a gross overestimate of America's capacity to trigger the growth of democracy in other nations and cultures, contributed significantly to errors of strategy in Iraq.

Political scientist Daniel Mahoney has written sagely of neoconservative overreach, which he sees as a betrayal of the conservative principles of prudence and moderation in foreign policy. President Bush's speeches, Mahoney argues, have been ennobling in a rhetorical sense but misleading about the human condition. In proposing that "the love of liberty is the predominant, even the overarching motive of the human soul," the president "downplays the cultural prerequisites of ordered liberty or democratic self-government" and "the decidedly 'mixed' character of human nature."[67]

U.S. policy makers should be cautious about the potential for development of Islamic foundations for stable democracy, such as universal human dignity and ordered liberty. In a 2006 paper on religion and state informed by Pope Benedict XVI's Regensburg lecture, Catholic natural law philosopher John Finnis voiced an important reservation about Islam. Finnis concluded that Islam "appears to me to offer unsound accounts of God, and human destiny, and to be anti-humanist and unclear about free will.... Mohammed's ... account of God and salvation lacks philosophical, moral or historical merit..."[68]

Finnis echoes the reservations about Islam held by many contemporary Catholic thinkers who, like him, oppose the modern secularist project and believe that democracy cannot be sustained without religion. Their views demand, like Mahoney's, a strong dose of prudence in assessing the capacities of human beings and religious communities as U.S. foreign policy is formulated. A policy of religious realism would accept that advice.

But many foreign policy thinkers appear to have concluded from American difficulties in the Middle East that democracy promotion should be significantly scaled back or abandoned. In effect, this is a call for the status quo ante, a return to the policies that viewed political Islam as a pathology to be controlled by despots. Diplomacy is said to be the answer, by which realists (and many liberal internationalists) mean U.S. negotiations with a widening circle of players, from bordering states to regional powers to the members of the UN Security Council. State-to-state negotiations must, of course, remain part of the effort. But they cannot, by their nature, resolve the underlying problem, which is Islam's internal war.

The United States cannot abandon the field in this conflict. While avoiding utopianism, it must also avoid a return to the pieties that facilitated the attacks of 9/11. It must use all the means at its disposal, including maintaining a robust military presence in the Middle East and seizing opportunities for bilateral and multilateral negotiations that can help. But the answer is not to abandon democracy promotion in the Muslim world. The answer is to understand the cultural prerequisites for liberal political development, especially the role of religious stakeholders in Muslim societies, and to learn how to influence their implantation, growth and maturation.

American democracy has succeeded in large part because of the successful covenant between religion and state, not its strict separation. That covenant includes a theistic premise that has enabled differentiation, pluralism, and religious freedom, and should not be abandoned in the conduct of U.S. foreign policy.

To accept this proposition does not require anyone to conclude that "America is a Christian nation," or that nonbelievers are lesser citizens than believers. It does require American officials to understand that America is a religion-friendly nation, and that (whether they believe the proposition true or not) it was founded on the proposition that God exists, that God created and creates all that is, that God is involved in creation, and that natural rights derive from man's duty to God.

Our policy makers should at least acknowledge that the search for God and the attempt to fulfill a duty to God has historically been understood as supporting both the character of citizens and the quality of their arguments in the public square. The questioning of this religion-state covenant—a questioning that is protected by the U.S. regime of religious freedom—has come late in our history. Whatever its effects domestically, it has proven to be a liability in the nation's engagement of a religious world.

Michael Novak has argued that the American covenant with religion is best understood within the framework of what he calls "Hebrew metaphysics." He argues that the U.S. democratic experiment was grounded in Jewish and Christian theistic assumptions.[69] Secularists should consider the wisdom of Novak's argument. It is difficult to imagine the U.S. system of religious freedom emerging solely from Enlightenment rationalism, Kantian philosophy, or atheism. Here is the point for skeptics to ponder: while more secular traditions would not highly value, let alone nourish, public religious expression (witness France), the American compact with religion would, and does, protect the right not to believe and the right to challenge religion in the public square.

Perhaps the best example of the importance of theism and religion in the American polity is the life and work of Thomas Jefferson, who was certainly not a Christian in any conventional sense of the term. But Jefferson's understanding of human equality, rights, and public virtue are incomprehensible without reference to a Creator heavily involved in his creation. To this extent Jefferson's thought mirrored Madison's—religious freedom is born in man's duty to God and this duty requires liberty for all. It *requires* men to protect the liberty of others. Jefferson also agreed with his peers that the American system could succeed only if it nourished both the natural desire of men to know the Creator and the public morality that flows from the religious enterprise.[70]

Jefferson's life also mirrored the imperfections of the American system in practice. When he wrote the Declaration's magnificent religious truth claim about God and man, Jefferson lawfully owned human beings as slaves. But as Abraham Lincoln, William Brennan, Martin Luther King, and countless other Americans have attested over the centuries, the promise of human equality and freedom, even when unrealized, remains grounded in the theistic premises of the founding. Again, the challenge to this grounding has arrived late in the nation's history. Contemporary warnings about the dangers of "theocracy," as well as the rejection of any theistic underpinning to American democracy, pose a serious threat—not simply to religious believers but to the rights of all Americans.

Given the strength of that challenge, it is unsurprising that the practitioners of U.S. foreign policy have often lost sight of America's debt to a theistic understanding of human rights. Too many have concluded that the founders saw no role for religion in public debates or public policy and that religious expression must be privatized. This, as much as anything else, has led to U.S. diplomacy's impoverished understanding of the possibilities for Islam and democracy. That understanding must be revised and enriched.

Concrete Steps

Proceeding from these principles, what actions might U.S. foreign policy take to engage and influence religious actors and the development of democratic political Islam? What arguments might American officials make? And how might we begin the critical process of opening American diplomatic culture to the opportunities presented by a world of faith?

The following steps and arguments are illustrative, not exhaustive, but they can point the way to a recalibrated policy of advancing regimes of religious freedom.

Steps to Take

1. Reestablish as the overarching U.S. policy in every state of the greater Middle East the encouragement of those democratic actors capable of adopting liberal, stabilizing reforms.
2. Develop the expertise and means to empower and influence democratic religious actors—religious elites who can influence the climate of opinion, as well as the processes and principles of democracy, by employing arguments drawn from their own comprehensive doctrines.
3. Develop guidelines for analyzing religion-state issues. For example, discern within each country the obstacles posed, or the opportunities presented, by dominant interpretations of *shari'a*. Where obstacles exist, determine what would be required of Muslim leaders and Islamic parties to overcome them. Among religious communities, what are the prevailing political theologies? Which religious actors and political theologies either reject, or are capable of rejecting, the use of coercion by the state to privilege their communities, forms of worship, or revealed truths? Which religious actors are open to ideas like differentiation, pluralism and the twin tolerations? How can the "spiritual capital" of each religious tradition be tapped and developed? Be alert to the importance of jurists and courts to the development of Islamic democracy.
4. Articulate an appealing religion-state model that can be adapted to different cultures, religions and nations. Extremists have framed the

debate over secularism by identifying it with France and opposition to Islam. The French/Kemalist model seeks to repress religion, as does the Mubarak/Assad authoritarian model. On the other end of the spectrum, the extremist Islamist model corrupts *shari'a* and harms Muslims by empowering despots. The model that can work for Muslims is a democratic bargain between Islam and the state, a mutual toleration in which Islam flourishes, as does religious pluralism and human rights.

5. Systematically target religious communities and Islamic parties in U.S.-funded democracy programs, including "civil society" programs. Develop strategies for encouraging religious behavior as social or spiritual capital. Take steps to overcome concerns that such programs are unconstitutional.

6. Expand the State Department's International Visitors program. Welcome into the United States Muslim scholars and jurists who seek to teach at American institutions, even those whose ideas are considered problematic. This does not mean admitting terrorists. It means getting over our fear that influential scholars such as Tariq Ramadan are dangerous because they are believed to be (and may be) dissimulators, speaking one way to Muslim audiences and another to non-Muslims. The answer to that problem is more direct public exposure to American critics, not less. If it is true (as I believe it to be) that the vast majority of American Muslims are anti-extremist precisely because of the American system of religious liberty, then more Muslims from Europe and the greater Middle East should be exposed to that system.

7. Exploit the Internet. For example, engage in Web-based discourse with members of Islamic parties, many of whom have their own Web sites and chat rooms. Encourage similar projects by U.S. academic and civic institutions, secular and religious. In order for such discourses to add value, that is, to challenge Islamic thinking, the American skeptics of Islam must be involved.

8. Engage the Islamic feminists. They are elements of a fascinating skirmish within the Muslim war of ideas, one that could become a full-fledged battle. Muslim feminists are drawing on sacred texts to demonstrate the potential for development and reform from within the heart of Islam.

9. Engage the economic sector. We have long sought, with very modest success, to encourage economic development in Middle Eastern nations. We should redouble those efforts and also build institutions to involve capitalists in the debate over political Islam. For example, what would a Muslim Brotherhood-led government in Egypt mean to Toyota, and vice versa?

10. Establish a privately funded Islamic Institute of American studies on American soil. Its purpose would be to bring the best jurists and

political leaders from across the Muslim world to study American history, society, politics, and, especially, religion. Unlike the International Visitors program, which exposes foreigners to America for a few weeks, this Institute and its work would be long term.

11. Engage the American Muslim Community and the broader U.S. public in supporting a refurbished international religious freedom policy. The State Department should listen to American Islam through institutions such as Ambassador Robert Seiple's Islamic Roundtable.

Arguments to Make

1. Religious pluralism—the free and peaceful contention of differing religious traditions within the democratic system—and religious competition both work to the benefit of religion and of democracy. As such, they can benefit Muslims religiously, economically, socially, and politically.

2. Religious communities contribute to democracy and their own flourishing when their adherents participate in civil society, including in secular organizations. Religious groups can contribute social and spiritual capital by bringing to voluntary associations, and to the democratic public square, not only their good works (which can develop spiritual and social capital) but also arguments about the common good grounded in their beliefs. Those arguments might include issues such as justice, mercy, human dignity, the family, poverty, disease, economic development, and the nature of political authority.

3. Private religious schools and systems of public education can complement and strengthen each other. The American system demonstrates that.

4. Successful democracies require moral teachers. They do not rely on the state to be a source of moral teachings but have vigorous contention within the public square over right and wrong. Muslim communities should engage in this process of democratic bargaining. Within the United States, for example, Muslims should articulate what they mean by *shari'a* and whether it contains any principles applicable in a pluralist democracy. This is the kind of democratic debate that if held in Afghanistan or elsewhere might lessen the power of extremist interpretations of *shari'a*.

Retooling American Diplomacy

1. Revamp training for American diplomats on religion. The goal should be to integrate thinking about religion into the entire range of diplomacy. Every foreign service officer, civil service employee, and political appointee, especially ambassadors, should receive general training

about religion as part of their orientation to the foreign service or the State Department. Later they should receive training particular to the country and region in which they will serve.

2. For foreign service officers, create a subspecialty in religion under both political and economic career tracks.

3. Provide opportunities and incentives to excel in integrating religion into American foreign policy, for example in assignments, promotions, and awards.

4. In the State Department, require a religion specialist for the country desk of every country in which religion plays a significant role in political or economic life—which is today virtually every country in the world. Although these specialists may necessarily be outside experts in the beginning, over time they should become trained, effective, engaged members of the American foreign service.

5. Elevate the role of democracy promotion at the State Department by integrating it, along with religious freedom, into the mainstream regional bureaus. This function should be carried out under the leadership of the under secretary for political affairs, not the under secretary for global affairs.

6. Grant the ambassador at large for international religious freedom the authority currently provided by the IRF Act as the principal adviser to the president and the secretary of state on the promotion of religious freedom. The ambassador and his office should be directly under the secretary, the deputy secretary, or the under secretary for political affairs. The ambassador should be an integral part of all senior meetings that implicate U.S. policy in states or regions where religion is a significant factor.

From the Middle East to the Far East

Again, these steps and arguments are illustrative, not exhaustive. But what about the world outside the greater Middle East? There are many non-Islamic cultures and nations whose internal developments and policies have enormous implications for American interests. Among them are Russia, Japan, India, as well as several countries in Europe, Latin America, and sub-Saharan Africa. But no county is more important to American well-being and security than is China, the largest country in the world, to which we now turn.

10

～∞∞～

Riding the Dragon

The Case of China

The size of China's displacement of the world is such that the world must find a new balance in 30 or 40 years. It's not possible to pretend that this is just another big player. This is the biggest player in the history of man.
    —Lee Kuan Yew[1]

Religion may outlast the [Communist] party and the [Chinese] state.
    —Jiang Zemin, Chinese president[2]

Kill the chickens and warn the monkeys.
    —Chinese proverb that describes Beijing's policy in Tibet[3]

Of Rice and Men

"Stale fried rice. For Mr. Farr to think Chinese officials are going to meet with him after all this reminds me of stale fried rice."

The message came to the American embassy in Beijing from Mr. Ye Xiaowen, director general of China's State Administration of Religious Affairs (SARA), and it provided an occasion for worried reflection. Ye was telling me not to come to China, and we had a decision to make. It was March 2001, one of the periodic low points in the U.S.-China relationship. Two years earlier during the Serbia-Kosovo conflict, the United States had inadvertently bombed the Chinese embassy in Belgrade. Many Chinese were convinced it had been deliberate. Just a month after Ye's fried rice message an American reconnaissance aircraft would collide with a Chinese fighter that had flown too close, precipitating a genuine crisis in Sino-American relations.

273

The immediate problem, however, was less dramatic but more revealing of the long-term problems besetting U.S.-China relations. The State Department had just released its worldwide *Country Reports on Human Rights*. Echoing the *Annual Report on International Religious Freedom*, which had been published the previous fall, the department had condemned the Chinese government for a worsening in its treatment of religious communities and individuals. Now, just before my planned departure for Beijing, the newly arrived George W. Bush administration had announced that it would seek a resolution condemning China at the United Nations Commission on Human Rights. Predictably, the Chinese were not pleased, and Ye's sarcasm conveyed their displeasure.

Still, the Chinese embassy in Washington had granted me a visa, and I was not disposed to put the trip off. After the bombing of its embassy China had suspended the human rights dialogue begun under the Clinton administration. The last official talks had been held in 1998, when Ambassador for International Religious Freedom Robert Seiple and Assistant Secretary for Democracy, Human Rights, and Labor Harold Koh had traveled to Beijing. Seiple had departed (as had Koh) and the new administration's replacement had not yet been identified. Over two years had passed without any official contact between the office of international religious freedom and Chinese officials, and I was determined that we not lose whatever advantages we had gained from Seiple's visit.

Beijing had been unhappy that when Seiple returned to Washington China was designated as a "country of particular concern (CPC),"[4] but that made it doubly important to follow up. As I saw it, there was little point in condemning the Chinese publicly without presenting sound arguments in private about why it was in China's interest to alter its policies. Without substantive exchanges of this kind, the only result of our denunciations would be dueling accusations by press spokesmen while religious persecution continued apace. Among other things, it would be useful to communicate what the Chinese government needed to do in order to remove itself from the CPC list.

Just days before my State Department colleague Paul Martin and I were to get on the plane, we received Ye's message. Our plan had been to meet with him and other senior officials in Beijing, and to do the same in Shanghai, Nanjing, and other locations throughout China. But our China desk was convinced that Ye's stance would color the trip, and that no senior officials would see us. They urged us to consider canceling for that reason, although they also observed that we might restructure our goals. After discussing the matter within our office, we decided to go ahead. We would ask our embassy to continue to press for appointments with Chinese officials and "official" religious leaders, but if those did not come through we would see a different China.

It was a good decision. The two-week trip took us to areas we would not have otherwise seen and into unscripted conversations that doubtless yielded

more insights than would have been the case had they been planned and supervised by Chinese officialdom. We traveled first to Beijing, and then to Nanjing,
Wenzhou, and Shanghai in eastern China. We then flew west to Chengdu in
the province of Sichuan. From there we drove ten hours north to the edges of
ancient Tibet. What we learned would help me prepare the next ambassador
for future encounters with Ye Xiaowen, SARA, and those areas of the Chinese
government responsible for the control and management of religion.

The Importance of China to American National Interests

Next to Islamist terrorism and Iran, China presents the most significant U.S.
foreign policy challenge of the early 21st century. This ancient east Asian land
of 1.3 billion people has experienced stunning economic growth in recent
decades and is in the midst of a socioeconomic transformation with enormous
international, regional, and domestic implications. China seeks, and is clearly
achieving, a growing role in international affairs. It is one of the world's longest
standing nuclear powers and possesses the means to deliver nuclear weapons
over long distances. It is a permanent member of the United Nations Security
Council, and as such is a powerful player in any attempt to build international
consensus on major issues. It is an important partner in our attempts to deal
with North Korea, traditionally a Chinese ally and a rogue nuclear regime that
poses a potential threat to the security of the region and the United States.[5]

China's economic might alone makes it the single greatest force for stability or instability in Asia and arguably in the world. It has now replaced Japan as
the world's second largest consumer of energy, behind only the United States,
which it will surpass within a few decades. Its enormous energy consump-
tion increases China's need for allies in the Middle East, resulting in a growing Sino-Muslim relationship.[6] Its economy, along with the Chinese diaspora,
influences the economic development, culture, and politics of its East Asian
neighbors, including the world's largest Muslim country, Indonesia.[7]

In short, China's regional and international influence, already great, is
growing. Samuel Huntington has written that Chinese economic and military power is likely to lead to an assertion of regional hegemony with international implications. Should its economic growth and political unity continue
for another decade, Huntington wrote in 1996, "East Asian countries and the
world will have to respond to the increasingly assertive role of this biggest
player in human history."[8] Other scholars argue that China requires peace in
order to achieve the modernization that it seeks.[9]

Two core questions emerge for American national security. The first is
whether China's foreign policy will be peaceful and stabilizing or aggressive
and a danger to American interests. In the best case, China would continue to
exercise a calming influence on its neighbors, in particular North Korea, which

Beijing would encourage in the direction of economic and political reform and away from its dangerous dalliance with nuclear weapons, arms sales to rogue states, and support of terrorism. China would also manage carefully its relations with India, Japan, South Korea, Vietnam, Singapore, Taiwan, and Hong Kong (now part of China), encouraging each to see the Chinese as partners rather than a threat. In the worst case, Chinese policies could lead to conflict with one or more of its neighbors. For example, a military attack against Taiwan would probably produce a serious crisis in Sino-U.S. relations.

In the long run, however, the nature of Beijing's relations with its Asian neighbors, as well as its overall international role, will turn on the answer to the second question: What will be the fate of China's internal political regime? Put simply, can the country's leaders continue moving toward a controlled market economy while successfully managing the domestic consequences of growth? Those consequences include massive internal problems, such as unemployment, internal dislocation, the breakdown of families, a demographic excess of young males, huge income inequities, enormous environmental degradation, HIV AIDS and other major diseases, and a slow but growing demand for political reform. Can the Chinese manage all this without a radical political retrenchment or a violent internal upheaval, the consequences of which could be catastrophic for China, its neighbors, and the United States?

The fact is that China's internal stability remains a serious long-term issue, called into question by the sea change wrought by modernization. Neither official nor private resources have been able to cope with massive internal emigration into the cities, where thousands move each year from surrounding villages. The health industry has been in shambles, unable to keep up with the need for hospitals and doctors. As China moved into the 21st century the ancient problem of leprosy hung on like a ghost of China's past, and new, more modern and virulent plagues such as AIDS began to wreak their devastation. As central government controls were relaxed in some areas, corruption increased. Families came under stress, with adultery, suicide, and the increasing rebellion of China's youth part of the result. China's leaders soon discovered that modernization brought traumas of a different sort, and they struggled to find solutions within the "socialist" model. Chinese planners furiously amended the Leninist construction of reality to fit the challenges of modernity.[10]

Although its accommodations with capitalism proved remarkably flexible, Chinese communism, like its dying counterparts elsewhere in the world, was built on a false anthropology, a grossly distorted understanding of human nature and human freedom. Among other things, it was utterly unable to account for man's longing for transcendence and the need to respond to it in freedom, much less accommodate such a natural right. Inevitably, the socioeconomic transformation of the country created a huge moral and spiritual vacuum, one that was rapidly filled by religion. After having been viciously and systematically suppressed during the Cultural Revolution (1966–1976), many of China's religions had quickly begun to revive. By the 1990s many were steadily increasing in the numbers of adherents with various strains of Christianity leading the way. By 2007, although government estimates suggested 100 million religious adherents, a government sponsored poll suggested there were three times that many.[11]

The growing phenomenon of religion naturally worries the Chinese political class. Unlike Tibetan Buddhism or Islam (both of which have their own problems), Christianity is directly associated with Western imperialism and, in the minds of many, China's humiliation. Adding to the anxieties associated with religion, China's new economic growth is inevitably producing pressures for political reform, which threatens the Communist regime. In 1989, the government arrested or killed the leaders of a protest in Beijing's Tiananmen Square, demonstrating a resolve to control, rather than be controlled by, internal movements for change.

There is in these trends a fundamental contradiction that must be resolved and to which American foreign policy must attend. On the one hand, the Chinese government has apparently succeeded in replacing a Marxist economy with carefully managed but increasingly free market practices that are producing not only impressive economic growth but an enormous reduction in poverty.[12] On the other hand, the government holds tight to outmoded and potentially disastrous methods in managing the consequences of economic growth. It is trying to midwife a stable political transition from the top down, controlling and manipulating with the deadening hand of socialist bureaucracy the activities of 1.3 billion citizens whose lives have been turned upside down. Some have been freed by new wealth; others plunged into despair by modernization.[13]

China has made the transition to the third generation of leaders after Mao Zedong, whose visage still dominates the entrance to the Forbidden City that housed Chinese emperors for centuries. To their credit, political leaders are asking tough questions about national policy. After all, a country capable of abandoning Marxist and Maoist economic theory in the course of a few years ought to be able to adjust its other principles in accordance with social and political realities.

As they look at the enormous problems they are facing, their doctrines tell them to repress, using party and state to keep the lid on. But their common sense, and the success of their economic pragmatism, tells them that other solutions must be considered as well. It is in their search for those solutions—ones consistent with their sense of Chinese greatness and national unity—that an opportunity to influence China emerges. In few areas is that opportunity greater, and in the long run more important for China's internal transformation, than the question of religion.

Some of China's leaders are beginning to grasp a fundamental reality. Religious belief and practice, particularly among the country's Christians, is growing and will not—as Marxist doctrine held along with the secularization theory—wither away with the movement of history. The long-standing solution has been to manage and if necessary suppress any organization or activity that might challenge the government's authority and China's sense of national unity while the nation modernizes. Religion is among those forces it has traditionally feared most, in part because Chinese history has provided ample evidence of its destabilizing potential.

Today religious devotion is moving with perplexing force to fill a void in the Chinese spirit. China's bosses, whose failure to understand religion adds to their fear, cling to party-related mechanisms of social control, including "official" oversight institutions within each religious group and the State Administration for Religious Affairs, often staffed by atheist ex–military officials at the national, provincial, and local levels.

The quixotic task of these functionaries is to ensure that religious practice accords with national policy. Their efforts have had some qualified success, producing a squad of five "official" religious groupings (Buddhism, Islam, Taoism, Protestantism, and Catholicism) that together claim some 150 million adherents, about 12 percent of the total population.[14] But they have also produced a growing religious "underground" of individuals and groups refusing government registration or resisting government control of religion. Estimates of both "official" and underground adherents vary widely, but the numbers of China's religious believers clearly exceed 200 million, and may be closer to 300 million, almost 25 percent of the total population. Most important, the trend is upward, and perhaps dramatically so. One recent estimate suggests that within 30 years China's Christian population alone could reach between 20 and 30 percent of the total.[15]

Awareness of these trends has alarmed Chinese officials, whose official ideology continues to view China as an atheist state and religion as a troublesome residuum of imperialism or the practice of ethnic minorities, to be managed and controlled. One result of their alarm has been persistent religious discrimination, which is inherent in the whole system of managed "official" religious groups. Far worse are the periodic crackdowns and bouts of harsh persecution.

Both discrimination and persecution have induced discontent and fear within China's religious population and a growing gap between government policy and social reality. The United States has at least recognized the problem, designating China a "country of particular concern" for its egregious violations of religious liberty in each year since the designations began in 1999. But despite the efforts of both IRF ambassadors, American policy has had little real impact on China's treatment of religion.

The Beijing government faces a deepening dilemma that must be resolved if the nation's economic growth is to move it toward stable and peaceful democratic governance in the coming decades. History suggests that rapidly increasing, diffuse religious devotion is not susceptible to the kind of control that China continues to impose. Religion can be forcibly suppressed for a time, as it was during the Cultural Revolution, and as it continues to be in various locations around the world. But China decided in the 1980s that the costs to the nation of Maoist savagery were too high. It has rejected Maoist methods, including the attempt to abolish religion altogether. In fact, since the days of the Cultural Revolution the government has refurbished tens of thousands of houses of worship and built even more.

Beijing's hope has been to domesticate and bureaucratize religious bodies under a neo-Confucian, patriotic umbrella of authoritarian control. But there is little in Chinese Christianity, Tibetan Buddhism, or the Islam practiced in the northwestern province of Xinjiang that suggests such a goal is feasible. Traditional religions that are energized and growing must either be ruthlessly suppressed or nourished and channeled into efforts for the public good. The movement of modern history, including in China, suggests that religious groups cannot over the long term be manipulated into an extension of bureaucracy by altering their doctrinal or moral imperatives to suit government policy.

Religious people and institutions have the potential for significant influence over China's development in coming decades by providing, inter alia, a source of social and spiritual capital. As noted, the questions now being asked by China's leaders provide an opportunity for governments that China respects, and also for China's religious groups themselves, to make the case for their inclusion as a positive force in the nation's socioeconomic and political development.

But the trajectory of current Chinese policy suggests that the government is likely to continue its counterproductive understanding of "unofficial" religious practice as China's enemy and to continue its efforts to restrain and manipulate that practice as a result. This will mean more religious persecution and a deepening of the social crisis standing in the way of China's peaceful movement toward stable representative government. It will also mean a continuing obstacle to U.S.-China relations.

To date, U.S. religious freedom policy has been sporadic in its application and minimal in its effects. It has succeeded in China, as it has elsewhere, in the occasional release of religious prisoners. It can also be said to have habituated China's leaders to U.S. interest in the issue, although they are doubtless aware of how erratic that interest can be. It cannot be lost on China's leaders that U.S. religious freedom proposals such as those presented by Ambassador John Hanford are for the most part left by the U.S. government to lay fallow on the table.[16] The most consistent elements of U.S. policy have been the annual public denunciation attending the CPC designation, which has never been followed by action, either positive or negative, and the annual attempt during the 1990s to condemn China at the U.N. Commission on Human Rights in

Geneva, which in every case was defeated by Chinese lobbying. One wonders whether Chinese Foreign Ministry officials on the America desk take bets on what their clients will do next.

Beijing, Heresy, and Abortion

During the two years prior to my arrival in China, a Chinese health group with elements of Daoism and Buddhism called Falun Gong had alarmed Chinese officials by demonstrating a capacity to attract tens of thousands, perhaps more than a million, of Chinese adherents without the knowledge of Beijing. The resulting crackdown was thorough and vicious, and its ripples were still spreading to the more traditional religious groups when Paul and I landed in Beijing.[17]

When we arrived at the U.S. embassy compound we learned that State's China desk had been correct. Ye's refusal to see me had been coordinated with other officials, all of whom had either responded in the negative to appointment requests sent by the U.S. embassy or had canceled appointments to which they had already agreed. After a meeting with Ambassador Joseph Prueher and an extensive briefing by the American country team, we began our own Beijing adventure.[18] Instead of meeting with Chinese officials, we had long, probing conversations with various actors in the drama of Chinese religions. Some were parts of religious communities and some were academics whose interest in the subject of American religious freedom policy exceeded their fear of official disapproval. Several met with us at their peril—we were almost certainly being observed by Chinese security agents.

One member of the quasi-official Chinese university system risked a rendezvous at a local hotel. China's academics, although their activities are often monitored by party officials, enjoy an elevated status because they are viewed as the gateway to knowledge and power. This man was a specialist on religion at the Chinese Academy of Social Sciences, and our discussion confirmed the importance of that and similar organizations to religious freedom in China. The Chinese government fears religious faith as unpredictable and unmanageable, largely the result of superstition. But they are increasingly willing to approach religion through the door of science and scholarship.

Accordingly, the Chinese government established the Institute of World Religions at the Academy of Social Sciences. The Institute is staffed by Chinese scholars who travel extensively to develop data and produce studies on the world's religions. This phenomenon reveals an interesting irony. Universities in the West, like the few remaining Communist governments in the world, remain for the most part fiercely resistant to the value and validity of the religious impulse. But scholars in Communist China, acting with the support of their government, are reaching out to religion.

We also met with Christians in Beijing. Some, like American Protestant minister Ellyn McGinnis, defended the Chinese approach to religion as understandable in light of Chinese history. She politely but firmly criticized official American ignorance of government-sanctioned Christian churches in China, which were, she insisted, clearly making inroads. McGinnis had a television program that she said was well received because she spoke of Christian themes, such as forgiveness, but not of Jesus. The best course for U.S. religious freedom policy, she told us, was to leave China alone.[19]

Although I understood her point—there is indeed a scarcity of understanding in the United States for the complexity of religion in China—McGinnis's "Jesus-free" approach to Christianity on Chinese television made me reflect on the phenomenon of heterodoxy among Chinese religions in general. Her own ministry is doubtless entirely orthodox, and the practice of trumpeting Christian virtues minus the revelation is certainly understandable in a country that is officially atheist.

I later discovered, however, that both Catholic and Protestant Chinese practices had yielded bizarre offshoots that bordered on heresy. The issue was to become a source of heated discussion, both with the Chinese and within the State Department. The question was what, precisely, ought to be the role of government in policing heresy? The answer for the U.S. government seems quite simple: none, unless criminal or civil laws are broken, in which case the issue is enforcing the law rather than religious orthodoxy.

In China, the problem is more complicated. Criminal and civil laws are regularly used by the state to control religious individuals and groups, whether religiously orthodox or not. In practice, "orthodoxy" is defined as adherence to government-supported religious umbrella organizations. This system of managing religions had encouraged breakaway groups that were not only doctrinally heretical (e.g., sect leaders claiming to be the second coming of Christ), but also socially disruptive and sometimes violent.

In one particular case, we discovered that unsanctioned but orthodox Protestant house churches were cooperating with local Chinese authorities in locating and arresting leaders of a competing, heretical sect. The case led to disagreements within the department over what our message to Chinese authorities should be. Some liked the idea of official Chinese support for orthodox Christian groups over heterodox cults. My view was that we had to tread carefully on this issue. Orthodoxy in any religion should be under the control of its adherents. We should encourage the government to let each religious group manage such affairs internally via training of clergy, teaching of adherents, and the like. It was a mistake in my view to encourage Chinese authorities to get involved.

Of course, those authorities were generally indifferent to questions of orthodoxy or heterodoxy but would clearly play one off against the other in order to control all religious expression. Our goal should be to convince government authorities it was in their interest not only to stay out of such matters, but also to support the religious infrastructure that would allow each group to "police" its own house. That, in turn, would provide benefits for Chinese social and economic development.

Other Beijing Christians, including a Catholic priest close to both official and underground Catholics, met with us at some risk. The priest was very wary about discussing his concerns but in the end decided it would be worthwhile. We purposely met in a noisy coffee shop and I had to strain to hear his quiet voice. However, his message was clear: the United States should do everything it could to improve cooperation between the "two wings" of Catholicism in China—the officially sanctioned Catholics and the underground Catholics who did not accept government regulation, especially of bishops. The two are not in reality separate entities. Theologically, there is only one Catholic Church. Also, in practice, lay Catholics who sympathize with the underground church sometimes attend mass at official churches. Bishops and priests on both sides of the divide know each other and sometimes cooperate. But sometimes they clash.

According to this priest, it was vital for his underground colleagues to get better seminary educations than were available to them in China, and the only remedy was to send them overseas. This, however, could not be done surreptitiously. Travel by underground priests generally required the agreement of the official bishop in the diocese where they resided. Our interlocutor urged us to press for more cooperation between underground and official clergy.

In the ensuing years I would come to see the wisdom of this advice, although it too has its limits. Most sympathetic observers of the underground Chinese Catholic Church recognize that a lack of sound religious formation is a growing problem. Underground seminaries lack the resources and, often, the stability to provide the kind of training needed for a priest in modern China. All Chinese priests (and indeed all Chinese clergy of every religion) are under enormous strain as they attempt to deal with the effects of their country's burgeoning moral and spiritual crisis while the numbers of adherents grow, sometimes quite rapidly.

The indispensable element for all clergy in modern China is sound doctrinal formation combined with exposure to the social sciences and humanities. One solution is to send seminarians and young clergy overseas for training, but this often leads to discontent upon their return to China, if they return at all. The durable solution is wholesale acceptance by Chinese government and society of the value of religion, and therefore religious education. For the Chinese Catholic Church, a solution will also require a dissolution of the boundaries between the "official" and underground churches. That cannot happen, however, until the Vatican and the Chinese reach an agreement.

Our coffee shop conversation also revealed one of the explosive moral and spiritual problems besetting Catholic priests in China—the issue of abortion. China's deficient understanding of human freedom is manifest in its notorious "one-child policy," which mandates that most families may not have more than one son or daughter. For one thing, this means that abortion is virtually a government-supported industry, used routinely as a method of birth control or sex selection. In some places, it also means that women are forced against their will to have abortions. One of the many terrible results of this misguided policy has been the tendency to favor male children, which sometimes has led to the abandonment or deliberate abortion of females. It has also produced a surplus of young males, a demographic distortion that has historically meant trouble for other societies, and very likely will increase the chances of aggressive Chinese policies.

For Catholic priests who follow the teachings of their church, China's abortion policy amounts to a multidimensional tragedy. Quite aside from the moral and social calamity of forced abortion, it is quite dangerous for priests to speak publicly, especially in an "official" church, against the practice of voluntary abortion, which Catholicism teaches is a grave sin. Even in the confessional or during private meetings, the coffee house priest told us, it was virtually impossible to instruct Catholics to avoid mortal sin without at the same time counseling them to flaunt Chinese law, which could put them in grave physical danger. Although forced abortion is a human rights abuse of major proportions, government policies that require people by law to defy the core teachings of their religious communities constitute a fundamental abuse of religious freedom.

After hearing the priest's concern, I decided to include the abortion issue in the China chapter of our next *Annual Report on International Religious Freedom*. I knew that some in the State Department would oppose this as "mixing two unrelated issues," or appearing somehow to assert the priority of religious freedom over the right of abortion. Ultimately I succeeded in getting a single reference into the text, but not without experiencing the distaste among some of my colleagues for that version of religious freedom that defends the right of religious groups to teach what they believe to be the truth, and their adherents to follow that truth, even when opposed by governments.[20]

Our final evening in Beijing provided a sobering glimpse into the fruits of China's socioeconomic transformation and, for some, a justification for the nation's need to control its population growth. We were returning from an off-the-record dinner with Western journalists at a local restaurant. The distance to our hotel was more than a mile, but it was a pleasant evening and we decided to walk. We strolled along for some time, chatting about what we had learned in Beijing, when a tiny Chinese girl appeared beside me. She was 4 or 5 years old and begging for money. "Don't do it, Tom," said my colleague Mark Lambert, who was walking behind me. Mark was the American embassy's veteran human rights officer, and I was to come to value his expertise on all matters Chinese.[21] I probably should have listened to him that night.

The little one was pitiful and adorable at the same time—a dangerous combination for the father of three daughters. I slowed my pace and reached into my pocket for some Chinese currency. Unfortunately, I had not mastered the exchange rate. The smallest coin I had was ten yuan, about a dollar I learned later, and I gave it to the little girl. Immediately an older woman appeared out of nowhere. She was the grandmother version of the little girl. Poorly dressed, she was wizened and stooped. But she was also agile. Speaking in urgent, thoroughly pitiable Chinese tones, she ran beside the little girl, exhorting her to greater effort and me to cough up more yuan. Clearly the transaction had not ended, as I had hoped.

"Tom, leave it at that and move faster. Let's get back to the hotel." The wisdom of Mark's counsel was becoming more and more apparent. Other children were emerging from the shadows and along with them other grandmothers. Reaching into my pocket one last time, I pulled out what I thought was my last ten Ruan and thrust it at one of the children. In fact it was 100 yuan, the equivalent of $12 and probably several days' income for a Chinese peasant. This occasioned a near riot. The crowd had grown to a dozen or more children and their grandmothers. "ARE YOU CRAZY? GET MOVING!" Mark's advice was now irresistible. We sprinted the last several hundred yards to our hotel, chased by a gaggle of children and old women, where we gathered breathlessly like escapees from the Boxer Rebellion.

What we had encountered, I then learned, was a tiny proportion of the thousands of beggars in Beijing. Many of them were there for short periods from surrounding villages and towns. Others had migrated from other parts of China. Some of the children had parents, others were orphans. The older women may have been grandmothers of the children, or not. Their job was to oversee the children and their pitiful take. There are millions of these internal exiles in China's cities, and the government does not know what to do with them. Periodically they are rounded up and sent back to their villages.

It is, of course, precisely this problem that China's "one-child" policy is designed to mitigate. There are many in the West, including in the United States, who are sympathetic to the goals of that policy. Although they do not endorse forced abortion, they consider it madness for the Catholic Church or any other organization to argue against easy access to abortion as means of reducing China's excess population. This dispute would later emerge when the Bush administration decided to withhold funding for the United Nations Development Agency, which the administration charged was encouraging forced abortions in China.

American reactions to the funding ban highlighted two competing concepts of human rights. The Bush administration's decision outraged those who believe population growth fuels human rights abuses and who see voluntary abortion as a means of abating the problem. Their view presumes a government's right, or, in the case of countries with huge populations, such as China, a responsibility to control population growth. A necessary component of managing this problem includes a right to choose abortion, protected by enabling laws.

Those who see even voluntary abortion as unacceptable hailed the Bush decision. Their view presumes a government's responsibility to protect innocent human life at all stages, and the right of religious communities (in this case the Catholic Church in China) publicly to proclaim its teachings, whether they are based on theology (abortion constitutes a radical turning away from God) or public philosophy (abortion is a human rights abuse that coarsens society and encourages other abuses).

China and Religion: A Brief Tour

Chinese history is replete with religions. Most are either indigenous (Taoism, Confucianism, ancestor worship) or imported many centuries ago (Buddhism) and are heavily ethical and philosophical in emphasis. These ancient religions tend to be supportive of the institutions of family and central authority that are, to this day, seen as the fundamental components of Chinese society.[22] None has yielded the kinds of nongovernmental voluntary institutions prevalent in contemporary Christian societies, and that are seen, albeit to a lesser extent, in Tibetan Buddhism and Uighur Islam. The characteristics of traditional Chinese religions have contributed to the fact that, in modern times, Chinese culture has been resistant to the development of a dynamic civil society—those associations of citizens that act as intermediary institutions between the government on the one hand and the individual and family on the other.

Moreover, Tibetan Buddhism, Christianity, and Islam are all viewed, to one degree or another, as alien to Chinese culture and potentially subversive of the authoritarian management policy now under way. Two—Christianity and Islam—are doctrinally separable from traditional Chinese religions by their emphasis on the one God and their acceptance of a unity of truth, characteristics that induce spiritual and moral action (such as proselytizing) often seen as threatening to Chinese culture and politics.

Tibetan Buddhism is seen as alien primarily because it is at the core of an ethnic culture that defines itself as distinctive and separate from China. Buddhists of the majority Han ethnic group number approximately 100 million, but they are spread throughout the country and have few difficulties with Chinese authorities.[23] Tibetan Buddhists number only about five million. Most inhabit Tibet, a province located in China's southwest and labeled misleadingly by the Chinese as an "autonomous" region. A considerable minority of Tibetan Buddhists remain outside the Tibetan autonomous region, mostly in the western parts of Sichuan, Yunnan, Gansu, and Qinghai provinces.

The Sino-Tibet problem is centered in the person most Tibetans see as their spiritual and political leader, the fourteenth Dalai Lama. For almost half a century the Dalai Lama has refused to accept China's brutal authority over Tibet and has sought to raise international awareness of the terrible injustice represented in Chinese rule. The relationship between China and Tibet had been a source of contention for centuries. During the 20th century, Chinese nationalist governments had sporadically asserted Chinese suzerainty, but in 1950 the new communist government invaded, establishing a direct regime of terror that continues to this day. In 1959 the Dalai Lama fled his country and established a government in exile.[24]

During the Cultural Revolution thousands of Tibetan monasteries were destroyed, and thousands of monks and nuns were imprisoned, tortured, and executed. In the decades since the end of the Cultural Revolution Beijing has experimented with various means of control, as it has with other religious groups, including an extended crackdown beginning in 1994. It has rebuilt some of the destroyed monasteries, but it also has initiated a transfer of populations, intensified reeducation and indoctrination campaigns against monks and nuns, and built discos, gambling houses, and brothels in an attempt to erode the traditional moral and spiritual pillars of Tibetan Buddhism. Its one-child policy has been applied with particular cruelty, including forced abortions and late-term abortions.[25]

The status of the Dalai Lama lends a more pointedly political element to Tibetan Buddhism than other religions in China (although Roman Catholics have a somewhat analogous problem). No solution to the issue of Tibet is conceivable without an agreement between China and the Dalai Lama. Although there are many factors involved in brokering such an agreement, the opportunities afforded by China's overall struggle to address the role of religion in its social and political transformation can and should be exploited. If China can learn to accommodate religions and religious actors as net contributors to Chinese society and economic development, it can move closer to an appreciation of Tibetan Buddhism as the energizing force of Tibetan culture and a source of strength and stability for its southwestern Tibetan province. Until that happens, however, the United States must press even harder on the Chinese government, publicly and privately, to cease the despoliation of Tibet and the religion that forms its culture.

Islam in China has shared some of the difficulties experienced by both Tibetan Buddhism and Christianity. The first Muslims arrived on the borders of China during the 8th century, defeating Chinese armies in Central Asia. Unlike their brethren in Arab lands, Persia, the Asian subcontinent, and much of central Asia, however, Muslims did not succeed in conquering and converting China. Rather, pockets of Chinese over the centuries gradually converted to Islam.

Today there are some nine million Hui Chinese Muslims, who are ethnically similar to the majority Han Chinese group. Hui Muslims live throughout the country and in general have little difficulty with the Chinese government, although they are quite aware of and attendant to government sensitivities about religion. The Hui tend to benefit from the geopolitical comparison with Christianity prevalent in Chinese schools, where students learn that the Christian West is an imperialist aggressor and Muslims, including those in China, are victims. Many Hui Muslims are subsidized by the government in fulfilling their religious duty of Hajj, the pilgrimage to Mecca that every Muslim is enjoined to make at least once in life if circumstances and resources permit.[26]

The one exception to this pattern of assimilation has been the Turkic Muslims who settled in the outlying regions of central Asia. In the 17th century, the Qing Dynasty (1644–1911) brought into China's borders what is today Xinjiang province in the northwest. Today Xinjiang borders the post-Soviet republics of Tajikistan, Turkmenistan, and Kazakstan, and the world's first Islamic nation, Pakistan. The nine million Turkic Muslims of Xinjiang province are ethnically distinct from the Hui and are called Uighurs. Many of them practice the Sufi variety of Islam. Their difficulties with the Chinese government stem in part from their status as an ethnic minority with a history of separatist movements supported by Russia during the 19th century. Today, however, the crucial problem is the fact that a tiny minority of Uighur Muslims have become Islamist extremists operating in China and internationally. A few are known to have been among those captured by the United States and held at Guantanamo Bay.[27]

As a result, Chinese officials in the region have had a legitimate security concern with some Uighurs. But like their counterparts in Central Asia, such as the government of Uzbekistan, they have used this concern as a pretext to persecute Muslims who are not extremists and have nothing to do with terror.[28] Many in the West have charged that U.S. human rights and religious freedom advocacy for Uighur Muslims has been compromised by America's own war on terror, which (or so the argument goes) has led Washington to pull its punches regarding Chinese treatment of the Uighurs. I am not convinced that this is the true source of the U.S. failure to have an impact on China's Uighur Muslim policy, but I agree that it has been a failure. That policy will require a recalibration and renewed consistency as part of a redirected and reenergized American policy in China.

The story of Christianity in China, better known in the West than Tibetan Buddhism and Islam, has been addressed elsewhere in this book and will be treated only briefly here. Christianity first appeared in China in the 7th century and had mixed fortunes in succeeding centuries. By the 16th century, Catholicism had been in precipitous decline for some time, until the arrival of the Jesuits—beginning with Matteo Ricci, whose impact on China is being felt to this day. Arriving in the Portuguese-controlled island of Macau off the south China coast in 1582, Ricci slowly worked his way onto the mainland and toward Beijing to the north, impressing his Chinese hosts with his mastery of their language and customs and his remarkable scientific and technological expertise. He finally reached the capital in 1601, where he lived for nine years until his death.[29] Three hundred years' later, the anniversary of his arrival in Beijing was commemorated in Rome by an international conference of China scholars and religious leaders. It was at this Ricci conference that Pope John Paul II issued an apology for the errors of Catholics in Chinese history in hopes of reestablishing a dialogue with the Chinese government.

One of the principle effects of Ricci's efforts was the rooting of Roman Catholicism in China, where it has survived despite considerable obstacles. Christianity was banned outright by the Qing dynasty in 1724, but by the dawn of the 19th century there were still some 200,000 Chinese Catholics. Their ranks, along with those of newly arrived Protestants, would increase during the 19th century as a result of the concessions forced upon China by Western nations. But it was well into the 20th century before Rome began a sustained effort to replace its European bishops with Chinese prelates. By 1949, when the victorious Communists established the People's Republic of China, there were some three million Chinese Catholics.

The 19th century was a fundamental turning point for religion in China, especially Christianity. Until the intrusion of the great powers, signaled by the Opium War with Britain (1839–1842), China had sustained a tradition of state dominance over religion that had lasted more than a thousand years. Historian Daniel H. Bays has observed that the intervention of the Western powers initiated a period in Chinese history that has proven to be an anomaly in the long tradition of state control of religion, a period during which the state was too weak to extend its bureaucratic tentacles into the religious life of the country. It was during these years that Christianity, especially Protestant Christianity, sunk its roots.[30] The hiatus in statist policy ended with the victory of the Communists in 1949, and their policies have reestablished the tradition of state control. This interpretation is plausible and helps locate the stubbornness of Chinese resistance to religious freedom in traditional Chinese culture and political behavior. It suggests that the obstacles to religious freedom in China are more than mere communist atheism.

It is also important to understand, however, that the period of Western intervention begun in the 19th century had a dual and contradictory effect on Chinese history. On the one hand, the Western powers required the Chinese government to tolerate Christianity, and the result was vigorous activity by Protestant and Catholic missionaries throughout the country. More important for the future success of Chinese Protestantism, the dominance of a foreign hierarchy did not hamstring the spread of Protestant Christianity as it did Roman Catholicism. By their nature more egalitarian in ecclesiology, Protestant denominations with Chinese pastors spread rapidly and easily.

On the other hand, both Protestantism and Catholicism became associated with Western imperialism during the 19th and early 20th centuries, a connection that to this day is emphasized by the Chinese government. Their complaints have some basis in fact, although they are routinely exaggerated, sometimes hypocritically so. I am reminded of the story of the Chinese official complaining in a speech to a party plenum about the illegitimacy of foreign influences in China, while behind him loom huge photos of Marx and Lenin (a German and a Russian, respectively).

Civil Society, Bishops, and Betrayal

As my colleagues and I prepared to explore Tiananmen Square and the Forbidden City in Beijing, I had occasion to recall an earlier visit there during the summer of 1998 by President and Mrs. Clinton. The president had showcased his desire to influence economic development and civil society in China, both worthy goals that should be integrated into U.S. religious freedom policy (and vice versa). Unfortunately the presidential trip also provided a glimpse into the weaknesses of official America's understanding of religion in China.

The Forbidden City is one of the most popular destinations for foreigners in China. Among other things it is a natural place for the government to demonstrate the majestic ties between the nation's history, its present, and its future. The entrance is located literally across the street from Tiananmen Square, the site of Mao Zedong's mausoleum and of the 1989 massacre. A visitor approaching the Forbidden City cannot help seeing a huge portrait of Mao above the entrance, as if to serve warning not to be swept away by the upcoming scenes of China's imperial past. Nothing in China, Mao seems to say, should be romanticized. All is instrumental to the purposes of the state.

We paid a visit to Tiananmen Square, noting the lines waiting to see the chemically preserved body of Mao in the mausoleum. We then entered the Forbidden City and were immediately impressed by the meticulous work which had protected the ancient palaces and residences of China's pre-Communist history from the depredations of time, as well as the raids of the Cultural Revolution's Red Guard. We were shown the location of the palace and grounds where the government had permitted the filming of *The Last Emperor*, a Hollywood production that flattered neither the emperor nor the communists and provided another indication (no doubt to the distress of Mao) of the emerging priority of economics over ideology in China's communist system.

Another example of economic globalization was the Starbucks coffee shop smack in the middle of the ancient pagodas. It was here that we heard the story, told with bemusement and a touch of exasperation by one of our foreign-service colleagues, of the Clintons' trip to the Forbidden City. All American presidential trips abroad are, as a rule, elaborately planned affairs, each preceded by many weeks of planning. Typically, the American embassy or consulate in the target area is besieged in the two weeks leading up to the president's arrival by White House advance teams, each of whose members feels empowered to make life miserable for the foreign service officers (FSOs) who will carry out various supporting tasks when the president arrives. I had experienced this unpleasant precursor ritual as an FSO in Bonn several years before during one of President Clinton's trips to Germany.

Ironically, even in the pre-9/11 world, security was a greater problem for presidents in Western Europe than it was in places such as China, where the prospects of violence were seen to be less severe. But there were other problems in China. When President and Mrs. Clinton visited the Forbidden City, there was the delicate question of restrooms. The Forbidden City is huge, comprising many acres, and a complete visit requires time. There were, of course, public restrooms available, but they were not, to put it tactfully, considered appropriate for presidential use. The president (known as POTUS, or President of the United States) and the First Lady (FLOTUS) were thus accompanied by their own dedicated portable facilities, dubbed the POTUS potty and the FLOTUS potty, respectively, by the FSOs given the honor of accompanying them.

This trip was designed, inter alia, to parry criticisms in the United States of President Clinton's proposal to bestow on China the status of normal trade relations, a step that would facilitate an increase in the commercial relationship between our two countries. It was also designed to highlight and encourage the development of China's nascent civil society of nongovernmental associations. It was the latter goal that led to the president's encounter with the Catholic bishop of Shanghai, Aloysius Jin Luxian, and inadvertently illustrated the prevailing confusion within U.S. policy circles over the state of Catholicism in China. The venue was a public discussion in Shanghai with a variety of Chinese citizens representing civil society. The subject was "shaping China for the 21st century," and the roundtable included a university president, a novelist, a consumer advocate, a professor, and others. And then there was Bishop Jin.

To observers of religious freedom in China, Jin is one of the most controversial and fascinating figures in the country. Eighty years old at the time of Clinton's visit, young Jin had been ordained as a priest in 1945. He had become a close associate of Shanghai's bishop in the early 1950s, Ignatius Kung Pin-Mei. Kung had thought highly of Jin, and had appointed him rector of the Shanghai seminary after the communist takeover. It was at this seminary that Kung is said to have warned Catholics of the terrible persecution to come, and exhorted them to stand fast in resistance to Communism. Both Kung and Jin were arrested in 1955 and thrown into prison. Both had been tortured, sent to labor camps, and offered freedom if they would abjure their allegiance to the Roman Catholic Church and support the Communist government.[31]

Some Catholics, including some in the United States, believe that Jin, unlike Kung, had broken under the abuse and had betrayed the Church in order to win better treatment in prison and approval by the Chinese government after his release.[32] Whether these accusations are true or not, Jin served over two decades in prison. In 1985, he was ordained bishop under the supervision of the Chinese government without the agreement of the Vatican. Kung was released that year and put under house arrest for another two years, after which he was permitted to emigrate to the United States. Here he learned that, in 1979, Pope John Paul II had named him a cardinal *in pectore* (in secret), and in 1991 Kung traveled to Rome to receive the red hat. For 30 years, Kung had been denied the right to say mass, to read religious books, to receive mail, or to have visitors. According to one report, the man who was assigned to guard Kung after his release from prison and during his house arrest in Shanghai was its new official bishop—Aloysius Jin.[33]

It was therefore something of a risk for the Clinton White House to invite Bishop Jin to the roundtable of civil society leaders. Back in Washington, the debate over China's human rights record was in full swing, as was the administration's attempt to defeat or drastically change the Nickles-Lieberman International Religious Freedom Act. The American embassy had probably recommended Jin as the "religion" participant in the discussion. He was a good contact for the U.S. consulate general in Shanghai. As I learned in a later meeting with him, he spoke excellent English and came across as a modest and pious man. Unlike his official church counterpart in Beijing, Bishop Michael Fu Tieshan, Jin was known to have been in communication with the Vatican and to have avoided public criticisms of the Roman Catholic Church of the kind that Fu often levied. As for the American critics of Jin's alleged betrayal of the Church and of Cardinal Kung (then living in Connecticut and approaching his 100th birthday), the White House was either ignorant of or discounted their political significance.

When it came time for Jin to speak, Mrs. Clinton introduced him. The bishop of Shanghai, she told the audience, "had been on the front lines of religious freedom in China." Jin proceeded to paint a bright picture of Catholicism in Shanghai, at one point making the interesting assertion that he had sent about 40 of his seminary students to Princeton to study canon law. He then provided an object lesson in how he had survived (some would say flourished) for almost 15 years as one of China's most visible bishops. Religious beliefs, he told POTUS, FLOTUS, and the assembled audience, are not restricted in China:

> People are often asked...if the Chinese Catholic Church was cooperating with the Communist Party. And the answer is simple: Why should the church believers here do something against our government, which is a government of ours?...And about the underground religion...my understanding is that, well, those people who were going what we call underground or having covert religious activities because of the fear of...some negative effects on them—I don't quite understand why those people should do this kind of thing.[34]

When Jin was finished, President Clinton thanked the bishop and moved on to the next subject. Clinton's purpose was not to debate the roundtable participants, and, even if he were aware of the tragic irony in the bishop's remarks, it would have made no sense to point them out in that venue. But the episode revealed the U.S. government's tin ear when it comes to religion in China. It was not simply that Jin's comments represented a willful dismissal of recent Chinese history, offensive to all who had experienced or knew of the suffering endured by underground Catholics in the past and in the present. Jin's very presence as a representative of "China in the 21st century" demonstrated that short-term public relations supersede substance in U.S. policy calculations, especially when it comes to religion. This myopia did not leave office with the Clintons.

Changing U.S. Religion Policy in China

Two new dimensions are called for in American religious freedom policy toward China. The first is a recalibration of the task ahead. Although it can (and indeed must) continue to target particular cases of injustice against religious people, as it does against injustice to political dissidents and other human rights abuses, the United States must also develop a medium and long-term strategy of fundamentally altering China's perception of religion. The doors to influencing China's official understanding of religion are several. They include its economy, the law, Chinese patriotism, and the nation's growing platoons of academic experts, whose job is to gather the information and provide the analysis needed to usher China to the next level of modernization.

The second dimension of U.S. religious freedom policy in China, as elsewhere, must be consistency and institutionalization. Under the IRF Act the United States has denounced China each year since 1999 as a particularly severe violator of religious freedom. We have traditionally tried to talk to the Chinese about religious persecution and other human rights abuses in annual human rights dialogues, but these too often devolve into humanitarian pleading, at the end of which the Chinese release a few prisoners. To be fair, American human rights officials do wrestle with how to build bridges in these talks, so that they might have some cumulative effect on Chinese law and culture—in other words on the long-term structures of persecution. But my experience is that the talks just don't work that way. The Chinese, like most other countries with which we have human rights dialogues, see them as an America-management task, rather than an integral part of U.S.-China relations and the vital interests that the two countries share.

Those interests center on trade, nuclear proliferation, and the stability of East Asia, especially North Korea. Underlying all of these issues is a shared interest in avoiding a catastrophic economic, social, or political meltdown within China, as it tries to manage the internal dissent that inevitably attends enormous economic growth. As noted, part of that internal volcano is the explosion of religious communities, which the Chinese Communist government does not understand and, ironically, fears far more than the effects of capitalism. It is a fundamental reason that China remains a severe violator of religious freedom. If the United States were going to integrate its religious freedom policy into its larger strategy for China, it would worry less about prisoner releases and more about Chinese religious communities, their relationships to Chinese laws designed to control them, and the elements of the Chinese government that design and implement China's religion policy.

How would a new religious realism be manifested in IRF policy? Among other things, it would mean transforming the case we make. Currently we threaten sanctions if persecution continues and offer better relations if it doesn't. This has not worked and is unlikely to do so over the long term. A broader policy would not abandon sticks and carrots but would nest them in a different logic, which goes something like this: religion and religious communities are natural and inevitable. Persecution induces social instability, even extremism, and harms the economy. Accommodate and nourish religious groups and they will benefit your economies and increase internal stability. This logic has been used by some U.S. officials, including, to a degree, both IRF ambassadors. But it must be used by all U.S. officials and it must be institutionalized in U.S. funded programs and in permanent U.S.-China bilateral organizations.

The goal of U.S. IRF policy in China should be to communicate a consistent, clear message that can overcome cultural and ideological resistance: it is in China's national interests not simply to end persecution, but also to favor the religious life. To be orderly and productive, it must be nurtured, not controlled and suppressed. Freed to pursue their beliefs, facilitated by Chinese laws and policies, Chinese religious communities will contribute to the economic, social, and political strengthening of China. This is as true of Tibetan Buddhists and Uighur Muslims as it is Chinese Christians.

We have been passing such messages willy-nilly to the Chinese for years, but we have done it inconsistently and have undermined the appeal to China's national interests with mixed signals and an emphasis on prisoner releases. Some religious freedom activists argue that we have complained about persecution without ever taking punitive action, such as economic sanctions. This criticism is correct to a point. Like other governments, the Chinese exploit our inconsistencies, including when we cry "wolf." But neither threats of sanctions nor sanctions themselves can alone solve the long-term problem of persecution, let alone religious freedom.

The Seminarian Rebellion and the Great Buddhist Sidewalk Debate

After leaving Beijing we traveled to Shanghai, where we were not surprised to hear confirmation that Bishop Jin had refused the consulate's request for an appointment with me. In the following year, I would have a fruitful meeting with the bishop and come to appreciate firsthand his charm and personal persuasiveness.[35] For the moment, however, Paul and I—along with our experienced consulate escort, Foreign Service Officer Peter Roe—set out to do what FSOs the world over love to do. We went to Jin's offices at the Sheshan seminary without an invitation, hoping to talk to whomever would see us. Good FSOs are detectives by nature. Although they don't particularly relish wading into foolish or dangerous situations, they consider it part of their profession to talk to people, ask questions, challenge the premises of interlocutors, and figure things out. Many of them become experts by steeping themselves in the language and culture where they serve; a few delve into religion and the religious actors that drive culture. Fortunately, several of the American FSOs in China were in the latter category.

Our visit to Sheshan provided a wealth of information, some moving scenes, and even some humor. Bishop Jin was not there, so we simply asked questions and, as luck would have it, got some answers. Among other things, we learned details of an important incident that had occurred in Beijing the previous year. Just as predictions of a Sino-Vatican agreement were reaching fever pitch, Beijing's Bishop Fu had arranged in January 2000 the ordination of six new bishops without Vatican approval, thus leading to a year of recriminations and a distinct downturn in the possibilities for an agreement. Ordained in the 1950s, Fu was made Bishop of Beijing in 1979 and was considered by the government the senior Chinese Catholic prelate. Fu's death in April 2007 was to raise expectations for the possibility of a thaw in Sino-Vatican relations.

The deterioration in those relations seemed to reach a nadir in late 2000 when the Vatican canonized dozens of Chinese Catholic martyrs, many of them killed during the 1900 Boxer Rebellion. The Boxers were treated as anti-imperialist heroes in Chinese schools. Worse, October 1, the date of the canonization, was also the anniversary date of the Communist takeover in 1949. Bishop Fu publicly condemned the martyrs as "criminals," a statement not calculated to endear him to the Vatican or to bring the two sides closer together. To Catholics, canonized martyrs are saints, not criminals.

The Vatican had learned of Fu's plans to ordain six new bishops without the pope's agreement just a few days prior to the event. The ordination of Catholic bishops has periodically been a source of controversy over the centuries. Although accommodations were sometimes made with European monarchs, canon law requires the prior approval of the pope in order for a bishop to be considered "licit" in the eyes of the Church. Should he willfully reject papal authority, a bishop is in schism with the Church, and may excommunicate himself *latae sententiae,* or automatically, by virtue of the act. Some suggest that both Bishops Fu and Jin have incurred such a penalty, although the Vatican has never publicly declared that status for either. What it has made clear is that the sacramental acts of even an illicitly ordained bishop are valid, provided that his ordination was carried out in the proper manner (apart from the issue of papal approval). This is why priests ordained by schismatic bishops are considered real priests and can administer the sacraments.

Laying aside such fine points of canon law and theology, few sane men would have any desire to enter the Roman Catholic priesthood, or become a bishop, in defiance of the pope. Given the clear meaning and reach of Catholic doctrine, both are acts that on their face would be self-defeating. Only in a system such as that of China, where control of all religions is standard policy and where Pope John Paul II in particular was feared because of the solvent effects of his actions on Eastern European Communism, could such ecclesiastical distortions appear routine.

In Shanghai we were told that Vatican officials learned of Bishop Fu's plans to ordain bishops illicitly a few days in advance of the January 2000 ceremony. The Vatican immediately communicated the pope's disapproval (via e-mail, telephone, and fax) to the prospective bishops and to the seminarians of the official Catholic seminary in Beijing who were to attend and assist. As a consequence, some of the former pulled out and a majority of the latter, about 100 seminarians, simply refused to attend the ceremony. For their trouble, many of these young men were expelled from the Beijing seminary. At Sheshan, the official church seminary in Shanghai, there was widespread support for this minor rebellion among their counterparts to the north. There was also a clear recognition that many of their lives had likely been ruined as a result.

While at Sheshan we also experienced another of the odd but routine distortions produced by a system that is trying to manage religion while also exposing children in China's atheist school system to some of religion's accoutrements. We followed a steep path to the magnificent Basilica Minor of St. Mary. Built over ten years between 1925 and 1935, the beautiful old building combines Romanesque and Gothic styles, and its spire is surmounted by a 3.87 meter bronze statue of the Blessed Mother of Sheshan, the Virgin Mary. We were told that apparitions of the Blessed Mother had been reported there in recent years, but no one dared to make them public. During the Cultural Revolution the statue of Mary had been destroyed, as were parts of the basilica itself, but like so many religious buildings in China it was restored by the government in the 1980s. The statue was not replaced until 2000.

When we entered the main church, we were surprised to see a group of several hundred young Chinese public school students. There are officially no other kinds of young students in China. Religious schools of any kind are forbidden, and the constitution does not guarantee freedom of religion for anyone under the age of 18. As a result, many local authorities ban any kind of religious instruction for children. These kids, the vast majority very likely the children of atheist parents, were sitting in the pews patiently but wearily listening to a droning recorded lecture on the architecture of the building. In front of them was a photographic display of various events in the church. Surprisingly, there was also a photo of none other than Pope John Paul II. The lecture did not, it is safe to say, provide much information about the pope or Catholicism, much less the significance of Mary in the Church. But the pictures themselves made it clear to the children that they were in a place where people worshipped.

I told my family about the scene in an e-mail that night. "They each had their little red bandannas around their necks, trying to endure this [lecture] with 8–9-year-old dignity, when you-know-who appeared (my colleagues and me, not the Blessed Mother) much to the amusement of the children. When they escaped from the lecture, they crowded around us and asked pertinent questions learned from their English classes, such as 'How old are you?' (A: 'Very old.'), and 'Do you have any money?' (A: 'No.') They were not begging, mind you, but were extremely curious."

Concerning religion, some might have been intrigued by the marble altar or the stained glass windows. But most, influenced by atheist parents, atheist teachers, and droning taped lectures, probably concluded that the subject was both boring and irrelevant. The message intended by Chinese school authorities, however, was probably more functional. Religion, they seemed to say to the children, is something that a few people do in China, some in large buildings like this one. They are nothing to fear, because we know what they do and have them under control. That message is, of course, a dangerous one if your object is control. The whole scene was emblematic of the thin line China is attempting to walk when it comes to religion.

While in Shanghai, we also visited two mosques and a Buddhist temple, both securely under the control of the government. In general, Muslims and Buddhists have few problems in the main parts of China (outside Tibet and the Uighur Muslim province of Xinjiang). But they know how to accept government instructions when necessary. At one of the mosques, we had an appointment with the chief imam. We visited twice, and each time we were told to wait, but he did not appear. Quoting from my e-mail home: "After cooling our heels for some time, and returning later to get the same story, we figured out he was not going to show. (I'm not stupid, just slow.) Later we learned that he was probably there the whole time—having received instructions from above (and I don't mean Allah) not to see me."

The Buddhist temple provided a more invigorating experience and yielded a revealing message about Chinese citizens. When we approached the temple, in this case completely unannounced, a Buddhist man was leaving the area and saw us. He immediately walked over in a friendly, open manner and began to chat. There on the sidewalk next to the temple, we discussed the issues of religion and religious freedom in China, and America's China policy. Before long, locals gathered around and, as the "great Buddhist sidewalk debate" (as we later dubbed it) continued, chairs were provided.

We talked for almost an hour, and the Buddhist gentleman proved to be a worthy supporter of his government's policy. The local audience was polite, but smiled broadly when the man asserted that America did not understand China. I took away from this "debate" a feeling of powerful, unalloyed Chinese patriotism. It was not triggered by any aggressiveness on my part; I took great care to praise China for its accomplishments and to emphasize my respect for Buddhism. But I was nevertheless a foreigner and an American defending an American policy. With friendliness, but utter confidence, they rejected my concerns about their country's deficiencies in religious freedom.

Our final visit in Shanghai was in some ways the most interesting. I had already met in Washington the American rabbi of Shanghai's only synagogue, David Greenberg, and we had become friends. Greenberg is a Lubavitcher— an orthodox grouping within Judaism which is the most active organization dedicated to serving the Jewish diaspora in difficult areas around the world. In Washington I often met with Rabbi Levi Shemtov, director of the American Friends of Lubavitch, who brought to our offices Lubavitchers serving their religion in countries such as Russia, Uzbekistan, and Turkmenistan.

Rabbi Greenberg told me the story of the Shanghai Jews, who had fled Germany prior to World War Two and had ended up in this city where they were permitted to build a synagogue. The Chinese Communist government has never recognized Judaism as a religion and does not permit the Shanghai synagogue to be used regularly for religious services. As a consequence, Greenberg works carefully to provide services for Shanghai Jews and to convince the Chinese that his community is an asset that should be welcomed in all its dimensions, especially its religious beliefs and practices. In a real sense, this ought to be the content of America's message to China. Shanghai's Jews are a source of social and spiritual capital that could be multiplied exponentially by freeing them and other religious communities to worship and contribute in public ways to China.

Thinking with the Chinese about Religion

If the United States is to break out of the cycle of empty threats (CPC designations), largely unavailing diplomatic dances (annual human rights dialogues), and being relegated to accepting a single, high-profile prisoner release as "progress," it needs to think differently and act differently when it comes to religion in China. Here are some ideas, by no means exhaustive, that could point the way.

The Economy, Civil Society, and Modernization

Economic activity is a major engine of Chinese policies, both domestic and international. China's economic development and modernization, and the small but growing civil society that has accompanied both, have occurred in significant measure because of adjustments in China's Confucian culture. The Culture Matters Research Project describes the changes this way:

> For reasons of national security and prestige, economic activity, which was traditionally the lowest rung on the Confucian prestige ladder, below scholars, soldiers, and farmers, has been promoted to high prestige—witness Chinese Communist leader Deng Xiaoping's exhortation: "To get rich is glorious." The effect has been to liberate those values that Confucianism shares with the Protestant ethic: education, merit, frugality, achievement, the lesser virtues.[36]

If Chinese authorities became interested in the growth of its religious communities as an economic asset and a driver of modernization, rather than a source of social and political instability, they would be far more open to arguments against discrimination and persecution. If they saw, for example, that unregulated Protestant house churches were factories for "the lesser virtues," that is, the social habits that yield economic productivity, they might reassess the role of the Three Self Movement as a means of controlling, or when necessary repressing, Protestant movements. The religion-economy connection could work to the advantage of other religious groups as well.

Consider the issue of religious education for young people. To date the arguments put forth by American human rights officials have been mainly humanitarian and rights based, that is, it is unjust, and a violation of the rights of children and their parents, to prevent religious education. As we have seen, these arguments and complaints about specific cases of abuse have yielded largely empty pledges by Chinese officials that there are no official barriers to childhood religious education in China. In fact, the severity of this problem varies from province to province and religion to religion. For example, outside Tibet, most Buddhist monks have little difficulty entering monasteries at very early ages, the norm for that religion. Inside Tibet, however, the entire system of Buddhist monasteries is under constant scrutiny, and China's goal is to undermine Buddhism's capacity to shape Tibetan culture.[37]

Religious education is not for the most part a problem for Hui Muslims around the country, but within Xingjiang province Uighur parents are often prevented from sending their young people to religious schools.[38] Within the varieties of Christian communities around China, Catholics and Protestants are subject to the whims of local authorities, largely because both local governments and the central government see religious education as a threat to the official atheist ideology. Officials from the State Administration of Religious Affairs (SARA) will occasionally respond to complaints by American or other foreign human rights officials about specific cases of abuse. But the Chinese do not see it in their interests to worry much about the biases currently in place against the religious education of Chinese youth.

One way to approach this problem is to facilitate a change in the calculus of self-interest and to tap into the Chinese Confucian evaluation of education as the highest rung on the prestige ladder. If the Chinese became interested in religious education as a way to reinforce the attitudes and virtues that yield economically productive behavior, they might look differently at their policies. The issue here is not which religions are more amenable to economic development than others. The idea is to get the Chinese to think seriously about the relationships between religion and sustaining economic growth. Such thinking would implicate much more than youth education; it would also raise questions about the treatment of "unofficial" or underground religious communities, the building of houses of worship, the training of clergy, and the involvement of religious people in government. Although this change in focus might prove more advantageous to Protestant groups in China, the economic logic of loosening restrictions on religious activity would be very likely to spill over to other religious groups as well.

To repeat: the premise of China's policy toward religion is that it is destabilizing and a threat to the socialist state. Part of this fear is ideological and derives from the Marxist-Leninist understanding of history and human nature. As China moves away from that understanding, U.S. policy makers should be attentive to opportunities for suggesting that religion is an inevitable part of society and can be married to the common good. Security concerns can be addressed by empirical studies showing that repression of religion tends to trigger radicalism and aggression, not contain it.[39]

The huge and growing need in China for social and spiritual services provides another opportunity for making the case that religion is good for China. As we have noted, the problems are enormous: infectious diseases from leprosy to AIDS, increasing numbers of old people without resources, continuing abject poverty for tens of millions of people, environmental degradation, massive migrations into cities and accompanying homelessness, the breakdown of the family, moral degeneracy, and more. Religious communities around the world are uniquely positioned to deal with such problems and to deliver the services that government cannot. China is no different. U.S. diplomats "raise these points" with the Chinese from time to time, but a sustained initiative would be very likely to prove more availing. For example, the United States could deploy its development grants to organizations, religious and secular, who work with local religious groups to provide social services.

The path from here to there is a long one. The obstacles to changing Chinese thinking about religion are significant, although it is always possible that a single authoritarian exhortation, such as Deng's "To get rich is glorious," can change official Chinese policy rather quickly. Moreover, as Francis Fukuyama has pointed out in his study of social capital, the Chinese state can play an enormous role in creating that capital itself.[40] Indeed, China's path to modernization for the most part "has relied on ideological and institutional innovations" from above.[41] If Chinese authorities conclude that freeing religion, or significantly loosening its ideological and institutional controls, can benefit Chinese modernization, a great deal might be accomplished. Still, the very engine of democratization is the development of civil society, voluntary and private organizations that limit the reach and the corruptibility of government. U.S. policy in China must balance its efforts on both government and civil society.

The United States should begin to integrate the religion-economy-civil society nexus into the full range of its discussions with China, including private diplomacy, public diplomacy, and foreign aid. In particular, it should realign spending through U.S. funded democracy and development programs administered through the National Endowment for Democracy, USAID, the State Department's Human Rights and Democracy Fund, and others. The executive and legislative branches should require a focus within all U.S. grant programs on religion and economic development, religion and civil society, and religious education. It might also apply some judicious diplomacy in convincing other nations to support this effort, especially those, such as the United Kingdom and Canada, that have existing human rights dialogues with the Chinese.

The Law

China's self-understanding is grounded in the rule of law, not in the democratic sense, in which law restricts the power of government and protects individual rights, but in the sense of defining and protecting the interests of the nation from the top down, that is, by the actions of the government. Implicit in the Chinese view of law is a view of the common good which is highly collectivist and paternalistic. As economic development continues to create a middle class and a civil society of voluntary associations, this view of law may begin to shift. But for the foreseeable future, religion will be addressed in China through the laws that are intended to regulate, control, and, if necessary, suppress it.

Working within that framework, U.S. foreign policy should systematize what are now ad hoc and inconsistent efforts on the part of various organizations inside China to encourage legal reform. We should encourage these disparate programs, some of which are U.S. funded but many of which are not, toward employing the law for the benefit of religious groups. For example, legal programs should target local and provincial officials who, in the course of crackdowns on religious groups, abuse laws and regulations now on the books. U.S. grants should encourage NGOs to train and support cadres of Chinese defense attorneys who are experts in existing legal codes and who can defend in Chinese courts religious groups suffering discrimination or abuse.

These litigators will need a secure grounding in China's constitution and those international covenants that China has ratified. They will also need to be experts in Chinese religious law and regulations, as well as the increasing use of administrative procedures by local authorities to place religious actors under arrest without trial. These procedures have been used for years against all religious groups in China. Elderly Catholic bishops, for example, some of them well into their 80s and 90s, are routinely rounded up and put into administrative detention. One particularly haunting case is that of Bishop Su Zhimin, who was detained in 1997. Despite repeated pleas by U.S. officials, including myself, he has not been seen and in 2006 was rumored to have died in custody. Su and others like him may not be physically tortured, but their treatment is nonetheless barbaric. It is intended to be a warning for others, a version of the old Chinese proverb: "Kill the chickens and warn the monkeys."

The Chinese revised their laws on religion in 2004, and they periodically hold national and provincial conferences to educate local officials about the statutes and the regulations that stem from them. These officials are generally guided by the national and provincial SARA but include security and other personnel. Sometimes they also include representatives of the official religious groups.

For the most part, this exercise is one of sharing information about a national problem and refining control and management techniques. The tone is one of deciding how best to address a thorn in China's side that is unlikely to be eliminated—indeed it cannot be—but also cannot be permitted to grow any worse than it is. In effect, a huge part of China's bureaucracy has as its *raison d'être* the management of the religion problem. That bureaucracy, especially SARA, is heavily invested in ensuring that religion does not get out of control. It is even more heavily invested in ensuring that the problem itself is not solved. In short, if there were no religion problem in China, there would be no need for SARA.

If China begins to move toward political democracy, the United States should be prepared to make cogent arguments for the dramatic scaling down of SARA on the grounds that it is a barrier to the full integration of Chinese religions into civil society. Such arguments are now unlikely to get a sympathetic hearing, but they should be made in a preliminary sense. For example, the U.S. embassy in Beijing, and consulates throughout the country, should increase their awareness of SARA activities, particularly in cases in which SARA officials are engaging in illegal or corrupt behavior. Litigators defending religious groups should be encouraged to focus on this problem as well, building a case that national Chinese authorities can understand.

One additional point bears repeating. The United States should consistently make the argument to officials and to religious actors that China will profit from allowing each of its religious communities to police its own notions of orthodoxy. Local police and security agents often encourage the groups themselves to provide evidence against others, which some groups use to their advantage. This is a dangerous and destructive game for all sides. The solution for China is to encourage each religious tradition to develop inside China the peaceful institutions of orthodoxy, the monasteries, seminaries, colleges, and schools that provide the normal scaffolding for any religion.

The Academy

The Chinese have traditionally venerated learning. When controlled religious activities became permissible after the Cultural Revolution, one result was a powerful policy need to understand better that which must be controlled. Accordingly, as Chinese institutions of higher learning developed during the 1980s and 1990s there was a natural interest in the "scientific" study of religion. Under Jiang Zemin, this interest expanded significantly, in large part because of the personal religious devotion exhibited by presidents Clinton and Bush. Jiang made it clear to the entire Chinese establishment, including its embassies abroad and its institutions of higher learning at home, that he wanted more study and greater understanding. Knowledge is power.

As a result of these imperatives, this officially atheist nation pays more attention to religion in its universities than most other countries of the world (including, ironically, many of the elite institutions in the United States). Chinese scholars travel the world in order to gather materials for detailed analyses of various religious traditions as they are developing in particular countries and regions. For example, Islam is of growing interest to the Chinese, both because of the nation's energy needs in the Middle East and because of concerns about Islamist radicalism coming from the Central Asian countries on its northwest borders. There are opportunities for U.S. policy in this native, and burgeoning, academic and policy interest in religion.

The United States should allocate significant resources to stimulate greater discourse on religion with Chinese academics. This can take many forms, all of which now exist but, as with most things involving U.S policy on religion, operate in an entirely ad hoc fashion. They include university exchange programs of both faculty and students, reciprocal conferences on religious topics, curricula development initiatives, discussion of the value of religious education for the common good, various models for encouraging doctrinal development and the like.

Focus on Nongovernmental Organizations and Work with the Chinese Diaspora

Much of the activities of NGOs would fall under the heading of "track two diplomacy," that is, diplomacy conducted by private associations with a variety of capabilities and interests. Empowering that kind of diplomacy has long been part of U.S. foreign policy.

Veteran China expert Carol Hamrin has provided an innovative and highly useful set of proposals designed to marshal and channel the talents of NGOs into the task of advancing religious freedom in China. Her study emphasizes as well the importance of the Chinese diaspora in directing progressive and pro-religion ideas back into China. These ideas should be incorporated into U.S. policies on China.[42]

Permanent U.S.-China Institutions

The Sino-American discussion of religious persecution and religious freedom is currently proceeding in its occasional "raising the issue" format. U.S. embassy and consulate officials have their regular contacts within official Chinese channels and these are quite valuable—for the most part they are the only channels we operate on a regular basis. Until May 2008 the last human rights dialogue was the one described in chapter 7, held in Beijing in December 2002. The Chinese had refused to reconvene these talks, although there was a senior bilateral dialogue on various issues, including human rights.

Each of these efforts has been of some value, but none has succeeded in institutionalizing communication between the two countries on religion. It is probably not too far off the mark to say that neither country is eager to formalize such communication. This must change. The United States, as part of a broader policy to address religion around the world, should develop a proposal for a permanent bilateral institution that has a chance of withstanding the ups and downs of U.S.-China relations and, at the same time, facilitates true dialogue.

One vehicle to this goal would be similar to the one proposed by IRF Ambassador John Hanford in the summer of 2002: a standing bilateral working group on religion, chaired by very high-level U.S. and Chinese officials. The group would be multilayered and interagency, drawing on government and related private sectors. This would at least create the possibility of continued communication between sectors even when official U.S.-China relations are in the tank, or when the Chinese have been offended by U.S. religious freedom or human rights reports.

The working group might include, for example, officials from national and provincial government and party organizations, security and law enforcement, minority and ethnic affairs, economic development officials and business leaders, academics, democracy advocates, and religious leaders. The overarching goal of the working group would be exchange of information, scholarship, and national experience on the issue of religion and its relationship to good governance. The group could make recommendations to both governments, and under its aegis could sponsor private and public programs to address religion as a matter of law and science.

To China's Jerusalem and Back Home Again

From Shanghai, we traveled to Wenzhou, a center of Protestant house churches on the country's east coast, just across the straits from Taiwan. Wenzhou has become known, somewhat ironically, as "the Chinese Jerusalem." Unlike many areas of China where the presence of Christianity dates back several centuries, Christians came to Wenzhou only in the late 19th century. Even though it is located on the east coast, it is an isolated city, surrounded on three sides by mountains and on the fourth by the sea. Incredibly, neither air nor rail access to the city were established until the 1990s. Until then, travel to Wenzhou involved a trip by boat from Shanghai or other coastal cities.

This geographic isolation has produced an unusual combination of circumstances in Wenzhou, one with implications for U.S. religious freedom policy. The central government has tended to avoid investment or other involvement in the city both because of its forbidding topography and because of its proximity to Taiwan, which increases the likelihood that it would quickly be attacked, and perhaps destroyed, in any China-Taiwan military conflict. But Beijing's hands-off approach triggered a remarkably dynamic group of small businesses that account for much of the city's economy. The products of these firms—electrical appliances, shoes, textiles, and the like—are sold primarily in the city itself, although exports to the rest of China are growing.

Wenzhou's isolation and economic liberty have been handmaidens to another startling development—religious freedom, or at least a degree of freedom unusual to China. Compared to the rest of the country, Christianity (especially Protestantism) and Buddhism have, until very recently, been left to grow. One estimate indicates that the numbers of Christians in the greater Wenzhou population of about seven million people is approaching one million (about 14 percent), many of them members of unofficial Protestant house churches. This kind of freedom has also encouraged emigration, and Wenzhou's Christian merchants have taken their businesses and their religious beliefs to other cities of China and beyond—for example, to Russia and to Europe.[43]

In his book *Jesus in Beijing,* David Aikman reports that in 2003 there were no fewer than 11 Wenzhou Chinese churches in Italy alone. This kind of evangelical mobility, aided no doubt by economic incentives, leads Aikman to speculate that China's growing international power could include a substantial influence on worldwide Christianity.[44] This may well turn out to be the case. It brings to mind the connection, raised by the German sociologist Max Weber, between Protestantism and capitalism. It also raises the intriguing question of whether there is a functional relationship within China between economic liberty and religious freedom. If so, can China's government and society come to see and appreciate that relationship and conclude that religious liberty will help broaden and sustain the economic growth now under way in that country?

Whatever the answers to those questions are in the future, the contemporary answer is a resounding "no." As recently as late 2000 and early 2001, Chinese officials in Wenzhou began a campaign of demolishing Protestant house churches, underground Catholic churches, and even Buddhist temples. The demolitions were apparently spurred by disapproving comments from Communist officials in Beijing, including President Jiang Zemin, concerning the numbers of overtly religious buildings visible in Wenzou. In response, local officials destroyed hundreds of buildings, many of them in residential areas.

It was for this reason that we flew into Wenzhou, again uninvited and without appointments. We wanted to see at least one of those demolished churches.

Our first impression of this city of dynamic small businesses was not a good one. Landing at the airport on a dark, foggy evening, we gathered our luggage and went immediately to a line of cabs, whose drivers were standing at various positions along the line haggling with what appeared to be customers. Given the difficult Wenzhou dialect, we had a separate interpreter with us, and I figured we would have no problem getting a cab. I was wrong. Again, from my e-mail home: "[O]ur two Chinese speakers...haggled without success to get someone to take us, and were about to despair enough to take a bus. Whereupon I, disgusted, simply got in a cab. The others followed and we were fine...until we got under way. The cabbie drove like a madman, talking on his cell phone, wiping the inside of the befogged window shield with a crumpled piece of paper, honking the horn constantly, and dodging the cars, trucks, carts, women, and children who moved across our path as we sped. Needless to say, there were no seat belts."

Remarkably, we made it safely to our hotel. There we plotted the next day's course over a memorable meal that included ginger frog and duck tongue. Although we were unannounced, we were throughout this trip constantly on the lookout for silent Chinese government "escorts." We assumed we were being followed, which was more or less routine for the suspicious Chinese. We were going to attend a Catholic mass at an official church in the morning and would certainly be noticed by the officials there, who would probably notify local officials. But given our mission tomorrow afternoon, which was to travel to a demolished house church in a residential neighborhood, we wanted to take extra care to avoid provoking an incident.

At 5:30 A.M. the next morning we were on the empty streets of Wenzhou looking for the Catholic church. After many false starts quite literally down dark alleys, we finally arrived. The mass was already under way and we slipped into the pews relatively unnoticed. In Catholic masses the world over there is a typical progression of stages in the service, culminating in the liturgy of the Eucharist and, as Catholics believe, the appearance of Christ himself—body, blood, soul, and divinity—in the consecrated host and the chalice. As far as I could tell, this mass was being celebrated according to the *novus ordo,* the new order established at the Second Vatican Council (1962–1965). Contrary to popular wisdom, pre–Vatican II masses were quite legal as well. In a 1992 encyclical, John Paul II had sanctioned them as a means of satisfying the longings of some Catholics for the traditional beauty they associated with the old mass. In China, I surmised that many older Catholics wanted the older mass, but that the official church preferred the new, if for no other reason than its celebration is in Chinese rather than Latin.[45]

As we finished the "liturgy of the word" (scripture readings) and prepared for the homily, I motioned to our interpreter to move next to me so that she could give me a sense of what the priest was saying. She was an American citizen, born and raised in China, and a professional interpreter. As we listened to the homily, I noticed her frown and, in due course, asked her what was happening. "I can't understand a word he is saying," she replied with some distress. "His dialect is just too bizarre." This, I came to learn, is not unusual. Wenzhou's isolation had produced a variation of Chinese that was virtually unintelligible to those who have never been exposed to it.

When the mass was over, we approached the priest and asked if we could chat. After some hesitation, he agreed, and summoned one of the laymen who had been in the service. We adjourned to his nearby residence, where we were joined by two other men. During our conversation, we learned that at least one was from the local Catholic Patriotic Association (CPA), the official "umbrella" organization which owned all Catholic properties and was responsible for ensuring the proper control and management of the official church. We inquired about the status of Wenzhou's underground Catholic bishop, who was rumored to be under house arrest. The CPA official assured us that he was not under arrest but that he was showing signs of Alzheimer's disease and had been moved to a nursing home. This story could have been the gospel truth, but it also could have represented an out-and-out lie. We were powerless to help the old man in any direct sense, but we expressed our government's concern for his welfare.

Leaving the church by mid-morning, we walked through the bustling streets with their rows and rows of small businesses. The city had high-rises, but the skyline was not dominated, as was Shanghai, by commercial buildings, corporate headquarters, and proliferating construction projects. There appeared to be relatively few banks for such a booming economy. In some ways it was like a huge medieval town of artisans and shopkeepers, rather than one of the most prosperous cities in the Far East. After a lunch that was mercifully free of frog and duck tongue, we caught a cab and headed for the residential area where lay the ruins of a recent Protestant house church demolition. We were not particularly concerned that the Chinese knew we were aware of this site. Indeed, we wanted the authorities to know that the United States was concerned enough to monitor the situation. But we did not want to provoke them unnecessarily, so we went as unobtrusively as we could.

When we arrived at the site, I was stunned. There on an empty concrete floor stood piles of bricks, neatly stacked in front of a chaotic dump of wood framing and wall board. This had once been a room, or several rooms, connected to another building that stood in a peaceful domestic neighborhood of small apartments, huts, and houses. A neighbor told our interpreter that the authorities had simply arrived one day with sledgehammers and axes and taken the building apart. She said that the members of the church were now meeting elsewhere. As we surveyed the wreckage, taking photographs as we talked, we noticed on the wall a posted notice, which said that the demolition had taken place because an illegal church had existed there. This notice was to provide important evidence for me in later conversations with Chinese officials.

Within ten minutes of our arrival at the demolished house church, we were treated to a sobering example of Chinese efficiency. Suddenly, men in military uniforms appeared, accompanied by civilians. They did not appear to be armed, but we did not stick around to find out. We calmly, but with all deliberate speed, walked away from the site and back to the main road. They did not follow.

When I returned to the United States, I attended a meeting on China hosted by Prison Fellowship International in Reston, Virginia. There I participated in discussions with clergy from the Shanghai Three Self Movement, the official Chinese Protestant umbrella organization analogous to the Catholic Patriotic Association. When one of them was asked by an American participant about the Wenzhou destructions, he answered that the actions were merely the result of changes in zoning regulations and had nothing to do with religion. Protestantism was, he insisted, flourishing unrestricted in China. I then told the assembled crowd of my visit to Wenzhou, and what we had seen on the posted notice next to the former house church. It was quite clear, I said, that this policy was directed against the Protestants who refused to join the Three Self Movement in Wenzhou.

It was a nice debating point, but I was doubtless telling this man nothing he didn't already know. The plight of house church leaders in China is similar but in some ways worse than that of underground Catholics. Although Chinese officials fear the pope and those in China who insist on professing their loyalty to him, at least the structure and ecclesiology of the Roman Catholic Church is no mystery to them. Protestantism, however, is by its nature diffuse in belief, authority, and structure. All Protestants share a commitment to the authority of scripture, but they manifest their beliefs in unpredictable and, for the Chinese, maddeningly disparate ways. Accordingly, crackdowns on Protestant house churches are sometimes even harsher and more energetic than those on the Catholics.

At the meeting in Reston, I encountered one other disturbing reality that was to form a theme for me in the months and years to come. The Shanghai officials at that meeting knew I had been in China, and they thought that I had come as a member of the U.S. Commission on International Religious Freedom. They were utterly unaware of the difference between that quasi-governmental commission of private U.S. citizens, charged with a watchdog role, and the office of the Department of State charged with carrying out American foreign policy.

Thus was revealed yet again a small example of the broad disarray that attends America's policy of "advancing religious freedom," a disarray that reigns both abroad and at home. It is a problem with many dimensions, as we have seen. And it is a problem that must be attended to, for the sake of the persecuted, for the sake of religious freedom, and for the sake of the American people.

Conclusion

Whither Religious Freedom?

A state will defend or seek to further a vital interest...because it perceives it as bearing directly on its continued existence as an independent entity, its territorial integrity, or the lives of its people.
—Thomas Jefferson[1]

With nations as with individuals our interest soundly calculated will ever be found inseparable from our moral duties.
—Thomas Jefferson[2]

Culture and values are the soul of development.
—*Arab Human Development Report,* 2002[3]

On a fine fall morning in Washington, D.C., we left the State Department quite early in order to avoid some of the city's notorious traffic. Turning left out of 21st Street onto Constitution Avenue, we caught a brief glimpse of the Lincoln and Vietnam memorials. As we drove east on Constitution, we noticed the colorful trees that surrounded the reflecting pool, a stark but pleasant contrast to the majestic pinnacle of the Washington Monument, high on a grassy hill and surrounded by American flags. It was October 2001.

Just below the U.S. Senate office buildings, we turned left onto North Capitol Street and headed toward another part of the nation's capital, its northeast quadrant, where crime-ridden neighborhoods and boarded storefronts compete with periodic stabs at urban renewal. Turning east again, this time on Rhode Island Avenue, we soon approached our destination. In a large lot on Otis Street, set in a very modest residential neighborhood, stood an old building that housed two groups of people that I wanted my guests to meet: an order of nuns and some men and women suffering with AIDS.

Just a month before, on the morning of September 11, my department colleagues and I had obeyed the alarms at Foggy Bottom and walked calmly out of the building. Some had seen television tapes of the first airliner hitting the Twin Towers, but none of us could know the severity of the crisis. Even when we saw plumes of smoke rising from the Pentagon across the Potomac River, it was difficult to fathom precisely what was happening and why. Only when we reached the safety of our homes did most of us even begin to ponder the fullness of the catastrophe that had struck our nation.

In the days to come, Americans would learn much about the religious ideology underlying the attacks. Then, slowly, the political strategy of democracy promotion, designed to counter this extremist interpretation of the Islamic faith, began to be implemented. Only later would the irony become apparent: our forward strategy of freedom failed to credit the critical role that religion must play if freedom is to endure.

The morning after 9/11 we were back at our desks at the State Department. The day before, when I heard the call to evacuate the building, I had been on the phone discussing preparations for a dialogue between the United States and the People's Republic of China on the subject of human rights. This was the first meeting since the Chinese had suspended the talks in 1999, and most of the event would involve set-piece exchanges at the State Department. But we also wanted to do something to show the Chinese how America handled issues of human rights. Various ideas were bandied about, including visits to a secular human rights institution, looking in at the federal courts, briefings at the Justice Department, and the like.

It had occurred to me that the Chinese might also profit from visiting a place called the Gift of Peace. Run by the Missionaries of Charity, the order established by Mother Teresa of Calcutta, the hospice cared mainly for men and women who were diagnosed with AIDS, most of them in their final weeks of life. Many of the sisters were in their 20s and 30s, and all of them wore the familiar white habits with blue lines across the top.

There was not much enthusiasm for this idea at the State Department, but we persevered, seeking and getting the assistance of outside supporters. When the day arrived, we met the Chinese delegation at Otis Street and took them into the building. Passing the chapel on the right, they saw the nuns on their knees in prayer.

We proceeded to a room where a sister briefed the delegation about the hospice. AIDS was a growing problem in China and, given the sorry state of the country's health care system, it was a very serious problem. As she chatted amiably with the delegation, the Chinese were puzzled by what they were seeing. There were no gleaming tables of hospital paraphernalia, no doctors and nurses rushing about, no intercom calls. There was only quiet and cleanliness. And compassion. Some in the West criticized Mother Teresa and the Missionaries for their efforts, describing them as little more than cynical fronts for conversion.

Behind the two speakers, the nuns had carefully placed a map of the world. On it were colored pins showing all the locations where the Missionaries of Charity had homes like this one, places where the sick and dying, the homeless and the outcast, were welcomed. There were red pins in India, blue pins in Russia, orange pins in Japan. Across the great expanse of China, however, the map was bare. Before she died, Mother Teresa had sought approval for her nuns to enter China. The government had turned her down.

We left the meeting room to see the facility. Some of the delegation went to the women's part of the building, others to the men's. As we walked, we were able to observe the nuns at work. They seemed to be of many nationalities, although, as I told my guests, it's hard to tell in America. We reached the room of an old man, weak and dying. He looked at us with sunken, hollow eyes. When the sisters approached, he brightened.

The Chinese officials saw it. Did they understand?

Will we?

Notes

INTRODUCTION

1. *The National Security Strategy of the United States*, 2006, section II. Accessed at www.whitehouse.gov/nsc/nss/2006/sectionii.html.

2. *National Strategy for Combating Terrorism*, September 2006, 1. Accessed at www.whitehouse.gov/nsc/nsct/2006/.

3. The State Department's 2006 *Annual Report on International Religious Freedom* (hereafter IRF Report) reported: "The Government [of Afghanistan] also responded positively to international approaches on religious freedom and worked effectively on high-profile cases such as [that of] Abdul Rahman." Available at www.state.gov.

4. At a March 6, 2006, press conference Under Secretary Nicholas Burns related his private remarks to Afghan Foreign Minister Abdullah: "I said on behalf of our government that we hope very much the judicial case...would be held in a transparent way. And of course, as our government is a great supporter of freedom of religion and as the Afghan constitution affords freedom of religion to all Afghan citizens, we hope very much that...the right of freedom of religion will be upheld in Afghan court." On March 20, spokesman Sean McCormack: "it's important...that the Afghan authorities conduct this trial...in as transparent a manner as possible. Our view...is that tolerance, freedom of worship is an important element of any democracy and these are issues...that they are going to have to deal with increasingly." Statements accessed at www.state.gov/r/pa/prs/2006/html.

5. For a compendium of critical comments on the administration's handling of the Rahman affair by religious supporters, including Colson's, see Rob Moll, "Should Evangelicals Support Bush's Foreign Policy If He Can't Guarantee Religious Freedom?" Accessed at www.chrisitianitytoday.com/ct/2006/117/13.0.html.

6. Statement of ambassador at large for international religious freedom to the Congressional Human Rights Caucus, April 7, 2006.

7. The Constitution of Afghanistan, Preamble, paragraph 8.

8. Zalmay Khalizad,"Afghanistan's Milestone," *Washington Post*, January 6, 2004, A17.

9. IRF Report for 2005, issued November, 2005.

10. Commission on International Religious Freedom (hereafter CIRF) Press Release, "Afghanistan: Freedom and Electoral Democracy," September 13, 2004. Available at www.uscirf.gov.

11. U.S. Institute of Peace, "Establishing the Rule of Law in Afghanistan," Report 117, March 2004, 7.

12. CIRF, Press Release, September 13, 2004.

13. CIRF Press Release, April 17, 2003, with text of CIRF letter to the president.

14. Articles 2 and 3 of the Afghan Constitution. The latter added, "and the values of this Constitution."

15. Nina Shea, "Conclusion: American Responses to Extreme *Shari'a*," Paul Marshall, ed., *Radical Islam's Rules: The Worldwide Spread of Extreme Shari'a Law* (Lanham, Md.: Rowman & Littlefield, 2005), 209.

16. 2006 IRF Report.

17. Daniel Philpott, "Explaining the Political Ambivalence of Religion," *American Political Science Review* (August 2007), 522–523.

18. Jeremy M. Sharp, *U.S. Democracy Promotion in the Middle East: The Islamist Dilemma* (Washington, D.C.: The Congressional Research Service, June 15, 2006), 10; David E. Kaplan, "Hearts, Minds and Dollars," *U.S. News and World Report*, April 25, 2005; Government Accounting Office, "U.S. Public Diplomacy: State Department Efforts to Engage Muslim Audiences Lack Certain Communication Elements and Face Significant Challenges (GAO-06–535)" (Washington, D.C.: GAO, May 3, 2006).

19. Interview with senior State Department official, July 27, 2005. Also see David E. Kaplan's update on his 2005 article ("Hearts, Minds and Dollars"; see n. 18) in 2006: "Of Jihad, Networks and the War of Ideas," *U.S. News and World Report*, June 22, 2006. Accessed at www.usnews.com/usnews/news/articles/060622/22natsec.htm.

20. Madeleine Albright, *The Mighty and the Almighty: Reflections on America, God, and World Affairs* (New York: HarperCollins Publishers, 2006), 8.

21. *The National Security Strategy of the United States*, September 2002, 3.

22. Todd M. Johnston and David B. Barrett, "Quantifying Alternate Futures of Religion and Religions," *Futures* 36 (2004), 947–960. The issue of religious demography is discussed in chapter 1.

23. A good analysis of how domestic religion is affecting U.S. foreign policy is Walter Russell Mead, "Religion and U.S. Foreign Policy," *Foreign Affairs*, September/October 2006, 24–44.

24. Liora Danan and Alice Hunt, *Mixed Blessings: U.S. Government Engagement with Religion in Conflict Prone Settings* (Washington, D.C.: Center for Strategic and International Studies, 2007), 3.

25. See the Henry Luce Initiative on Religion and International Affairs. Available at www.hluce.org/hluceinitiative.html.

26. Kevin Seamus Hasson. *The Right to Be Wrong: Ending the Culture War Over Religion in America* (San Francisco: Encounter Books, 2005), 40–42.

27. E-mail exchange with a legal expert at an executive branch agency with foreign affairs responsibilities.

28. According to the CSIS study, "Many government officials remain skeptical or concerned about engaging religion abroad because of the domestic and legal tradition surrounding the separation of religion and state.... Some officials said they believe the Establishment Clause categorically limits government activities related to religion, while many others said they were not sure of the ways the clause should shape their actions and decisions." Danan and Hunt, *Mixed Blessings*, 39. For a discussion of the effects of the Establishment Clause on foreign aid, see Jessica Powley Hayden, "Mullahs on a Bus: The Establishment Clause and U.S. Foreign Aid," *Georgetown Law Journal* 95:171 (2006).

29. Quoted in John I. Jenkins and Thomas Burish, "Reason and Faith at Harvard," *Washington Post*, October 23, 2006. Ultimately Harvard considered adding religion to its core curriculum but rejected the idea.

30. See, for example, my exchange with a retired diplomat on this subject in *First Things*, Letters to the Editor, October 2006.

31. The IRF Act states (section 2 b) that "It shall be the policy of the United States...to condemn violations of religious freedom and to promote, and to assist other governments in the promotion of, the fundamental right to freedom of religion."

32. In a 2006 briefing the IRF ambassador, asked whether religious freedom had increased or declined over the past year, answered that the trend over 30 years had been toward democracy and therefore greater religious freedom. He also argued that there had been a gradual easing of persecution in the communist world, most notably in Vietnam but also over time in China. He acknowledged that persecution in China had increased over the last two or three years, and that a worldwide growth in religious fundamentalism was increasing persecution (accessed at www.state.gov/g/dlr/rls/rm/2006/72303.htm). In 2007, one of the world's leading authorities on religious persecution, Paul Marshall, wrote that "violations of religious freedom worldwide are massive, widespread, and, in many parts of the world, intensifying." See Marshall, "The Range of Religious Freedom" in Paul Marshall, ed., *Religious Freedom in the World 2007* (Lanham, Md.: Rowman and Littlefield, 2007), 11. This phenonmenon is not limited to what used to be called "the Third World." Marshall notes that "Despite these countries' continuing openness, much of Europe seems to be becoming less religiously free." Ibid., 8.

33. Philpott, "Explaining the Political Ambivalence of Religion," 506–507.

34. Brian J. Grim, "The Social and Political Impact of Religious Freedom Worldwide," a paper presented to a Georgetown University symposium on U.S. IRF policy, February 25, 2008. A version of Grim's paper appears as "Religious Freedom: Good for What Ails Us?" in *The Review of Faith and International Affairs*, June 2008. Also see Grim and Roger Finke, "Religious Persecution in Cross-National Context: Clashing Civilzations or Regulated Religious Economies," *American Sociological Review* 72:4 (2007). For a discussion of the religious competition model of religious freedom, and how it can lead to social capital, see Rodney Stark and Roger Finke, *Acts of Faith: Explaining the Human Side of Religion* (Berkley, Calif.: University of California Press, 2000). For the relationships between religious belief and economic growth, see Robert J. Barrow and Rachel M. McCleary, "Religion and Economic Growth Across Countries," *American Sociological Review* (October 2003). We return to the subject of religion and democracy in chapter 3.

35. Philpott, "Explaining the Political Ambivalence of Religion."

36. I am indebted for this formulation to Kevin Seamus Hasson. See his *The Right to Be Wrong: Ending the Culture War Over Religion in America* (San Francisco: Encounter Books, 2005). My views on the meaning and reach of religious freedom have been influenced by, inter alia, Hasson; the Roman Catholic Church's *Declaration on Religious Freedom* (Walter M. Abbott, S.J., ed., *The Documents of Vatican II*, Piscataway, N.J.: New Century Publishers, Inc., 1966); John Courtney Murray, S.J., *We Hold These Truths: Catholic Reflections on the American Proposition* (New York: Sheed and Ward, 1960); Robert George, *Making Men Moral* (New York: Oxford University Press, 1995); Keith J. Pavlischek, "Questioning the New Natural Law Theory: The Case of Religious Liberty as Defended by Robert P. George in Making Men Moral," in Kenneth L. Grasso and Robert P. Hunt, eds., *A Moral Enterprise: Politics, Reason and the Common Good* (Wilmington, Del.: ISI Books, 2002); Christopher Wolfe, *Natural Law Liberalism* (Cambridge: Cambridge University Press, 2006); George Weigel, *Freedom and Its Discontents: Catholicism Confronts Modernity* (Washington, D.C.: Ethics and Public Policy Center, 1991). None, of course, is responsible for any errors of fact or interpretation on my part.

See also Farr, "Religious Realism in American Foreign Policy: Lessons from Vatican II," in *The Review of Faith and International Affairs* (Winter, 2005–2006), 25–33.

37. *Zorach v. Clauson*, 343 U.S. 306, 313 (1952) (Douglas, J., concurring).

38. For a discussion of the relative merits of theological discussions within Shiite and Sunni Islam, and in comparison with Christianity, see James A. Bill and John Alden Williams, *Roman Catholics and Shi'i Muslims: Prayer, Passion and Politics* (Chapel Hill: The University of North Carolina Press, 2002), 17–20.

39. The Regensburg speech of September 13, 2006, is widely available. See, for example, www.ewtn.com. See also the response by a variety of Muslim jurists, "Open Letter to His Holiness Pope Benedict XVI," dated October 12, 2006, at www.islamicamagazine.com. Also see a further Muslim response in January 2008: "A Common Word Between Us and You," at www.acommonword.com.

40. Michael J. Sandel, "Freedom of Conscience or Freedom of Choice," in James Davison Hunter and Os Guinness, eds., *Articles of Faith, Articles of Peace: The Religious Liberty Clauses and the American Public Philosophy* (Washington, D.C.: The Brookings Institution, 1990), 74–92.

41. Ibid., 77.

42. Albright, *The Mighty and the Almighty*, 104, 160–61.

43. For a sampling of the literature on what constitutes "religion," see William James, *The Varieties of Religious Experience* (New York: Mentor Books, 1958), esp. 39, 42. Two treatments by historians are Arnold Toynbee, *An Historian's Approach to Religion* (London: Oxford University Press, 1956) and Huston Smith, *The Religions of Man* (New York: Harper Colophon Books, 1958). Also see Jude P. Dougherty, *The Logic of Religion* (Washington, D.C.: The Catholic University Press, 2003). I am aware that my definition will seem simplistic to some, especially the incumbents of religious studies departments at American universities whose professions seem to require complexification. For a sober analysis of the difficulties in defining religion, see T. Jeremy Gunn, "The Complexity of Religion and the Definition of 'Religion' in International Law," *Harvard Human Rights Journal* 16 (2003), 189–215.

44. See Richard Dawkins, *The God Delusion* (New York: Houghton Mifflin, 2006); Christopher Hitchens, *God Is Not Great: How Religion Poisons Everything* (New York: Hachette Book Group, 2007).

45. Grim, "The Social and Political Impact of Religious Freedom Worldwide."

46. On the freedom of religious communities within civil society, see Robert P. George and William L. Saunders, Jr. "Dignitatis Humanae: The Freedom of the Church and the Responsibility of the State," in Kenneth Grasso and Robert P. Hunt, eds., *Catholicism and Religious Freedom: Contemporary Reflections on Vatican II's Declaration on Religious Liberty* (Lanham, Md.: Rowman and Littlefield, 2006), 1–17.

CHAPTER I

1. Mary Habeck, *Knowing the Enemy: Jihadist Ideology and the War on Terror* (New Haven, Conn.: Yale University Press, 2006), 7.

2. Quoted in Owen Chadwick, *The Secularization of the European Mind in the 19th Century* (Cambridge: Cambridge University Press, 1990), 10.

3. Edward Luttwak, "The Missing Dimension," in Douglas Johnston and Cynthia Sampson, eds., *Religion, the Missing Dimension of Statecraft* (New York: Oxford University Press, 1994), 12.

4. James E. Bill, *The Lion and the Eagle: the Tragedy of American-Iranian Relations* (New Haven: Yale University Press, 1988), 403. Just as little seems to have changed at the State Department, the CIA still seems hesitant to engage in analysis of religion. Former

CIA analyst Reuel Marc Gerecht recently wrote that "In the nine years (1985–1994) that I spent in the Central Intelligence Agency working on Middle Eastern issues, especially on the 'Iranian target,' I cannot recall a single serious conversation about Islam as a faith.... Friends at Langley tell me that even today there remains little sustained attention to the question of how believing Muslims, country by country, view the outside world...." See Gerecht, "Mirror Imaging the Mullahs: Our Islamic Interlocutors," January 23, 2008. Accessed at www.aei.org/include/pub_print.asp?pubID=27405.

5. Vali Nasr, *The Shia Revival: How Conflicts within Islam Will Shape the Future* (New York: W.W. Norton and Company, 2006), 217.

6. Ibid., 122.

7. Luttwak, 11; Barry Rubin, "Religion and International Affairs," in Johnston and Sampson, 33.

8. There have been some improvements in Vietnam's attitude toward religious persecution. See chapter 7.

9. Luttwak, ibid.

10. Stanton Burnett, "Implications for the Foreign Policy Community," in Johnston and Sampson, 289.

11. Quoted in George Weigel, *The Final Revolution: The Resistance Church and the Collapse of Communism* (New York: Oxford University Press, 1992), 140.

12. Ibid.

13. See Daniel Philpott, "The Catholic Wave," *Journal of Democracy* (April 2004), 32–46.

14. Samuel Huntington, *The Third Wave: Democratization in the Late Twentieth Century* (Norman: University of Oklahoma Press, 1991), 77–85; Lawrence E. Harrison, *The Central Liberal Truth* (New York: Oxford University Press, 2007), 98–101. Harrison argues that Catholic countries, especially in Latin America, have had difficulty consolidating democracy. Ibid., 92–94.

15. Robert D. Woodberry and Timothy S. Shah, "The Pioneering Protestants," in Larry Diamond, et al., eds., *World Religions and Democracy* (Baltimore: The Johns Hopkins University Press, 2005), 117–131.

16. One notable exception has been the U.S.-funded Asia Foundation, which has initiated several programs with religious communities in Indonesia. See http://asia-foundation.org/project/projectsearch.php?country=indonesia. In addition, the National Endowment for Democracy has begun to fund a variety of Muslim reformers. NED funds the International Forum for Islamic Dialogue, including its "Islam 21" project, which is building a core of educators among Muslim youth and a network of liberal Islamic intellectuals and activists. The related Muslim Civic Participation Project is developing a generic civic curriculum to conceptualize and articulate a pluralist and modernist Islamic discourse, using a "training the trainers" approach to create a network of educator activists in Bahrain, Egypt, Iraq, Jordan, Morocco, and the UK. NED grantees also include the Center for the Study of Islam and Democracy, specifically its work in developing a Muslim democrats network. I am grateful for these references to Michael Allen, editor of the NED's *Democracy Digest*.

17. Douglas Johnston, ed., *Faith-Based Diplomacy: Trumping Realpolitik* (New York: Oxford University Press, 2003), 3.

18. Peter L. Berger, ed., *The Desecularization of the World: Resurgent Religion and World Politics* (Washington, D.C.: Ethics and Public Policy Center, 1999), 2, 9–10.

19. Jose Casanova, *Public Religions in the Modern World* (Chicago: The University of Chicago Press, 1994); David Martin, *A General Theory of Secularization* (New York: Harper and Row Publishers, 1978) and *On Secularization: Towards a Revised General Theory* (Aldershot, England: Ashgate Publishing, Ltd., 2005). For an early theological perspective on desecularization, see Harvey Cox, *The Secular City: Secularization and*

Urbanization in Theological Perspective (New York: The Macmillan Company, 1965). On secularization in American culture, see Christian Smith, ed., *The Secular Revolution: Power, Interests, and Conflict in the Secularization of American Public Life* (Berkeley: University of California Press, 2003).

20. Daniel Philpott, "The Challenge of September 11 to Secularism in International Relations," *World Politics* (October 2002), 67.

21. Pavos Hatxopoulos and Fabio Petito, eds., *Religion in International Relations: The Return from Exile* (New York: Palgrave Macmillan, 2003), 1–20. A major voice on religion as an international issue after the Cold War was Samuel Huntington. See *The Third Wave*, ibid., and Huntington, *The Clash of Civilizations and the Remaking of the World Order* (New York: Touchstone, 1966); also Gilles Kepel, *The Revenge of God: The Resurgence of Islam, Christianity and Judaism in the Modern World* (University Park: The Pennsylvania State University Press, 1994).

22. Scott M. Thomas, *The Global Resurgence of Religion and the Transformation of International Relations: The Struggle for the Soul of the 21st Century* (New York: Palgrave Macmillan, 2005), 10.

23. Jonathan Fox and Shmuel Sandler, *Bringing Religion into International Relations* (New York: Palgrave Macmillan, 2004), 2. For other post-9/11 reassessments, see John D. Carlson and Erik C. Owens, eds., *The Sacred and the Sovereign: Religion and International Politics* (Washington, D.C.: Georgetown University Press, 2003) and Ted G. Jelen and Clyde Wilcox, eds., *Religion and Politics in Comparative Perspective: The One, the Few, and the Many* (Cambridge: Cambridge University Press, 2002). On modernity and religion, see Timothy Samuel Shah and Monica Duffy Toft, "God is Winning," *Foreign Policy* (2006), 39–43.

24. Philip Jenkins, "The Next Christianity," *Atlantic Monthly* (October 2002). Accessed at http://www.theatlantic.com/doc/200210/jenkins.

25. See, for example, the work of Iranian dissident Abdolkarim Soroush, *Reason, Freedom and Democracy in Islam: Essential Writings of Abdolkarim Soroush* (Oxford: Oxford University Press, 2000). Soroush spent a semester at Georgetown's Berkley Center for Religion, Peace and World Affairs, where I am a senior fellow. He participated in one of three symposia on U.S. international religious freedom policy held at Georgetown during 2008. See his comments from that symposium in a forthcoming publication by the Berkley Center, at www.berkleycenter.georgetown.edu.

26. Vali Nasr, *The Shia Revival: How Conflicts Within Islam Will Shape the Future* (New York: W.W. Norton and Company, 2006).

27. See Marc Gopin, *Between Eden and Armageddon: The Future of World Religions, Violence and Peacemaking* (Oxford: Oxford University Press, 2002); Marc Gopin, *Holy War, Holy Peace* (Oxford: Oxford University Press, 2002); and Mohammed Abu-Nimer, *Nonviolence and Peace Building in Islam* (Gainsville: University of Florida Press, 2003). I am grateful to Professor Daniel Philpott for these sources.

28. Philip Jenkins, *The Next Christendom: The Coming of Global Christianity* (New York: Oxford University Press, 2002).

29. George Weigel, *Freedom and Its Discontents: Catholicism Confronts Modernity* (Washington, D.C.: Ethics and Public Policy Center, 1991), 25–50.

30. Todd M. Johnston and David B. Barrett, "Quantifying Alternate Futures of Religion and Religions," *Futures* 36 (2004), 947.

31. Testimony of Tsultrim Dolma, Hearing before the House Committee on International Relations, September 10, 1997: *Freedom from Religious Persecution Act, Part II—Private Witnesses*," 6–9, 15.

32. For a good discussion of American efforts on religious persecution prior to the 1990s, see T. Jeremy Gunn, "The United States and the Promotion of Religion and

Belief," in Tore Lindholm, W. Cole Durham, Jr., Bahia G. Tahizib-Lie, eds., *Facilitating Freedom of Religion or Belief: A Deskbook* (Koninklijke Brill, NV: Martinus Nijhoff, 2004), 723–28. Much of the U.S. effort centered on international institutions and covenants, such as the 1948 Universal Declaration of Human Rights, or the creation of a UN Special Rapporteur on Religious Persecution in 1986. Key domestic developments included the establishment of a congressional-executive committee on human rights and a congressional human rights caucus. Gunn also highlights the work of David Little, then at the U.S. Institute for Peace, and the growing academic interest in "freedom of religion and belief" as precursors of the American legislative campaign.

33. Samuel Huntington, "Religious Persecution and Religious Relevance in Today's World," in Elliott Abrams, ed., *The Influence of Faith: Religious Groups and U.S. Foreign Policy* (Lanham, Md.: Rowman and Littlefield, 2001), 58.

34. John T. Noonan quoted in W. Cole Durham, "Perspectives on Religious Liberty: A Comparative Framework," 1, in *Religious Human Rights in Global Perspective: Legal Perspectives*, eds. Johan D. van der Vyver and John Witte, Jr. (The Hague: Martinus Nijhoff, 1996), 1.

35. John Shattuck, Testimony before the House Committee on International Relations, September 9, 1997: "Freedom from Religious Persecution Act, Part I—Administration Witnesses," 37.

36. For the IRF Act's policy goals, see the statute, Section 2 (b) Policy.

37. See, for example, the *Country Reports on Human Rights* between 1995 and 1998. Available at www.state.gov.

38. J. Bryan Hehir, "Religious Freedom and U.S. Foreign Policy: Categories and Choices," in Abrams, *The Influence of Faith: Religious Groups and U.S. Foreign Policy*, 36.

39. See chapter 4.

40. See, for example, Gregory J. Moore's Christian-based argument for PNTR: *Human Rights and United States Policy Toward China from a Christian Perspective* (Wynnewood, Pa.: Crossroads, 1997).

41. Bernard Lewis, *The Crisis of Islam: Holy War and Unholy Terror* (New York: The Modern Library, 2003), xxiv. The date of the statement's publication was February 23, 1998.

42. Many first heard the term in 1989 when Iran's Grand Ayatollah Ruhollah Khomeini issued a fatwa against Salmon Rushdie for his authorship of *The Satanic Verses*, a novel that was widely perceived by Muslims to slander the prophet Mohammed. Khomeini called on Muslims to kill Rushdie. Ibid., 139.

43. Ibid., xxv–xxvii.

44. Ian Kershaw, *Hitler: 1889–1936—Hubris* (New York: Norton and Co., 1998), 244; Robert Payne, *The Life and Death of Adolf Hitler* (New York: Praeger Publishers, 1973), 197.

45. *The 9/11 Commission Report: Final Report of the National Commission on Terrorist Attacks Against the United States* (New York: W.W. Norton and Co., 2005), 108–143; Daniel Benjamin and Steven Simon, *The Age of Sacred Terror* (New York: Random House, 2002), 219–255.

46. David E. Kaplan, "Of Jihad, Networks and the War of Ideas," June 22, 2006. Accessed at www.usnews.com/usnews/news/articles/060622/22natsec.htm.

47. The report, *Changing Minds, Winning Peace*, was submitted to Congress on October 1, 2003. Accessed at www.state.gov/r/adcompd/rls/prls/24777pf.htm.

48. Accessed at www.house.gov/international_relations/108.

49. Presentation by Scott Carpenter, Deputy Secretary of State for Near Eastern Affairs, April 27, 2006.

50. Wilfred M. McClay, "The Soul of a Nation," *Public Interest* (Spring 2004), 5.

51. The text of Clinton's November 7, 2001 speech was accessed at http://www.freerepublic.com/focus/f-news/567115/posts.

52. *New York Times*, November 4, 2004, A31.

53. Robert Satloff, *U.S. Policy Toward Islamism: A Theoretical and Operational Overview* (New York: Council on Foreign Relations, 2000), 1–2.

54. See Richard John Neuhaus, "The Two-Hundred-Year War," *First Things* (April 2006), 63–67.

55. Huntington, *Clash*, 217.

56. *Report of the 9/11 Commission*, 47–70; 363. Buried in the commission's recommendations is one brief reference to "Education that teaches tolerance, the dignity and value of each individual, and respect for different beliefs is a key element in any global strategy to eliminate Islamist terrorism." It is a pity that the commission, perhaps unaware of the U.S. international religious freedom policy, did not elaborate the importance of this issue. See page 378.

57. See, for example, the president's remarks at the Islamic Center of Washington, D.C., on September 17, 2001. The White House press release was entitled, *"Islam Is Peace," Says President*. Accessed at www.whitehouse.gov/news/releases/2001/09/20020917-11.html.

58. See White House Fact Sheet: *President Bush Remarks on the War on Terror*, October 6, 2005. Accessed at www.whitehouse.gov/news/releases/2005/10/20051006-2.html

59. See a January 2008 document from Homeland Security's Office of Civil Rights and Civil Liberties, "Terminology to Define the Terrorists: Recommendations from American Muslims." Accessed at www.investigativeproject.org/documents/misc/126.pdf.

60. Ximena Ortiz, "Geopolitical Jihad," *National Interest* (Spring 2006), 6. According to Ortiz, "while many jihadists probably take solace in visions of celestial rewards, including chaste (if spirited) maidens, they are probably not driven to violence by those visions.... Jihadists are probably motivated more by a zeal to destroy or avenge than to create much of anything, caliphates or VIP spots in paradise included. The impulse appears to be more nihilistic and, arguably, hormonal."

61. Quoted by Richard John Neuhaus in "The Anatomy of a Controversy," Mitchell S. Muncy, ed., *The End of Democracy? The Judicial Usurpation of Politics: The Celebrated First Things Debate with Arguments Pro and Con* (Dallas: Spence Publishing Company, 1997), 175.

62. Nicholas Kristof, "Believe It or Not," *New York Times*, August 15, 2003.

63. John Rawls, *A Theory of Justice—Revised Edition* (Cambridge, Mass.: The Belknap Press, 1999), originally published in 1971; *Political Liberalism* (New York: Columbia University Press, 1996); *Justice as Fairness: A Restatement*, ed. by Erin Kelly (Cambridge, Mass.: The Belknap Press, 2001).

64. Rawls, *Political Liberalism*, 1.

65. Michael Dorf, "In Praise of John Rawls, the Man Who Made Moral Philosophy Respectable Again–And Whose Views Also Profoundly Informed American Legal Thought," accessed at http://writ.news.findlaw.com/dorf/20021211.html.

66. Alfred Stepan, "Religion, Democracy and the 'Twin Tolerations,'" in Larry Diamond, et al., eds., *World Religions and Democracy* (Baltimore: The Johns Hopkins University Press, 2005), 11.

67. Robert P. George, "Public Morality, Public Reason," *First Things*, November 2006, 21–26.

68. See Daniel Philpott, "Explaining the Political Ambivalence of Religion," *American Political Science Review* (August, 2007), 505–525; Timothy Samuel Shah,

"For the Sake of Conscience: Some Evangelical Views of the State," forthcoming in Sandra Joireman, ed., *Christian Perspectives on the State* (New York and Oxford: Oxford University Press, 2009).

69. Philpott, "The Challenge of September 11," ibid.

70. Robert P. George and William L. Saunders, Jr. "Dignitatis Humanae: The Freedom of the Church and the Responsibility of the State," in Kenneth Grasso and Robert P. Hunt, eds., *Catholicism and Religious Freedom: Contemporary Reflections on Vatican II's Declaration on Religious Liberty* (New York: Rowman and Littlefield Publishers, Inc., 2006), 4–5.

71. Quoted in Robert Louis Wilken, "Augustine's Enduring Legacy," The Bradley Lecture (Washington, D.C.), January 9, 2006. Accessed at www.aei.org.

72. Peter Gay, *The Enlightenment: An Interpretation—The Rise of Modern Paganism* (New York: Vintage Books, 1966), 207. See also Paul Hazard, *The European Mind, 1680–1715* (Cleveland: Meridian Books, 1968), esp. 119–154, and Frederick B. Artz, *The Enlightenment in France* (Kent, Ohio: The Kent State University Press, 1968), 30. The understanding of the Enlightenment associated with these works (especially Gay's), i.e., as a unified historical climate of opinion, has been challenged on several post-modernist fronts. Michel Foucault condemns Enlightenment reason as being just as tyrannical as religion. Robert Darnton argues that focusing on the "high Enlightenment" hides its social significance. See Gertrude Himmelfarb, *The Roads to Modernity: The British, French and American Enlightenments* (New York: Knopf, 2004), 4.

73. Carl Becker, *The Heavenly City of the Eighteenth-Century Philosophers* (New Haven: Yale University Press, 1965), 15.

74. Quoted in Rodney Stark, *The Victory of Reason: How Christianity Led to Freedom, Capitalism and Western Success* (New York: Random House, 2005), 6.

75. John Finnis, "Religion and State: Some Main Issues and Sources," in C. S. Titus, ed., *God, Religion, and Civil Governance* (Arlington, Va.: The Institute for the Psychological Sciences, forthcoming).

76. Stark, 11–12.

77. The locus classicus on this theme is Alasdair McIntyre, *Whose Justice, Which Rationality?* (Notre Dame: The University of Notre Dame Press, 1988).

78. Chadwick, *The Secularization of the European Mind in the 19th Century,* 162–163.

CHAPTER 2

1. Robert D. Kaplan, "Interventionism's Realistic Future," *Washington Post,* November 22, 2006, A21.

2. George Weigel, "Symposium on the Bush Doctrine," *Commentary* (November 2005), 65.

3. Michael Rubin, "Rumsfeld and the Realists," *Wall Street Journal,* November 13, 2006, A16.

4. Daniel Philpott, *Revolutions in Sovereignty: How Ideas Shaped International Relations* (Princeton, N.J.: Princeton University Press, 2001), 64.

5. Gary Rosen, "Bush and the Realists," *Commentary* (September 2005), 31–32. For a defense of realist thinking applied to the freedom agenda see Henry A. Kissinger, "Realists vs. Idealists," *International Herald Tribune,* May 12, 2005, accessed at www.iht.com/bin/print_ipub.php?file=/articles/2005/05/11/opinion. For a stern realist critique of the freedom agenda by Brent Scowcroft, see Jeffrey Goldberg,

"Breaking Ranks," *The New Yorker*, October 31, 2005, accessed at www.newyorker.com/printables/fact/051031fa_fact2.

6. Daniel Philpott, "The Challenge of September 11 to Secularism in International Relations," *World Politics* (October 2002), 66, 72.

7. See, for example, Robert F. Ellsworth and Dimitri K. Simes, "Realism's Shining Morality: The Post-Election Trajectory of U.S. Foreign Policy," *The National Interest* (Winter 2004–2005), 5–10.

8. Henry A. Kissinger, "Implementing Bush's Vision," *Washington Post*, op-ed, May 16, 2005.

9. Kissinger uses the same word, "passions," often in referring to religion. See Kissinger, "Realists vs. Idealists," ibid. The extensive index to Kissinger's 900 word *magnum opus, Diplomacy*, does not contain the word *religion*. See Kissinger, *Diplomacy* (New York: Simon and Schuster, 1994), 877–912. I am grateful to *Economist* magazine for pointing this out: "In God's Name," *economist.com*, November 1, 2007.

10. Henry Kissinger, "Implementing Bush's Vision," *Washington Post*, op-ed, May 16, 2005.

11. Alfred Stepan, "Religion, Democracy and the 'Twin Tolerations,'" in Larry Diamond, et al., eds., *World Religions and Democracy* (Baltimore: The Johns Hopkins University Press, 2005), 21. Also see Pratap Bhanu Mehta, "Hinduism and Self-Rule," in Diamond, ibid., 58.

12. Krauthammer, "In Defense of Democratic Realism," 16.

13. Robert F. Ellsworth and Dimitri K. Simes, "Realism's Shining Morality: The Post-Election Trajectory of U.S. Foreign Policy," *The National Interest* (Winter 2004–2005), 5–10.

14. *The Washington Quarterly* (Autumn, 2005) 121–134; e-mail communication with Ms. Bronson, June 27, 2006.

15. See chapter 9 for a discussion of the Iraq Study Group's report.

16. See Richard Haass, *The Opportunity: America's Moment to Alter History's Course* (New York: Public Affairs, 2005). Haass was director of the State Department's Office of Policy Planning under the Bush administration and left in 2003 to head the Council on Foreign Relations. He is considered a realist and often clashed with neoconservatives in the administration.

17. My tenure as a diplomat began in 1982 under the Reagan administration. By 1985 I was heavily involved in Cold War issues, including Reagan's Strategic Defense Initiative and arms control in general. I believe it is fair to say that many American diplomats were opposed to Reagan for his foreign, as well as his domestic, policies. With the election of William Clinton in 1992, however, there was substantial support at Foggy Bottom for the new administration. See chapters 6 and 7.

18. Kevin Phillips, *American Theocracy: The Peril and Politics of Radical Religion, Oil and Borrowed Money in the 21st Century* (New York: Viking, 2006); James Rudin, *The Baptizing of America: The Religious Right's Plans for the Rest of Us* (New York: Thunder's Mouth Press, 2006); Michelle Goldberg, *Kingdom Coming: The Rise of Christian Nationalism* (New York: W.W. Norton, 2006); Randall Balmer, *Thy Kingdom Come: How the Religious Right Distorts the Faith and Threatens America: An Evangelical's Lament* (New York: Basic Books, 2006); Damon Linker, *The Theocons: Secular America Under Siege* (New York: Doubleday, 2006).

19. Ronald Inglehart and Pippa Norris, "The True Clash of Civilizations," *Foreign Policy* (March/April 2003), 63–70.

20. Ibid., 65.

21. Lawrence Harrison, *The Central Liberal Truth* (New York: Oxford University Press, 2007), 96.

22. Inglehart and Norris, ibid., 69.

23. Michael J. Sandel, "Freedom of Conscience or Freedom of Choice," in James David Hunter and Os Guinness, eds., *Articles of Faith, Articles of Peace: The Religious Liberty Clauses and the American Public Philosophy* (Washington, D.C.: The Brookings Institution, 1990), 75.

24. The Culture Matters Research Project found the family to be integral to child rearing and education, a critical component in development and democracy. Harrison, ibid., 207–211.

25. Christina Hoff Sommers, "The Subjection of Islamic Women," *Weekly Standard,* May 21, 2007, 18–19.

26. Ibid., 19.

27. Lawrence A. Uzzell, "Religious Human Rights Discrimination?" *The Public Justice Report,* July 2005, accessed at www.cpjustic.org.

28. Jean-Paul Marthoz and Joseph Saunders, "Religion and the Human Rights Movement," accessed at http://hrw.org/wr2k5/religion/1.htm.

29. Ibid., 3, including footnote 4; 22.

30. Ibid., 3–4.

31. Sandel, ibid., 75.

32. On Koh, see chapter 5.

33. On Shattuck, see chapters 1 and 3.

34. Harold Hongju Koh and Ronald C. Slye, *Deliberative Democracy and Human Rights* (New Haven: Yale University Press, 1999).

35. Ibid., 6–7, 41–47, 50–51.

36. Ibid., 51–54.

37. Jeremy Waldron, "Deliberation, Disagreement, and Voting," in ibid., 217.

38. Some would object that neoconservatism is not a "school of American foreign policy" so much as a persuasion or a tendency within American conservatism. For an excellent analysis from this point of view see Adam Wolfson, "Conservatives and Neoconservatives," *Public Interest* (Winter 2004), accessed at www.thepublicinterest .com/current/article2.html. I believe, however, there is such ample evidence of the intellectual contributions of neoconservatives to the Bush administration's reaction to 9/11, especially the invasion of Iraq and the "freedom agenda," that it warrants consideration as a distinct school of opinion. See the usage adopted by one major neocon, Charles Krauthammer, who sees neoconservatism (in various forms) as one of "the three major American schools of foreign policy." Krauthammer, "The Neoconservative Convergence," *Commentary* (July–August), 2005, 21.

39. Joshua Muravchik, "Can the Neocons Get Their Groove Back?," *Washington Post,* November 19, 2006, B3.

40. See, for example, Robert P. George, *The Clash of Orthodoxies: Law, Religion and Morality in Crisis* (Wilmington, Del.: ISI Books, 2001), esp. 153–168.

41. Novak was head of the U.S. delegation to the most critical Cold War institution for human rights—the Conference on Security and Cooperation in Europe. See George Weigel, *Tranquilitas Ordinis: The Present Failure and Future Promise of American Catholic Thought on War and Peace* (New York: Oxford University Press, 1987); *American Interests, American Purpose: Moral Reasoning and U.S. Foreign Policy* (New York: Praeger, 1989); *Idealism Without Illusions* (Washington, D.C.: Ethics and Public Policy Center, 1994).

42. In 1986 I served as State Department adviser to the U.S. negotiating team in its Geneva talks with the Soviets on SDI.

43. See George Weigel, *The Final Revolution,* 77–102.

44. Francis Fukuyama, *America at the Crossroads: Democracy, Power and the Neoconservative Legacy* (New Haven: Yale University Press, 2006), 116.

45. Andrew J. Bacevich, *First Things* (March 1998), 24–25.

46. A sampling: Thomas E. Ricks, *Fiasco: The American Military Adventure in Iraq* (New York: The Penguin Press, 2006); Larry Diamond, *Squandered Victory: The American Occupation and the Bungled Effort to Bring Democracy to Iraq* (New York: Times Books, 2005); Michael Gordon and Bernard Trainor, *Cobra II: The Inside Story of the Invasion and Occupation of Iraq* (New York: Pantheon, 2006); David L. Phillips, *Losing Iraq: Inside the Postwar Reconstruction Fiasco* (New York: Westview Press, 2006); George Packer, *The Assassin's Gate: America in Iraq* (New York: Farrar, Straus and Giroux, 2005).

47. Reuel Marc Gerecht, "Mirror-Imaging the Mullahs: Our Islamic Interlocutors." Accessed at www.aei.org.

48. Noah Feldman, "Imposed Constitutionalism," *Connecticut Law Review* (Summer 2005), 866.

49. Ibid., 867.

50. Ibid., 876–877. Feldman notes that Senators Brownback and Santorum (both Catholics) pressed publicly and privately for religious liberty and secularization. He cites a letter making the same argument, signed by Brownback, Santorum, Joseph Lieberman (Jewish), and Lindsay Graham (Protestant). See Feldman's footnote 76.

51. See, for example, Richard John Neuhaus, *The Naked Public Square: Religion and Democracy in America, 2nd ed.* (Grand Rapids, Mich.: William B. Eerdmans Publishing Company, 1987); Michael Novak, *On Two Wings: Humble Faith and Common Sense in the American Founding,* expanded edition (San Francisco: Encounter Books, 2002); George Weigel, *Freedom and Its Discontents: Catholicism Confronts Modernity* (Washington, D.C.: Ethics and Public Policy Center, 1991).

52. Rosen, ibid., 32.

53. For the views of Weigel and Novak, respectively, during the year prior to the U.S. invasion of Iraq, see "George Weigel on Pre-Emption, Just War and the Defense of World Order," Zenit News Agency, September 22, 2002, accessed at www.ewtn.com/library/ISSUES/ZPREEMPT.HTM; Michael Novak, "'Asymmetrical Warfare' and Just War: A Moral Obligation," *National Review Online,* February 10, 2003, available at www.nationalreview.com/script/printpage.asp?ref=novak/novak021003.asp.

54. George Weigel, *Idealism without Illusions: U.S. Foreign Policy in the 1990s* (Washington, D.C.: Ethics and Public Policy Center, 1994), 189.

55. Ibid., 189–191.

56. See in particular George Weigel, "Just War and Iraq Wars," *First Things* (April 2007), 14–20.

57. George Weigel, *Faith, Reason, and the War Against Jihadism: A Call to Action* (New York: Doubleday, 2007), 85.

58. Ibid., 112.

59. Ibid., 112–113.

60. Ibid., 128.

61. Francis Fukuyama, *The End of History and the Last Man* (New York: Avon Books, 1992), 211. The book became a bestseller and the winner of the Los Angeles Times Book Prize. George Gilder called it "a landmark work...profoundly realistic and important...timely and cogent...the first book to fully fathom the depth and range of the changes now sweeping the world" (from the book cover). Fukuyama's original essay was "The End of History?" *The National Interest,* Summer 1989, 3–18.

62. While he acknowledges that "there is no inherent conflict between religion and democracy," Fukuyama argues that "Christianity in a certain sense had to reinvent itself through a secularization of its goals before liberalism could emerge.... By making religion a private matter between the Christian and his God, Protestantism eliminated the need for...religious intervention into politics...." *The End of History,* 216.

63. George Packer, *The Assassin's Gate*, 54–56.

64. Fukuyama, *America at the Crossroads*, 28.

65. Ibid., 30

66. Ibid., 114–154. Fukuyama also credits Olivier Roy's "brilliant and persuasive argument that contemporary jihadism cannot be understood in cultural or religious terms." Ibid., 72.

67. James Q. Wilson, "The Reform Islam Needs," *Wall Street Journal*, November 13, 2002, accessed at www.opinionjournal.com/extra/?id=110002613.

68. Ibid.

69. See his discussion of the founding in ibid.

70. Muravchik, "Can the Neocons Get Their Groove Back," ibid.

71. See *The National Security Strategy of the United States*, September 2002, chapter 2, second paragraph.

72. See Andrew J. Bacevich and Elizabeth H, Prodomou, "God Is Not Neutral: Religion and U.S. Foreign Policy After 9/11," *Orbis* (Winter 2004), 43–53.

73. See Jim Hoagland, "Diminishing the U.S. Footprint," *Washington Post*, March 13, 2006, B7.

74. *The National Security Strategy of the United States*, March 2006, chapter 2, numbered paragraph 2.

CHAPTER 3

1. For a creative approach to this problem, which could be adapted for training U.S. diplomats on the relationships between religion and state, see Daniel Philpott, "Explaining the Political Ambivalence of Religion," *American Political Science Review* (August 2007), 505–525.

2. See Noah Feldman's discussion of Islamic majoritarianism in Feldman, "Imposed Constitutionalism," *Connecticut Law Review* (Summer 2005), 857–889.

3. Arch Puddington, "The 2006 Freedom House Survey: The Pushback Against Democracy," *Journal of Democracy* (April 2007), 135–137.

4. Samuel P. Huntington, *The Third Wave: Democratization in the Late Twentieth Century* (Norman: University of Oklahoma Press, 1991), 16–21.

5. Puddington, "The 2006 Freedom House Survey," 127.

6. Robert A. Dahl, *On Democracy* (New Haven, Conn.: Yale University Press, 1998), 145–146.

7. See Michael E. Brown, et al., eds., *Debating the Democratic Peace* (Cambridge, Mass.: The MIT Press, 1996).

8. See the *National Security Strategy of the United States*, 2002.

9. For example, see Fareed Zakaria, *The Future of Freedom: Illiberal Democracy at Home and Abroad* (New York: Norton, 2003).

10. For a critique of the sequencing approach, see Thomas Carothers, "The 'Sequencing' Falacy," *Journal of Democracy* (January 2007), 12–27. For a cogent discussion of the shortcomings of existing U.S. civil society programs, see Daniel Brumberg, "Beyond Liberalization?" *The Wilson Quarterly* (Spring 2004).

11. George Packer, *The Assassin's Gate: America in Iraq* (New York: Farrar, Straus and Giroux, 2005), 137–139.

12. Yochi J. Dreazen, "New Rebuilding Plan in Iraq Stirs Debate About Tactics," *Wall Street Journal*, April 19, 2007, A1.

13. Gary Rosen, ed., *The Right War? The Conservative Debate On Iraq* (Cambridge: Cambridge University Press, 2005).

14. Joseph S. Nye, Jr., "Transformational Leadership and U.S. Grand Strategy," *Foreign Affairs* (July/August, 2006), 139.

15. Francis Fukuyama, *America at the Crossroads*, 46.

16. Zbigniew Brzezinski, "Terrorized by 'War on Terror,'" *Washington Post*, March 25, 2007, B1.

17. Puddington, 136.

18. Gregory Gause, "Can Democracy Stop Terrorism?" *Foreign Affairs* (September/October 2005), 62–76.

19. See, for example, Steven R. Weisman, "Democracy Push by Bush Attracts Doubters in Party," *New York Times*, March 17, 2006, A1, and Jeffrey Goldberg's exploration of the views of Brent Scowcroft, "Breaking Ranks," *The New Yorker*, October 31, 2005.

20. See, for example, Peter Beinhard, "The Rehabilitation of the Cold-War Liberal, *New York Times Magazine*, April 30, 2006.

21. Fukuyama, *America at the Crossroads*, 46. Also see George Packer, *Assassin's Gate*, 54–55. Packer mounts a scathing attack on the neoconservative plans to employ U.S. military force against Iraq. He claims that the influence of Leo Strauss led to a "Strauss cult," a form of neoconservative Gnostic Puritanism that fed war fever. Neocons first imbibed Strauss's belief in "a secret body of understanding to which only a select few would be admitted." Then they "seized and distorted his teachings, ironing out every irony in pursuing their rigidly virtuous and peculiarly American crusade against the malaise of the modern world."

22. Peter Beinhart, *The Good Fight: Why Liberals—and Only Liberals—Can Win the War on Terror and Make America Great Again* (New York: HarperCollins, 2006), 198–199.

23. Beinhart, *The Good Fight*, passim; Tony Smith, "Its Uphill for the Neoliberals," *Washington Post*, March 11, 2007, B1.

24. Philip J. Costopolous, in Larry Diamond, et al., eds., *World Religions and Democracy*, ix.

25. For a useful exploration of Jefferson's profound contradictions, including the relationship between his private religious beliefs and his public evocations of religion, see Kevin Seamus Hasson, *The Right to Be Wrong: Ending the Culture War over Religion in America* (San Francisco: Encounter Books, 2005), 76–77, 83–93. Hasson concludes that judgments about Jefferson's public claims concerning God and man, claims that have had a profound impact on the American way of democracy, should not be tied to the inconsistencies of Jefferson's own life. The fact that he owned slaves when he claimed universal human equality should not undermine that claim, if the claim is indeed true.

26. Quoted in James R. Stoner, "Is There a Political Philosophy in the Declaration of Independence?," *The Intercollegiate Review* (Fall/Winter 2005), 5; also see Michael Novak, *On Two Wings: Humble Faith and Common Sense at the American Founding,* expanded edition (San Francisco: Encounter Books, 2002), 33.

27. Michael Novak, *On Two Wings*, 58–59.

28. On Madison's views concerning the importance of religion, and the role of the First Amendment, see John T. Noonan, *The Lustre of Our Country: The American Experience of Religious Freedom* (Berkeley: University of California Press, 1998), 61–91; James T. Hutson, *Religion and the Founding of the American Republic* (Washington, D.C.: Library of Congress, 1998), 70–76; Philip Hamburger, *Separation of Church and State* (Cambridge: Harvard University Press, 2002), 105–106, 165–166, 181–185; Novak, *On Two Wings*, 52–61, 131–141. For a contrary view on Madison and the founders, see Walter Berns, "Religion and the Founding Principle," in Robert H. Horwitz, ed., *The Moral*

Foundations of the American Republic, 3rd ed. (Charlottesville: University of Virginia Press, 1987).

29. Hutson, *Religion and the Founding of the American Republic*, 79–80.

30. Ibid., 80.

31. Hamburger, *Separation of Church and State*, 297–299, 324–326. On the views of 19th-century American Catholic bishops, see Gerald P. Fogarty, S.J., *The Vatican and the American Hierarchy from 1870 to 1965* (Wilmington, Del.: Michael Glazier, Inc., 1985), 40–41, 154–155.

32. Noonan, *The Lustre of Our Country*, 136.

33. Cf. James P. Moore, Jr., *One Nation Under God: The History of Prayer in America* (New York: Doubleday, 2005).

34. Lawrence E. Harrison, *The Central Liberal Truth: How Politics Can Change a Culture and Save It from Itself* (New York: Oxford University Press, 2006), 92–94.

35. Ibid., 92–98.

36. Alfred Stepan, "Religion, Democracy and the 'Twin Tolerations,'" in Larry Diamond, et al., eds., *World Religions and Democracy* (Baltimore: The Johns Hopkins University Press, 2005), 10.

37. In 2007, Indonesia and Senegal became the second and third Muslim nations to be ranked as "free." See www.freedomhouse.org.

38. Harrison, *The Central Liberal Truth*, 118.

39. Ibid., 119.

40. Murray, *We Hold These Truths*, 55, 126. Richard John Neuhaus, *The Naked Public Square: Religion and Democracy in America*, 2nd ed. (Grand Rapids: William B. Eerdmans Publishing Co., 1986). Also see Neuhaus, "A New Order of Religious Freedom," *First Things* (February 1992), 13–17.

41. Philpott, "Explaining the Political Ambivalence of Religion," *American Political Science Review* (August, 2007), 506–507. See the discussion of consensual differentiation in the Introduction to this book.

42. Stark, *The Victory of Reason*, 197–199.

43. See the discussion of this issue in the Introduction.

44. Michael J. Sandel, "Freedom of Conscience or Freedom of Choice," in James Davison Hunter and Os Guinness, eds., *Articles of Faith, Articles of Peace: The Religious Liberty Clauses and the American Public Philosophy* (Washington, D.C.: The Brookings Institution, 1990), 74–92.

45. Robert D. Woodberry and Timothy S. Shah, "The Pioneering Protestants," in Larry Diamond, et al., *World Religions and Democracy*, 119.

46. It should also be noted that Saudi Arabia and Iraq are religiously diverse because of the presence of a significant minority of Shiites in the former and Sunnis in the latter. To date, however, this kind of plurality is a cause of tension and conflict rather than a basis for religious pluralism.

47. Stark, *The Victory of Reason*, 199.

48. John Rawls, *Political Liberalism* (New York: Columbia University Press, 1996), 10. Rawls argued that it was possible, in effect, for "citizens of faith" to translate their arguments in ways consistent with public reason and therefore acceptable to his concept of political liberalism. But this Rawlsian "carveout" for religion seems to me highly problematic and unconvincing. His description of Christianity's contribution to liberalism is essentially that the Protestant Reformation led to religious pluralism, grounded in conflicting doctrines on the authority for salvation (the Church or the Bible). This conflict led to the wars of religion, because the "competing transcendent elements do not admit of compromise. Their mortal combat can be moderated only by circumstance and exhaustion, or by equal liberty of conscience and freedom of

thought." Ibid., xl–xli. Rawls seems to be unaware of any contributions by Christian doctrines to the idea of limited government, universal human dignity, natural law or natural rights.

49. See, for example, Russell Hittinger's analysis of what he characterizes as the Supreme Court's "motivational analysis, which first emerged in connection with religion." Hittinger argues that the Court, implicitly at least, overturned a Colorado referendum because the Court discerned "religious animus" on the part of the people of that state. Hittinger, "A Crisis of Legitimacy," in Muncy, ed., *The End of Democracy? The Judicial Usurpation of Politics: The Celebrated First Things Debate with Arguments Pro and Con* (Dallas: Spence Publishing Company, 1997), 25, 29. The issue also arises when Catholic bishops deny communion to Catholic politicians who reject the teachings of the Church. Some argue that this constitutes the unconstitutional intrusion of religion into politics. In fact, it constitutes an exercise of religious freedom.

50. Alfred Stepan, "Religion, Democracy and the 'Twin Tolerations,'" 11.

51. Ibid., 5.

52. Ibid., 5, 10–11.

53. See Francis Fukuyama, *Trust: The Social Virtues and the Creation of Prosperity* (New York: The Free Press, 1995); Robert D. Putnam, *Bowling Alone: The Collapse and Revival of American Community* (New York: Simon and Schuster, 2000), 65–79.

54. Putnam, 74. Here Putnam is not referring per se to religious communities active in the political arena, but to the act of religious community itself.

55. Corwin Smidt, ed., *Religion as Social Capital: Producing the Common Good* (Waco, Tex.: Baylor University Press, 2003).

56. Ibid., 218–218.

57. A recent exploration of this issue is provided by Theodore Roosevelt Malloch, *Spiritual Enterprise: Doing Virtuous Business* (New York: Encounter Books, 2008).

58. Robert D. Woodberry, "Researching Spiritual Capital: Promises and Pitfalls," a paper delivered to a Forum on Spiritual Capital, January 14, 2005.

59. Ibid.

60. Richard Madsen, *China's Catholics: Tragedy and Hope in an Emerging Civil Society* (Berkeley: University of California Press, 1998), 135.

61. Harrison, *The Central Liberal Truth*, 145–147.

62. Robert W. Hefner, "Muslim Democrats and Islamist Violence in Post-Soeharto Indonesia," in Hefner, ed., *Remaking Muslim Politics: Pluralism, Contestation, Democratization* (Princeton: Princeton University Press, 2005), 273–301.

63. In early 2006 an Iranian newspaper editor noted that Iranian civil society associations and movements had been flourishing a mere four or five years before, but the autocratic counter-reaction had depleted civil society. See "U.S. Role Complicates Iranian Efforts for Change from Within," *Washington Post*, March 14, 2006, A16.

64. Harrison, *The Central Liberal Truth*.

65. See, for example, Abdullah Ahmed An-Naim, *Toward an Islamic Reformation: Civil Liberties, Human Rights and International Law* (Syracuse: Syracuse University Press, 1996).

66. Khaled Abou El Fadl, *The Great Theft: Wrestling Islam from the Extremists* (San Francisco: HarperSanFrancisco, 2005), 22.

67. See Zakaria, *The Future of Freedom*.

68. Jose Cassanova, "Civil Society and Religion: Retrospective Reflections on Catholicism and Prospective Reflections on Islam," *Social Research* (Winter 2001), 16.

69. Harrison, *The Central Liberal Truth*; Woodberry and Shah, "The Pioneering Protestants."

70. Harrison, *The Central Liberal Truth*. Harrison's study categorizes countries by Protestant, Jewish (Israel), Catholic, Orthodox, Confucian (more an ethical system than a religion), Buddhist, Islamic, and Hindu. Table 4.1, 88–89.

71. Ibid.

72. Woodberry and Shah, "The Pioneering Protestants," 119.

73. Harrison, *The Central Liberal Truth*, 89.

74. Ibid., 94–95.

75. See Daniel Philpott, *Revolutions in Sovereignty: How Ideas Shaped Modern International Relations* (Princeton: Princeton University Press, 2001).

76. Woodberry and Shah, "The Pioneering Protestants," 118.

77. Ibid., 120.

78. Ibid., 118–119.

79. Max Weber, *The Protestant Ethic and the Spirit of Capitalism*, trans. Talcott Parsons (New York: Charles Scribner's Sons, 1958).

80. Peter Berger, "Christianity: The Global Picture," in Diamond, et al., *World Religions and Democracy*, 146–150.

81. Philip Costopoulos, "Introduction," in Diamond, et al., *World Religions and Democracy*, xix.

82. George Weigel, *Witness to Hope: The Biography of Pope John Paul II* (New York: HarperCollins Publishers, Inc., 1999), 531.

83. Huntington, *The Third Wave*, 75.

84. Ibid., 77, 78, 83.

85. The classic Catholic treatment of doctrinal development is John Henry Cardinal Newman, *An Essay on the Development of Christian Doctrine* (New York: Longmans, Green and Co., 1949). For an excellent contemporary exploration of the issue see Avery (Cardinal) Dulles, "True and False Reform," *First Things* (August/September), 2003.

86. Quoted in George Weigel, *Freedom and Its Discontents: Catholicism Confronts Modernity* (Washington, D.C.: Ethics and Public Policy Center, 1991), 12.

87. Brian Tierney, *The Idea of Natural Rights: Studies on Natural Rights, Natural Law, and Church Law, 1150–1625* (Grand Rapids: William B. Eerdmans, 1997), 36. On the inquisitions, see Henry Kammen, *The Spanish Inquisition: A Historical Revision* (New Haven: Yale University Press, 1997) and Edward Peters, *Inquisition* (Berkeley: University of California Press, 1998).

88. Brian Tierney, *The Idea of Natural Rights*, 36–37.

89. Ibid., 43.

90. Tierney concludes that "The idea of natural rights grew up—perhaps could only have grown up in the first place—in a religious culture [i.e., "the Christian jurisprudence and philosophy of the Middle Ages"] that supplemented rational argumentation about human nature with a faith in which humans were seen as children of a caring God." Ibid., 343.

91. John Paul II, "*Veritatis Splendor*," in J. Michael Miller, C.S.B., ed., *The Encyclicals of John Paul II* (Huntington, Ind.: Our Sunday Visitor, Inc., 1996), 701.

92. See, for example, Sandel, "Freedom of Conscience or Freedom of Choice?," 485.

93. "Declaration on Religious Freedom: On the Right of the Person and of Communities to Social and Civil Freedom in Matters Religious," in Walter M. Abbott, S.J., ed., *The Documents of Vatican II* (Piscataway, N.J.: New Century Publishers, Inc., 1966), 675–696. The American Jesuit John Courtney Murray, widely acknowledged to have influenced the Declaration, wrote in a footnote that religious freedom was not based on the modern concept of "freedom of conscience," because that phrase was often interpreted to mean radical moral autonomy in human affairs, or, as he put it, that "I have the right to do what my conscience tells me to do, simply because my

conscience tells me to do it. This," Murray argued, "is a perilous theory. Its particular peril is subjectivism—the notion that, in the end, it is my conscience, and not the objective truth, which determines what is right or wrong, true or false." See footnote 5 of the Declaration.

94. This does not mean, of course, that all Catholics manifest such virtues. The Culture Matters Research Project included measurements of levels of corruption within societies formed by religion, including Catholicism. It is striking that in Latin America, levels of corruption are particularly high. Lawrence Harrison credits Max Weber's observation that the "Catholic cycle of sin/confession/absolution/renewed sin" results in a "more flexible Catholic ethical code." Harrison, *The Central Liberal Truth*, 106.

95. For an excellent discussion of the Catholic doctrine of religious liberty in civil society and how it provides an antidote to the monism of modern democracy, see Robert P. George and William L. Saunders, Jr., "*Dignitatis Humanae*: The Freedom of the Church and the Responsibility of the State," in Kenneth Grasso and Robert P. Hunt, eds., *Catholicism and Religious Freedom: Contemporary Reflections on Vatican II's Declaration on Religious Liberty* (New York: Rowman and Littlefield, 2006), 1–17.

96. Quoted in Weigel, *Freedom and Its Discontents*, 26. The Magisterium made a distinction between "freedom of conscience" (the false notion of an inherent right not to believe in God) and "freedom of consciences" (the right of all people to worship God). Pope Gregory was condemning a radically relativistic, atheistic notion of "freedom of conscience." This issue is addressed in Leo XIII's encyclical *Libertas Praestantissimum*, June 20, 1888.

97. Weigel, *Freedom and Its Discontents*, 28–29.

98. Ibid., 27–29.

99. Hamburger, *Separation of Church and State*, 201–219. The anti-Catholic provisions were called the Blaine amendments. See 297–299, 324–328.

100. See Thomas F. Farr, "Religious Realism in Foreign Policy: Lessons from Vatican II," *Review of Faith and International Affairs* (Winter 2005–2006), 25–34.

101. The dissidents were headed by Archbishop Marcel Lefebvre, whose objections to the Second Vatican Council in general, and to *Dignitatis Humanae* in particular, led him into schism with the Church. After years of attempted reconciliation, the Church excommunicated Lefebvre in 1988. For his views on *Dignitatis*, see Lefebvre, *Religious Liberty Questioned*, tr. Rev. Fr. Jaime Pazat de Lys (Kansas City: Angelus Press, 2002).

102. Walter Isaacson, *Benjamin Franklin: An American Life* (New York: Simon and Schuster, 2003), 459.

CHAPTER 4

1. The Senate vote was 98–0. The House passed the IRF Act on a voice vote.

2. White House Presidential Signing Statement, October 27, 1998.

3. "Senate Puts Aside Bill to Punish Nations That Persecute Religion," *New York Times*, July 24, 1998, A1.

4. Allen D. Hertzke, *Freeing God's Children: The Unlikely Alliance for Global Human Rights* (Lanham, Md.: Rowman and Littlefield Publishers, Inc., 2004), 234.

5. For example, Congress had during the Cold War created the position of "ambassador at large for burdensharing." This official's job was to press European governments to share more equitably the burden of fighting the Cold War. I had the opportunity to work with two of these ambassadors and witnessed persistent attempts by the department under the Bush I and Clinton administrations to downgrade it because of a perception that, along with the congressional scrutiny it entailed, it complicated U.S. relations with the Germans, French, British, and others. For a congressional view on

this position, see Senator Lautenberg's comments of May 2, 1994, at http://thomas .loc.gov/cgi-bin/query/z?r103:S02MY4–52:. Another example of this phenomenon was the congressionally imposed "special Cyprus coordinator," whose job of managing the Cyprus problem was (and is) complicated by the dominance of the Greek lobby in the U.S. Congress. For my views on this issue, see Thomas F. Farr, "Overcoming the Cyprus Tragedy: Let Cypriots Be Cypriot," *Mediterranean Quarterly* (Fall 1997), especially 51, 60.

6. The account that follows will draw to some degree on Allen Hertzke's excellent study of the domestic campaign that led to the International Religious Freedom Act, *Freeing God's Children*. This account differs from Hertzke's in at least two respects. First, I am less concerned with providing a comprehensive explanation of the campaign that led to the act than to identify those trends that affected its implementation. Second, Professor Hertzke sees the critical division over the bill as between those who sought to punish religious persecution through punitive actions and those who sought to promote religious freedom through quiet diplomacy. I agree that this was a fundamental division among those who supported the law, but I see it as one of several critical disputes.

7. A few Roman Catholics were present at the meeting as well, including former Reagan speechwriter Peggy Noonan.

8. For an insightful survey of the movement, Michael Horowitz, and Nina Shea, see Jeffrey Goldberg, "Washington Discovers Christian Persecution," *The New York Times*, December 21, 1997.

9. Title V, sections 501–504, of the International Religious Freedom Act of 1998.

10. See, for example, John Shattuck, "Religion, Rights and Terrorism," *Harvard Human Rights Journal* (Spring, 2003), 183–188. Also see the remarks in Jean-Paul Marthoz and Joseph Saunders, "Religion and the Human Rights Movement," accessed at http://hrw.org/wr2k5/religion/1.htm. This essay is discussed in chapter 2's section, *Liberal Internationalism*.

11. On domestic church-state issues, Clinton himself seemed to have conflicting views. Marci A. Hamilton criticized the Clinton administration for too much free exercise and too little attention to the restrictions of the establishment clause. See Hamilton, "Religion and the Law in the Clinton Era: An Anti-Madisonian Legacy," 2000. Accessed at www.law.duke.edu/journals/64LCPHamilton.

12. During the Congressional hearings on Wolf-Specter in September 1997, this suspicion was on full display. Some of the animus was also directed toward the Clinton administration itself. On the issue of religious persecution, according to Richard Land, the State Department had been "woefully negligent." Don Argue: the U.S. government had been "a silent and indifferent witness to intolerable religious persecution." Fr. Drew Christiansen: training was needed at State and INS to counter "ignorance or indifference to violations of religious liberty." *Hearing Before the Committee on International Relations*, House of Representatives, First Session, September 19, 1997, 22, 24, 26.

13. For Horowitz' pre-Wolf-Specter views on the issue of Christian involvement in American democracy and of persecution of Christians abroad, see his articles in *Crisis Magazine*, "Bridges Crossed—and yet to Cross: A Sympathetic Jewish Writer Speaks to Evangelicals," (September 1994), 33–39; and the op-ed that many credit as the opening salvo in his campaign against Christian persecution: "New Intolerance Between Crescent and Cross," *Wall Street Journal*, July 5, 1995.

14. Michael Horowitz, speech at an international conference in Washington, D.C., in Dan Fefferman, ed., *Religious Freedom and the New Millennium* (Falls Church, Va.: International Coalition for Religious Freedom, 2000), 61–66. For a revealing Horowitz interview after the passage of the IRF Act, see Michael Cromartie, "The Jew Who Is

Saving Christians," *Christianity Today*, March I, I999. In this interview, Horowitz continues to insist that "if the facts are told openly, the goodness of the American people...will ensure serious action against persecuting governments."

15. The statute did require the director to "consult" the secretary of state in making policy recommendations to the president and to "coordinate" with the secretary "to ensure that the provisions of the Act are fully and effectively implemented." See H.R. 1685, May 20, 1997, Section 5 (e). But this language did not provide any direct authority to the secretary and, in any case, did not affect the sanctions decision, which rested with the director alone.

16. One problem with the original Wolf-Specter bill was figuring out precisely which countries were to be covered in the report and therefore targeted by the new policy. Rather than simply name all the countries outright, the statute includes cross references both to particular countries named within the statute and to earlier congressional resolutions that had specified other countries that are not named in the statute. Those named in the statute were "Communist countries, such as Cuba, Laos, the People's Republic of China, North Korea and Vietnam"; [H.R. 1685, Section 2 (3)] and Sudan [Section 2 (5)]. Other countries named in stipulated resolutions [Section 2 (8)] were Morocco, Saudi Arabia, Pakistan, Iran, and Egypt. For the Annual Report, see Section 6. For the sanctions provisions, see Section 7.

17. H.R. 1685, Section 3 (4); Section 7.

18. Hertzke, *Freeing God's Children*, 218.

19. For an example of a faith-based argument against sanctions see Gregory J. Moore, *Human Rights and United States Policy Toward China from a Christian Perspective* (Wynnewood, Pa.: Crossroads, 1999).

20. See the op-ed by National Security Advisor Sandy Berger, "Wrong Approach to Religious Freedom," *Washington Post*, May 14, 1998, A23.

21. It is interesting that some putatively informed observers continued to believe that the IRF Act, after its passage, contained a White House office of persecution monitoring. See William Martin, "With God on Their Side," *Georgetown Journal of International Affairs* (Winter/Spring), 2000, 10. For the changes that essentially gutted the Wolf-Specter bill, see *HIRC Markup*, March 25, 1998, 29–66.

22. "News Release," Office of Senator James Inhofe, May 20, 1997.

23. Hertzke, *Freeing God's Children*, 190; on Wolf-Specter's chances in the Senate, see Rosalind I.J. Hackett, Mark Silk, and Dennis Hoover, eds., *Religious Persecution as a U.S. Policy Issue* (Hartford, Conn.: Center for the Study of Religion in Public Life, 2000), 8–9.

24. Hertzke, *Freeing God's Children*, 211.

25. Interview with John Hanford, May 20, 2004. Hanford met with Horowitz and other supporters of Wolf-Specter on at least two occasions to persuade them to alter what he considered to be potentially harmful provisions of the draft bill. Only when they resisted his suggestions did he decide to begin researching and drafting an alternative.

26. The phrase "truth patrol" is that of Steve Moffit, who was Senator Don Nickles' staffer and a key member of the team that drafted the IRF Act. Interview with Moffit, July 9, 2004. The fear that the department would "fudge the facts" was intensified when President Clinton suggested Wolf-Specter would lead to that outcome. Hertzke, *Freeing God's Children*, 204.

27. An example of liberal concern was Stacey Burdette of the Anti-Defamation League. Although she was uncomfortable with the anti-State Department attitudes of Wolf-Specter supporters, she believed that the department had generally ignored the issue of religious persecution. Hertzke, *Freeing God's Children*, 198.

28. Hertzke, *Freeing God's Children*, 231–233.

29. The commission has an excellent web site, at which all its publications and policy recommendations can easily be accessed: www.uscirf.gov.

30. I encountered this confusion during a trip to China, where (I later learned) a Chinese religious official thought I was a member of the commission. See chapter 10. Confusion about the difference between the commission and the State Department office of international religious freedom was, alas, not limited to foreign governments. One senator involved in the IRF Act told me several years later that he thought John Hanford had been a perfect choice to head the commission. Hanford had by that time been IRF ambassador at the State Department for well over a year. Slips of the tongue happen, of course, but they are abetted by ambiguity and confusion.

31. Wolf-Specter in its initial stages had an entire section devoted to sanctions on Sudan. Clearly the tragedy of Sudanese Christians was a major force in garnering support among Protestants and Catholics alike.

32. Nina Shea, *In the Lion's Den: A Shocking Account of Persecution and Martyrdom of Christians Today and How We Should Respond* (Nashville, Tenn.: Broadman and Holman, 1997); Paul Marshall, with Lela Gilbert, *Their Blood Cries Out: The Untold Story of Persecution Against Christians in the Modern World* (Dallas, Tex.: Word, 1997).

33. *United States Polices in Support of Religious Freedom: Focus on Christians* (Report Consistent with the Omnibus Consolidated Appropriations Act, Fiscal Year 1997, House Report 3610).

34. For example, *Congressional Quarterly* reported that under the bill "the religious persecution monitor's task would be to determine whether those [targeted] countries were persecuting or allowing the persecution of Roman Catholics, evangelical Christians, non-Muslims and moderate Muslims." *CQ Special Report*, September 13, 1997, 21–22. CQ's description was a typical extrapolation from the bill's convoluted language, which clearly targeted the named categories but also permitted the director of persecution monitoring to include within his scope of action "any community within any country or region thereof that the Director finds...is the target of religious persecution." See H.R. 1685, May 20, 1997, Section 2, (3)-(8), and Section 4 (a).

35. See Horowitz, "New Intolerance Between Crescent and Cross," *Wall Street Journal*, July 5, 1995, and Nina Shea, "Terror Against the Church," *Crisis* (March 1997), 18–20.

36. No doubt many Wolf-Specter supporters included Tibetan Buddhists and Baha'is in the bill because of genuine concern for those groups. And, much to their credit, the lobbyists for the two groups are among the most effective in Washington, largely because they are credible. But the rationale for naming only those victims and excluding others proved weak and unsustainable. The Baha'is, whose beliefs require them to avoid any involvement in partisan politics (and who did not endorse any of the IRF bills), expressed their concern when approached about inclusion in Wolf-Specter but did not object. As one Baha'i representative put it to me, including the Baha'is in the bill was clearly understood as "an opportunity to include other groups so that [Wolf-Specter] won't be seen as a Christian bill."

37. See, for example, the story of an Iranian convert to Christianity who was granted refugee status by the UN High Commissioner for Refugees but denied entry to the United States by a U.S. immigration official. Nina Shea, "Terror Against the Church," *Crisis* (March 1997), 19. See also my experience in a similar case, chapter 8.

38. The Catholic Bishops Conference was particularly opposed to "expedited removal" procedures, which the conference staff believed were unjust. The conference initially sought an amendment of these procedures in the IRF Act but later settled for giving the responsibility for studying the matter to the U.S. Commission on International Religious Freedom.

39. See the Annual Reports on International Religious Freedom at www.state.gov
. The Executive Summaries of each report give a quick view of the levels of persecution
in such countries.

40. See the statement at http://www.nae.net/index.cfm?FUSEACTION=editor
.page&pageID=48&IDCategory=9.

41. See the testimony of Fr. Richard John Neuhaus: "This legislation is about
the persecution of all believers, not just Christians." Rev. Don Argue: "This bill is
not a Christian bill. This bill speaks to all issues of religious persecution and violations of conscience." *Hearing Before the Committee on International Relations,* House
of Representatives, First Session, September 19, 1997. Fr. Neuhaus has written extensively on the importance of religious freedom as a universal human right. Rev. Argue
was appointed to the IRF Commission in 2007.

42. The Human Rights Reports are available at www.state.gov.

43. In an e-mail to me after reviewing a draft of this chapter, John Shattuck took
issue with this assertion. Because he was the head of DRL in the mid-1990s, his views
carry particular weight. His experience was that "the DRL officers were generally all
over the map in political and religious orientation, and some of the civil-service officers were holdovers from the Reagan-Bush era, although it is certainly true that the
political appointees were from the President's party." Some of our disagreement may
be semantic. As noted in the Introduction, my argument is not that most people in DRL
or elsewhere at the State Department were irreligious, but that many were secularists
who thought of religion as a private matter, not properly part of public policy. As for
Reagan-Bush holdovers among the civil service staff, when I arrived in DRL in 1999,
I encountered only one. Others had no doubt been present during Assistant Secretary
Shattuck's tenure, but, in any case, I believe my argument about the secularist views in
DRL to be sound.

44. During the Cold War conservatives focused on human rights in communist
countries but were suspicious of those who saw U.S. interests primarily through the
human rights lens. For a critique of the Carter administration's human rights "pur-
ism" see Jeanne Kirkpatrick, "Human Rights and Foreign Policy," in *Human Rights and
American Foreign Policy* (Gambier: Public Affairs Conference Center, 1982), 1–11.

45. See Hertzke, *Freeing God's Children,* 99–101.

46. Steven A. Holmes, "G.O.P Leaders Back Bill on Religious Persecution," *New
York Times,* September 11, 1997, A3.

47. From a 1997 speech accessed at http://publicaffairs.cua.edu/speeches/
albright97.htm.

48. Personal conversation with senior staffer.

49. As noted, there was anecdotal evidence of U.S. discrimination against religious applicants for asylum or refugee status. Interestingly, Secretary Albright in 1997
asserted that "we are modifying our procedures for reviewing requests for political
asylum to ensure that those fleeing religious persecution are treated fairly." Accessed
at http://publicaffairs.cua.edu/speeches/albright97.htm. This language suggests that
existing procedures did not already ensure fairness. See similar assertions in the State
Department's 1997 report on Christian persecution, *United States Polices in Support of
Religious Freedom: Focus on Christians (Report Consistent with the Omnibus Consolidated
Appropriations Act, Fiscal Year 1997, House Report 8–9).*

50. See, for example, Jeremy Gunn's comments in Hackett, *Religious Persecution,*
49. Also Stephen Rickard, "Religion and Global Affairs: Repression and Response,"
SAIS Review (Summer/Fall), 1998, 56.

51. David Little, "Does the Human Right to Freedom of Conscience, Religion and
Belief Have Special Status?" *Brigham Young University Law Review,* 2001.

52. See Noah Feldman, "Imposed Constitutionalism," *Connecticut Law Review* (Summer 2005).

53. Shattuck served as assistant secretary from 1993–1998, and as U.S. ambassador to the Czech Republic from 1998–2000. See his memoir of those years, *Freedom on Fire: Human Rights Wars and America's Response* (Cambridge: Harvard University Press, 2003).

54. Rev. Thomas D. Williams, L.C., "The Myth of Religious Tolerance," *Crisis* (June 2006), 31–35.

55. Shattuck, "Religion, Rights and Terrorism,"183–188.

56. Pew Forum on Religion and Public Life, May 8, 2007. Accessed at www.pewforum.org/events/?EventID=139

57. Ibid.

58. E-mail from John Shattuck to the author, June 26, 2007.

59. Article 18 of the ICCPR reads: "Everyone shall have the right . . . to have or to adopt a religion or belief of his choice, and freedom, either individually or in community with others and in public or private, to manifest his religion or belief in worship, observance, practice and teaching."

60. Press Briefing of February 1, 1995. Available at www.state.gov. The quotation on population was accessed at www.hwy9.com/psp/twirth.htm. In the overview to that year's Human Rights Reports, such non-traditional human rights issues were duly emphasized, whereas religious persecution and religious freedom—quite extraordinarily—received virtually no attention. In a summary of human rights problems in countries where religious persecution was severe—Sudan, Afghanistan, Nigeria, Egypt, India, Indonesia, and Algeria—there was no mention of religious persecution. Only in the discussion of Saudi Arabia was there any reference to the matter and there but a mild notation of "restrictions on freedom of speech and religion." *Overview of Country Reports on Human Rights Practices for 1994*. The Overview, usually written by the DRL assistant secretary's staff, was a good reflection of the priorities given by the political leadership at the State Department. It is important to note, however, that the individual chapters of this report were initially drafted by the respective U.S. embassies abroad and did not uniformly ignore religious persecution as was sometimes alleged. The 1994 chapter on China, for example, was strong. Finally, by the mid 1990s, the State Department's Human Rights Reports had begun sporadically to cover sexual orientation as a human rights issue. See the 1994 Reports for Denmark and the Netherlands, section 5.

61. For a Catholic view of the Cairo conference, see George Weigel, "What Really Happened at Cairo," *First Things* (February 1995), 24–31.

CHAPTER 5

1. Much of the account that follows results from either the author's personal involvement, his discussions and interviews with the principals, or both.

2. From Matthew 16:18.

3. Robert Seiple, *A Missing Peace—Vietnam: Finally Healing the Pain* (Downers' Grove, Ill.: Intervarsity Press, 1991), 158–159.

4. The three were Reverend Don Argue, Rabbi Arthur Schneier, and Archbishop Theodore McCarrick.

5. Clinton's comments accessed at http://www.clintonpresidentialcenter.org/legacy/061898-speech-by-president-to-religious-leaders.htm.

6. Robert Seiple, "Religious Liberty: How Are We Doing?" *Christianity Today*, October 10, 2001. Accessed at www.christianitytoday.com/global/ph.cgi?/ct/2001/013/12.98.html.

7. Some in the department argued that situating the new office in the human rights bureau assured its "mainstreaming" and that its establishment as a stand-alone office under the secretary, or the under secretary for global affairs, would ensure its isolation. Although a few held this view out of concern for the office, it was largely a spurious argument. Other ambassadors at large had offices independent from bureaus with similar interests, such as the ambassador at large for counterterrorism. The key to success for these offices was support from senior officials and sufficient personnel and funding to accomplish the mission. None of this was available to the religious freedom office.

8. More wary of the long-term significance of this arrangement, Jeremy Gunn, one of the office's earliest staff members and a lawyer, advised Seiple to insist on the right to communicate in writing directly to the secretary. But the ambassador was confident he could manage this problem and accepted the arrangement.

9. The article was accessed at www.christianitytoday.com/ct/ 2000/128/31.0 .html.

10. See the declaration, "We Hold These Truths," in *First Things* (October 1997).

11. Michael Horowitz, "Cry Freedom: Forget 'Quiet Diplomacy'—It Doesn't Work," *Christianity Today.* Accessed at www.christianitytoday.com/ct/2003/003/6.46.html

12. Allen Hertzke, *Saving God's Children: The Unlikely Alliance for Global Human Rights* (Lanham, Md.: Rowman and Littlefield, 2004), 231, 233, 379 (footnote 107).

13. Robert Seiple, "The Light of Religious Freedom," *The Washington Times,* December 24, 1998, A17.

14. Letter from Neuhaus to Seiple, dated January 4, 1999.

15. Under the International Religious Freedom Act, the authority and responsibility to designate countries of particular concern was vested in the president. In the summer prior to the first designations, however, President Clinton delegated this authority to Secretary Albright. When the Bush administration took over, the authority remained with the secretary of state. This was a decision that should have increased the effectiveness of the ambassador at large, but neither ambassador was able to employ the "CPC" process with consistent effectiveness. Both Ambassadors Seiple and Hanford, however, gained significant, if isolated, victories in the CPC process that could, and should, be expanded by their successors—Seiple with China and Hanford with Vietnam and Saudi Arabia. On the latter, see chapter 7.

16. When he signed the act, President Clinton had issued a "signing statement" drafted by the State Department's lawyers that included an interpretation of the standard for designating a country of particular concern that appeared to raise the bar even higher. Whereas the statute listed rape, torture, and the like as *examples* of "systematic, ongoing and egregious violations," the Clinton interpretation asserted that such violations must be "accompanied by" rape, torture, etc. The Clinton language has not yet, to my knowledge, been evoked in a CPC finding, but could conceivably be employed to avoid designation.

17. "Religion Today by the Associated Press," September 30, 1999.

18. Robert Seiple, "Speaking Out: The USCIRF is Only Cursing the Darkness," *Christianity Today,* October 16, 2002. Seiple said that Congress should cease funding the commission "soon" if it did not change its ways, which he described as "unconscionable. At $3 million a year, this ought to inspire a taxpayer's revolt. More to the point, that which was conceived in error and delivered in chaos has now been consigned to irrelevancy."

19. In 2002, Congress amended the IRF Act and extended the commission's life to 2010.

20. This amount swamped the budget of Seiple's tiny office, which was funded in 1999 at less than $300,000, including salaries and travel funds. There was no funding for IRF programs.

21. After leaving the State Department, Seiple formed the Institute for Global Engagement (www.globalengage.com).

CHAPTER 6

1. Chas. W. Freeman, Jr., *The Diplomat's Dictionary* (Washington D.C.: National Defense University Press, 1994), 155 (Kennan), 112 (Stinnett).

2. On Bush's faith and the Iraq war, see Paul Kengor, "What Bush Believes," *New York Times*, October 18, 2004.

3. See, for example, Wilfred M. McClay, "Bush's Calling," *Commentary*, June 2005, 49–53. McClay is a professor of history at the University of Tennessee at Chattanooga. Also see David Aikman, *A Man of Faith: The Spiritual Journey of George W. Bush* (Nashville: Thomas Nelson, 2004).

4. After leaving the State Department, Harold Koh became dean of Yale Law School and a fierce critic of the Bush administration's policy in Iraq.

5. On March 21, 2001, Senators Joe Lieberman and Don Nickles, co-sponsors of the IRF Act, sent a letter to President Bush urging him not only to appoint an ambassador at large "soon," but also insisting "that the office be maintained as a distinct entity within the State Department as required under the Act." The letter was also signed by nine other Senators of both parties.

6. David Jones, "The Joy of Sects: Religious Freedom Reporting," *Foreign Service Journal* (January 2001), 26.

7. In fact, we deliberately chose categories that cut across the CPC standards so that we would not have a single section in the executive summary that indicated which countries were going to be designated. This was necessary both because the official designations were officially based on the IRF report itself, and by definition could not precede it, and because the country desks would have yet another reason to resist including their countries in the summary.

8. See a vigorous discussion of this issue in Rosalind I. J. Hackett, Mark Silk, and Dennis Hoover, eds., *Religious Persecution as a U.S. Policy Issue* (Hartford, Conn,: Center for the Study of Religion in Public Life, 2000), 25–32.

9. *Annual Report on International Religious Freedom for 1999* (Washington, D.C.: U.S. Government Printing Office: 2000), 3.

10. Before publishing this paragraph, we ran it by the Muslim member of the IRF Commission, Laila al Maryati, who said she considered it a fair treatment of the subject. Serbia was included in the first list of "particularly severe violators" of religious freedom in 1999.

11. Annual Report for 2002, Executive Summary, xvii.

12. This problem is elaborated in chapter 7.

13. For example, I addressed audiences at Trinity College (Connecticut), Brigham Young University (Utah), George Washington University (Washington DC), Florida Atlantic University, Virginia Wesleyan College, American University (Washington, D.C.), Victoria College (British Columbia), and the Army's School of the America's (Ft. Benning, Georgia).

14. Rosalind I.J. Hackett, Mark Silk, and Dennis Hoover, eds., *Religious Persecution as a U.S. Policy Issue* (Hartford, Conn.: Center for the Study of Religion in Public Life, 2000), 20.

15. Ibid., 54. The speaker in this case was Professor Winnifried Fallers Sullivan, a widely respected scholar of American religion and the author, in later years, of a book entitled, *The Impossibility of Religious Freedom* (Princeton: Princeton University

Press, 2005). Professor Sullivan and I discussed these issues in a joint appearance on a panel at the Library of Congress in November, 2006, which is available at http://www .pewforum.org/events/?EventID=133

16. The text of the First Amendment reads as follows: "Congress shall make no law respecting an establishment of religion, or prohibiting the free exercise thereof; or abridging the freedom of speech, or of the press; or the right of the people peaceably to assemble, and to petition the Government for a redress of grievances."

17. Introduction to the 1999 *Annual Report on Religious Freedom.* Available at www .state.gov.

18. This is not the real name of the family, some of whose members remain in Iran.

CHAPTER 7

1. I met Coats when I briefed him on religious freedom issues in Germany prior to his departure for his new post. He was clearly interested, and when I asked, confirmed that the prospect of his becoming ambassador at large for international religious freedom had earlier been raised.

2. Abrams had been indicted by the Iran-contra prosecutor for lying to Congress. He pled guilty to two lesser offenses and was pardoned by George H. W. Bush.

3. I had briefed him on the State Department's bureaucratic organization and who did what, and had given him my views on options for various administration positions. Hudson had met George W. Bush when *Crisis* magazine published an article on the Catholic voter that had caught the candidate's eye.

4. Al Kammen, "In the Loop," *Washington Post,* May 2, 2001.

5. On March 6, co-sponsors of the IRF Act, Senators Nickles and Lieberman, along with a few of their colleagues, wrote the president to urge quick action on a nominee. This letter was sent, apparently, before an internal White House decision was made on Hanford.

6. David Aikman, *Great Souls: Six Who Changed the Century* (Nashville, Tenn.: Word Publishing, 1998).

7. Aikman later published his much awaited analysis of the problem of Christian persecution in China, *Jesus in Beijing* (see chapter 10).

8. Office of Inspector General,. U.S. Department of State and the Broadcasting Board of Governor, *Monthly Report of Activities* (September 2003), 13.

9. Senator Rick Santorum mentioned the IG report in his column for the Catholic monthly, *Crisis* magazine. See "Rattle the Cages for Religious Freedom," *Crisis,* November 4, 2003.

10. The listing of senior State Department officials was accessed on May 31, 2007, at www.state.gov/r/pa/ei/biog/c7647.htm. On the IRF ambassador's title and responsibilities see the IRF Act, Title 1, section 101 (b) (1).

11. David Jones, "The Joy of Sects: Religious Freedom Reporting," *Foreign Service Journal* (January 2001), 28.

12. See the *Annual Report on International Religious Freedom,* Tibet Chapter (under China). Available at www.state.gov.

13. Fu Tieshan died in April 2007. His death provided an opportunity for moving the Sino-Vatican relationship forward, and with it religious freedom in China. Fu's replacement, Fr. Joseph Li Shan, pastor of St. Joseph's church in central Beijing, was elected by a committee of priests, nuns, and Catholic laymen. Although the procedure was not orthodox, the Vatican had apparently approved in advance. This could provide an opportunity for a breakthrough, but other such opportunities in the past have not materialized.

14. The Commission finally visited China in 2005, but the Special Rapporteur has not yet done so.

15. For an insightful discussion of Kamm's work in China, see Tina Rosenberg, "John Kamm's Third Way," *The New York Times Magazine,* March 3, 2002, 58–63; 81.

16. See Ann Noonan, "Blind Faith: Is the State Department Soft on China?," *National Review Online,* October 25, 2005.

17. Nailene Chou Wiest, "Reform of Religious Policy Is on the Agenda," *South China Morning Post,* December 17, 2002. On Jiang's statement, see John Pomfret, "Protestantism Rise in the Land of Mao," *Washington Post,* December 24, 2002, A1.

18. Hearing before the Sub-Committee on International Operations and Human Rights of the Committee on International Relations, House of Representatives, October 9, 2002, "An Evaluation of the Annual Report on International Religious Freedom," 20.

19. The annual human rights dialogues, which had been suspended in the late 1990s, were once again suspended after the December 2002 meeting. They were reconvened in May 2008.

20. November 13, 2006, "Release of the 2006 Designations." Accessed at www .state.gov/r/pa/prs2006/75927.htm.

21. November 13, 2006 Press Statement. Available at www.uscirf.gov. Paul Marshall's *Religious Freedom in the World* (Lanham, Md.: Roman and Littlefield, 2008) continued to rank Vietnam among the worst persecutors in the world. See his essay, "The Range of Religious Freedom," 3.

22. May 8, 2007, available at www.pewforum.org.

23. Conversation with Chris Seiple, president, Institute for Global Engagement, June 5, 2007.

24. Hanford used data from a study of Saudi textbooks compiled by the Hudson Institute's Center for Religious Freedom. Available at http://crf.hudson.org/index. cfm?fuseaction=publication_details&id=4454&pubType=CRF_Reports.

25. A Senate resolution in August 2004 had called on the State Department to designate Saudi Arabia. The IRF Commission had recommended Saudi's designation every year since 2000. See CIRF press release, "Saudi Arabia: Senate Resolution on CPC Designation and Exportation," August 9, 2004. Available at www.uscirf.gov.

26. Many officials were involved in this working group. One in particular was helpful to Hanford. He was Deputy Assistant Secretary Scott Carpenter.

27. Transcript of the May 8 Pew Forum event, accessed at www.pewforum .org/events/?EventID=139.

28. See chapter 4.

29. See Introduction.

30. In July 2008, ten years after the IRF Act passed, the department finally put out a "request for proposals" for monetary grants to advance religious freedom. The money had been appropriated by Congress against the resistance of the State Department.

31. Pew Forum transcript, accessed at www.pewforum.org/events/?EventID=139.

32. Natan Sharansky, with Ron Dermer, *The Case for Democracy: The Power of Freedom to Overcome Tyranny and Terror* (New York: Public Affairs, 2004), 138–139.

CHAPTER 8

1. See *The 9/11 Commission Report: Final Report of the National Commission on Terrorist Attacks upon the United States* (New York: W.W. Norton, 2004), esp. chapters 8, 9, and 11.

2. Michael Wolfe, ed., *One Thousand Roads to Mecca: Ten Centuries of Travelers Writing about the Muslim Pilgrimage* (New York: Grove Press, 1997), xvii.

3. Ibid., xxiv.

4. See the discussion of the Saudi pledge in chapter 7.

5. Lawrence Wright, *The Looming Tower: Al-Qaeda and the Road to 9/11* (New York, Alfred A. Knopf, 2006), 65–67.

6. Hamid Algar, *Wahhabism: A Critical Essay* (Oneonta, N.Y.: Islamic Publications International, 2002), 27.

7. On Wahhabism, see Algar, *Wahhabism*. For a different interpretation, see David Commins, *The Wahhabi Mission and Saudi Arabia* (London: I. B. Tauris, 2006). Commins stresses the distinctions and conflicts between Wahhabis and the Muslim Brotherhood, including the Wahhabi tendency to avoid criticizing rulers. He also emphasizes the Wahhabi desire to avoid all contact with infidels. I am grateful to Hillel Fradkin for recommending this work. My own view, reflected in the current chapter, is that Wahhabism provided distinct theological warrants for violence and coercion that were appropriated by Bin Laden and his movement. Although other influences doubtless played a part, this form of Sunni extremism can neither be understood by Americans, nor eliminated as a theological imperative by Muslims, without reference to Wahhabism.

8. Bernard Lewis, *The Crisis of Islam: Holy War and Unholy Terror* (New York: The Modern Library, 2003), 76–81.

9. Wright, *The Looming Tower*, 78–80.

10. Ibid., 157–161, 209–210.

11. http://newsvote.bbc.co.uk/mpapps/pagetools/print/news.bbc.co.uk/2/hi/middle_east/29667.

12. See the report at www.state.gov.

13. The IRF Act requires an annual review of the status of religious freedom in each country "to determine whether the government of that country has engaged in or tolerated particularly severe violations of religious freedom in that country during the preceding twelve months…" Such governments are to be designated CPCs. Section 402 (b) (1) (A).

14. Technically the latter two were not CPCs under the IRF Act, because neither were governments recognized by the United States. Accordingly, we decided to "identify" them as particularly severe violators. Although the Act did not mandate action against them de jure, they were treated substantially the same as the others, which is to say that no action was actually taken. In cases in which governments recognized by the United States were designated, existing sanctions were reaffirmed or "double hatted." This largely empty gesture was not made against Serbia or the Taliban, because the IRF Act did not require it. See chapter 4.

15. See Introduction.

16. Wright, *The Looming Tower*, 174–175.

17. The Crusades had temporarily succeeded in recapturing parts of the Christian Levant, including Jerusalem. But the Crusades were at the time (unlike today) not viewed by Muslims as a major threat to Islam. There was, in fact, little interest by Muslims in the Crusades until the 19th century. See Lewis, *The Crisis of Islam*, 50–51.

18. Wright, *The Looming Tower*, 174–175; David Benjamin and Steven Simon, *The Age of Sacred Terror* (New York: Random House, 2002), 41–52. For a useful thumbnail sketch of various extremist arguments and their support within Islamic tradition, see Michael Moss and Souad Mekhennet, "The Guidebook for Taking a Life," *The New York Times*, "Week in Review," June 10, 2007, 1, 3. For a different take on Ibn Taymiyya, see Reza Aslan, *No God But God: The Origins, Evolution, and Future of Islam* (New York:

Random House, 2005), 85–86. Also see Mary R. Habeck, *Knowing the Enemy: Jihadist Ideology and the War on Terror* (New Haven: Yale University Press, 2006), 19–26.

19. Khaled Abou El Fadl, *The Great Theft: Wrestling Islam from the Extremists* (San Francisco: HarperSanFrancisco, 2005), 221. See also David Cook, *Understanding Jihad* (Berkeley: University of California Press, 2005) and Michael Bonner, *Jihad in Islamic History: Doctrines and Practice* (Princeton: Princeton University Press, 2006).

20. Abou El Fadl comes close to making such an argument in his treatment of jihad by emphasizing the terrorists' psychological insecurity and their abuse of the texts to strike fear as a tactic in the pursuit of power. That analysis is doubtless accurate in part, but it fails to acknowledge the authenticity of radical views of jihad that can be found in Islamic tradition (*The Great Theft*, 249). That said, Abou El Fadl has been at the forefront of Islamic attempts to teach a moderate view of Islam from the texts, rather than ignoring them.

21. Habeck, *Knowing the Enemy*, 20.

22. For example, "intellectual jihad" can be seen as part of ijtihad (interpretation of the texts). See Fazlur Rahman, *Islam and Modernity: Transformation of an Intellectual Tradition* (Chicago: University of Chicago Press, 1982), 7–8.

23. Lewis, *The Crisis of Islam*, 31.

24. bin Bayyah, H. E. Allamah Abd Allah bin Mahfuz, et al., "Open Letter to His Holiness Pope Benedict XVI." Accessed at http://www.islamicamagazine.com/letter/.

25. Lewis, *The Crisis of Islam*, 46. For a very different treatment of this subject, see Bat Ye'or, *The Decline of Eastern Christianity under Islam: From Jihad to Dhimmitude*, tr. by Miriam Kochan and David Littman (Madison, N.J.: Fairleigh Dickinson University Press, 1996). Ye'or emphasizes the persecution of Christians and Jews under the dhimmi system.

26. Ye'or made these comments in a 1998 interview with Michael Cromartie. Accessed at www.christianitytoday.com/bc/8b5038.html.

27. Algar, *Wahhabism*, 11–13, 9; Benjamin and Simon, *The Age of Sacred Terror*, 52.

28. Abou El Fadl, *The Great Theft*, 113.

29. Ibid., 126–27.

30. Cf. Seyyed Hossein Nasr, *The Heart of Islam* (HarperSanFrancisco, 2002), 22–3.

31. Abou El Fadl, *The Great Theft*, 143–44. Abou El Fadl, a major Muslim jurist, employs the term "moderate," a concept that he argues captures the essence of Islam. Other Muslims object to it precisely because they believe it implies the opposite, namely "that orthodox Islam entails violence." Michelle Boorstein, "From Muslim Youths, a Push for Change," *Washington Post*, July 15, 2007, A15.

32. Ibid., 28–38; 23.

33. Ibid., 49; Algar, *Wahhabism*, 31–34.

34. Algar, *Wahhabism*, 2.

35. Ibid., 42–43.

36. Michael J. Perry, *The Idea of Human Rights: Four Inquiries* (New York: Oxford University Press, 1998), 78; For a useful discussion of Islamist feminism and its increasingly influential Koranic interpretations, see Christina Hoff Sommers, "The Subjection of Islamic Women," *The Weekly Standard*, May 21, 2007, 14–20.

37. One celebrated case involved the abduction of Dria Davis, the American Christian daughter of a divorced Saudi father. At the age of 11, she visited him in Saudi Arabia but was not permitted to return to the United States. The child's mother alleged that the U.S. embassy said it could do nothing, so she hired mercenaries to retrieve Dria. See Dria Davis, "Elian, Here is My Story," *Wall Street Journal*, January 28, 2000.

38. See Roush's Web site, www.patroush.com. She has written a book on the ordeal: Patricia Roush, *At Any Price: How America Betrayed My Kidnapped Daughters for Saudi Oil* (Nashville: Thomas Nelson, Inc., 2003).

39. Abou El Fadl, *The Great Theft,* 250–255.

40. On the Mortara case, see Bertram Wallace Korn, *The American Reaction to the Mortara Case: 1858–1859* (Philadelphia, Pa.: American Jewish Archives, 1957). A more recent work, although marred by rhetorical excess, is David I. Kertzer, *The Kidnapping of Edgaro Morara* (New York: Knopf, 1997). During its meeting of May 2001, the International Catholic Jewish Liaison Committee, established after Vatican II, affirmed that the Mortara case "exemplifies the historical problem that Nostra Aetate and subsequent statements of the Holy See have solved 'in our time.'" Accessed at Vatican. va/roman_curia/pontifical_councils/chrstuni/relations-jews-doc.

41. See chapter 6.

42. The Koran refers to *da'wa* as the summons to the way of Allah, to the true religion. In contemporary Islam, it is often used to denote "the effort to spread the teachings of Islam, and in this sense is roughly equivalent to the concept of 'mission' in Christianity." John Bowker, ed., *The Concise Oxford Dictionary of World Religions* (Oxford: Oxford University Press, 2005), 149.

43. Christians were resettled to Iraq, the Jews to Palestine and Syria. Lewis, ibid., xxix–xxx. Lewis notes that "[c]ompared with European expulsions, 'Umar's decree was both limited and compassionate." Also see Aslan, *No God But God,* 94.

44. Annual Report on International Religious Freedom for 2000. Available at www.state.gov.

45. Aslan, *No God But God,* 179–80; Nasr, *The Heart of Islam,* 71.

46. In India and elsewhere, the concept of peoples of the book is extended by Muslims to Hindus and Buddhists.

CHAPTER 9

1. Berman's statement may be found in "The Philosopher of Islamic Terror," *New York Times Magazine,* March 23, 2003. Quoted in Michael Novak, *The Universal Hunger for Liberty: Why the Clash of Civilizations Is Not Inevitable* (New York: Basic Books, 2004), xi. Also see Paul Berman, *Terror and Liberalism* (New York: W.W. Norton, 2003).

2. Quoted in Olivier Roy, "Liberte, Egalite, Laicite?," *The American Interest* (Jan–Feb 2007), 130.

3. Vali Nasr, "The Rise of Muslim Democracy," *Journal of Democracy* (April 2005), 13–27.

4. Vali Nasr, *The Shia Revival: How Conflicts within Islam Will Shape the Future* (New York: W. W. Norton, 2006), 119–145.

5. On the influence of all three, see Mary Habeck, *Knowing the Enemy: Jihadist Ideology and the War on Terror* (New Haven: Yale University Press, 2006), 22–26, 37–39, 57–69.

6. See, for example, Thomas Donnelly, "A Question of Faith: Conflicts Driven by Religion Can Be Long and Bitter," American Enterprise Institute for Public Policy Research, December 27, 2006. Available at www.aei.org.

7. Vali Nasr, "When the Shiites Rise," *Foreign Affairs,* July/August 2006, 58–74; see also Gal Luft and Anne Korin, "Islam's Divide—And Us," *Commentary* (July–August), 2007, 41–45.

8. Nasr, "When The Shiites Rise," 59–60.

9. *The Iraq Study Group Report* (New York: Vintage Books, 2006), 28. Accessed at http://www.usip.org/isg/iraq_study_group_report/report/1206/iraq_study_group_report.pdf

10. For a catalogue of Islamist terrorist groups, see Richard A. Clarke, ed., *Defeating the Jihadists: A Blueprint for Action* (New York: The Century Foundation, 2006), esp. chapter 3.

11. Another example of this religion-avoidance syndrome is the persistent use in the West of the term "ethnic cleansing" to describe religiously inspired butchery that has little or nothing to do with ethnicity, such as that which occurred in the Balkans during the 1990s, or in Iraq between Shiites and Sunnis. See Robert Satloff, *U.S. Policy Toward Islamism: A Theoretical and Operational Overview* (New York: Council on Foreign Relations, 2000), 1–2. On the 9/11 Commission, see chapter 1.

12. *Declassified Key Judgments of the National Intelligence Estimate "Trends in Global Terrorism: Implications for the United States,"* dated April 2006. Accessed at http://www.cfr.org/publication/11545/.

13. Habeck, *Knowing the Enemy*, 7.

14. See chapter 1.

15. Robert Satloff, *U.S. Policy Toward Islamism*, 1–2.

16. Ibid., 3.

17. Ibid., 2.

18. Ibid., 17.

19. A 2006 study by the Congressional Research Service notes that although the Bush administration's democracy agenda has forced an internal debate over whether the United States should engage Islamist groups, the policy has been "left somewhat vague, perhaps even deliberately so...." In fact, that policy has not been one of directly engaging Islamists or Islamic groups. See Jeremy M. Sharp, *U.S. Democracy Promotion Policy in the Middle East: The Islamist Dilemma* (Washington, D.C.: Congressional Research Service, June 15, 2006). Quote from page 6.

20. Graham Fuller, *The Future of Political Islam* (New York: Palgrave Macmillan, 2003), xi–xii.

21. The reaction to the ISG report of the neoconservative journal the *Weekly Standard* was decidedly negative. See its lead editorial, "A Perfect Failure," *Weekly Standard*, December 11, 2006, 11–12.

22. *The Iraq Study Group Report*, 46–50.

23. David Ignatius, "Baker Hamilton Does Its Job," *The Washington Post*, December 7, 2006, A31.

24. An advisor to the ISG, Marc Reuel Gerecht, noted that "In its deliberations and its final recommendations, the ISG barely acknowledged Islam." See Gerecht, "Mirror Imaging the Mullahs: Our Islamic Interlocutors," accessed at http://www.aei.org/publications/filter.all,pubID.27405/pub_detail.asp

25. *Iraq Study Group Report*, 13–14.

26. Ibid., 67.

27. Ibid., 68.

28. Ibid., 46.

29. Ibid., 48

30. Bernard Lewis, *The Crisis of Islam: Holy War and Unholy Terror* (New York: The Modern Library, 2003), 15–16.

31. David Ignatius, "Wise Advice: Listen, and Engage," *Washington Post*, June 24, 2007, B7. Kissinger was secretary of state under Presidents Nixon and Ford. Brzezinski was national security adviser under President Carter. Scowcroft was national security adviser for Presidents Ford and George H. W. Bush.

32. David B. Rivkin Jr., "Diplomacy in the Post-9/11 Era," *Wall Street Journal,* November 17–18, 2007, A11.

33. Bernard Lewis, "The Roots of Muslim Rage," *The Atlantic Monthly,* September 1990.

34. A compelling question for U.S. interests is possible links between Iranian extremist Shiism and Iran's procurement and possible use of nuclear weapons. For example, Iranian President Mamoud Ahmedinejad has recklessly suggested a connection between nuclear war and the return of the Hidden Imam. The United States has made many mistakes by ignoring what extremists say, and they should not ignore Ahmedinejad. Yet the real power in Iran rests with the clerics, especially Supreme Leader Khamenei. Neither his theology nor his behavior suggests he seeks his own destruction or that of Iran, which would be the likely consequence of the *use* of nuclear weapons, either against Israel or U.S. interests in the region. That said, there does seem to be a link between Khomeinst Shiism and the drive to become a nuclear power. That link is the power of Sunni states in the region (including a nuclear Pakistan). The United States and the international community should do all it can to prevent a nuclear Iran. The very existence of this problem, however, increases the critical importance of the emergence of stable, liberal democracies in the region and, within Shiism, the triumph of Sistaniism.

35. Cheryl Benard, *Civil Democratic Islam: Partners, Resources and Strategies* (Santa Monica: The RAND Corporation, 2003); Angel Rabasa, et al., *The Muslims World After 9/11* (Santa Monica: RAND, 2004); Angel Rabasa, et al., *Building Moderate Muslim Networks* (Santa Monica: RAND, 2007).

36. Benard, *Civil Democratic Islam,* 3, fn. 3.

37. Ibid., 5.

38. Ibid., 33.

39. Ibid., 26.

40. Ibid., 37, and fn. 10.

41. Ibid., 85.

42. Ibid., 121–122.

43. Ibid., 123.

44. Khaled Abou El Fadl, *The Great Theft: Wrestling Islam from the Extremists* (San Francisco: HarperSanFrancisco, 2005), 142–179. For an attack on Abou El Fadl on the grounds that he is a covert Islamist who "wants Muslims to live by...the Shari'a" and who whitewashes the militant meaning of jihad, see Daniel Pipes, "Stealth Islamist: Khaled Abou El Fadl," *Middle East Quarterly* (Spring 2004).

45. In fact, Abou El Fadl explicitly rejects the "modernist" label. He argues that all Islamic groups are influenced by modernity, including fundamentalists. More pointedly he notes that "liberal values are not always achieved by moving forward; sometimes they are achieved by harkening back to tradition." Khaled Abou El Fadl, *The Great Theft,* 16–17. See his exchange with Muqtader Khan in Abou El Fadl, *Islam and the Challenge of Democracy* (Princeton, N.J.: Princeton University Press, 2004), 63–68; 122–125.

46. See chapter 3.

47. On the influence of Rawlsian secularism, see chapters 1 and 3.

48. For a discussion of Sandel's use of this concept, see Introduction.

49. Lewis, *Crisis,* 20–21.

50. Vali Nasr, *The Shia Revival,* 125.

51. Satloff, *U.S. Policy Toward Islamism,* 1–4.

52. Lewis, *Crisis,* 108–109.

53. For a trenchant criticism of the Democratic Party's backtracking on democracy promotion, written by a Democrat, see Ronald D. Asmus, "The Democrats' Democracy Problem," *Washington Post,* June 17, 2007, B3.

NOTES TO PAGES 261–274   345

54. See, for example, *The Pew Global Attitudes Project*, July 14, 2005, p. 2. Available at www.pewglobal.org.

55. April 17, 2007 interview in Washington, D.C., with U.S.AID official from U.S. Embassy, Islamabad.

56. See the Pakistan chapter of the 2006 *Annual Report on International Religious Freedom*. Available at www.state.gov.

57. Liora Danan and Alice Hunt, *Mixed Blessings: U.S. Government Engagement with Religion in Conflict Prone Settings* (Washington, D.C.: Center for Strategic and International Studies, 2007), 39.

58. Paul Marshall, *Radical Islam Rules: The Worldwide Spread of Extreme Shari'a Law* (Lanham, Md.: Rowman and Littlefield, 2005), 2.

59. See Satloff, *U.S. Policy Toward Islamism*, 26–31, for a classic statement of this view.

60. Robert Spencer, *Islam Unveiled: Disturbing Questions About the World's Fastest-Growing Faith* (San Francisco: Encounter Books, 2002), 109.

61. Mustafa Akyol, "Render Under Ataturk," *First Things* (March 2007), 16.

62. See Michael Rubin, "Turkey's Putin Deserves to Go," *Wall Street Journal*, June 6, 2008, A15.

63. See the *Annual Report on International Religious Freedom* for 2002–2008, including the Executive Summaries. The 2005 Executive Summary noted some regression on religious freedom, but subsequent reports have indicated that government policy "continued to contribute to the generally free practice of religion." Available at www.state.gov.

64. Akyol, "Render Under Ataturk," 16–17.

65. For an overview of U.S. policies, see Sharp, *U.S. Democracy Promotion Policy in the Middle East: The Islamist Dilemma*.

66. Daniel Philpott, "Explaining the Political Ambivalence of Religion," *American Political Science Review* (August, 2007), 505–525.

67. Daniel J. Mahoney, "Conservatism, Democracy and Foreign Policy," *The Intercollegiate Review* (Fall 2006), 11–12.

68. John Finnis, "Religion and State: Some Main Issues and Sources," in C. S. Titus, ed., *God, Religion, and Civil Governance* (Arlington, Va.: The Institute for the Psychological Sciences, forthcoming).

69. Michael Novak, *On Two Wings: Humble Faith and Common Sense in the American Founding*, expanded edition. (San Francisco: Encounter Books, 2002), 8–13.

70. See chapter 3.

CHAPTER 10

1. Quoted in Samuel Huntington, *The Clash of Civilization and the Remaking of World Order* (New York: Simon and Schuster, 1996), 231. Lee Yuan Kew was the prime minister of Singapore.

2. From Jiang's December 2001 speech to a Chinese conference on religious affairs. *Washington Post*, "Protestantism Rises in the Land of Mao," December 24, 2002, A1.

3. Mary Craig, *Tears of Blood: A Cry for Tibet* (Washington, D.C.: Counterpoint, 1999), 287.

4. In a later meeting with Ye Xiaowen, we learned that he actually believed the U.S. Commission on International Religious Freedom, not Seiple, was responsible for China being designated a CPC.

5. Wang Jisi, "China's Search for Stability with America," *Foreign Affairs* (September/October 2005), 45.

6. David Zweig and Bi Jianhai, "China's Global Hunt for Energy," *Foreign Affairs* (September/October 2005), 25–38.

7. David S. Landes, *The Wealth and Poverty of Nations: Why Some Are So Rich and Some So Poor* (New York: W.W. Norton and Co., 1999), 478.

8. Huntington, *The Clash of Civilizations*, 231.

9. Zheng Bijian, "China's 'Peaceful Rise' to Great-Power Status," *Foreign Affairs* (September/October 2005), 18–24.

10. Cf. Ross Terrill, "China Is Not Just Rising, but Also Changing," *New York Times*, September 9, 2006, A27.

11. Edward Cody, "Poll Finds Surge of Religion Among Chinese," *Washington Post*, February 8, 2007, A15.

12. Bijian, "China's 'Peaceful Rise' to Great-Power Status," 18–19.

13. Cf. Thomas L. Friedman, "How to Look at China," *New York Times*, November 9, 2005, A27. For a highly pessimistic view of China's modernization and its effects on poverty and stability, see Guy Sorman, "The Truth About China," *Wall Street Journal*, April 20, 2007, A15.

14. See the section on "religious demography" in the China chapter of the State Department's 2006 *Annual Report on International Religious Freedom*. Available at www.state.gov.

15. David Aikman, *Jesus in Beijing: How Christianity Is Transforming China and Changing the Global Balance of Power* (Washington: Regnery Publishing, Inc., 2003), 285. Aikman's book was banned in China in 2003 and remains so today. See the China chapter of the 2006 *Annual Report on International Religious Freedom*. Available at www.state.gov.

16. See chapter 7.

17. See Human Rights Watch, *Dangerous Meditation: China's Campaign Against Falungong* (New York: Human Rights Watch, 2002).

18. Every American embassy has a country team, headed by the ambassador and consisting of the deputy chief of mission, the political and economic counselors, the consul general, and other key embassy officials, including military attaches.

19. See David Aikman's brief discussion of McGinnis in *Jesus in Beijing*, 143–144.

20. The reference read as follows: "Catholic priests in the official church also face dilemmas when asked by parishioners whether they should follow Church doctrine about birth control or State family planning policy. This dilemma is particularly acute when discussing abortion." From the 2001 *Annual Report on International Religious Freedom*, China chapter. Available at www.state.gov. In the following years, this aspect of the report was altered to assert—incorrectly—that abortion and birth control were not issues of church doctrine but of papal authority: "The Government insists that Catholic Patriotic Association officials, clergy, and believers be 'patriotic' and 'law abiding.' When government policy and Papal authority conflict—as they do, for example, on abortion or birth control—state policy takes precedence, leaving priests with the dilemma of how to advise their practitioners."

21. Mark was later given the department's annual award for excellence in human rights reporting.

22. This paternalist aspect of traditional Chinese religions is sometimes labeled "filial piety." Lawrence Harrison, *The Central Liberal Truth* (New York: Oxford University Press, 2007), 7, 52.

23. See *Annual Reports on International Religious Freedom*, China chapter.

24. Craig, *Tears of Blood*, 23–39; For a good overview and a description of Chinese policy toward Tibetans outside the Tibetan Autonomous zone, see Tibet Information Network, *Relative Freedom? Tibetan Buddhism and Religious Policy in Kandze, Sichuan, 1987–1999* (London: Tibet Information Network, 1999).

25. Craig, *Tears of Blood*, 333–341.

26. See Dru C. Gladney, *Muslim Chinese: Ethnic Nationalism in the People's Republic* (Cambridge: Council on East Asian Studies, Harvard University, 1991).

27. Stephen Schwartz, "Beleaguered Uighurs," *The Weekly Standard*, June 21, 2004, 16–17.

28. See the China chapter of the 2006 *Annual Report on International Religious Freedom*. Available at www.state.gov.

29. Jean-Paul Wiest, "Setting Roots: The Catholic Church in China to 1949," in Jason Kindrop and Carol Lee Hamrin, eds., *God and Caesar in China: Policy Implications of Church-State Tensions* (Washington, D.C.: Brookings Institution Press, 2004), 83.

30. Bays focuses on the period between 1900 and 1949 as the period of anomaly, but his analysis seems to me valid for the period beginning with the "unequal treaties" of 1842 and after, when the Chinese religion bureaucracy was increasingly ineffective because of the preferences provided Christianity in the treaties themselves. Whatever the duration of the period, Western intervention clearly induced a hiatus in the historical pattern of state control of religion, a pattern to which Chinese Communists returned. See Daniel H. Bays, "A Tradition of State Dominance," in Jason Kindopp and Carol Lee Hamrin, eds., *God and Caesar in China: Policy Implications of Church-State Tensions* (Washington, D.C.: Brookings Institution Press, 2004), 28–26.

31. M. A. Thiessen, "A Tale of Two Bishops," *Crisis* (February, 2002), 13–19.

32. Ibid.

33. Ibid.

34. The White House, Office of the Press Secretary (Shanghai, People's Republic of China), "Remarks by the President and the First Lady in Discussion on Shaping China for the 21st Century," June 30, 1998. Accessed at www.whitehouse.gov/WH/New/China/19980630-3597.html.

35. During this meeting I implored Bishop Jin to write his memoirs so that people would know his version of the events that had formed his life. He responded that, sadly, it would not be possible.

36. Lawrence Harrison, *The Central Liberal Truth*, 44.

37. Ellen S. Reinstein, "Turn the Other Cheek or Demand an Eye for an Eye? Religious Persecution in China and an Effective Western Response," *Connecticut Journal of International Law* (Fall 2004), 7–8.

38. Ibid.

39. Philip Jenkins, "The Politics of Persecuted Religious Minorities," in Robert A. Seiple and Dennis R. Hoover, eds., *Religion and Security: the New Nexus in International Relations* (Lanham, Md.: Roman and Littlefield, 2004), 25–36. This issue is also discussed in Carol Lee Hamrin, "A New Framework for Promoting Religious Freedom in China," *TheReview of Faith and International Affairs* (Spring 2005), 8. For a broader analysis of government repression and religious violence, see Brian Grim and Roger Finke, "Religious Persecution in Cross-National Context: Clashing Civilzations or Regulated Religious Economies," *American Sociological Review* 72:4 (2007).

40. Francis Fukuyama, *Trust: The Social Virtues and the Creation of Prosperity* (New York: The Free Press, 1995), 16–17.

41. Zheng Bijian, "China's Peaceful Rise," 20.

42. Carol Lee Hamrin, "A New Framework for Promoting Religious Freedom in China," 3–10.

43. David Aikman, *Jesus in Beijing* (Regnery, 2003), 181.

44. Ibid., 181, 290–292.

45. It is, however, entirely acceptable to celebrate the novus ordo in Latin as well. Further, on July 7, 2007, Pope Benedict XVI issued an apostolic letter, *Summorum Pontificum*, expanding opportunities for the use of the older Roman rite. See the letter at www.ewtn.com/library/papaldoc/b16SummorumPontificum.htm.

CONCLUSION

1. Chas. W. Freeman. Jr., *The Diplomat's Dictionary* (Washington, D.C.: National Defense University Press, 1994), 183.

2. Ibid., 185.

3. Quoted in Lawrence Harrison, *The Central Liberal Truth* (New York: Oxford University Press, 2007), 6–7.

Index